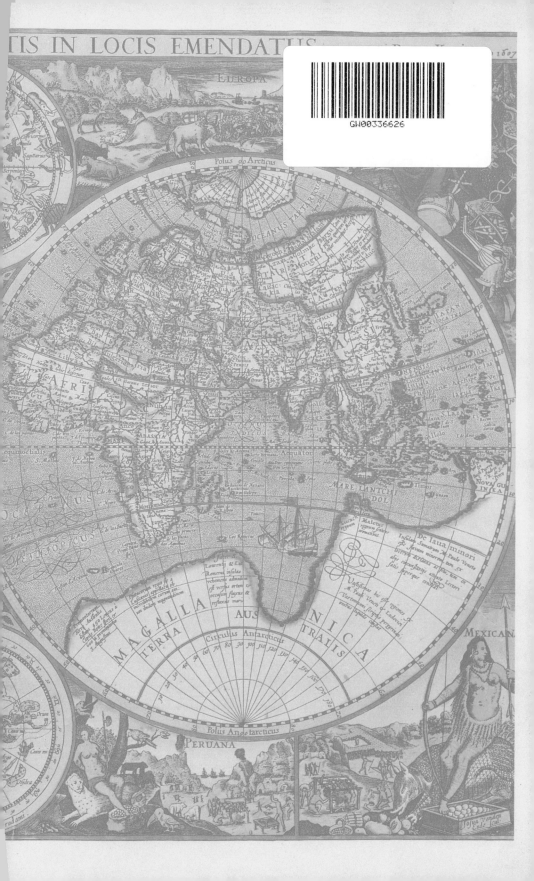

Asia Pacific:

A View on its Role in the
New World Order

Michael S. Dobbs-Higginson

Longman 朗文

First published in 1993
Reprinted 1993

Longman Asia Limited
18/F Cornwall House
Taikoo Place
979 King's Road
HONG KONG
Tel: 811 8168
and associated companies through the world.

ISBN 962 00 0105 2

Produced by Longman Asia Limited
Printed in Hong Kong
NPC/02

DEDICATION

To my mother who started me off on this extraordinary voyage of discovery. To my wife, Marie-Thérèse, who provided the sane other half to balance the equation. To our children, Julien, Justine and Charlotte, who with often considerable amusement have either watched or helped with the whole process. To them all, for giving me their trust, love and, most importantly, the physical and emotional room in which to write this book. Finally, to Kevin O'Sullivan who has been an integral part of my family's life for the last thirty years.

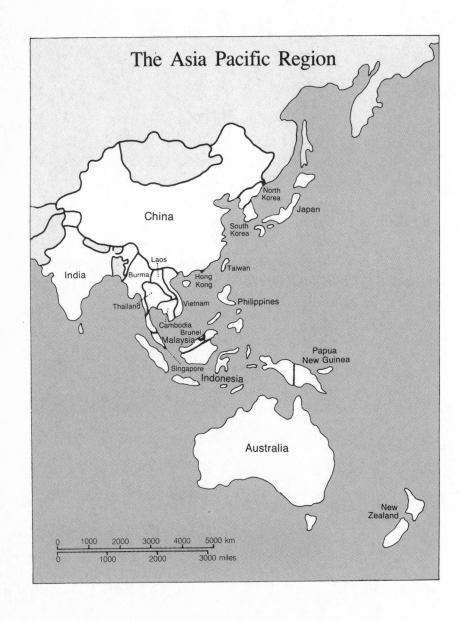

The Asia Pacific Region

China

North Korea

Japan

South Korea

Taiwan

Laos

Burma

Hong Kong

India

Thailand

Vietnam

Philippines

Cambodia

Brunei

Malaysia

Singapore

Indonesia

Papua New Guinea

Australia

New Zealand

| 0 | 1000 | 2000 | 3000 | 4000 | 5000 km |

| 0 | | 1000 | 2000 | | 3000 miles |

Contents

Advance Reviews

'While I do not agree with some of the author's views, these disagreements are just a few pebbles, so to speak, on the foot-hills of a towering mountain of convincing logic and vision.'
Yoo Chang-Soon, Chairman, Korean Federation of Industries, former Prime Minister and former Governor, Bank of Korea, Korea

'With his understanding of the cultures and values of both East and West, the author is well qualified to publish this objective study.'
Tun Ismail bin Mohamed Ali, Chairman, Permodalan Nasional, Malaysia

'The author is unique amongst businessmen in having such a deep understanding of the primary characteristics of the region's countries, including Japan.'
Yoh Kurosawa, President, The Industrial Bank of Japan, Japan

'Many Westerners have tried to explain Japan, but few have taken on all of Asia Pacific. No one, before now, has succeeded in translating thirty years of inside knowledge of the region into information that is understandable, logical, and useful to business people.'
Per-Olof Eriksson, Chief Executive Officer, Sandvik AB, Sweden

'This is the work of an expert geopolitical and historical scholar, not of an investment banker. This is the highest compliment I can pay the author.'
Chen S. Yu, Deputy Governor, The Central Bank of China, Taiwan

'An excellent effort. For anyone interested in the region this book will become an invaluable and inseparable companion.'
R.P. Goenka, President, CACCI, India

'A must for the informed CEO!'
Tan Sri Haji Basir bin Ismail, Chairman, Petronas, Malaysia

'Dobbs-Higginson traverses the Asia Pacific countries, identifying their hopes for, and the impediments to, achieving a better and more tolerant world.'
John Ralph, Chief Executive, CRA Limited, Australia

'Although the market is littered with numerous attempts to define parts, or all, of the region, this book stands out as one of exceptional worth.'
Tomomitsu Oba, President, Japan Center for International Finance and former Vice-Minister, Ministry of Finance, Japan

'This masterpiece is a must for anyone wanting to become an insider in Asia Pacific.'
Göran Lindahl, Executive Vice President, Asea Brown Boveri, Switzerland

'This book is a fascinating *tour de force*. Highly recommended!'
Nukul Prachuabmoh, former Minister of Transport & Telecommunications, and former Governor of the Bank of Thailand, Thailand

'This book is a brave attempt to provide a contemporary view of Asia Pacific at a time when the region is undergoing rapid and momentous changes. Highly recommended for the lay reader.'
Sim Kee Boon, Chairman, Keppel Corporation, Singapore

'... a comprehensive and in-depth analysis of the region, enabling the reader to better appreciate why it has developed so rapidly, and how it may develop in the future.'
Dr. Fritz Leutwiler, former Governor, Swiss National Bank, Switzerland

'Few businessmen have either the intellectual training or interests of Michael Dobbs-Higginson. Even fewer have tried, and succeeded, in understanding different cultures from their own. This book gives a remarkable insight into the region and those who read it will be better equipped to meet the challenges which await it.'
Malcolm Turnbull, Managing Director, Turnbull and Partners, Australia

'This book includes sensitive and perceptive analyses of the region's nations, presented in a lucid style and with great attempts at objectivity.'
Dr Helmut Sohmen, Chairman, World-Wide Shipping Agency Limited, Hong Kong

'With keen insight and satirical humour, Dobbs-Higginson ambitiously attempts to unravel the complexities of thousands of years of history and culture. A thoughtful book and well worth reading.'
Minoru Murofushi, President, Itochu Corporation, Japan

'Dobbs-Higginson has written a fresh, unbiased observation on a concept barely touched on. His analysis is well-informed and eloquently written. It is a superb contribution to, and a must for anyone interested in, Asia Pacific relations.'
Shigekuni Kawamura, President, Dainippon Ink & Chemicals Inc., Japan

'A fascinating analysis of the crucial subject of the future of Asia Pacific by a European with an impressive knowledge of, and experience in, the region.'
Dr. H. Onno Ruding, Vice Chairman, Citicorp, United States and former Minister of Finance, The Netherlands

'Dobbs-Higginson's thesis is sound and often highly persuasive. This book will serve as an important contribution to serious discussion on the region's future.'
Yuji Tsushima, Member of the House of Representatives, Japan

'A stimulating, lively, and thoughtful book. It provides many new and original perspectives on the region.'
Antoine Jeancourt-Galignani, President, Banque Indosuez, France

'A must-read for anyone wishing to come to grips with the historical, cultural, and geopolitical features of Asia Pacific. This book shows a rare understanding of the region.'
Koji Kakizawa, Parliamentary Vice Minister for Foreign Affairs, Japan

Preface

I was twenty. A wintry dawn filled the sky above the low buildings of Shino-In, a small Buddhist temple forming part of the main monastery complex of the Shingon sect situated at the top of Mount Koya in Japan. In the silent room of *tatami* mats, plastered walls and paper windows, beside my *futon*, my tea, left in a cup from the night before, had frozen solid. I had not slept much; it had been too cold. The night had passed as a kaleidoscope of images: the African savannahs of my childhood; the great cities of the West where I had studied and worked; the beaches and palm trees of Hawaii, left only days before. With morning, these familiar images slipped away. Alone in the monastery, I felt completely disconnected from everything.

Wood rasped against wood, breaking the silence. A black-robed monk entered, bringing the Japanese version of a continental breakfast: seaweed floating in a strange soup, pickled roots, some rice. Setting it down, he greeted me. Not a word made sense. The only Japanese I knew was *sayonara*, meaning 'goodbye'. It was a tempting, but hardly appropriate, response. Sitting on the *tatami*, freezing, starving and confused, I faced the reality of Buddhist monastic life. This moment, over thirty years ago, was the beginning of my personal odyssey through the cultures and countries of Asia Pacific.

For the three months I spent at the temple, I endured massive sensory deprivation. The food remained as strange as the first breakfast. I could talk to no one; no one talked to me. I could not read. Everything I could see was alien. Even the sounds were unfamiliar. The experience stripped me culturally naked. All I was able to do was hear and see, and attempt to imitate. For weeks and months, I could not understand, but in the end I would begin to. And during this experience, my personal philosophy began to take on a more concrete form.

I was not the first of my family to reach out to the East. My mother's Anglo-Irish family had been involved with India since the late eighteenth century. My father, the son of a British general, was born in Tientsin, China. I was brought up in Africa, in the isolated British colony of Southern Rhodesia — now known as Zimbabwe. After World War I, my grandfather had retired there to carve a farm out of the bush, and when my father left his British public school, he joined him. When my mother left her English public school, she went to the United States and in the 1930s travelled across the country and then worked her way through university. After earning a degree in medical osteopathy, she set off to practise in Africa. She showed up in Rhodesia knowing no one other than her future mother-in-law, whom she had met on the ship bringing them both to Cape Town. It was an adventurous step even now, but particularly brave in the 1930s. There she met and married my father, and passed on to me her fiercely independent nature.

Among my Rhodesian schoolmates, I was always the maverick. In the cultural and intellectual backwater of colonial Africa, my mother taught us that anything is possible, it just depended upon one's perspective. She also insisted that we never accept any belief or maxim until we had metaphorically tasted, touched, and kicked it. Her attitude was by no means the norm in that colonial society of God and Empire. I learned not to fear being an outsider and to take risks at an early age. By the time I was a teenager, Rhodesia had become too small. Leaving my family behind, at the age of eighteen, I set off on my odyssey.

For the next seven years I travelled around the world — fortunately, long before the hordes of hippies took to the road. I first went via South Africa to medical school at Trinity College in Dublin and then to a series of universities and monasteries in Europe, North America, and Asia. I did not graduate from any of these universities — I studied whatever interested me, and I left when I felt I had had enough and needed to go on to the next stage. Nor did I decide to spend the rest of my life in any of the monasteries. Early on, I chose to learn by doing things myself rather than by reading about what others had done.

My travels were financed by work: inspecting pork pies; selling oil paintings in Frankfurt; being a newspaper photographer and selling encyclopaedias in Alberta; logging on Vancouver Island; being a stevedore on the Alameda docks in San Francisco; running a laboratory on a US geodetic survey ship in the northern Pacific and a surfboard concession on Waikiki Beach in Hawaii; teaching English in Japan and mathematics in Thailand; being effectively press-ganged into the temporary service of a major Western intelligence agency; playing the foreign gangster in cheap Japanese movies; and antique art and gem dealing in Southeast Asia among many other jobs of all descriptions.

Intense curiosity gave me a craving for different experiences: studying German culture in a German Heimvolkshochschule; living with an artist, his wife, and his mistress in Frankfurt; discovering Longhead Indian burial caves in the northwest of Vancouver Island; being a Buddhist monk in monasteries in Japan and the Himalayas; studying the Japanese tea ceremony and flower arrangement; earning a black belt in Japanese *kendo* (sword fighting); studying sixteenth-century Japanese history and traditional Japanese architecture at Kyoto University; visiting the then legal opium dens of Vientiane; living in an ashram in Old Delhi; taking LSD with a Tibetan lama in the depths of the Himalayas (before the drug was generally known about, let alone illegal); exploring in remote areas of Asia and the Middle East (before they became much more accessible); living in an olive grove high above Beirut; participating in London's 'Debutante Season' (a fascinating anthropological experience); sailing the Atlantic in a seven-metre sloop; and studying at London University. Such diverse experiences helped me to appreciate how wonderfully strange, varied, and endlessly fascinating the world is.

These jobs and experiences reinforced my independent pursuit of philosophy, history, art, architecture, and adventure. By the time I was twenty-five, I had lived in more than a dozen countries, and had visited many more. I spoke almost fluent Japanese, reasonable French, and some German. I had developed a deep appreciation for Buddhism from monasteries in Japan, Thailand, and the Himalayas. The 'little discipline' of my monastic years — prioritisation, sense of purpose, and considerable objectivity — would have given me an edge whether I had decided to be a dustman, a rock singer, a banker, or a politician. But when I stopped wandering, I turned to commerce. Buddhism and business may seem incompatible, but an entrepreneur — like a monk — can cultivate his own identity while participating in the greater whole.

My business life began in London in 1967. At the same time, I met a woman who was equally independent and different. Marie-Thérèse, a French student studying English, impressed me with her clear sense of moral values, remarkable self-possession, and ability to create an oasis of calm around her — as well as with her ability to consume a bottle of whisky during an all-night discussion without being unduly affected. At midnight one night in 1967, we climbed to the top of a crane in St. Malo in Brittany and there, we decided to get married — but only if Marie-Thérèse would learn Japanese. By then I expected to be involved with Japan for the rest of my life.

I moved to Tokyo, and when Marie-Thérèse had passed her exams after studying Japanese in various parts of Japan for a year, she joined me there. We were married in the municipal city hall of Chiyoda-ku, Tokyo. During our five years in Japan, I started five companies with an American ex-GI partner, who also spoke Japanese — in wholesale travel, real estate, business consulting, automotive engineering, and a petrol-station, with a little export business on the side. I began to feel at home, even seeking out the soup I used to think so strange. But as I became comfortable with the East, I became disconnected from my Western roots. So in 1973, at the age of thirty-two, I returned to London to reconcile the two. I became a banker with a small investment bank, which would later become Credit Suisse First Boston.

Eleven years later, I joined Merrill Lynch, the then largest investment bank and brokerage house in the world. In 1985, I moved to Hong Kong to become chairman of Merrill Lynch's operations in the Asia Pacific region, which included all of the countries east of Pakistan, except Japan. My business and my personal life by then spanned cities from Salisbury to London, Frankfurt, and Montreal, from San Francisco to Tokyo, Sydney, and Bangkok, and from New Delhi to Stockholm and New York. My family and I enjoyed the privileges of three different nationalities, yet escaped feeling enclosed by any of them. Thirty years after first sitting, forlorn and bewildered, in a Japanese monastery with a bowl of seaweed, I felt equally at home in almost any country, East or West.

Initially, it did not bother me that Japan was not part of the region I was responsible for at Merrill Lynch. Its exclusion gave me a better chance to broaden further my knowledge of the rest of Asia Pacific. However, over the years, I came to believe that the future of the region must include Japan, and therefore, that it made sense for Japan to be included as part of my territory. For a variety of internal reasons this was not possible. So, in 1990, Merrill Lynch and I agreed to a friendly parting of the ways.

Working as an investment banker, and subsequently in pursuing my various interests, I have been constantly reminded how easy it is for Westerners to misunderstand the countries belonging to the Asia Pacific region (by my definition, the inverse triangle of India down to New Zealand and up to China and Japan). It should not be difficult to appreciate Asia Pacific's economic and political dynamism, but to understand this dynamism requires knowledge of more than just Asia Pacific's markets. It is the region's discipline and focus, its culture and philosophy, more than its investment strategies and corporate structures, that have created its trade surpluses. It is its newly evolving middle classes' 'people-power' that is causing such political change over such a short period of time. And it is the lack of understanding of these characteristics — rather than of its politics, science, and economics — that has created the barriers which still exist between the East and the West. Indeed, the same principles apply to the peoples of Asia Pacific themselves; they often misunderstand each other and, as a result, create barriers.

My current business and other interests have remained primarily focused on Asia Pacific. I now have the majority ownership of Processing Technologies International Limited, a processing technology (research and licensing) company, with activities worldwide; shareholding interests in the Royal Chiang Mai Country Club in Thailand, a horticultural company in Australia, a trading company in Burma, and a glass foam insulation manufacturing plant in Shanghai; an advisory role to Banque Indosuez, Paris, to a major Asian trading company, and to an Asian government ministry, all with regard to their activities in Asia Pacific; the sponsorship, with my family, of a small Foundation; and directorships in both Luthy Baillie Dowsett Pethic & Co. Holdings Limited, a UK private company, and Hotel Properties Limited, a major, publicly listed Singapore company.

Today, the Tourreau Foundation, which my family and I created in 1988, uses our French home, *Château de Tourreau*, in Provence, as its main base. We bring together at our home for two or three days at a time, politicians, bureaucrats, academics, and businessmen from both the West and Asia Pacific. We provide them with an opportunity to meet one another in agreeable surroundings, on a personal and individual basis (rather than as representatives of their organisations), and in complete privacy — and with all discussions being strictly off-the-record. Thus, this process of frank discussion hopefully creates an opportunity for strong personal friendships (if not at least respect) to develop. These relationships, in turn, will also hopefully lead to a marked improvement in communication and understanding between the individuals concerned and, by extension, ultimately between the peoples and cultures of their respective countries. This book, which has taken me five years to finish, is part of the same effort, and all its royalties will be donated to the Foundation.

At this point, I wish to emphasise that this book is not an academic one and, further, that I am not an economist. Rather, this book is written for the general reader, Asian or Western, who is interested in obtaining an overview of the Asia Pacific region, its past, present, and my vision as to its likely future. It is the result of my own motivation in trying, in some small way, to improve people's understanding of the region. It also derives from more than thirty years of passionate involvement both in the affairs of Asia Pacific and in how it and the rest of the world, Europe in particular, relate to each other. This book is specifically, therefore, my personal view on how the countries of the region are made up and why and how they should come together in order to create a regional forum. Further, my views are based primarily on the history, culture, and politics, rather than the economics, of the region's countries, with these views being coloured by my Buddhist philosophy of balance. However, I have, where relevant, included some general economic statistics which support my views.

For those who wish to obtain a more economic perspective, I can recommend Lester Thurow's *Head to Head: The Coming Economic Battle among Japan, Europe and America* (1992) which I have read with interest and profit. The reader will notice a number of references to Professor Thurow's work in Part Three of my text. I can likewise strongly commend the *International Herald Tribune*, *The Economist*, and *The Far Eastern Economic Review* for their general coverage, albeit in very different ways, of the region's affairs. In my opinion, these three latter publications, together with a local newspaper of one's choice, provide an ideal combination of international and regional reporting on the region's affairs. The reader will also note numerous references to these three publications in my text.

My hope is that with a better grasp of this vast subject, Western readers will be able to cope more empathetically, and thus more efficiently, with the countries of Asia Pacific in this time of extraordinary change. I hope, too, that readers in Asia Pacific will gain new insights into their region, into each of the countries within it, and into how they might collectively respond to each other and to the rest of the world in the new world order.

I see the world primarily in terms of whether or not it is in balance — both in the macro sense (of a country, a region, and the world itself) and in the micro sense (of the local community and the individual person). Everything one does, or the world does, affects and is also affected by whether the world, and oneself within it, is in a state of balance or not. Unless one understands oneself within oneself, oneself within the world, and then the world around one, how can one possibly achieve this balance in order to live (and work) effectively? Without proper balance, considerable energy needs to be used either to compensate for such imbalance or to attempt to achieve such balance. Correspondingly, with proper balance, considerable energy is freed up and can be used productively for achieving other, more rewarding, internal and external goals of both a spiritual and worldly nature.

Michael Dobbs-Higginson
March 1993

Introduction

As we all now know, the world is moving towards a different order. With the effective demise of communism, and of the superpower rivalry which has predominated since World War II, we are facing such a completely new set of operating conditions that most people haven't really begun to comprehend the ramifications, either in political or, more importantly, in economic terms. In the new world, our definitions for even common terms have changed. Our concepts of defence, government, leadership, and nationality have also begun to change dramatically.

In the West, two trading communities, the European Community (EC) and the North American Free Trade Agreement community (NAFTA), are emerging to fill at least a material part of the power vacuum caused by the Cold War's end. In the East, I believe that another such community is forming, and that its progress should be encouraged. If the Americas and the EC become increasingly protectionist as they organise themselves in these communities, countries in the East will become increasingly isolated and dependent upon one another in order to survive. Yet together these Eastern countries could command great strength and a force for the continuance of free trade, thus providing a genuine counterweight to the West — a balance the world requires.

My aim in the following pages is to describe and explain those countries encompassed in the triangular region, from India down to New Zealand and up to China and Japan, all of which I have chosen to define as Asia Pacific. I do this not only with reference to the region's internal changes over the centuries, and particularly since World War II, but also in terms of the way the region is most likely to adapt to the recent extraordinary developments in the rest of world.

In Part One of this book, I consider the Asia Pacific region as a whole.

It is standard to argue that the countries in this area are too diverse, too hostile to one another, and too geographically separated ever to come together as a coherent regional force. However, it is not often recognised that far from being divided, the region's peoples have benefited from a gradual blending of ethnic groups over the last two millenniums. In the broad sweep, the early history of Asia was similar to that of Europe — a never-ending succession of governments, wars, and regional mixing. Despite their variety, the religions and other philosophical beliefs of Asia Pacific share the same ideas of kinship, discipline, tolerance, and death. In today's technological world, travel and telecommunications have made physical barriers insignificant. Although there still remain significant barriers of understanding and there are many different national objectives, far less now divides Asia Pacific than ever before. Thus, in Part One, I have attempted to identify these changes and to demonstrate how the remaining barriers are eroding in such a way that some of these national objectives have, or will, become common ones.

I should make it clear from the outset that, in my view, the Asia Pacific region is really two sub-regions. One is from India to Indonesia and up to China and Japan. The second sub-region includes only Papua New Guinea, Australia, and New Zealand, which sub-region I have termed for the sake of convenience 'Australasia'.

In view of this point concerning the two sub-regions, I would ask the reader to indulge me in my approach to Part One in that most of the identified regional common factors are, in fact, common to the countries of the Asian sub-region, *or* to Australia and New Zealand, rather than to the Asia Pacific region as a whole. Thus, while my central argument is that all the region's countries today have more and more in common, Australasia does not yet have all that much in common with Asia. However, because Australasia, in my view, has no alternative but to look north for its long-term future, I believe my argument will become valid over the medium term. Furthermore, if one extrapolates on the existing Asian immigration to Australasia, the cross-fertilisation of business interests in both directions, and the current and future student generations' similar cross-fertilisation of career, intellectual, and other interests, the two sub-regions of Asia and Australasia will soon have more in common than otherwise. Finally, this tendency will be reinforced by the coming regionalisation of the world, which theme I develop further in Part Three.

Part Two examines the region country-by-country; in each case with a historical overview and an analysis of the culture, particularly the business culture, based on my own experience of many years' living and working in the region. While outlining each of the major countries' unique qualities, their strengths and weaknesses, I have tried to determine the positions they should and/or might take as they go forward into the future *vis-à-vis* both the other countries of Asia Pacific and the world as a whole. In these country chapters, it is only at the end of each chapter that I refer to the reasons why each country would benefit from supporting a regional forum and to the consequences of not doing so. It is in Part Three that I develop a detailed argument concerning the benefits of a regional forum.

I would like to draw the reader's attention to two further points. First, despite the vitally important role that I believe the countries of Southeast Asia will play in bringing the region together in the future, particularly the countries of the Association of South East Asian Nations (ASEAN), due to constraints imposed by my publisher I have had neither the time nor the space to do them full justice here. Secondly, I should point out that, due to the vast size and complexity of this region, I have deliberately left out a number of the smallest countries (either in general size or in economic terms), such as Nepal, Bhutan, Sikkim, Bangladesh, Sri Lanka, and the islands of Melanesia and Polynesia. This decision was taken simply on the grounds that, although they are geographically a part of Asia Pacific, and while in theory they could belong to a new Asia Pacific regional forum, their future involvement, if any, will probably only occur several stages later in the region's attempts to develop its own community forum — just as the country membership of the EC (and, for that matter, NAFTA) has evolved, and is still evolving, in stages over time.

In Part Three, I identify four major issues facing the world as a whole, namely the changes in the traditional East–West defence axes to North–South trade axes, in the nature of government, in the relevance of nationality as geographically defined, and in the definition of leadership. These issues are particularly relevant to the countries in the emerging Asia Pacific community. I also provide a suggested, general blueprint to show how an Asia Pacific regional community might evolve.

During the Cold War, world balance was maintained by the two superpowers on a defence/security-related East–West axis. In the new order, another kind of superpower rivalry will develop, based on North–South trade axes. Governments in the developed world will concentrate more on a new form of cold warfare, in the arena of trade and economics. And now that the threat of a superpower-initiated global nuclear holocaust has lessened, the man on the street will be much more vociferous about what he wants. Financial gain seems now to be his rationale, not fear or ideological or moral conviction. The world's different 'tribal communities' and its middle classes, including businessmen, will want to take a much more active role in deciding what their governments should and should not do for them, both domestically and in the domestic and global marketplaces respectively. Their demands will also call into question the relevance of national borders — and of national, particularly federal, governments. During the Cold War, many borders were drawn essentially to keep people in, or to keep people out; in most cases, this is no longer necessary. Ultimately, with the development of 'regional' and, conversely, 'tribal communities', the meaning and relevance of the current 'nation state' structures will be increasingly questioned.

All these factors will combine to produce a new form of world leadership — 'multi-polar' leadership — in which the power is shared by the world's leading economic powers on a pragmatic, business-like basis, rather than on an ideological one. At the same time, people all over the world are slowly forming both new regional groupings and, at the same time, tribal, or smaller community groupings. These new, geopolitical groupings are thus appearing on two levels: one is up in the stratosphere where people feel that a regional grouping such as the EC and NAFTA will provide them with the best 'club' to join, i.e. in contrast to the smaller, national government clubs which are proving to be so confused and ineffective at dealing with national, regional, and global issues. The other level is down below, in the provincial, sub-provincial, or tribal world of Karens, Sikhs, Quebeçois, Scots, Tamils, Latvians, Eritreans, Serbs, and Kashmiris, and finally down to municipal halls and other small community associations around the world where people feel they can fully participate in, and be responsible for, the proper functioning of such communities.

Separate from this process, these new macro- and micro-groupings, as well as existing nations, are all now likely to look more to the United Nations (UN) as the only truly neutral, supranational political entity. As long as it is appropriately funded and otherwise supported by its member states, the UN should become increasingly important as a forum for resolving global, regional, and even 'tribal community' problems. Its ability to fulfil this role was demonstrated during the Gulf War and its aftermath. But this exercise was a relatively simple one, namely the removal of the Iraqis from Kuwait. Since then, its interventions have become much more complex and the UN is not yet organisationally or intellectually prepared for such a role, which contrasts strongly with its traditional role of providing economic and social programmes. It must also be acknowledged that the UN management is ill-accustomed to managing directly military administrative matters, let alone military exercises. There appears to be considerable on-the-ground frustration — for example, in Yugoslavia and Cambodia — by senior military UN personnel about the responsiveness of their civilian masters, who are bureaucratic ones to boot! With all its peacekeeping initiatives around the world, many of them aimed at stopping countries with internal, hate-driven tribal warfare from becoming unglued, something has to be done before the UN loses its credibility. According to the Secretary General, in 1992 the UN was involved in thirteen peacekeeping operations around the world, with a total of 53,000 troops and at a cost of more than US$3 billion! The UN has a steep learning curve and some major structural adjustments to deal with before it can become fully effective. The endless self-interest and political indecisiveness of its member states will also continue to hamper its full evolution to such a Utopian position.

There is little doubt that the existing EC will grow in terms of its collective economic ambitions (rather than necessarily its collective political ambitions) to encompass a large part of Eastern Europe, Russia and, possibly, even North Africa. Similarly, the emerging free trade relationship between the United States, Canada, and Mexico will no doubt come to incorporate at least part of the Caribbean and Central and South America. If these initially trade-based communities in Europe and the Americas tend towards protectionist policies, this could leave other countries out in the cold; the booming economies of Asia Pacific will be particularly hard hit. It is essential, therefore, for the countries of Asia

Pacific to organise together and cultivate new markets in the vast and underdeveloped populations of their region. Not only will they become more self-sufficient, but collectively they will be in a stronger position to negotiate bilaterally with the other two economic communities.

Japan has a vital role to play in Asia Pacific. The old rhetoric is that, owing to its behaviour in World War II, Japan is mistrusted and feared by the rest of Asia Pacific. But I believe that Japanese co-leadership of Asia Pacific is not only needed but will, in fact, be largely welcomed by the other countries of the region. If Japan acts with sensitivity and discretion, it could also convert its peacekeeping initiatives in the region (Cambodia) into a contribution towards regional unification, as well as providing economic co-leadership. While Japan is far more vulnerable than is generally supposed, in the near term it is the only Asia Pacific country with the economic credibility and strength to negotiate with the rest of the world. The other countries of the region should harness this power for the collective good of the whole.

India must also be considered part of the Asia Pacific equation. India's loss, both of its historical ties with Europe, in particular with Britain, and of its more recent close relationship with the Soviet Union, has left it in potential isolation. Asia Pacific needs India. Its long history, the size of its markets, and the quality of its workforce are all factors which can help to counter-balance the huge potential of a future 'Greater China', namely the People's Republic of China, Taiwan, Hong Kong, the 'Overseas Chinese' spread throughout the rest of the region — and, possibly, Singapore. In this connection, the countries of ASEAN (namely Brunei, Indonesia, Malaysia, the Philippines, Singapore, and Thailand) will also have a major role to play. The same general principle possibly applies to offsetting the potential strength of a future Asiatic Russia.

Southeast Asia, Japan, China, Korea, Australasia, India, even Asiatic Russia and all the other nations of Asia Pacific, have something to offer and something to gain from a regional community. Their future success lies in establishing an equilibrium, or a state of balance, between them, and, from such a position, with the rest of the world. Thus, in my proposed general blueprint for such a regional community, I have taken the pragmatic view that none of the countries of the region will accept Japan attempting to provide the primary leadership (as opposed to their co-leadership) for such a community and that China has too much on its plate to be able to even contemplate such a role. Further, it is my view that Australia and its Asia Pacific Economic Co-operation (APEC) initiative, which also includes the United States and Canada as members, has tried and will fail (for reasons I explain later), that India has first to be generally accepted as a real member of the region and, finally, that there is no other single country with the ability and clout to launch with credibility any such initiative. Therefore, I have suggested that ASEAN is the most viable and credible locomotive for negotiating into place such a regional community forum. It has the structure in place, the neutrality *vis-à-vis* the bigger regional players, and its members individually have much to gain.

I should re-emphasise that I have based my vision of such a regional community forum on historical, cultural, geopolitical, and philosophical arguments. I have not attempted to provide a detailed economic analysis of the effects of creating such a forum.

I believe that the new trade cold war is already almost upon us. The skirmishing has begun: the testing both of the various parties' will to tough it out (and not bluff it out) when making threats, and to stand their ground before such threats. All this is not helped by the high probability that the Uruguay Round of the General Agreement on Tariffs and Trade (GATT) will miss its next deadline and thereafter no doubt continue to lurch from deadline to deadline. This will probably occur without giving any comfort that a resolution will be forthcoming. It will no doubt turn into a kind of trade-war version of the nuclear superpower confrontation which itself lurched from crisis/deadline to crisis/deadline until the Soviet Union collapsed. Unfortunately, in this new equation, there is really no party that will or can actually collapse and thus allow a final resolution as in the case of capitalism versus communism.

I must also emphasise that I do not envisage (sadly) any immediate attempt by the countries of Asia Pacific to form a regional forum. It will no doubt take years, but I have no doubt that one will eventually be formed from the ASEAN base building blocks. My only hope is that such a forum is formed for the right reasons (i.e. because it makes intrinsic sense) and at the right time (from a position of strength and peace), rather than as a defensive reaction at a time of weakness and fear.

Therefore, the primary purpose of this book is not only to provide the reader with my view on these issues but, more importantly, to provoke as widespread a debate as possible on such issues, particularly within the region.

In Part Four, the Epilogue, I have attempted to address some of the fundamental issues, such as moral versus economic objectives and the paradoxical long-term trend towards both smaller and larger communities, which issues I believe will face the Asia Pacific region, and indeed the world, during the next twenty-five to fifty years.

On a final, general point, I should confess that this book could be viewed by the purist or the technically or academically inclined reader as being three books rolled into one. In such case, there could be some cause for criticism. More specifically, the first 'book' could be defined as Parts One and Two, which describe the countries of the region, with it being deemed that some of the countries reviewed have not received equal or sufficient treatment. The second 'book', Part Three, could be defined as being primarily an argument on why and how an Asia Pacific regional forum should be formed, with it being deemed that there is insufficient economic data and, in turn, insufficient economic justification for such a forum. The third 'book', being Part Four, could be defined as a preliminary philosophical argument as to the diminishing moral value system in the new world order, with it being deemed that, while the subject has been clearly identified, no solution has been suggested. I would, however, beg the reader's indulgence concerning these views.

In defence, I would claim that the three 'books' are related in historical, cultural, economic, geopolitical, and philosophical terms. The world's national and regional geopolitical and economic conditions are in a considerable, and in many cases an extraordinary, state of flux, and in Asia Pacific there is a greater positive, potential convergence of these general factors than elsewhere. I have consequently taken the view that the generalist reader would rather have an overview of these separate, but interlinked, subjects presented in one book that is easy to read, than have a detailed analysis presented in a much more academic manner in three volumes.

Overview

Overview
It is Time to Abandon the Old Orthodoxy

It seems sensible to begin with the obvious question: 'Why Asia Pacific?' What do these countries and peoples have in common which might lead us to believe that a new geopolitical/economic community is a real possibility? The Asia Pacific region has known little unity in the past. East from India to China and Japan, and south through Asia to Australasia, hundreds of languages are spoken; people pray to Allah, Christ, Buddha, and Mammon; socialists and capitalists vie for power; silicon chip factories thrive next to rice paddies ploughed by water buffalo; and people live in Stone-Age villages and crowded into futuristic cities. Many of these societies have followed divergent traditions for centuries. The Koreans and the Japanese have long been rivals, while the distrust between Cambodia and Vietnam goes back millenniums.

However, despite the incredible diversity of Asia Pacific, there are common themes, and changes elsewhere are forcing countries in the region to rely more upon these commonalities than their differences. In the future, the countries of Asia Pacific won't be able to ignore each other. Nor, for that matter, will the rest of the world be able to ignore a more united Asia Pacific. The region is stronger than ever before. Japan has developed into an economic superpower. Korea, Taiwan, Singapore, and Hong Kong are growing so quickly that they will soon be on a par with the already-industrialised countries. Thailand and Malaysia are not far behind. China will, and India may (if it can get its act together), catch up soon. For continued success, all these countries are counting on free trade. None has a market large enough or affluent enough to support expansion by itself. None has all the resources necessary for a modern economy. Traditionally, all of Asia Pacific has relied upon Europe and the United States for investment, technology and, most importantly, for export markets. With the rise of new economic groups and the possibility of protectionism and economic and trade competition, Asia Pacific may not be able to continue to rely on these regions in the same manner as before. It will have to look within.

Scholars have traditionally asserted that the Asia Pacific region will always be divided. Until a few years ago, everyone assumed that Russia would hold Eastern Europe for the foreseeable future. As we have seen, however, orthodoxy can be turned on its head in the space of a few months. Not to take account of the discipline, determination, focus, and overall economic strength of a united Asia Pacific could prove to be very costly in the race for a share of the global marketplace. It is my view that many of the divisive forces which pertained in the past are no longer relevant. In fact, as a result of the recent tumultuous changes in the world, many of these forces will now become unifying factors.

The first argument against the idea of Asia Pacific unity is usually the geography of the region. About the only generalisation upon which scholars can agree is that the countries of this region possess sweep and drama: vast plains, soaring mountains, volcanoes, deserts, and dense jungles. Neither palm trees, nor terraced rice fields, nor steppes predominate. Asia Pacific has the earth's highest point and its lowest, and some of the world's wettest, and driest, spots. It has the deepest lake and the deepest river. But Asia Pacific has little to compare with the immense plains of European Russia, the American Midwest, and Northern Europe. Their unrelenting, fertile flatness is somehow reassuring to farmer and city dweller alike; it is solid, manageable. Asia Pacific poses a challenge to man: an interlocking complex of dominant mountain ranges alternating with plateaux, basins, rich river lowlands, and island arcs.

Unlike the United States and Europe, where the mountains mostly run north–south, the mountains of Asia Pacific (excluding Australia) run mostly east–west, to form an immense amphitheatre facing north, and blocking the beneficent influence of the warm coastal waters to the south and east. Thus the interior two-thirds of these vast land masses are either too cold or too dry to support more than isolated nomadic tribes. The great civilisations of Asia Pacific have tended to rise on the golden edges of the Asian and Australian continents and in the valleys and plains along the Indus and the Ganges rivers in India; the Yellow and Yangtze rivers in China; the Mekong, Irrawaddy, and Salween rivers in Southeast Asia; and the Murray and other rivers in Australia. People have also settled and terraced the edges of the lower mountains: the Eastern and Western Ghats which flank south–central India's Deccan plateau; the curving ranges of Southeast Asia; the hilly, river-threaded landscape of China; and the profusion of mountains which from the air make Japan, Korea, and New Zealand look like seas in a heavy gale. The dry, cold vastness of the interior creates monsoon weather patterns on this periphery, which makes possible the intense cultivation necessary to feed the vast populations that live there.

Island groups fringe much of this varied, crowded region — great unsolved jigsaw puzzle pieces separated by lagoons, straits, seas, and even oceans. Volcanoes and earthquakes threw up most of these island chains, which are partly submerged mountain belts branching off the Himalayas and Karakoram.

Until modern times it was true that no interconnection, no community could arise in such a vast, varied expanse of land and water, but now the once insurmountable barriers are being overcome. Air travel and telecommunications have opened the nations of Asia Pacific to the world and to each other. Asia Pacific is no longer at the ends of the earth. The aeroplane, the telephone, the fax machine, and as yet undreamed-of technologies, are making the physical barriers irrelevant. In the coming century, Asia Pacific will be less hindered by geography than at any time in the past.

The barriers that remain — the sheer distance from Europe and the Americas — will actually make it more natural and convenient for Asia Pacific to focus in on itself. It makes more sense for Korea to import Chinese or Australian coal than to import it at a higher cost from America or Africa. Minerals from Australia can support industries in Japan. Food from Australia and New Zealand can fill the supermarkets of Hong Kong and Tokyo. Indian exports will find ready markets in nearby Asia Pacific, rather than in distant Europe which has been India's traditional, major trading partner. Common economic interests will lead to more personal and political ties, further encouraging the nations of Asia Pacific to a union of interest, and therefore of purpose.

Even if barriers of geography now mean less than they once did, it is still a fair observation that there are a dizzying number of peoples in Asia Pacific between whom discord could arise at any moment. Yet in prehistoric times, the Asia Pacific peoples mixed slowly but thoroughly.

The Chinese came originally from the west and settled along the Yellow River valley. From there, they moved north into Siberia, Korea, and Japan, assimilating with the native populations. Tribes of Chinese descent also travelled down into Southeast Asia. The Khmers came from the northwest to settle the interior of what is now Cambodia. The Lao also came from China originally. The Thai peoples, known as Shan in Burma (Myanmar), were the last major group to move from southwest China into Southeast Asia, where they mixed with the Caucasoid races which had moved into the region from India. The tribes of the Central Asian plateaux are also Caucasoid, and although they were never ethnically dominant in Asia Pacific, their marauding migrations did much to stir up the ethnic pot. They were probably responsible for the Caucasians found in pockets of Asia — the Papuans in New Guinea and a tribe in northern Japan known as the Ainu.

During the last 300 years, Asia has been not so unlike Europe. Poverty, war, politics, religious differences, and economic opportunities have caused people to migrate from country to country. During China's imperial rule, poverty drove tens of millions of Chinese to spread throughout Asia Pacific and beyond. Several hundred thousand Koreans were forced to move to Japan to replace Japanese soldiers fighting in World War II. Since then, waves of refugees have fled the turmoil in Indochina. There have also been economic refugees: would-be business-men travelling abroad to look for better opportunities; Vietnamese boat people sailing to Hong Kong in search of a better life (and now being sent back); Filipinos taking domestic positions in the homes of expatriates all over the world, but mostly in Asia; and, most recently, Asians have begun to move to Australia and New Zealand, to take advantage of the open space, economic opportunities, and greater political freedom.

When outsiders have moved into already-inhabited areas, friction has usually ensued. But often this has been followed by gradual assimilation. When the Mongols took over China, they became more Chinese than the Chinese. India, home to successive waves of immigrants — the Aryans, the Greeks, the Moguls — is a complex, undefinable mix of peoples and cultures. In southern Asia, the cuisines of the region follow a natural progression — Indian dishes and flavours gradually adapting to become more and more Chinese — reflecting the peoples there. The Chinese communities all over Asia Pacific share in both their host culture and their Chinese heritage. Many Southeast Asian languages incorporate words from Chinese and from the Indian Hindi, as well as from its ancestors Sanskrit and Persian. Thus, far from being always sharply divided, the peoples of Asia Pacific have participated in a slow mixing and sharing.

As the recent changes in the world make borders more symbolic than physical, the peoples of Asia Pacific will begin to mix even more freely, following the imperatives of business and a natural desire to explore. The Indians living in India, Singapore, Hong Kong, and Japan will do business with each other, as will the Chinese in Australia, Thailand, and the Philippines, and the corporate Japanese everywhere they travel in Asia Pacific. Australasian and Southeast Asian students will enrol at universities in Japan and vice versa.

The skies are already full of Boeing 747s carrying newly affluent Asia Pacific tourists in every direction: from Bangkok to Tibet and Mandalay, from Goa to Darwin, from Pusan to the ski slopes of New Zealand, from Bombay to Bali. The Pacific Area Travel Association has published figures showing that the number of Asia Pacific people travelling within the region has increased from just under 11 million in 1980 to approximately 26.5 million in 1990. As commerce and tourism between the nations of the region become more common, tourists and businessmen are pushing their governments to allow freer travel and trade between nations, just as earlier in this century the Europeans started pushing their governments to do the same.

Links between families also tie the region together. The only constant in the cultures of the various Asia Pacific peoples is the primacy of the family, which is encouraged by most of the religions. The anthropologist who called the Philippines an 'anarchy of families' could have been speaking of almost any Asian country. In China, the word for country is made up of two characters, 'nation' and 'family'. In virtually all the great traditional societies of Asia, it is the family that preserves social cohesion and solidarity. Although this generalisation does not apply to Australia and New Zealand, with the passage of time and with greater Asian involvement in Australasia through increasing immigration, student exchanges, and business, it will have more relevance in the future.

In most Asian countries, it is the custom to be extremely indulgent and permissive in bringing up young children, so that they feel totally secure in the family's warm embrace. This means that as adults, they fear social rejection above everything; dissent and non-conformity often become psychological impossibilities. So strong are these feelings that, for instance, the chief minister of an Indian state resigned in 1968 because his mother disapproved of his activities and ordered him to give them up.

Other relationships are modelled on the family. Political parties tend to be a cluster of patron–client relationships. A local landowner or businessman who wishes to enter provincial or national politics offers himself as the patron of the peasants in his district. Like a father, he secures for them government development projects and tax exemptions. And like sons, they vote for him at elections and bring their disputes to him for arbitration. Similarly, the legal systems of Asia Pacific are expected not merely to judge, but also to conciliate, in the manner of a father. According to the Japan Research Institute, 35 per cent of all cases that actually went to court in Japan in 1991 were settled out of court.

Family ties are the best indicator of the winners in Asian elections. About 40 per cent of Japanese politicians are sons or adopted sons of politicians—in effect, politics in Japan have become a kind of family business. For most of the years since independence in 1947, India has been ruled by a single family: first Jawaharlal Nehru, then his only daughter Indira Gandhi, then her son Rajiv Gandhi. They were a dynasty without a throne. The same was the case with Chiang Kai-shek's son in Taiwan. In North Korea, Kim Jong-Il is the front runner to succeed his father.

These patterns also hold in business. In China, preferential hiring of workers' children has made many factory jobs essentially hereditary positions. The Marwaris, from a village in the Indian region of Rajasthan, have risen to business prominence all over the country but remain linked by the greater family of the ancestral village. All over Asia, there is a preference towards doing business with one's own ethnic family. Ethnic Chinese will always have a predisposition to deal with other ethnic Chinese; Sindhis will instinctively prefer to do business with other Sindhis. And taking this one step further, it may be generally said that Asians will always feel more comfortable doing business with other Asians than with Americans or Europeans.

The diversity of religious belief — too many gods representing too many different value systems — is another argument used against regional unity. Some joke that the region produces religions like an apple tree bears apples. The Hindus, for example, have some 300 million gods, while the Bon Tibetan pantheon claims 70,000 second-rank deities in addition to the 20 top-ranking gods and goddesses. The Chinese, who are sometimes accused of being irreligious, actually feel that there can never be too many gods or practical rites. Chinese emperors had a minister whose sole responsibility was overseeing rites. Today, so some will argue, this is one of the principal roles remaining for Japan's emperor.

At least part of the religious argument against Asia Pacific unity is true. Islam has always been the odd man out in Asia and a definite force for disunity and conflict. So also, to the surprise of many, has Hinduism been, as evidenced in the sectarian riots in India in the early 1990s. Additionally, Hinduism and Confucianism have been forces for social inertia. And yet there is no time when someone in Asia Pacific is not offering a chant, a song, a call, or a prayer to the Almighty, the Jade Emperor, Allah, Shiva, Brahman, the Sun Goddess, Buddha, or Jesus. Asia Pacific overflows with serene and monstrous images, painted and carved, smiling and grimacing, before which the faithful prostrate themselves, pray, and meditate.

Religious influence is a decisive factor everywhere. The manufacturer of some of the best Japanese cameras has named the most perfect after Kwannon, a great deity of the Buddhist pantheon — Canon. The relationship between Asian peoples and their gods is so intimate that it is impossible to draw a hard and fast dividing line between them. In Thailand or Hong Kong, and in many other parts of Asia, people don't think twice about having a picnic in a temple. The temple is a home.

The roads of the region have been pounded by the feet of countless pilgrims making holy journeys to sacred mountains, enshrined relics, famous monasteries. Saffron-robed monks in the third century BC first carried the Buddha's message from India to the rest of Asia, where it has played a part in the cultural history of almost every country. As Buddhism expanded into Asia, it gradually lost strength in the land of its birth — today Buddhism is no longer one of the main religions of India. Where it has established itself in other countries, followers have divided into two camps: in Sri Lanka and Southeast Asia, believers preach the *Hinayana* or

'Lesser Vehicle', so called because it holds out salvation only to a committed few; in the rest of Buddhist Asia, the *Mahayana* or 'Greater Vehicle' lets everyone have a chance. Practices vary from place to place, as the Buddha's message has often mixed with native theologies — in the process becoming practically a new religion. And yet, throughout the region, there are people travelling towards the same goal — *nirvana*, the ultimate extinction of the self. It is in concepts such as this that the detachment of the East lies, a detachment often very difficult for the occidental mind to comprehend.

The peoples of Asia also share numerous other related forms of belief in the 'undefinable', such as their faith in the various kinds of fortune telling. Astrology is taken very seriously in Asia, and many senior politicians, bureaucrats, and private-sector businessmen are influenced in their decision making by the configurations of the stars. Indonesia's President Suharto regularly consults astrologers on the timing of his actions. While it is true that the American president Ronald Reagan allegedly did the same, the practice of astrology in the West is generally perceived to be a rather fringe activity and not to be taken seriously.

The major faiths of Asia have tended to influence the development of highly organised, stratified societies, and while religion solidifies ties within certain groups — marking them off from their neighbours — in some ways it ties groups together. When Indians from Hong Kong do business with Indians from Singapore, it brings these nations one step closer. Even though the Japanese and the Koreans have difficulties with each other, their Confucian, family-based societies have a similarity in structure, which at least allows them common ground from which to express their respective positions.

Throughout the region, religion and culture have created governments which almost instinctively prefer to develop policy by consensus rather than by the open cut and thrust of Western politics. Tolerance is one trait shared by all the Asian beliefs, except those which have their origin in the Judaeo-Christian and Islamic heritages. In Asia, a person's intolerance towards other religions is more often than not considered proof of his spiritual unfitness. Buddhism spread and endured, unstained by religious wars or holy inquisitions. Daoists find proselytism repugnant. In Asia, whatever belief an individual or a group might have about God, it is not considered final. There are thousands of gods. As the Great Khan Mongka put it, 'The various religions are like five fingers on one hand.'

Once again, in this equation, the sub-region of Australasia is the odd man out. Yet the basic Christian beliefs of Australia and New Zealand are not entirely at odds with the rest of the region. Japan, Korea, and China have substantial, strong Christian communities. Other countries in the region also have, and give recognition to, their Christian communities. Many such communities are a result of former colonial ties and related Christian missionary work, yet many new and younger converts have been exposed to Christianity when studying abroad. Conversely, the Asian immigrants to Australasia have taken with them their ancient beliefs; as more join them, these linkages will strengthen.

In addition to providing a little-recognised common ground between different cultures, Asian religions impart many lessons which make the peoples of Asia Pacific better prepared for the new world of economic trade. The most important of these is the Asian concept of death. Because Asians believe the spirit is in a constant state of evolution, taking one's own life, either to make a political statement or to accept responsibility for one's actions, has had a long, honourable tradition in Asia. Japanese *samurai* were able to face ritual suicide with bravery. At the beginning of the Vietnam War, monks immolated themselves in fire to protest the abuses of the American-backed regime. A more recent example is the Indian students who burned themselves to death in protest against the Indian government's proposed new legislation to reserve a percentage of jobs for the lower castes. All these actions required a dispassionate conviction, common to the Asian, that death is not the end. This belief freed them to act. It has allowed people to conquer pain, to be willing to take more risks, and to take a longer-term view.

T he peoples of Asia Pacific are by no means unique in their distrust of strangers; a history of battles with outsiders is common to every region of the world. However, for all the countries in Asia Pacific, the most frightening outsiders were the 'Western barbarians', and conflicts with Western barbarians form a shared experience over several centuries. Nothing was so strange nor so threatening to the average Asian as the Caucasian Westerner. In China, they are called 'foreign ghosts'(Chinese ghosts and monsters are usually blond and blue-eyed); or *ang mo gau* ('red-haired monkey'); *or yang gee tzu* ('overseas devil'); and many other uncomplimentary names. In Japan, Westerners were once called *ketojin* ('hairy, red-nosed barbarians'). The Australian Aborigines called them *gaba* ('government men'), while the Maoris in New Zealand called them *pakeha* ('white strangers'). And yet, for most of Asia Pacific's history, Westerners were isolated curiosities with little influence on the places they visited, and none at all beyond.

The first Westerner to exert a profound influence on the Asia Pacific region was probably Alexander the Great who, advancing south to conquer Greece, Egypt, and the great Persian Empire, mused that if the Egyptians could be folded into his dominion, so might the Asians. Moving eastward, the conqueror burst through the Khyber Pass and into India, overwhelming the various city-state kingdoms in the Punjab. Alexander wanted to press on to the Ganges River, where he believed Asia came to an end, but his troops refused to move further east and so Alexander moved down the river valley of the Indus, conquering its peoples in a campaign of horrible slaughter.

Throughout the age of Alexander, and from the fourth century BC to the waning days of the *Pax Romana* in the first century AD, trade links were open from the West to the Orient. Yet India and Central Asia remained barriers to direct cultural exchange because few, if any, individuals made the entire journey from West to East or from East to West. Those who did were usually slaves who had little impact on the cultures to which they were taken. Instead, traders played a game of cultural telephone which stretched across the Eurasian continent from the Mediterranean through Samarkand to China. Western culture faded imperceptibly into Eastern with each step of the camel trains, until, towards the end of the fourth century AD, Central Asian tribes severed these lines of communication.

Almost a millennium later, after the depredations of the Mongol hordes in Europe, Western governments sent emissaries to Asia to see whether there was a possibility of re-establishing trade links. John of Plano Carpini returned to France with a letter from the Khan inviting the Pope to pay him homage and to send a hundred Europeans to his court at Xanadu outside Beijing. The Pope sent five men, amongst them Marco

Polo, who became famous for his tales of huge walled cities and highways, strange animals, and empires of gold.

Marco Polo, and the friars that went before him, were more influenced by the East than vice versa. The accounts written by Polo and Carpini resonate with their superior disdain and yet are full of their worries about the potential threat from the allegedly inferior Asian 'barbarians'—while the Khan regarded their Christianity and clocks as nothing more than vulgar curiosities.

In 1498, Europe opened the door between East and West again, this time by sea. When Vasco da Gama and a party of 160 men made a landfall at 'Calicut' on the southwest coast of India, nobody in the East or the West fully appreciated the importance of the moment. India's rulers felt they had little to fear from a few bold men and three puny ships. But the fantastic profits earned by da Gama's voyage ensured that soon more and more Europeans would be landing at Calicut. From there, European interests expanded eastward. Soon, most of Asia had to bow before the bigger guns, faster ships, and more advanced military and industrial technology of the Europeans.

The Western assault caused tremendous pain in a region where 'face' is one of the central concepts of society. And the Western assault did not long remain confined to the material level of trade. Missionaries quickly followed in the wake of the merchant galleons. Their evangelising called into question the definition and future evolution of not only each of the Asian countries' governments and cultures but of their very souls.

While the missions may not have been particularly successful, the mission schools were. After the arrival of the Jesuits in Macau in the sixteenth century, networks of missionary schools sprang up throughout Asia Pacific, teaching the élite the tenets of Western liberalism. Christian schools established by the British survive to this day in India and elsewhere in Asia. In 1905, the Chinese government abolished the imperial examination system, based on rote learning of Confucian precepts of behaviour and government. Great Christian educational and medical institutions were constructed, and many who would become leaders of post-imperial China were educated in these schools, including Sun Yat-sen, who would be responsible for the downfall of the last Chinese dynasty, and Chiang Kai-shek, Sun's political heir.

As the Asia Pacific countries adapted to cope with the challenges set by the outside world, they were hampered by a number of obstacles for which the West was also responsible. Colonising nations often drew borders on maps without any consideration for ethnic or geographic boundaries. For this reason, for example, many Thais live outside Thailand. Malaysia has been defined politically and geographically, but it has found it difficult to construct a commonly accepted national culture for the Malay, Indian, and Chinese populations within its borders. Many nations in Asia Pacific are fighting guerrilla wars against minority races who feel no national loyalty to the 'country' in which they live. The collection of tribal island cultures that is the Philippines has little more than its colonial past to unify it. The same is true for Malaysia, India, and Indonesia.

After independence, those Asian nations which had previously been colonised returned to many of their old patterns where people were pitted against people, island against island, province against province. Only a few decades ago, village life in most of Asia was largely self-contained, with its own order and hierarchy. As the colonial governments receded, and faced with the necessity of having to survive in the global community, new governments have had to forge new nations from these constellations of villages. In the West, this process took four centuries. The nations of Asia Pacific have had only slightly more than four decades.

It has been a painful process. A crisis of identity could be said to exist in every country in Asia Pacific, while governments see-saw between rejection and acceptance of Western ideas and attempt to cope with the momentous changes following the end of the Cold War. Although Lee Kuan Yew has been referred to in England as the 'finest Englishman west of the Suez', he has in fact tried to create a model Confucian state. This dichotomy has played an important part in almost all of Asia Pacific's social upheavals, rebellions, or conflicts. In an effort to return to what was truly Cambodian, Pol Pot's regime brutally liquidated its European-educated intelligentsia — and millions of others besides. The Chinese spent most of the first half of the twentieth century debating and fighting over how to incorporate Western ideas into their society, before finally bowing to a government based on their own version of Marxism, a Western philosophy. Throughout Asia Pacific, intellectuals are trying to recover from the impact of Western power and are learning to discriminate between the desirable and the undesirable, to digest one and reject the other. In the meantime, the skylines of Bangkok, Seoul, Jakarta, Taipei, and other Asian cities are in a constant state of dramatic flux, throwing up buildings with classical Doric columns, mock Tudor restaurants, and fake-rustic native buildings floored with linoleum and lit with neon.

Although it is usually concluded that the Western influence on Asia has been divisive, there is a unity in the form of the struggle against this influence. China and India may disagree, may be very different culturally, but they have the colonial experience in common. When Britain, France, and the Netherlands withdrew from their Asian colonies, they all left an imprint of Western law, Western bureaucracy, and a sense of structure. Unlike Europeans and Americans, who have been able to remain comfortably smug about their own superiority, the peoples of Asia Pacific have been forced to embrace and understand foreign cultures. There are not many Western masters of Korean drums or Chinese opera, but there are many concert-calibre violinists and pianists in the East—in Korea, Japan, and China, for example. The facility the citizens of Asia Pacific have developed for learning about foreign ideas, whilst remaining within their own native culture, gives them a significant advantage over their Western peers. However, it should be recognised that this phenomenon is certainly not universal, as there are a number of minority races, such as the hill tribes of Thailand, Burma, and elsewhere, as well as the Aborigines of Australia and the Maoris of New Zealand, who have not benefited in the same way.

Should it become necessary to rally for fierce competition against the United States and Europe, Asia will also enjoy some psychological advantages. The most important of these is, ironically, the fact that Asia has suffered from, and thus has been substantially influenced by, what I call the 'pain factor'. Wars are not, of course, unique to Asia, but in this region they have been particularly brutal and have endured until very recently. Since the beginning of the twentieth century, the Japanese have contributed considerable pain in the process of furthering their territorial ambitions. Their efforts culminated in World War II, when they imposed their dream of a Japanese-led 'Greater East Asia Co-Prosperity Sphere'. Subsequently, between 1966 and 1976, China's Cultural Revolution brought death or persecution to most families. Napalm and other bombs have rained down on Vietnam. The Khmer Rouge buried millions in mass graves in Cambodia. In India, Partition led to huge massacres; rioting has plagued the country ever since. More than a million Indonesians died in the 1965 communist insurrection. The Korean War killed one and three-quarter million people. Both Korea and Taiwan are in a constant state of military preparedness. Filipino peasants have been caught in the crossfire between the army and communist guerrillas. Military coup has followed military coup in Thailand. Burma, now called Myanmar, has repressed its own people, as well as fighting ongoing wars with separatist hill tribes. While the United States and Europe have enjoyed relative peace in the post-World War II era, it has seldom been possible to escape the sound of gunfire in some part of Asia Pacific.

The region has also been steadily battered by natural disasters. Since 1900, earthquakes have killed almost 850,000 in Asia Pacific, more than twice the number killed in major quakes in all the other regions of the world. Asia Pacific's typhoons have killed some 450,000 in the same period. Floods have washed away more than 4 million people. Outside the region, only some 25,000 have died from similar causes. It is a tough part of the world. Hundreds of millions live lives of unremitting drudgery and hopelessness. Of the estimated fifty-plus major famines in the world since the Middle Ages, nineteen have been in Asia: sixteen in the Indian subcontinent and three in China. In 1987, the Food and Agriculture Organization of the United Nations (FAO) summed up the harshness of life in the region: 'In many parts of Asia, the human achievements of the twentieth century have made no mark. The rural poor continue to carry the burden of contaminated water, hunger, malnutrition. They stand by, helpless, as their babies die. For those who survive their first year, the average life span will be barely more than half that enjoyed in richer countries, or in the richer sections of their own countries.'

With chaos ever a possibility, prosperity is never taken for granted in Asia. In China and India, people often ask 'Have you eaten yet?' before asking 'How are you?' The Japanese from the Osaka area ask, 'Are you making a profit?' Most Asians live as peasants, and their lives are a tough, relentless cycle of field work, debt, uncertainty, and early death. Eleven of the world's twenty-five most populous areas lie within Asia Pacific, where more than half of the people live on less than one-quarter of the world's land area. There is always a shortage of something: privacy, food, education, medicine, land. People get used to doing without.

This experience has given Asians a different outlook on life. While Westerners have grown rich, comfortable, often lazy, and often feeling that their government owes them a living, most Asians have remained tough and willing to make personal sacrifices for the benefit of future generations. In Asia Pacific, people prioritise. On a personal level, this means that small businessmen are willing to work eighteen hours a day to make their ventures successful. Their children come home and help them even though they may have six hours of homework. In Europe, Filipinos take jobs as servants, and send the money home so that the next generation can be educated and have a better chance. In Britain, the small, Indian-owned supermarkets have carved out a market niche by staying open late at night. This kind of commitment and sacrifice is the reason why Korean grocers have been able to take over the vegetable business in many of the main metropolitan cities of the United States in the space of a few years.

Most of the generation now in power in Asia Pacific has lived through World War II, the pain of reconstruction, and the upheaval ever since. In most countries, especially those with a Confucian ethos, people find the motivation to work long hours out of a determination that the younger generation will never suffer as they have. These survivors seldom squander their money. Savings rates in Asia are typically considerably higher than in Europe and, especially, the United States. Between 1980 and 1986, the citizens of Japan and the Four Dragons — Hong Kong, Singapore, Korea, and Taiwan — saved the equivalent of one-third of their countries' Gross Domestic Product (GDP).

Huge savings are made on a national level. In order to build a modern industrial infrastructure on the devastation left by the Korean War, the South Korean government exhorted their people to eat barley, tradition-ally a famine food and usually only eaten by the poor, and not rice, which was then considered a luxury food. Barley, as a cold-climate crop, could be grown and harvested during the fallow, winter and spring season for rice. They did this, not for a year or two, but for fifteen years. Ironically, today, barley is considered a fashionable health food and it commands a premium! Japanese management and workers will frequently take a voluntary cut in their regular bonuses or even in their pay in order to see the company through hard times, something virtually unheard of in American or European firms. On the base of these sacrifices, Asian countries have poured their initially scant resources into building ship-yards, steel plants, high-technology factories, and so on. Such a strategy has brought great wealth to Japan, the first to start this process after World War II, and since then to Korea, Taiwan, Hong Kong, and Singapore. Now it is beginning to bring wealth to the next round of countries: Malaysia, Thailand, Indonesia, China, and India.

Governments in Asia, both socialist and capitalist, plan far into the future. Taiwan determines its economic strategy in five-year plans. In the early stages of Japan's industrialisation, government policy performed a valuable and important role by choosing to concentrate on certain industries and avoiding duplication of effort. Today, Japanese companies commonly have strategies worked out for the next twenty years. In Korea, the industrial conglomerates known as '*Chaebol*' had, and to a large extent still have, close relationships with government. Central planning has not always guaranteed success — governments have picked some initial losers, for example petrochemicals in Singapore and shipbuilding in Taiwan — but in the main, it has helped to create many of Asia's success stories.

Suffering has not only made the nations of Asia Pacific more likely to succeed in business, it has also prepared them to deal with a world in which changes come quickly and often without warning. A hundred years ago — despite the inevitable wars, depressions, and confrontations — the world was much more stable. It was divided into countries, and the countries were organised into separate economic and political sectors. Although there was communication between these sectors and countries, they were to a large degree independent entities. If they affected each other it was usually by a slow process which took years. Even twenty to thirty years ago, most people counted on this stability and made long-term investments. People bought bonds and held them until they came to term. They held stocks for decades. Speculators accounted for only a small percentage of investors, and were considered rapscallions by the others.

All that has changed. Now, given the rapidity of change, most investors are speculators. Capital chases around the world at the touch of a button. Since 1989, most currencies and many bonds and shares are traded globally. The new, freer atmosphere has allowed financial wizards to invent whole new ranges of highly sophisticated financial instruments. Currency and stock options and futures markets have sprouted in international markets. Companies have become less timid about making cross-border acquisitions. Some industries — chemicals, pharmaceuticals, media, advertising — went acquisition mad. Marketing companies now look for global opportunities to sell their products. Anything with the power to leap across a frontier — a consumer brand or patented intellectual property — increases in value. Uncertainty and change rule the day.

The world has become like a kaleidoscope. With each turn of the globe, everything changes. And with each turn, there is the danger of economic confusion. An economic falter in Australia can affect investors in Tokyo and London. The actions of Tokyo bond traders can dramatically affect those in New York. And these cause-and-effect relationships are not limited to the economic sphere. There is more and more contact between different spheres, between politics and economics, for example. In the mid-1970s when Libyan MIGs challenged American fighter jets over the Mediterranean, the price of gold shot up for a few days even though there was no actual combat. Even casual comments by heads of state or central bank governors can materially affect business. Every day, the relationships between different parties change, and change in one relationship affects change in all of the others. For example, when the dividing wall between East and West came down, the German equity market skyrocketed. The Deutschmark appreciated 30 per cent in the last six months of 1989 and again appreciated substantially in the latter part of 1992 during the chaotic European currency markets of that period.

The mid- to late 1990s are likely to see a further increase in the rapidity and degree of change, and on a global scale. Some people will find it difficult to adapt. But for those who live in Asia Pacific, uncertainty has been, and is, a fact of daily life. When typhoons hit Japan, people have traditionally gathered their belongings and calmly moved to higher ground. In the West, hysteria is usually the first reaction to any such crisis.

When American soldiers occupied Japan after World War II, they were astounded by the polite reception they received from the Japanese. But among many reasons for this, the Japanese knew from experience that it was wiser to adapt. As the Asian saying goes, the peoples of Asia have learned to bend not break, as bamboo bends before the wind — hopefully the Australasians will learn this philosophy from their northern neighbours so that they will be able to integrate with them more effectively. It is this flexibility, more than anything else, which will allow the peoples of Asia Pacific to meet the challenge of the future by turning conventional orthodoxy on its head and creating a regional forum to help them deal with the challenges of playing a major role on the world's economic and political stage.

PART TWO

The Principal Players
of Asia Pacific

JAPAN

In Search of Understanding
and a New Role for Itself

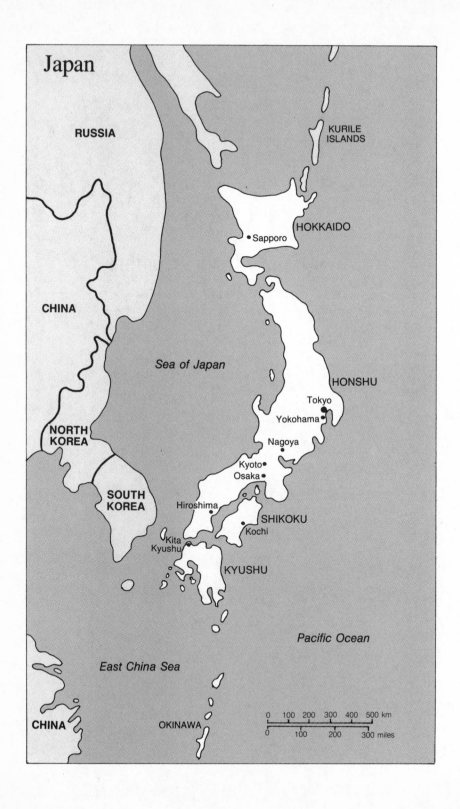

Japan

RUSSIA

KURILE
ISLANDS

HOKKAIDO

•Sapporo

CHINA

Sea of Japan

HONSHU

Tokyo
Yokohama•

Nagoya•

NORTH
KOREA

Kyoto•
Osaka•

SOUTH
KOREA

Hiroshima•
SHIKOKU

Kochi•

Kita
Kyushu•
KYUSHU

Pacific Ocean

East China Sea

CHINA   OKINAWA

0   100 200 300 400 500 km

0   100   200   300 miles

JAPAN

In Search of Understanding and a New Role for Itself

O rthodox critiques of Japan always seem to assume that, although the Japanese are perplexingly different, they are like the rest of the human race in their social structure, and thus entirely to blame for their various crimes, such as insensitivity, trade surpluses, and diplomatic ineptitude. But the Japanese are not like the rest of us. Place, time, and history have marked off Japan from the rest of the world, and although Japan's citizens have the same skyscrapers, wear the same clothes, and play the same golf, in most respects Japan remains as Japanese as it was four hundred or even a thousand years ago. But the signs of change are already clearly evident.

Most early societies, once they had the tools, tried to control their natural environment, and from there went on to try and control everything else. The Japanese have never tried to control nature; they have simply accepted that they were, and are, part of it. For all their sophisticated aesthetics and amazing technology, the Japanese still live closer to a state of nature than any other nation, both literally and figuratively. This is in part because the Japanese have never been able to escape nature's vagaries. Typhoons, volcanic eruptions, earthquakes, and tidal waves have over the centuries given the Japanese an absolute sense of the immutability of nature, and the impossibility of controlling it. Instead, they have learned to adapt by building their structures with flexible materials, which until the advent of the twentieth century usually meant wood, reeds, and paper. They blur the line between nature and the home, never marking themselves off from nature, never building huge stone edifices, victory arches, cathedrals, Great Walls, or Aswan Dams. Their language — with more than forty different words for rain — exhibits a finely-tuned appreciation of nature's nuances.

As less than one-third of the land is habitable, the Japanese people have also had to learn to live in close proximity to one another. With paper screens forming walls, privacy is impossible, and so the Japanese have developed a system of social filters. When confronted close-up with someone they don't know, the Japanese don't see him. When accosted by a stranger in a manner that is not polite, they don't hear him. When oppressed by an overcrowded environment like a rush-hour train, they don't sense it. When confronted by an inescapable embarrassment, they don't recognise it.

Concepts of morality and guilt distance a society from nature. It is entirely inappropriate to impose ideals of fairness and order upon nature's random acts and often brutal processes of self-correction. Too many Japanese do not experience guilt because they do not believe in fairness, even as an ideal, although this phenomenon is now becoming less true of the younger Japanese generations as they become more exposed to, and influenced by, the rest of the world. In nature there is only survival and balance. The Japanese have a different burden. They feel shame if the group judges their actions inappropriate. But if they can avoid the opprobrium of the group, they remain free of both guilt and shame no matter what their actions are.

With such different frames of reference, it is almost impossible for Westerners, and even the people of the rest of Asia Pacific, to judge Japan on common ground. There is virtually none. For example, although the behaviour of the Japanese and the Germans during World War II was equally appalling, while the Western world was perfectly entitled to damn the Germans, it cannot make as harsh a judgement of Japan. Hitler's regime departed from all the common values laboriously developed by Western civilisation during the previous two millenniums. In contrast, Japanese behaviour during World War II remained perfectly consistent with the standards evolved by their civilisation. The Japanese did what they had always done, and did unto others as they did to their own people. Some may insist that certain acts are universally wrong. This reaction is natural from a Western standpoint. It is certainly true in a moral sense. But it does nothing to advance the world's understanding of Japan, which has a completely different set of rules. Railing against this reality or assessing blame serves little purpose. Only through understanding — on both sides — can the chasm between Japan and the rest of the world be bridged.

One of the most compelling analyses of modern Japan has been advanced by the Dutch journalist and businessman Karel van Wolferen in his book *The Enigma of Japanese Power* (1989). Van Wolferen suggests that Japan's political system, its lack of absolute leadership, is the cause of Japan's inability to deal equitably with the rest of the world. Conversely, it is the cause of the rest of the world's inability to understand Japan, let alone deal with it. Van Wolferen has done a superb job of outlining the characteristics of what he calls, rather darkly, the Japanese 'System'. However, he falls into the typical trap of a Westerner—namely, using Western concepts and terminology to analyse a completely alien structure. Van Wolferen suggests that those ruling Japan have consciously decided to live in a system which most non-Japanese would find threatening from the outside and intolerable from the inside. But the Japanese have never made a specific, conscious decision to live as they do. Programmed over centuries as their society has evolved, the Japanese don't consider and then decide how to respond, they just react instinctively. The goal of ensuring the survival of their self-contained system remains their only constant.

In short, while the rest of the world (the West and East included) is largely populated by troups of bickering individualistic monkeys doing their own thing and often paying no more than lip service to the concept of good of the community or nationhood, Japan is a gigantic, rich, and frighteningly efficient ant colony.

No doubt many, both Japanese and others, will take offence at this analogy — but such a reaction will no doubt be rather emotionally based and possibly also demonstrate little knowledge of how ant communities actually work and of how fascinatingly complex and efficient they are. From many points of view, ants are more admirable than monkeys! Thus this analogy should not be viewed as absolute or pejorative but, rather, as one that makes the distinctions much clearer. Further, to reinforce this point, I wish to add that after more than thirty years of close involvement with Japan, I have a profound respect for its culture and most of its achievements. I also have a considerable, yet objective, affection for its people. Thus I wish to give no offence in using this analogy; rather, I wish to use it as a dramatic vehicle to highlight the marked differences between the Japanese approach to communication and life, and that of the rest of the world. I have learned a great deal from the Japanese, for which I am truly grateful. However, despite all this, I reserve the right to be objective in my views and I believe that many of the characteristics of the Japanese people can best be explained by using this analogy.

Ants have one of the most complicated social structures in the animal kingdom. Yet despite the many species of ant, this structure is based on a very few basic concepts: hierarchy, the subordination of individual desires, and an absolute commitment to collective goals, even to the point of death. Ant colonies, like most undisturbed systems in nature, tend to stay instinctively in balance. If one group grows too strong or strays too far from a collective goal, it is corrected, absorbed, or eliminated. Each task has its own set group of programmed ants. When there is no food, some volunteer to be eaten. When a colony becomes too big, young queens are produced to draw off a portion of the colony. Ants don't worry about abstract concepts of morality, freedom, or goodness, which transcend the colony system itself. Ants don't rely upon active, central leadership. The supposed leader of a colony — the queen — does nothing but lay eggs. Yet the worker ants, the warrior ants, and the food-gathering ants, amongst others, divide into their respective groups to pursue the colony's objectives almost as if by mental telepathy.

It may sound preposterous at first, but virtually all the things that can be said of ants can be said about the Japanese. They live according to a dizzyingly complex system of social rules. Japanese society emphasises hierarchy, subordination of the individual, and collective action. The overall society relentlessly programmes these ideas until they become instinctive. Left to itself, this society stays in balance. It hardly ever allows one family or one group to become too powerful. Collectively, the Japanese don't subscribe to any higher set of values that transcends their own self-interest. Japanese society divides into groups of endlessly diminishing sizes — political parties, ministries, companies, even criminal organisations, down to alumni groups for every conceivable activity.

To watch the Japanese in action, go to any major tourist attraction in the world. Sometime during the day, a group of Japanese travellers is sure to spill out of an air-conditioned tour bus. Carrying their tour group flags and their cameras, they will start frantically posing for photos in front of the landmark or descend *en masse* on some delighted shopkeeper. The Japanese do nothing solo. When they go on holiday they don't leave their neighbours and co-workers behind, they go as their representatives. Holidaymakers have a duty to bring back pictures and presents for those waiting at home.

You can take the Japanese out of the country, but you can't take the country out of the Japanese. Very few, if any, Japanese tourists, business-men, or diplomats blend into the life of a foreign country. The rest of the world is too different. So the Japanese bring their social patterns with them.

Japanese society can be supremely hierarchical, practical, and brutal in its competition — albeit subtly so. Ant colonies compete fiercely with one another when confronted; likewise, balance in Japanese society has been a result of fierce rivalry between competing groups. Even in the seventh century, when they had just adopted Chinese ideas of order and central rule, the Japanese provincial clans continued to compete compulsively. Shifting alliances of feudal clans remained the nexus of power until the modern age. Today, these clan groupings have been replaced by new groupings of bureaucrats, company executives, and politicians. Nothing has changed. The first goal of Matsushita electronics is to outsell Sony electronics — then to outsell Europe's Phillips electronics. Even within companies, divisions and subdivisions are set in competition with each other. Co-operation is a secondary and subsequent consideration.

The rule is survival of the fittest. It is not surprising that having survived the tests they set for themselves, Japanese companies often find foreign competitors, even in their foreign markets, a walkover. Systemic harmony and specific brutality is the rule of nature. In the case of the Japanese, it also results in extraordinary economic success.

While industry is divided into competitive *gurupu*, or conglomerates, government splinters into rival political parties and rival ministries. These groups, and the sub-groups in turn, exert ceaseless restraint, mutual scrutiny, and interference upon each other. Government in Japan is quite different from government in the rest of the developed world. No one is ultimately in charge. Of course, hierarchy exists, but in each group, not within society as a whole. No one rules the entire roost.

Japan's dominant Liberal Democratic Party (LDP) is not really liberal. In fact, it would be difficult to say that it is democratic, or even a party, in the Western sense of those words. The LDP and the other political parties are more a coalition of *habatsu*, or political factions. While these political parties have direct grass roots organisation, they rely more on other organisations to further their interests at the local level. These organisations in turn rely on the politicians for support in dealing with the bureaucrats who dispense government largess. In agriculture, a system known as the *Nokyo* ensures that farmers completely support the bureaucracy. The *Nokyo* is an interwoven network of agricultural co-operatives, subsidiaries, sister organisations, and specialised federations. Farmers must rely on the *Nokyo* for everything from fertiliser supplies and marketing networks to bank loans and insurance. In return for these services, the farmers must support the local candidates put up by the LDP or the other parties.

Political parties do not have an identifiable system to regulate leadership changes. Nor does the LDP, the only party that really matters, claim to support any identifiable principles. According to the constitution, executive power wielded by the LDP is vested in the cabinet. But most Japanese ministers do not run the departments whose portfolios they hold. They tend to have little or no influence within their ministries. The regular cabinet reshuffles do not give ministers time to absorb enough detail to outsmart their top bureaucrats. The very people who are supposed to lead can't really take individual charge — in any case, they don't actually wish to, as otherwise their position would become suspect and the system would fail.

If prime ministers and their cabinets had the time to develop decisive, central power, it would push the system out of balance. So that one group or person doesn't become too powerful and their followers too disaffected, leaders change like the seasons. The political factions ensure that no prime minister stays too long and that each faction gets a crack. Prime ministers come and go every couple of years. Very few rebel successfully against the seasonality.

In all this circus-like balancing act, what matters is loyalty to the group. While the idea of Japanese unity under the emperor was most often a fiction, it remains an important fiction. Without the concept that Japan and the emperor are one, the balance of the whole system could break down. In feudal Japan, it was vital that the nobility should profess notional loyalty to the emperor through the ruling lord (or *shogun*) of the time, to whom they also owed loyalty. The ruling feudal lord then claimed that the emperor had given him the exclusive mandate to rule in his name. The same applies today, except that the actors are different. They are the bureaucrats, the politicians, and the businessmen, all vying for power with no leader except the titular emperor. Without the veneer of this controlling untruth, absolutely nothing would check the vicious rivalries of the underlying real system and Japanese society could disintegrate into chaos.

This natural, self-correcting mechanism has kept overall order in Japan, but at the price of constant tension. In order to keep it from growing to overwhelming proportions, a delicate web of often conflicting obligations, debts, and favours has evolved. First there is *on,* or the obligation a person automatically has to his emperor, his parents, his teachers, and his company. No one can fully repay this obligation, and indeed no one is expected to, because it is infinite. In effect, it is a form of psychological bondage. The next system of linkages consists of formal obligations, or *gimmu,* which demand repayment and can encompass legal or contractual obligations. The remaining important form of social linkages is that of inter-personal obligations, or *giri.* These require acknowledgement and repayment: doing a favour for a friend, or giving a greater gift than one has received. One might even owe a return favour to a distant relative who once helped an ancestor.

Not only does every Japanese owe these obligations to others, but he also has obligations to himself, to clear his reputation of insult, to admit no failure, to respect all the Japanese proprieties. With so many duties and obligations to so many people, these must necessarily conflict. But in the overall structure, these obligations take precedence over everything, over concepts of morality, or personal preference. When the confused foreigner criticises and asks of a Japanese the 'why' of an action which to him appears wrong, the Japanese will often say, 'I could not do the "right" thing because of *giri.*' In fact, in such case, by following *giri,* the Japanese actually felt he did do, by his definition, the right thing! However, it is im-portant to point out that, since World War II, these obligations have generally begun to weaken — further evidence that the nature of the Japanese is changing, albeit slowly.

Another fascinating example of the complexity of Japanese life is the language itself. It is a generally accepted principle that language reflects the nature of a people. This could not be more true than in Japan. The Japanese language is imprecise. Rather than providing a means to state concepts logically, Japanese relies on suggestion and inference. Singular and plural forms exist only rarely in Japanese. The number, and indeed the sex, of a subject can often be construed only from the context. When one demands a direct response, a Japanese hardly ever answers with a simple 'yes' or 'no'. The Japanese 'yes' means, 'I hear what you are saying' rather than any confirmation, or indeed any understanding, of what was said. If inclined to be negative or uninterested, rather than say 'no' and have to give the appropriate justification, the usual Japanese response is '*kentoshimasho*' — 'Let's study it.' This is almost always the kiss of death, as it postpones the proposition indefinitely. Decisions that merit discussion are reached by consultation and committee. Consensus is the goal. If one man makes a decree, colleagues and subordinates resent him, regardless of his status. Any sharp conflict that might disrupt the group is avoided. In most societies, problems and issues can be resolved with a simple yes or no, and people move on to the next subject. In Japan, the impossibility of direct answers, which may be deemed confrontational, drags out this process. An answer may come eventually, but waiting requires the patience of Job. The Japanese have this in great quantity, but few outsiders do.

Collectively, these linguistic characteristics are designed to help eliminate friction. Some Japanese may hate each other, but not in an articulated personal way. For example, the Japanese language has almost no swear words. In times of fury, the Japanese can call each other stupid, very stupid, or blindingly stupid. These few epithets comprise almost the full range of Japanese profanity. In times of elation, the Japanese language similarly limits the choice of words. Expressions of extreme anger or happiness would take the person expressing these feelings into the realm of strong individual expression. As individualism is suspect, such expressions are very rare, unless to very close intimates.

Japan's various religions and beliefs have helped to reinforce the country's unique nature. As with other foreign elements, the Japanese did not adopt wholesale the religious influences which arrived in Japan. Buddhism, Daoism, and Confucianism were adapted and collectively blended together with Shintoism to become part of the structure which binds Japanese society together.

Shintoism is indigenous to Japan. The origins of this ancient and animistic belief go back before recorded history and encompass the worship of a variety of ancestors, village gods, and nature. At the head is the Supreme Sun Goddess, Amaterasu, who leads a complex pantheon of *kami*, or 'gods', divinities presiding over everything in old Japan. *Kami* live in rocks, trees, the family well, the yard, the gate. *Kami* preside over villages and over the processes by which people make their living: the looms, the pottery wheels, the anvils. Shinto deifies emperors as well as various national heroes. Shinto does not present a formal moral or philosophical system but a set of customs and rituals. A Japanese scholar once put it this way: 'We don't have theology, we dance.'

Shinto places of worship, like the central shrine facing the rising sun at Ise, remain simple without images, wonderfully roofed with parts painted a clear red. During a typical ceremony, Shinto priests, wearing spotless white vestments with black head-dresses and carrying evergreen branches, file back and forth in columns. Music rises, eerie, reedy, punctuated with heavy drumbeats and gongs, threaded with harplike plucks of a *koto*, summoning spirits. Then dancers appear, moving slowly, as if in a dream. The pines, the rocks, the forest, mountains, air, and sea of Japan seem to send forth spirits in response. And when the music dies, the dancers retire. The rocks and forests lie silent, and yet they are somehow alive, the tall conifers rising as natural ziggurats. Living Shinto demands gratitude and awe amidst the mystery of nature. Its rituals stress purity, especially bodily cleanliness, symbolic of the open, pure mind necessary to appreciate life's imponderables.

While Shinto ties believers to the rhythms of nature, it has also been used by the ruling élite as an instrument to reinforce the Japanese people's loyalty to society. Shinto fosters the belief that, since the Japanese have occupied their island as long as anyone can remember, they are all related to each other, to the divine emperor and, ultimately, to the Sun Goddess herself. In the 1930s and 1940s, these aspects of Shinto were used by the military rightists to whip the Japanese into a nationalistic frenzy. During World War II, this spirit sent many young pilots off to commit suicide — *kamikaze* — or, in the case of soldiers as well as civilians, to jump off cliffs rather than suffer the disgrace of being captured. After Japan's defeat, the American occupation government banned Shinto as an instrument of the state. That there are as many Shintoists today is due in part to the unchanging nature of the Japanese culture which still requires Shinto ritual to sustain it, viz. the ceremonies surrounding the late Emperor Showa's funeral in 1989 and the enthronement of his son, Emperor Akihito, in 1990.

Over the centuries, the Japanese appreciation for the beauty and wonder of nature fostered by Shinto merged with Buddhist ideas of unity and intuition. The ruling classes, who had the necessary time and sophistication, were greatly attracted to the austere Zen form of Buddhism which sought to open the way to spiritual insight by self-denial. Self and life were secondary to duty and obligation and, as with Shintoism, Zen brought society into nature while also providing the feudal leaders with a philosophical dogma to inspire absolute loyalty from their retainers.

Zen came into its full flower as an influence on Japanese culture during the feudal Ashikaga period, which lasted from the fourteenth to the sixteenth century. During this period, the feudal lords, or *daimyo,* and their warrior retainers, the *samurai,* lived by *Bushido* — the way of the warrior, a creed based on Zen Buddhism which enshrined honour, loyalty, fearlessness, and self-denial. Because it was espoused by these powerful and admired elements in society, Zen came to influence every aspect of Japanese life, from government, to the martial arts, architecture, flower arranging, and tea drinking.

While Zen created a philosophical motivation to adhere to the ant-like rules of Japanese social structure, China's Confucianism provided the hierarchical forms and the social rules of this structure. Confucian philosophies preach an idealistic, but resoundingly practical approach to life. According to Confucius, man is essentially good. Ministers should honour their emperors; sons, their fathers; wives, their husbands; the young, their elders; friends, each other. People should be honest, and should be prepared to sacrifice themselves for the good of the whole, the family, the state. All of these ideas appealed to the Japanese leaders; however, they also knew that a wholesale adoption of Confucianism would destroy the balance of their society. Confucius taught that benevolence was the most effective power for harmonisation of life on earth.

According to the Chinese interpretation, leaders had a moral obligation to act benevolently and the common people had a duty to rebel against them if they were unjust. The Japanese chose to interpret this message in another way. Leaders bestowed benevolence as a gift at their discretion; they had no sense of obligation to their subjects, nor did the subjects expect any. Absolute, unthinking loyalty and obedience were the rule.

The Japanese people still consider differing ranks and status immutable, like the sun and the seasons. Hierarchy dominates the school, the family, the office, even the tea ceremony. People exchange business cards before greeting each other so that each will know how deeply to bow. The superior bends slightly at the waist, the subordinate may bow 45 degrees. Within companies, people refer to each other by the year they joined the company — those who joined earlier have a higher rank. It is natural for a Japanese to shape his inter-personal relationships according to age, status, and affiliation. Japan is probably the only country in the world which publishes the equivalent of a *Who's Who* with a special section listing the schools, universities, and graduating classes of all the members of the Japanese establishment. This provides everyone with an immediate frame of reference as to each person's position relative to everyone else. Once these positions are clarified, everyone knows how to behave.

In modern Japan, the education system determines how and where individuals fit into the hierarchy. Education performs the same function in other countries, but not with the rigidity it does in Japan. In the West and in other countries of Asia Pacific, people can rise from nowhere to the pinnacle of society. Mao Zedong spent his childhood in a village, as did China's current leader Deng Xiaoping. Former British prime minister Margaret Thatcher started life as a grocer's daughter. However, once one has entered university, similar success stories, while not impossible, occur with much less frequency in Japan. A middle-sized company would not dream of trying to hire a graduate from the prestigious Tokyo University. Likewise, a graduate of a middle-level school like Hiroshima University would not dream of a career with a top-flight corporation or government ministry. The Japanese tend to stay where society has decided they belong.

Since the group is really a matter of life or death, parents teach their children loyalty and submission to the group almost from birth. When they start school, children have already accepted their place in, and their need for, the larger whole. Thus to remain included, they somehow endure the gruelling pressure and unrelenting regimentation of the Japanese education system. Success at school — and from there a place at the best university — provides the main opportunity for the Japanese to achieve a higher 'classification' in society.

Schools suppress spontaneous reasoning, as well as spontaneous behaviour. Teachers do not instruct their pupils in how to think logically, or how to ask the right questions — or really how to ask any questions at all. Instead, Japanese education stresses memorising, memorising, memorising, in this way embedding in the subconscious the idea that obedience is the prime principle — 'do as you're told, don't think, and we'll look after you.' Those who make it to college get a last chance to rebel, to ignore their studies, and to adopt wild fashions. However, almost all will shape up after graduation. Early lessons exert a powerful hold.

Over and over, in numerous ways, Japanese society hammers home the idea that the group is supreme, and loyalty to it essential. When young adults join a company, they go through a lengthy indoctrination. Although everyone starts at the bottom, all move up steadily. All workers in Japanese production companies become union members. Eventually, union members become management. It is difficult to take a hard line with a manager who was one's senior union colleague and mentor just a year before and who will continue to be one's mentor in the future.

Subtle leverage keeps the peace. In spite of the ideology of class struggle that colours union pronouncements, few Japanese plants are crippled by strikes. Few man hours are lost to absenteeism. Workers organise unions on the basis of companies, not occupations — making it difficult for them to take independent stands. On the other side of the corporate desk, managers don't fire people. As people move up the corporate ladder, and competition grows more fierce for a smaller number of jobs, those who lose out in the survival-of-the-fittest stakes are moved laterally to other divisions, to subsidiary companies, or to associated group companies. The company tries to find a place for everyone, even if it is pushing paper for most of the day.

About one-third of Japan's workers enjoy the security of lifetime employment and in return are steadfastly loyal to their employers. The other two-thirds may be loyal to their companies, but don't have absolute job security. This majority of the workforce either works for small firms which can't offer lifetime tenure or as non-tenured workers for large corporations. However, in order for this two-thirds to survive, they and their companies must be loyal to the larger corporations upon whose discretionary benevolence they rely.

Japanese law mandates that bureaucrats retire at age sixty, well before old age makes it impossible to work. The system provides that when they leave government, in a phenomenon called *amakudari*, or 'descent from heaven', many senior bureaucrats take jobs in industry, banking, or politics. Their new positions often double their income and give them significant influence and handsome fringe benefits. A firm that accepts an *amakudari* bureaucrat can usually expect a favour from the ministry concerned. As new businessmen, they, and their personal ties with the bureaucracy and with politicians, link business to government. Similarly, other former bureaucrats find second careers as politicians in the Diet, where they tie the political system into the bureaucracy. This process is a very important part of tying the Japanese system together.

The group does not require a loss of self. In fact, in Japan one really has no true self-identity without the group. Feudal Japan pitied a man without a master. *Ronin*, as the masterless *samurai* were called, could be desperate characters. In modern Japan, likewise, a man without a company is nothing. Everyone needs a *kamban* — a 'shop sign' or, more loosely, a 'label' — or company connection, otherwise people won't know how to deal with him.

In other countries, societies are composed of separate organisations — labour unions, stockholders, legislators, consumer groups, churches — which have at least one primary goal in common: they advocate individual rights. In Japan, these groups are just part of the social structure, constantly and instinctively supporting the establishment in their dissent, rather than trying to change anything. Consumer groups advocate protectionism. Japanese courts enforce laws selectively. If society's interests are threatened, these positions create a paradox: consumers lobby for prices to stay high and citizen protection groups advocate legislation that doesn't protect because society chooses not to enforce it. In fact, the legislature does not legislate. Stockholders do not demand dividends. Labour unions are usually considerate enough to organise strikes to be held during lunch breaks. When faced with the threat of a rebellious and independent union, companies often respond by sponsoring a rival, more moderate union. Before long, employees realise that continued rebellion would block their promotion prospects. Soon the new alternative union attracts more members than the troublesome union, and thus keeps the group whole.

Traditionally, in all these contexts, rebelling against the status quo endangers the society's collective programming. Thus rebellion in Japan has been almost invariably a pointless exercise, as the relentless nature of the system has been designed to maintain the group, and thus the balance, at any cost. The usual outcome is not that society changes but that the rebels are subsumed by the ant colony. In the most extreme cases, they are excluded, and relegated, in the Japanese sense, to non-existence. The old Japanese proverb '*deru kuge wa utareru*' — 'the nail that sticks up gets beaten down' — sums it up very well.

To call an Englishman an eccentric — in other words, a strongly individual person — is a compliment. To a Japanese, it's an insult. In the West, and indeed in most of Asia, individual vision and drive bring people to the top of their professions. In Japan, the recipe for success is generally just the opposite. Success almost invariably comes from being all things to all people, rather than from being a strong individual. To draw too much attention to oneself as an individual invites resistance from the rest of society.

With a sense of pleasure and relief, some Western observers have noted that the Japanese are becoming more individualistic, emulating the West in their feverish pursuit of consumer status symbols. Japanese consumers are indeed buying Gucci handbags, Burberry raincoats, and Rolex watches. In the West and in Japan, consumers buy signature goods because of strong brand recognition; Westerners also want an assertive symbol of material success to prove that they as individuals are 'as good as the Joneses'. In Japan, consumers buy the same goods for another reason as well; to prove they belong to the right group. Mr Watanabe does not want to be different from Mr Saito or better, he wants to be the same. It is a small difference, but a crucial one. Perhaps, the Japanese person might allow himself a small personal display of individualism in the choice of Rolex versus Cartier. Some hope exists that Mr Watanabe could become more like Mr Jones in the future — but for the present, the group remains supreme in Japan.

This collective system requires endless, circuitous discussion. But once a decision is made, the whole weight of the group is behind the action. Unlike in the rest of the world where the individual or group has to worry about in-fighting after the course is mapped out, Japanese organisations can charge ahead without such worries, like ants which can move objects several times their weight. So the Japanese can enter the American computer chip market and, within a few years, dominate it; go from a feudal society to a modern military power in a scant fifty years, as they did in the second half of the nineteenth century; and rebuild from atomic rubble to be an economic superpower in only forty years. Bookshelves groan with recent Western books trying to explain the roots of Japanese success. In many ways, it can be explained as their equivalent of what was called, in another century, the Protestant work ethic. But more than just this collective work ethic, it is Japan's ant-like social structure which has prevailed over the world's economy.

Just as an ant colony is self-contained, Japan has been self-contained for most of its history. Today, the Japanese sense of 'we-ness' versus 'they-ness' remains stronger than in any other modernised country. The Japanese have a sharp awareness of themselves as being Japanese and of others as being, first of all, 'not Japanese'. Officials have actually explained to foreign businessmen that medicine manufactured by foreign firms must undergo special tests before being allowed into Japan because of the different construction of Japanese bodies. Not so long ago, Japanese businessmen or tourists on arrival at JFK airport in New York could be heard whispering, 'Gosh, there sure are a lot of foreigners here.'

Given their unique history, it is not unreasonable for the Japanese to have developed a strong sense of being unique and isolated. They were. With the exception of primitive tribes in the dense jungles of the Amazon and of Papua New Guinea, no race has had the opportunity to develop a completely independent culture as the Japanese have had. Between the seventh century, when Japanese recorded history begins, and World War II, Japan was spared the military and ensuing cultural invasions which battered the rest of the world. For most of early history, the countries of mainland Asia largely ignored the island chain, if they even knew it existed. It was AD 57 before the first recorded blip of recognition appeared: a cursory note in Chinese court records mentions a visit by Japanese envoys. In the third century, the Chinese chroniclers of the Kingdom of Wei were amazed to discover that the Empress Himiko of the Kingdom of Wa (as the Chinese then called Japan) remained set apart from her people and ruled them via her younger brother. This was the earliest record of a common theme throughout Japanese history—namely, that titular power could be, or is, very different from real power. In subsequent centuries, few rulers on mainland Asia paid Japan much attention. Only one ruler, the ferocious Kublai Khan, the grandson of Genghis Khan, was interested enough to try to invade Japan; he failed.

No one knows the origins of the Japanese people with any certainty. Elements in the language hint at a Polynesian/Southeast Asian connection in early times. Intriguing bits of evidence — like tribes in the northern hills of India who eat sushi — point to even more distant connections. Recent archaeological evidence has indicated that the emperor may well be descended from a Korean prince or noble, but for nationalistic reasons any discussion of this has been effectively suppressed.

Japanese recorded history begins with the *Kojiki*, or Record of Ancient Matters, and the *Nihonshoki*, or History of Japan. These works are mostly make-believe. Both begin with the Japanese creation myth which chronicles the story of Ninigi, the grandson of the Sun goddess Amaterasu, who descended to the island of Kyushu with a mandate to rule in perpetuity. He brought with him the regalia that are still symbols of imperial authority in Japan. Ninigi's descendants, according to the tale, established the Japanese state on the Yamato Plain, and then conquered the barbarians of Kyushu, the Kanto Plain and, ultimately, southern Korea.

Japan emerged slowly as a tribal society, like that of the Germanic tribes of Roman times or the later Scottish clans. Tribes divided the land into dozens of fiefdoms. Historians believe the first historical Japanese state, Yamato, rose from a dominant 'sun-line' clan which gradually conquered other clans and turned their leaders into vassals or ministers. The Yamato gradually grew in strength and complexity, probably due in part to increased contacts with the continent as Korean traders appeared on Japan's shores.

From AD 400 to 900, a steady stream of Korean pilgrims and nobles, as well as some Chinese, landed on the islands, many taking court positions because of their knowledge and skills. Until the seventh century, Japan did not even have a written script. But after the Koreans brought Chinese characters with them, the Japanese adopted these and used foreign ideograms together with their phonetic script to write their own very unique language. Koreans also introduced the Confucian classics, the calendar, and improved irrigation techniques. In succeeding centuries, Japan tried to build a centralised bureaucracy on the model of China, and in 710 they built what was intended to be a permanent capital in Nara on the model of Chang'an, the glittering capital of China's T'ang dynasty. Nara even copied Chang'an's tiled roofs and grid street pattern, but when the Japanese adapted, they did it in their own particular way. They adopted the forms of Chinese government but kept the reality very Japanese. In the end, foreign imports always became far more Japanese than the Japanese became foreign.

This period of change and ensuing confusion provided the first opportunity for a provincial clan to usurp power and govern in the name of the emperor. From 868 until 1160, the Fujiwara clan completely dominated the court, creating the pattern which would be repeated throughout Japanese history. The Minamoto clan which followed it also dominated the emperor and obliged him to grant to Minamoto Yoritomo the military title of *Shogun*, or 'Barbarian-subduing Generalissimo'. By 1338, the Ashikaga clan had taken the shogunate from the Minamoto. Then, in 1467, the Ashikaga lost control completely. For the century that followed the fall of the Ashikaga — a period known as *Sengoku Jidai*— war between rival feudal lords raged throughout Japan.

Finally, after these many centuries of feudal musical chairs, three successive military leaders, Oda Nobunaga, Toyotomi Hideyoshi, and Tokugawa Ieyasu, managed in only thirty-five years (1568–1603) to create conditions which restrained Japan's competing groups from their endless warring. Completely united for the first time in 1603 by Tokugawa Ieyasu, Japan came to enjoy a period of order lasting nearly three centuries. During this time, Japan developed in complete isolation from the upheaval which Western colonialism was visiting upon the rest of Asia.

Tokugawa Ieyasu, as the self-elected *shogun*, reserved all important administrative functions for his *hatamoto*, or direct *samurai* retainers. He allowed the *fudai daimyo*, or 'inside feudal lords', those who had supported his rule, complete discretion within their domains, and this group over time supplied the ruling élite in the Tokugawa shogunate. He managed to keep power by balancing these favoured groups against those who had opposed him — the *tozama daimyo*, or 'outside feudal lords'. Ieyasu left these *tozama daimyo* in control of their fiefs and their *samurai*, but he kept them separated from each other and from playing any important role in the government of the nation. He further reinforced his hold over all the *daimyo* by instituting a hostage system, whereby members of all the *daimyo*'s immediate families had to live in Tokyo on a rotating basis. However, it was a coalition of certain *daimyo* that eventually brought about the downfall of the Tokugawa shogunate and gave rise to the Meiji Restoration.

Although Tokugawa Ieyasu unified Japan's competing lords, he did not eradicate the Japanese system's natural tendency to dilute the authority of any single leader. During the Tokugawa regime, the titular head of the shogunate became more and more removed from the actual exercise of power and the old pattern emerged: there was a titular emperor, a titular *shogun*, and underneath a diffusion of power through many different groups.

Japan faced its first wrenching confrontation with the outside world in 1853. In July of that year, the American Admiral Matthew C. Perry appeared in Tokyo Bay with his squadron of 'black ships' and refused to leave until a request for a trade treaty had been properly delivered. Perry returned eight months later, with more ships which could have easily destroyed the capital. The shogunate reluctantly concluded that it had no choice but to comply. The treaty Perry managed to negotiate did not give the United States substantial concessions — and it allowed the Japanese to wriggle out of what the Americans thought they had been promised (a phenomenon that persists until this day) — but the agreement set a precedent for treaties with other Western powers and spelt an end to

Japan's official seclusion policy. It also marked the beginning of Japan's modern problems.

Disagreement over this decision unleashed a power struggle within the country. Japan had never exposed its remarkably balanced system to such foreign destabilising influences in such quantities and it unleashed powerful feelings on both sides. The two fictions which had kept the Tokugawa system together — the shogunal boasts of loyalty to, and protection of, the imperial court — had proved patently false in the most public way. It became clear that the then Tokugawa *shogun* was unable to protect Japan from the barbarians, and furthermore that he had made concessions to the foreigners. Years of violence and extremism followed.

Reformers outmanoeuvred the *shogun*. Emperor Meiji finally ascended the throne in 1869 at the age of sixteen, and his ascension abolished the 'dual rule' of the *shogun* and the emperor. Technically, the emperor now reigned supreme — with the support of the right nobility.

Some of those nobles who had supported this new arrangement wanted to commit themselves to what was, by Western standards, a fiercely conservative isolationist policy. Perhaps this would have kept Japan from evolving into an economic juggernaut, but it remains a moot point because the majority of the reformers wanted to take an opposite course, drastically changing the direction Japan had followed for centuries. For this, they obtained the co-operation of the impressionable young emperor and thus they came to dominate the Meiji government.

The reformers took for granted that Western strength depended upon constitutionalism, which produced national unity; upon industrialisation, which produced material strength; and upon a well-trained military. They therefore overhauled the political system. To lessen the feudal decentralisation which they blamed for much of Japan's weakness, they called in land registers and established central authority over what were formerly feudal domains. They abolished all legal inequality among the classes, and diminished the influence of Buddhism on government. To undertake such drastic and unpopular reforms they relied upon a peculiar union of the lower-ranking *samurai* and the merchant class. These were the *samurai* retainers who had learned statecraft as chamberlains for the *daimyo*, and who had run the feudal monopolies in mines, textiles, and the like. They were young *samurai* of modest rank and did not represent a class interest in any sense. Indeed, their measures destroyed the class of feudal lords. By 1877, these one-time supporters had organised a full-scale social revolution, and they were able to placate the traditionalists with a trump card: the emperor.

Secure in their authority, the reformers then set about making Japan competitive with the outside world. Japan avoided the decades of hand wringing which paralysed most other Asian countries when first confronted with the West. While some elements of society may have opposed their reform, Japan's leaders spent far less time worrying about the rightness or the wrongness of the modern world. To them it was a simple Darwinian equation: adapt or be beaten. Japan's ease in entering the modern industrial world, in comparison with China and other Asian nations, was precisely because its ant-like society lacked strongly held precepts, based on transcendental beliefs, which would have distracted them from their ruthless determination to survive. The Meiji reformers, rooted in their ant-like traditions, had no fears that they would lose their Japaneseness if they acquired the trappings and forms of Western power.

As an ant colony might send out scouts, the reformers sent the nation's best and brightest to Europe and the United States. What these student 'emissary' *samurai* learned in the West strengthened the opinions the reformers had already formed as to how best to respond to the modern age. When they returned, the Meiji government appointed them to positions of authority. With the help of a handful of foreign advisers, these returned *samurai* carried out what came to be known as the 'Meiji Restoration'.

Wasting little energy, the Japanese sprinted to catch up with Europe and the United States. Universal education began. The new navy was modelled on the British navy. Gavels came down in modern courts enforcing a codified legal system, based on first a French and then on a German model. Modern banks opened in a country which not long before had paid bills in rice. The telegraph wired the country together.

As Meiji industrialisation took off, government control over the economy became automatic. Just as the feudal *shoguns* and their retainers had monitored and directed society, their new Excellencies arranged the game and set the rules. They not only planned, but built and financed with government money, the industries they decided they needed. This kept the nation from wasting precious resources by letting two competing companies do the same thing at the same time. Instead of beginning with light industries and consumer goods — the traditional first step in modernisation — Japan's planners first concentrated on key heavy industries: arsenals, shipyards, iron works. By the early 1880s, industries were well-organised and businesses prosperous, but state management soon became grossly inefficient. Recognising this, the government then sold the state concerns at absurdly low prices to a chosen, usually family-run, conglomerate — to one of the *Zaibatsu* groups — thus setting one of the world's first precedents for privatisation.

Japan earned the respect of Western powers after its victory in the Russo-Japanese War in 1905. By the second decade of the twentieth century, Japan had begun to influence the rest of the world. It had amassed enough strength to become the only Asian colonial power, governing Korea and Taiwan. Huge *Zaibatsu* built business empires throughout Asia. By 1919, Japan was recognised at the Paris Peace Conference as one of the 'Big Five', along with Britain, France, Italy, and the United States.

The Meiji reformers, for all their achievements, also laid the foundations of modern Japan's problems. They established a modern state with the idea that oligarchic rule would only be a temporary stage, to be replaced by a well-coordinated system of government blending Japanese and Western institutions. But understandably wary of diminishing their power, the Meiji reformers never took the final step to democratic rule, or to providing a system that defined clear leadership and accountability. Their ant-like characteristics remained constant even during this period of extraordinary change.

By the time the full success of the Meiji measures was achieved, the architects of these policies had reached their old age. Thus the constantly competing rivals for power had to cope with the problems of succession. With the death or enfeeblement of the first generation of leaders, the pattern of political manipulation changed. No group that followed could match the prestige the Meiji leaders had enjoyed. No group could hold the balance as the system, suddenly embroiled in international politics, began to tilt dangerously.

When the Meiji emperor died in 1912, he was succeeded by his son

Yoshihito, who took the reign name 'Taisho', or 'great righteousness'. Unfortunately, Yoshihito suffered from mental illness. Strokes greatly diminished his mental capacity to reason and carry on normal social intercourse. With his waxed handlebar moustaches and his slavish admiration of Germany's rather ridiculous Kaiser Wilhelm II, Yoshihito turned dandiness into a laughable, then pitiable, foppishness. His temper tantrums, combined with a personal inability to rule, made him a poor successor to his father.

Into the power vacuum rushed a collection of rival political parties and ministries, supported by the newly prestigious businessmen. This might have meant a growth in popular power. In 1918, the first non-titled prime minister seated the first party cabinet. But his assassination in 1921 cut short cautious efforts to extend the electoral franchise, as well as to reduce the power of the military and the bureaucracy. The businessmen who supported the parties, and the bureaucrats who led them, shared a fear of the social movements that followed Japan's industrialisation and the importation of foreign ideas.

The Japanese instinct for trying to balance opposing factions remained. Under the Meiji constitution, governments had to make their peace with the military, with the House of Peers, and with the conservative nobility close to the throne. Frequently, the Diet found itself virtually powerless and this encouraged corruption and disorder within it. The Meiji constitution was so ambiguous about the powers of the governing executive that prime ministers could achieve little unless they secured, through compromise, the co-operation of forces antagonistic to democratic government. This might have been effective if Japan had remained isolated and independent. But it led to confusion when, experimenting with the new concepts of democratic government, Japan found itself in a global community of nations whose respective leaderships were based on taking full responsibility, which generally meant that they were held fully accountable. Nor could the emperor solve Japan's problem. Emperor Hirohito, who succeeded Emperor Taisho in 1926, was a quiet, reflective man, ill-suited to lead in those tumultuous times.

Meanwhile, social currents outstripped political evolution. The franchise was finally extended to all men in 1925. It was a time of surging cultural freedom. People started to talk about Marxism and, what were to

Japan's leaders, other weird and dangerous ideologies. Western music, dancing, and sports became popular. In the cities, rising standards of living and increasing expectations created a need for more and better higher education. Western ideas and Western systems began to challenge the rigid social structure. At the same time, Japan's economy began to run into problems. Japan could not make modern products without importing the iron, coal, and other raw materials necessary for its factories. And the new industrial economy needed foreign markets to fuel its growth.

After the worldwide financial crash of 1929, international trade shrank. Just at the time Japan was reaching out to the world, countries retreated to nationalistic policies of self-sufficiency. Rejected, with its goods barred from many countries, Japan felt unjustly spurned. It was haunted by the vision of actual mass-starvation. The world recession had cut the prices of Japan's then principal export, raw silk, by 50 per cent, and the archipelago was then short of foreign exchange to buy rice. The United States' 1930 Smoot-Hawley Tariff destroyed Japan's American trade which had represented 15 per cent of its exports. Then Japan was pressed to sign the 1930 London Naval Treaty, restricting the size of the Japanese navy.

International diplomatic and economic hostility, combined with a leaderless government, confusing social changes, and discontent among the conservative rural population, all pushed the Japanese system dangerously out of its traditional state of self-correcting balance, creating a situation in which militarism could dominate. Confused, the ant colony veered out of control. Despite the modernisation that had created Japan's military strength, Japanese feelings of xenophobia and domination hadn't changed. Dealing with the rest of the world on equal terms went against the entire pattern of Japanese history. The Japanese weren't used to thinking of alliance and equality with other races and cultures. With the exception of China, which Japan saw as something of an elder brother, outsiders were considered as inferiors. Given their astounding success at modernisation, it was not unreasonable for the Japanese to see themselves as the natural leaders for Asia.

In the late 1920s and 1930s, many Japanese began to think their nation should make a conquest, any conquest. They believed that Western nations had ensured their economic and military strength by colonial conquest of other parts of the world, including Asia. They argued further that Japan's population had grown from 30 million at the beginning of the Meiji Restoration to 65 million in 1930. Each year, the population figures grew higher. Imports of needed foodstuffs increased. To balance the economy, Japan had to export more. Experience as the colonial overlord of Korea and Taiwan had shown that colonies — particularly those in Japan's immediate sphere of influence, Asia — would provide new markets for the archipelago's goods.

In 1931, the army decided unilaterally to experiment and, because of the confused nature of the times, it atypically was able to impose its own factional objectives on the rest of society. The Kwangtung army captured Mukden and occupied Manchuria. In response, again atypically, Tokyo's civilian government did little. Even today, many Japanese feel no responsibility for Japan's actions in China. It was not Japan's colony, it was the army's. But by acquiescing when the army occupied Manchuria, the Tokyo government proved that the military could usurp its decisions and go uncorrected. With new confidence, the military rightists went on to wreak havoc. In 1932, they murdered the Japanese prime minister. Others, certain right-wing factions outside the military, assassinated the former finance minister and several leading industrialists. These assassinations marked the end of effective government by parliamentary means.

The war minister, General Sadao Araki, became the most influential figure in Japan. Araki was a ferocious *Bushido* ideologue, who ran a Nazi-style youth movement and did everything he could to encourage totalitarian Shinto. In a European country he would almost certainly have become a dictator, and thus created a centralised focus of decision making and responsibility. But in a country which, in theory, was ruled by a living god-man, individual leadership was often punished by assassination — again, the natural Japanese social law of self-correction. Even the most authoritarian Japanese subscribed to clan or group rule. Small oligarchies met and argued in secret, making collective decisions which avoided individual responsibility.

In 1935, when Hitler repudiated the Versailles Treaty, members of the Japanese armed services carried law books to the roof of the Tokyo Military Club and burned them publicly. With this symbolic repudiation of the rule of law, Japan reverted to the pre-Tokugawa era, when feudal lords vied for power under the authority of the emperor. The state became a collection of warring factions, with the military predominating. History had transformed the feudal lords into generals and admirals surrounded by fanatical followers. Assassination became the general arbiter of disputes. Putting military men in charge of ministries did not solve any problems, since they were just as liable to be assassinated as civilians. Taking decisions collectively was no protection either, as the military rightists developed the technique of collective assassination.

Japan became virtually ungovernable due to faction-fighting among the élite. Foreign adventure became the only means by which the country could attain some semblance of unity. Japan withdrew to the age-old concepts of survival of the fittest. It rejected the League of Nations and the disarmament system set up after World War I, both of which focused on transcendental goals of peace and justice. Freed from the constraints of these organisations, Japan no longer tried to adapt to the mores of the Western-dominated international system, but instead started on a course of imposing itself on the rest of the world by brute force.

First, Tokyo financed a naval build-up. Before the European War even began, Japan had created a total war economy, including control of labour, prices, and wages. By 1938, rationing and shortages were already more severe than they had been in the Germany of 1918. In an attempt to find a leather substitute, people tanned rat skins. Major commodities, such as raw cotton, cloth, chemicals, leather, metals, oil, wool, and steel, disappeared from the market. Soon militarist Japan had moved closer to *rapprochement* with the fascist Western powers, Germany and Italy. The leaders of Germany and Italy had also rejected 'higher principles' in favour of absolute obedience to the state. These were also the only two Western countries dissatisfied with the disarmament system.

By 1941, Japan was formally allied with Germany. The war was going badly for Britain and France, and Japan moved into Asia to take over the French and British colonies there. Protesting against this move, the United States declared a total embargo on all exports to Japan, drastically cutting Tokyo's supply of oil. Japan, increasingly shut out by the world's markets, responded by sending its bombers to Pearl Harbor.

Japan's colonial empire, euphemistically called the 'Greater East Asia Co-Prosperity Sphere', already extended from the Japanese archipelago to Korea and Manchuria, through China to Southeast Asia. Once Japan became involved in the war, it tried to develop its empire and exploit it economically while the Allies assailed its periphery. In the colonies they occupied, the Japanese attempted to create a new cultural order where discipline and absolute loyalty to Japan were the key elements. But the effort of imposing its own system on the rest of Asia proved untenable. As Allied pressure stripped the empire of its natural and industrial resources, it brought Japan to its knees.

Japan's vulnerability had led it to try for an empire, but it also ensured Japan's defeat. In Southeast Asia, Japan had neither the time nor the resources to carry out programmes of mass education, to develop communications and industry, or to achieve advances in agricultural productivity, as it had done in Taiwan and Korea. Nor could its strained wartime economy supply the needed industrial products. As Japanese shipping dwindled in the last years of the war, Japan was unable even to obtain the raw materials these countries produced. Despite its strenuous efforts to exploit its vast conquests, it lacked the capacity for rapid expansion that the American economy possessed. Japan simply wasn't big enough. On top of all this, the 'monkey' culture countries it tried to convert to the Japanese culture were too different.

During the last months of the war, the Allied submarine blockade defeated Japan economically. Allied destruction of the Japanese navy and air force left the home islands vulnerable. None of Japan's largest armies ever suffered defeat. They wanted to fight on. But American bombing raids had brought the consciousness of defeat to the Japanese people. Thus, in 1945, after two years of suicidal battles, the Empire of the Sun vanished in the flashes of light from atomic blasts over Nagasaki and Hiroshima and in Emperor Hirohito's subsequent surrender to General MacArthur of the United States. When occupation forces made landfall on Japan, they found its cities destroyed, its stockpiles exhausted, and its plants gutted. The government had lost all prestige and respect. Food supplies had dwindled alarmingly. Rising inflation threatened to sap what little remained of national strength. The time was ripe for changes.

For the seven years between 1945 and 1952, Allied forces occupied the country. Japan endured the unendurable. The four Allied Powers charged MacArthur with removing undemocratic tendencies in Japanese society.

The occupation government was supposed to be run in consultation with Allied Pacific forces, but it quickly became an American affair. The Americans had clear ideas about how the new Japan should be run. They wanted to purge Japan of its militaristic tendencies, to modify its extremely hierarchical social tendencies, and to encourage democracy.

Accordingly, the occupation government tried to dismantle the Japanese society's traditional hierarchy. The Americans enforced demilitarisation, and the writing of a new constitution. The emperor, until recently considered an omnipotent god by his people, became, after his surrender, once again, as in feudal Japan, a largely empty symbol of the nation's unity. The American occupation forces engineered land reform and remade the Japanese government in the image of the American constitution. They redistributed two-thirds of the land, turning millions of tenant peasants into landowners, and broke up the large *Zaibatsu* which had powered Japan's thrust for an empire.

Yet the occupation government did not really understand Japan. Therefore it could not know how to follow through, to ensure that the reality of Japanese society changed. At the same time, the shock and shame of losing World War II made the Japanese psychological prisoners of their own defeat. In traditional Japan, to surrender was to become a nonperson. Without self-respect, all the Japanese had left was hierarchy and order. This reinforced the ant-like structure of their society. Increasingly concerned about the rise of communism in Asia, the United States switched its emphasis from restructuring Japanese society to encouraging and, by considerable investment, helping Japan to build up sufficient economic strength so that it could be a bulwark of capitalist democracy in Asia. With this change of focus by the Americans, Japan adopted many of the forms of democracy and developed, some argue in certain senses, a more egalitarian society than exists even today in the United States and Britain. However, without the necessary follow-through by the Americans to ensure their adoption of the substance that makes a true democracy, the basic system remained very Japanese.

Having been isolated for most of their history, the Japanese had never previously suffered defeat. But ever adaptable, they looked to their conquerors, the Americans, to teach them how to rise up again. They concluded (rightly) that American economic strength had been behind its victory in World War II. So the Japanese determined that the way to national rebirth was by building economic strength.

Japan's post-war governments tried to step into the leadership vacuum by directing industry. They encouraged citizens to commit themselves wholly to the pursuit of an alien goal: money, not as in the West for individual gain, but rather for national and corporate gain. The Japanese developed a new race of 'salarymen' working for large corporations. During the Meiji reforms, companies had pursued economic success, but they had done so in support of military goals, and in pursuit of a proper place in the world's international hierarchy. During and after the MacArthur reforms, Japan's leaders found themselves constitutionally bound to a policy of pacifism and non-interference in the affairs of other nations. Economic success was no longer the means to a goal, it was the goal itself — a striking development for a nation whose leadership and ruling classes had long disdained commercial activity and had for centuries measured its wealth in *koku* — units of rice.

To this struggle, the Japanese brought all their qualities of resourcefulness, hard work, and loyalty. Prosperity did not come immediately. In the early 1950s, Japanese incomes and technology lagged far behind those of the United States and advanced European countries. The world sniggered as Japan started making toys and gadgets. For most of the 1950s and early 1960s, the label 'Made in Japan' signified tacky, unreliable goods.

However, success would come, and with a vengeance. Japanese workers were industrious, literate, and advanced. Japan soon learned that it was cheaper to license or buy new technology than to develop it independently. It began to import technology and export products that were cheaper and better built than those produced by the West. In many cases, they improved on the technology that they licensed or bought. The Japanese used their new knowledge to foster the growth of five selected industries: steel, shipbuilding, coal, electricity, and fertilisers.

The particular combination of free enterprise and government guidance which other countries sometimes refer to as 'Japan Inc.' made a huge contribution to Japan's success. Banking credit made investment in heavy industry possible, on the assumption that increases in productivity would cancel out debts later on. The Japanese government followed the wartime strategy of linking banks with certain industries and instructing them to provide an immediate, unlimited money supply. The strategy worked. The Tokyo government involved itself intimately in plans aimed at emulating some of the policies of other countries' socialist governments, but its plans worked better than those of any socialist nation. The Ministry of Finance and the Ministry of International Trade and Industry co-operated in charting Japan's future growth. They targeted growth indus-tries, set production goals, and evaluated foreign markets.

At the same time that government encouraged and helped business, each company had to be financially independent. Fierce competition was the rule in the marketplace. There was no socialist safety net to lull Japanese business into a sense of security. By the mid-1950s, this industrial policy had refuelled Japan's economy, and it had regained the per capita production levels of the pre-war years. By the 1970s, Japan was the world's leading shipbuilder; and Japanese cars were driven in most of the world's countries. Increasingly, a Japanese label came to mean quality, reliability, and good after-sales service.

In less than two generations, Japan had rebuilt itself into one of the world's great economic powers. The technological gap had largely disappeared. Today, it produces the biggest tanker, the thinnest wrist-watch, the smallest television set. No longer a copycat, it has effectively taken over whole industries, such as consumer electronics, cameras, and certain categories of computer chips. It is moving into innovative indus-tries such as biotechnology and supercomputers. It counts itself as a member of all the international status clubs, the groups which have provided, amongst others, the chairmen of the UN Security Council and the Organisation for Economic Co-operation and Development (OECD). In the mid-1980s, Japan's banks dominated the international banking business and the country enjoyed record-breaking trade surpluses: US$44 billion in 1984, US$56 billion in 1985, and US$93 billion in 1986. In 1991, its trade surplus was US$103 billion. Japan is strong enough to finance a substantial portion of the United States' budget deficit and it is the world's largest net creditor.

Barred by its American-imposed constitution from developing an offensive military, Japan has relied upon America for defence, thus avoiding the extraordinary costs of being a modern, major military power. The United States has acted as Japan's foil in the international Western defence system. Although the Meiji reformers were taken with the idea that a strong military state was needed to deal with other states, from 1945 until well into the 1980s Japan had little need to worry. It was hardly ever called upon to participate directly in the defence-driven Cold War equation.

Liberated from the responsibility of coping with the rest of the world, Japan was able to return to its own intuitive system of natural checks and balances. It was allowed to deal with countries on the basis of purely economic priorities, with scant regard to political/defence consequences. Thus it has developed leadership qualities only in the economic sphere. Now that many look to Japan for political and social leadership, Japan cannot respond easily. Tokyo works in its own way. Starting after the Gulf War, after a seemingly endless and tortuous national debate on Japan's participation in the UN-sponsored peacekeeping forces in Cambodia, it finally sent, in September 1992, a military contingent of some 600 'Self-Defence Force' personnel to support passively the UN's peacekeeping forces there — accompanied by more than 300 members of the Japanese media! As a Japanese politician friend explained, the constant reportage on every aspect of these military personnel going about their daily activities in the Japanese media is immensely reassuring to the Japanese public. It also paves the way for the next stage, which is to seek Diet approval for such personnel to take part in active military engagements, if required in the course of their peacekeeping functions.

For years, the outside world has assumed that Japan was on the brink of change. In the 1960s, people said that Japanese youth would change things once they got to positions of influence. In the 1970s, observers predicted that employees who returned home from abroad would 'internationalise' Japan upon their return. Instead, such employees were often referred to by their domestic colleagues as being *bata kusai*, meaning 'smelling of butter'. In other words, they had been tainted by their foreign experience and were in thorough need of rehabilitation. Most recently, it has been fashionable to think that unstoppable economic developments and collective security would force Japan to join the international community. In the period 1987–1992, the pressure of a perceived public demand for change, coupled with the Recruit and other political and business scandals, including that involving Shin Kanemaru, vice chairman of the LDP, and the illegal donations to him by the transport company Sagawa Kyubin, reinforced the idea that the Japanese system was being forced to transform itself.

It is true that Japan is changing, but in its own way. Unlike the scandals in the West, where Western legal and moral systems clearly define the illegal actions, or amorality, of those involved, the scandals in Japan arose from the system being obliged to recognise that past practices were no longer acceptable given Japan's position of co-leadership in the global economic community.

Tokyo enjoys no close ties or alliances with anyone but Washington, and even that is a strange relationship, difficult to define and now weakening. The American leadership has become embattled by domestic economic, political, and social problems. With the disappearance of tension between the West and the former communist bloc, the United States as a whole is coming to view its relationship with Japan more as a rivalry than as a friendship.

While its wealth has created great envy in the rest of the world, Japan has done little of the global networking necessary to orchestrate the co-operation of other countries. The Foreign Affairs Ministry in Japan is one of the country's weakest. The Japanese have trouble with diplomacy, because they do not accept any common, internationally recognised value system of diplomatic *quid pro quo*, or fair play. Japan has collected few IOUs from past favours. It cannot prevail upon friends in an emergency, let alone ordinarily, because it basically has no friends. And other countries feel that Japan owes them. Tokyo is creating a Japan-dominated trade and industrial zone from Tokyo to Seoul, Bangkok to Sydney, but this economic influence is not coupled with any sense of moral, let alone other senses of, mutual obligation or diplomatic influence. Most Western countries, while clamouring for Japan's money, are anything but friendly.

Japan also finds it almost impossible to communicate effectively with the rest of the world in the human sense of one individual understanding another. The nation has instinctively thrown up a network of articulate 'establishment members' who appear to specialise in helping the poor, benighted foreigner to understand the 'perfectly ordinary system of Japan'. Resident foreign diplomats and businessmen often deal with Japan through this intermediary group of English-speaking and supposedly internationally-adept ombudsmen. Japanese leaders entrust these individuals with conveying a sense of reasonableness, if not of agreement. Sadly, these buffers — some would say 'duffers' — have no power to take any action. In many ways they are just like soldier ants whose sole job is to keep intruders out of the nest.

Foreign negotiators or trade representatives who go home reporting that 'this time we have talked to the proper authorities and these authorities are ready to take action', are almost always disappointed or embarrassed when their analyses prove wrong. While these intermediaries are supposed to smooth Japan's relationship with the outside, in fact they harm it by compounding the confusion. Negotiators who thought they had made a deal are bound to feel cheated when they learn the 'deal' never existed in the collective Japanese mind. When put under pressure, the Japanese tend to become more Japanese.

Much of the 'Japan problem' is a result of different types of understanding in the West and in Japan. The Japanese constantly endorse the idea that there is a need for a 'better understanding of their position'. But in Japanese, the term *'rikai shite kudasai'* — meaning 'please understand my position' — may follow a completely absurd statement underlining their patent self-interest. This response demands a recognition of the Japanese position, irrespective of whether it has any relevance to any commonly-accepted business values, let alone moral ones. In the context of disputes, 'understanding' to Westerners means finding out the reality of the matter under discussion, and trying to get both sides to define a common reality, one which is acceptable and more or less fair to both parties. In Japan, true 'understanding' means having to accept things the way they are, unless one is strong enough to change them.

In the West, 'reality' is seen as immutable, not something that can be managed, moulded, or negotiated. In Asia generally, people are more comfortable with the idea of multiple and contradictory truth. But nowhere is this more true than in Japan. Japanese leaders can move with agility from one 'reality' to another, in an attempt to explain 'facts' and 'motives' to Japanese counterparts and foreigners. In Japanese, being *makoto,* or sincere, means forcing one's thinking and emotions into line with what the surrounding society expects.

The Japanese approach in this sphere goes far beyond the lame excuses and self-serving untruths which other societies are prepared to tolerate. Japanese administrators and bureaucrats who show 'mental flexibility' — the ability to adjust, chameleon-like, to changing conditions — are highly appreciated. Those with a reputation for sticking to positions based solely on a single theory or outlook do not rise very high in their chosen fields. Similarly, many modern Japanese intellectuals adopt new or foreign ideas in rapid succession, primarily as an intellectual exercise. They need not make a conscious effort to test these new ideas against their established convictions; they certainly need not incorporate them into their lives.

The problem of different frames of reference repeats itself when the Japanese go abroad. The majority tend to go abroad not as individuals but as representatives of a ministry, a company, or an institution and they can only parrot the party line. Japan lacks true statesmen in the classical sense of the word — senior bureaucrats, politicians, or businessmen who have sufficient authority and self-confidence to improvise in pursuing general policies. Without the power to adapt policy quickly, the Japanese often cannot finesse themselves out of awkward situations. It is not surprising that people the world over — most of whom can and will improvise — find the Japanese extraordinarily frustrating.

Japan confuses the world. It has become a major power, but it does not behave the way most people expect a major power to behave. Most outsiders do not realise that the Japanese prime minister is not expected to lead. In 1964, a movement was launched to strengthen the office of prime minister, and thereby centralise control over the bureaucracy. The plan failed, due to strong opposition from both the LDP and the bureaucracy. Politicians didn't want it because they feared it would come between them and the ministries, endangering a source of influence that enabled them to extract political funds from their constituencies. The civil servants didn't want it because it might have endangered some of their prerogatives.

Yasuhiro Nakasone, prime minister from 1983 to 1987, broke with the tradition of 'team player' prime ministers by trying to lead his nation. He formed a new administrative agency with the rank of a ministry. He tried to improve the ability of the prime minister's office to react quickly to emergency situations and found new ways to pressure the bureaucrats to break through deadlocks. His reforms were popular, but in the end they were sabotaged by his fellow politicians and the bureaucrats.

The leadership mystery also holds in business. The disciplined array of firms which has made Japan famous in the post-war world are only semi-autonomous. Most of the large firms belong to *gurupu*, or conglomerates, such as Mitsui, Mitsubishi, Sumitomo, and others, heirs to the pre-war *Zaibatsu*. However, they are not true conglomerates as the term is generally understood elsewhere. There is no ultimate parent company. The Japanese version is a group of companies formed in almost self-sufficient clusters around their own banks and industrial, trading, real estate, and insurance companies. Cross-shareholdings and interlocking directorates tie all the parts together. But no one is actually in charge of a *gurupu*. They are essentially clubs sharing common interests — a repetition of an endless pattern in Japanese life.

Some Western theorists, nonplussed by the tangled web of Japanese politics and business, have concluded that the apparent confusion and naïve protestations of Japanese leaders must hide a conspiracy. These theories, while possible, are highly unlikely. Post-war Japanese society has simply been exhibiting ant-like behaviour. The experience of the post-war period and the instinctive reflexes of Japan's culture have created groups capable of masterminding operations but no single, central leader able to create a blueprint for Japan, as Margaret Thatcher did for Britain, as Lee Kuan Yew did for Singapore, or as Helmut Köhl did for Germany. Japanese society is as yet incapable of producing a single, responsible voice to deal with the rest of the world.

Japan's limited efforts at post-war foreign policy do not give any reason for optimism. Allowing itself to be intimidated by the Arab world has not made Japan's oil supplies any more secure — as, for example, during the Gulf War when no country in the Middle East (which supplies 70 per cent of Japan's oil needs) was prepared to make any special effort to ensure Japan's supply. For a while in the 1970s, it seemed that independent approaches to China and the Soviet Union were developing, but these were soon shown to be awaiting cues from the United States. Japan tried to get involved in resolving the Vietnamese occupation of Cambodia, but when the other governments expected commitments, no active policy was forthcoming. The credibility of its mediation in the Indo-Chinese conflict was also undermined by the anger of the ASEAN community at the way Japan, while going along with the United States in refusing to recognise Vietnam, was doing fairly large-scale business there — in fact, in the early 1990s, Japan became Vietnam's biggest trading partner. As usual, Japan was trying to have it both ways.

When Japan tried to respond to the Iraq–Kuwait conflict, its initial reaction was that of paralysed incoherence. Its first official statement was that the Iraqi invasion was 'very regrettable'. Others regarded Japan's reaction with a paroxysm of fury, contempt, and/or frustration. Subsequently, Japan, as the primary beneficiary of Middle East oil, was in stages shamed into coughing up some US$13 billion to finance the Allied task force. Japan then went into a series of convulsions over whether or not it could commit troops to join those from the rest of the world in Saudi Arabia. The farcical end to this saga was that the prime minister's lack of authority was exposed, and he risked losing his job as a result. Yet, in contrast, and to give Japan credit, in order to provide the necessary funds it imposed a specific one-off tax on the Japanese population — an impressive achievement when compared with Washington's past inability to increase tax, even on petrol, in order to help pay for its chronic deficit.

Japan's inability to respond was in part the result of its American-imposed constitution, which forbade Japan to develop an offensive army. Another contributing factor was Japan's 'nuclear allergy'. Having sustained the horror of two nuclear explosions over its cities, an unusual collective pacificism will remain a critical factor in Japanese politics for a long time to come.

Unfortunately, Japan has continued to treat its diplomatic bridge-building like a business proposition. Money can create power. Power creates responsibility. The Western world divides that responsibility into self-interest and, if there's enough left over, occasionally into unconditional altruism. In theory, through altruism, one can contribute to the global good. By doing so, friendships can be created. Trying to model itself on the altruistic aid standards of the Western world, Japan tried to do the same. Unfortunately, it hadn't understood the nature of altruism, another curious, universal Western standard. Japan instinctively created its own version: 'tied-aid', delivered for the good of Japan rather than for the good of the recipients. It tended in the past to grant aid only if the beneficiaries used the money to buy Japanese goods and services.

Japan's aid programme has since become the largest in the world. In 1987, at a seven-nation summit in Montreal, Japan pledged at least US$50 billion in aid through 1993. In response to criticisms that previous Japanese aid programmes were linked to contracts with Japanese firms, Japan announced that by 1990 all of its aid would be granted independently of any Japanese contracts. Japan has targeted much of its aid at the Asian region, which accounts for more than two-thirds of Japan's net disbursements; the American and EC shares were less than one-tenth and one-fifth of their own aid programmes respectively. However, to date, its aid has won it few, if any, lasting friends.

Although Japan's aid to China has been substantial, the country has often clashed with Japan over such issues as the portrayal of events before and during World War II. In 1982, and again in 1986, the Chinese denounced the revision of Japanese secondary school textbooks, which included diluted accounts of Japan's invasion and ferocious occupation of China in the 1930s. The Koreans, remembering Japan's past colonial exploitation, also nurture an animosity for Japan, and pass it on to the next generation through their schools. As soon as the United States began to talk of withdrawing some forces from Asia Pacific, Australia and Singapore immediately voiced concerns about a possible Japanese rearmament.

The Asian beneficiaries of Tokyo's largess are generally the first to voice worries about Japanese economic imperialism. Asia has joined the global clamour for access to Japan's markets. Editorials critical of Japan appear in newspapers throughout Asia. Politicians claim that Japan has only Japan's interests at heart. Environmentalists claim that Japan fishes the seas without worrying about the effect on the ecosystem. It is clear that Japan needs more than financial clout to secure it a co-leadership role in the new world order.

The world has a tendency to see Japan as invincible. Nothing could be further from the truth, as became apparent when, in 1990, Japan's economic bubble finally burst to the astonishment of all, including the Japanese. Japan, even more than other nations, cannot survive apart from the world it considers so foreign. All Japan's industries depend upon exports. And if the world chooses to shut Japan out, it can do so simply by freezing Japanese assets abroad or instituting domestic foreign exchange controls *vis-à-vis* Japan. The yen would plummet. There is no way the Japanese could win a trade war.

Additionally, Japan still has to import virtually all of its base materials such as oil, iron ore, lead, wool, and cotton. It imports more of these goods than any other nation on earth, not to mention countless container ships loaded with coal, copper, zinc, lumber, and a cornucopia of other raw materials. Most of these commodities come from distant corners of the world. Foreign countries supply more than four-fifths of the energy that powers Japan's assembly robots, smelts the steel for Toyota cars, and lights the ministries and laboratories where researchers and bureaucrats dream up tomorrow's growth industries. When it is a buyer's market for commodities, as it was after World War II, Japan has no need to be concerned about this. But of course, conditions change. When the Arab-Israeli War of October 1973 halted oil supplies from the Middle East, it almost destroyed the Japanese economy. It is not surprising that Japan had a rather confused response to the Iraq–Kuwait crisis.

Japan has always been terrified of being too dependent on food imports. In 1973, heavy Soviet imports of soyabeans created a shortage scare in the United States. The United States suddenly declared an embargo on soyabean exports to all countries, and Japan went into shock. The United States supplies almost all the soyabeans that go into such staples as *tofu* — soyabean curd — and *miso* soup served throughout Japan. The same is true of the wheat in Japan's noodles. Although the Americans soon lifted the embargo, the panic underscored Japan's vulnerability at the most basic level. Little has changed in this area. Fear of being deprived of food imports is one of the justifications the post-war Japanese government has used for subsidising rice farmers, even though this policy distorts both the country's politics and economics.

Although Japan's defence budget is substantial (for 1991, the 0.95 per cent of Gross National Product (GNP) that Japan spent on its national defence amounted to some US$36 billion), it can do little to force other nations to be co-operative. If the United States decided to stockpile soyabeans for a decade, or to freeze all Japanese assets in the United States, Japan could impose trade sanctions, but little else. And as Japan imports so little in the way of processed goods, cutting down on imports would in effect be almost meaningless.

Japan has very real strategic worries. As an island nation, by definition Japan is exposed on all flanks. After World War II, the Korean War shocked Tokyo into recognising this vulnerability. In the two decades after World War II, Japan has gradually recreated a new army, innocuously labelled the 'Self-Defence Force'. The United States has tutored the publicity-shy Force, and joint exercises and co-operation have strengthened the tie until it has become as strong as that between the United States and Europe. The United States and Japan have taken each other for granted. But like Europe, Japan has sometimes had reason to doubt American commitment. When the United States started to make overtures to China in the early 1970s, it did not bother to consult Japan. The implication of Japan's irrelevance threw the nation into consternation. Then, in the late 1970s, President Carter again threw American constancy into doubt when he decided to withdraw ground troops from Korea, only to reverse the decision. These actions by Japan's most important ally seemed irrational from Japan's vantage point, as have some of those that followed. In 1985, the Pentagon blocked Japanese attempts to buy a New Hampshire ball-bearing plant, saying it was a defence risk. Much more significantly, opposition in the United States Congress and the Bush administration in 1989 prompted a review of a joint United States–Japan project to build F-16 jet fighters. The implication that Japan was not trustworthy embarrassed and disturbed Japanese leaders. Now the Cold War is over, and as Japan's export machine is likely to continue to be successful, and the concerns of other countries of Asia Pacific as to a possible rearmament by Japan continue to be raised, the ambivalence of the United States about sharing defence technology is likely to increase, leaving Japan militarily vulnerable in the North Pacific — in an extreme scenario, an economic plum ready for plucking.

Two decades ago, the world started grumbling about Japan's trade policies. Those mutterings have become strident complaints. Since Japan grew into a regional economic power in the 1970s, old fears have been revived and new resentments have sprung up in neighbouring countries. Japan buys one-third or more of the exports of Australia, the Philippines, and South Korea. Less prosperous neighbours, who remember the

Japanese as ruthless colonial masters or cruel wartime conquerors, until very recently have strongly resented the success of the country they view as a defeated aggressor. They also fear that Japan might be using trade to create a new version of the old Greater East Asia Co-Prosperity Sphere.

People in other Asian countries have been heard to echo the comment of French president Charles de Gaulle, who in the 1960s was reported to have called Japan's prime minister a 'transistor salesman'. Americans complained bitterly of the 'free ride' Japan was taking at American expense. In 1971, President Nixon suddenly announced that the American dollar would no longer be convertible to gold and a temporary 10 per cent surcharge would be assessed on all imports. Some claimed that these measures were aimed primarily at Japan, which held large reserves of American currency and depended on the United States as an export market. When the Japanese prime minister made a goodwill trip to Southeast Asia in 1974, a barrage of anti-Japanese protests and rioting greeted him. In other parts of Asia Pacific, business leaders condemned Japan as being an 'economic animal'. As Japan has continued to grow, such criticism has followed.

In 1990, because he failed to obtain a directorship on the board of a Japanese company in which he had taken a substantial equity investment, American businessman T. Boone Pickens took out a full-page advertisement in *USA Today*, protesting about Japan's trade practices. According to the advertisement, 'Japan is laughing at the United States. We Americans are losing the economic war but not because Japanese workers are smarter or more industrious than Americans. We are losing the war because corporate Japan takes advantage of our open markets, but plays by an entirely different set of rules — rules that mock the American principles of free and fair trade.' Pickens's actual reasons for the position he took are highly suspect. But, as is often the case, it is the perception that counts and not the reality, which itself is often hidden or disguised. Pickens later gave up and sold his shares.

Japan has not followed the course used by Britain and the United States during their ascendancy. Instead of using its new-found riches to foster global economic development, Japan has chosen to use its capital to further strengthen its own economic position. While belatedly it has become the largest donor of international aid, it has not previously provided much aid to the Third World. Britain and the United States were able to surmount foreign opposition to their rise as trading and creditor nations, the British by building public works in the colonies, and the Americans by providing material assistance in the reconstruction of Europe after World War II. In any case, few countries had the strength to take on Britain or the United States at the height of their respective military and economic power. Conversely, today, despite its strength, Japan is in a much weaker position.

All over the world, trade ministers have criticised Japan for importing only raw materials and exporting finished goods. Officials and business-men have criticised the exclusionary nature of the Japanese market. Excessively detailed and even artificial standards ensure that it is as hard as possible for imports to enter Japan. Since tariffs and foreign exchange controls were lifted in the 1970s, Japanese non-tariff barriers have for the most part actively excluded non-Japanese manufacturers, both those with plants in Japan and those exporting into Japan. Big manufacturers like Sony and Matsushita, for example, used to control their own retail outlets and prevent these shops from selling competitors' products. Today, most consumer electronic goods, in terms of domestic sales volume, are sold through department stores and discount stores, both of which carry goods from many different suppliers, including Sony and Matsushita. The entire *keiretsu* system of cross-shareholding among Japanese companies ties suppliers to buyers, banks to borrowers, and so on, making it almost impossible for a foreign company to buy a Japanese one. However, it should be recognised that this system was not specifically designed to keep foreigners out of the domestic market. It developed naturally as a reflection of Japan's social and corporate structures. The fact also that many Japanese corporate owners do not want to sell to foreigners is a decision made of free choice, not necessarily a function of some dark conspiracy!

In effect, most Japanese manufacturers do not have to compete with foreigners in their home market. Although a degree of liberalisation in the financial market has taken place, this has not significantly increased the accessibility of the Japanese market to foreign financial institutions, particularly to commercial banks.

In Europe, EC officials have complained that the Japanese are getting around import rules by using assembly operations in the twelve member countries. At these factories, workers put together parts brought in from Japan with little or no local input. The goods produced in this way are technically European, but of course are really Japanese. In response, many of the EC governments have objected vigorously, and the EC's Single Market is not likely to be terribly friendly to Japan.

By early 1990, the American trade deficit with Japan had reached a colossal US$49 billion, although this was down from US$59 billion in 1987. Japanese officials contend the American troubles are rooted in its budget deficit, its consumer credit, and its poor education system. The United States counters that the deficits have as much to do with Japan's exclusionary policies as with any American malaise.

Bashing the Japanese has become a staple of American domestic politics. Hundreds of legislators have introduced protectionist trade bills aimed at Japan. In 1989, the Bush Administration threatened retaliation after Japan restricted imports of American satellites, supercomputers, and forest products. As complaints threatened to escalate into a trade war, the United States proposed talks.

Called by the US government the 'Structural Impediments Initiatives' (SII), the talks, which began in 1989 and lasted one year, sought to address more fundamental elements of economic imbalance on both sides of the Pacific. The talks produced a wish list of basic changes on both sides, changes that were admittedly hard to make. The US list targeted Japan's high savings rate, its complex distribution system favouring 'mom and pop' stores (keeping out large foreign discount stores), and a land-use policy that favours farmers and keeps housing prices extraordinarily high. The Japanese demands on the United States seemed equally intractable: an improvement in the low US savings rate, greater emphasis on invest-ment rather than consumption, and an improved educational system. Each side's demands touched on so many nerves that the two heads of government had to intervene to prevent relations deteriorating rapidly. In the end the United States agreed to try to increase its savings rate and reduce its fiscal deficit, while Japan pledged to spend more on public works in order to improve the country's inadequate infrastructure. Since the advent of the Clinton administration in January 1993, there have been calls for the reinstatement of the SII, which suggests that this mechanism may be used with at least the same, if not more, vigour than in the past.

The Japanese have tried to counter global hostility by making small adjustments at home, and investing in property and manufacturing abroad. This long-term strategy, they hope, will enable them to sustain their market share above the present level, while being insulated from currency fluctuations and the vagaries of protectionist sentiment. By the end of 1987, Japan had direct investments worth US$33 billion in the United States. When the Japanese started to buy things like Manhattan's Rockefeller Center, this struck an emotional chord in the United States and generated much hostility. Although Japan's investments in the United States are far smaller than those of Britain or the Netherlands, Americans feared they were losing autonomy to Japan. A 1989 poll found that eight out of ten Americans surveyed favoured limits on Japanese investments in American companies.

Past events have already shown Japan's vulnerability in the world market. At a 1990 meeting of the world's seven richest countries — the Group of Seven, or 'G7' — Japan had hoped to get reassurance that the other countries would continue to co-ordinate their policies and help to prop up the falling yen in order to stave off inflation in Japan. It was disappointed. The Americans pronounced 'satisfaction' with the state of the currency market. Japan, it seemed, would have to go it alone on inflation.

While Japan might be able to go it alone on inflation, it cannot afford to go it alone on every economic challenge. Japan's enormous wealth is in many senses an illusion — as has recently been proven in the dramatic decline in the Japanese share and real estate market values. Japan is only wealthy because the rest of the world permits it to be so. The great strength of the yen is only possible because of Japan's intrinsic manufacturing efficiency and because it makes highly efficient use of its access to free markets. In turn, the strength of the yen in foreign exchange markets greatly inflates the value of Japan's land and corporations. All this would change if other countries closed their markets to Japanese goods. This has led some economists in Tokyo to theorise that Japan will likely be running a trade deficit by the year 2000 — a perfectly possible scenario. As the world grows increasingly regionalised, Japan is likely to become more vulnerable both to pressure from its Asia Pacific neighbours to allow more imports and to general economic retaliation from the West.

Tokyo's economic power is a two-edged sword. Japan has supported the US deficit by buying Washington's federal bonds. In reality, in the 1980s, the Japanese had nowhere else to put their money, as there was no other economy large enough to absorb Japan's investments. Further, if Japanese investors had put all their wealth into the Japanese economy, it would have flooded the country with money and caused inflation. And if Japanese investors had pulled out of the United States, it could have destabilised the world economy. In the 1990s, things are different. Because of the collapse of Japan's 'bubble economy', many Japanese have had to sell off their foreign assets, often at substantial discounts, to raise funds to meet their obligations in Japan. This factor has obviously impacted negatively on the respective host economies.

There are some signs that attitudes in Japan may be changing. Japan's business leaders now realise that the West, in particular Europe, feels that Japan has been the 'winner' of a global trade competition. They also now understand that there is no longer much desire to negotiate the resolution of trade problems, but rather there is much more focus on creating defences against Japan's perceived economic onslaught. As the *Far Eastern Economic Review* stated in its cover story of 6 August 1992, *kyosei* (loosely translated as 'living together' or 'symbiosis') has become a top Japanese priority for dealing with this issue. Initiated by the *Keidanren* (the Federation of Japanese Industries) and certain senior corporate business leaders, the rest of the Japanese establishment has joined the debate. Topics such as, should the Japanese work fewer hours and have more holidays, should Japanese companies put more emphasis on profit and less on market share, and how can Japan make suitable changes to its own systems so that others will reciprocate, are being discussed seriously. This debate augurs well for the future, but only if it offers up real opportunities for a mutual recognition that Japan and the West must find an accommodation and only if the West, embroiled in its own current problems, can muster sufficient enthusiasm to join the process. However, if this *kyosei* process continues to be dictated from the top, in Japan's world of 'bottoms-up' management, it is not likely to succeed in any material way.

Today, also, the younger generation are a genuinely new breed. Older people call them *shinjinrui*, or 'new humans'. They are the first generation of Japanese to be brought up in affluence, and to have learned most of the things they know about life from the television screen and from international travel. They are adopting Western ideas of rebellion, job mobility, and self-gratification. They commit themselves to following fashions, buying magazines which chronicle global trends in clothing, to music, interior decoration, and food. These young Japanese are increasingly frustrated by Japan's poor living conditions, including the long commutes and the cramped and costly apartments.

Traditional Japanese values maintain that 'it is bad to borrow—better to balance your books; better still to save'. But young people, instead of saving, have started to buy on credit. They have quickly learned Western consumer credit habits. In a Japanese Ministry of International Trade and Industry report published in October 1992, the use of credit cards by the Japanese was reported to have increased dramatically. In 1983, only 40 million credit cards circulated in Japan, or one for every three Japanese. By 1991, 63 per cent of Japanese adults had credit cards, compared with 60 per cent in the United States. Put a different way, in 1991, 166 million credit cards had been issued to Japan's population of 123 million. As a result, while at the end of 1979 only some US$760 million of credit was outstanding, by the end of the 1980s, the total had leapt to some US$450 billion, a more than 500-fold increase. Again in 1991, of these credit card holders, approximately 40,000 Japanese had declared personal bankruptcy due to their inability to repay their credit card induced debt. It is interesting to note that most of the offenders were either young men in their late twenties or early thirties or young women in their mid-twenties. Through this new 'habit', and now having to undergo the pain of 'kicking the habit', they should have more in common with their 'monkey' society peers—at least with such peers in the West, who have had long experience with this form of addiction. However, not all of this can be blamed on the 'new humans', as the figures clearly suggest that older Japanese people are also starting to borrow. Even the older generations are starting to enjoy themselves, to assert individual wants. In the late 1980s, consumption came into the open. In the winter, women in fur coats throng the city streets. Japanese skiers not only want the best gear, they want the most expensive.

Japan is the second largest market for cut diamonds in the world.

A further reflection of the social changes taking place is the change in eating habits. Rice has, for over a thousand years, been an immutable corner-stone of Japanese life. Today, however, according to the Japanese Ministry of Agriculture in 1991, rice takes second place to meat and dairy products in terms of domestic market consumption. From a more technical perspective, the Ministry claims that in 1960, the Japanese received 48 per cent of their total caloric intake from rice. In 1992, they claimed the figure was only around 28 per cent. McDonald's and Kentucky Fried Chicken now rank the first and second most popular restaurants respectively in Japan. While many, both inside and outside Japan, make the general argument that the Japanese are highly resistant to change, certainly these dietary trends give evidence to the contrary.

The stress of Japanese business life has brought not only riches to the country but also *karoshi* to its executives — a new word coined to describe 'death by overwork'. While women still do all of the housework, many also have part-time jobs. They have started to complain about sexual harassment and job discrimination, and to demand the right to have real careers. More tangible changes are likely now that Japan's recent economic boom has ended, and as individuals begin to resent past practices.

Probably the most important evidence of change is the fact that the Japanese system of 'lifetime employment' may be coming to an end. As a result of Japan entering into a severe recession in the early 1990s, Japanese industry came to the reluctant conclusion that in order to make material cost savings, it had to adopt the pernicious Western practice of laying off employees. To the horror of many throughout Japan, this process has begun. By early 1993, Nissan had announced the closure by 1995 of its 5,000-employee Zama car factory near Tokyo, almost 10 per cent of its workforce. Sumitomo Metal Industries has stated that it would cut its workforce by 14 per cent (3,000 people) over the next three years. NKK Corp and Kyocera Corp announced cuts of 15 per cent and 8 per cent respectively. Many others are following suit. Although only some 30 per cent of Japan's labour force has enjoyed the privilege of such lifetime employment, this concept has been one of the absolute foundations of the Japanese system. A material change of this kind to the system will have serious repercussions on the nature of Japanese society. Additionally, a new, desperate cost-cutting measure was introduced in early 1993. Companies, many of them illustrious names in corporate Japan, that had extended firm job offers in 1992 to university students in their third year, unilaterally withdrew their offers, just as the hapless students were about to graduate. While this measure has engendered general outrage, it has certainly brought home the message to the new generation of prospective employees that, even in Japan, the world is changing.

These changes could lead to a breakdown of the values — loyalty, hierarchy, sacrifice, consensus — upon which Japan has relied for its success. The confusion is already palpable. Japanese society today resonates between tradition and change, swinging back in some areas and forward in others. In Kawasaki and several other cities, parents send their children to kindergartens where they play practically naked in all seasons, building snowmen with bare hands. These parents feel that enduring such hardship instills determination and provides some antidote to the affluence and unrelieved urbanisation of the modern world. Yet Japanese who travel abroad find it hard to understand why they should pay so much to subsidise Japanese farmers when people can live better for less in other countries. Parents struggle to understand the interests of their children, while sending them to the traditional crammer schools.

In some ways, the changes wrought by the new generations could be Japan's best hope for the future. Although Japan has become dislocated every time it has attempted to deal with the rest of the world, it can no longer avoid this painful process. Change is not an option, it is a necessity.

In particular, Japan must somehow reform its political system, which is almost dynastic and feudal in nature. For Japan to have increasing credibility, not only in the West but more importantly in the region, and for it to set itself, or be set up as a regional co-leader, it cannot allow the almost numbing repetition of political scandals to continue. From the former prime minister Tanaka and the Lockheed bribes in the 1970s (the first major post-war scandal to receive international notice) to the 1992 scandal of the 78-year-old Shin Kanemaru, vice president of the LDP receiving ¥500 million (US$4 million) from the transport company Sagawa Kyubin, the rest of the world has looked on in amazement. This was compounded by further revelations that Kanemaru might have previously used his influence with the Tokyo-based Inagawa-kai, a *yakuza* — criminal family — organisation to pressure successfully a right-wing political group, who were vigorously opposing Noburo Takeshita's then candidature for the post of prime minister, to stop. They did, and Takeshita was elected. Corruption is endemic in politics worldwide. However, it is the repetition and scale of Japanese political corruption that boggles the mind and reinforces the view that Japan is different from, if not alien to, the rest of the world. The Kanemaru case gives some indication that in Japanese politics too, there are glimmerings of change. If he had apologised and resigned as soon as the news broke, Kanemaru might have more or less retrieved his reputation. However, he used his power to plea bargain, and got off with a paltry fine of ¥200,000 (US$1,660) and a misdemeanour charge, without resigning. This event led to an unprecedented series of demonstrations, petitions, and hunger strikes around the country, and Kanemaru was finally forced to resign. As one Japanese television news anchor said, 'There is something completely new going on in Japanese politics. It is called people-power.' Subsequently, in March 1993, after an inquiry by the Japanese tax authorities, Kanemaru was arrested for tax evasion. The public prosecutors then discovered he had some US$50 million-plus in cash, bonds, and in over a hundred kilograms of gold bars, all secreted away.

There has been another development that could lead to a more representative system of politics. Following Kanemaru's resignation, including from the leadership of the 'Takeshita' faction which was by far the most powerful faction in the LDP party, considerable infighting broke out between his likely successors, Ichiro Ozawa and Keizo Obuchi, supported by the veteran senior LDP player, Seiroku Kajiyoma. In the event, Obuchi won and became the head of the Takeshita faction only to find that Ozawa, with some forty younger Diet members and with the former finance minister Tsutomu Hata fronting as nominal leader, set up a new break-away faction called the 'Reform Forum 21'. This could result in the LDP's stranglehold on Japanese politics weakening and, in turn, allow a less feudal and more representative system to evolve. Despite the fact that the Japanese public seems to have been either inured or indifferent to these antics in the past, they appear to be changing. It is now primarily up to them to provide the ongoing impetus for genuine reform. As I shall refer later, there is considerable precedent for this type of people-power induced change in other Asian countries.

The Japanese government must do more for its own people. Despite Japan's per capita income exceeding the other top six industrial economies, Japan lags behind most other industrialised nations in terms of the development of its infrastructure. For example, it has less area of parks per person and fewer expressways compared with other roads, and it falls dismally short in terms of housing area per person (*Far Eastern Economic Review*, 25 February 1993, p. 56). As it devotes more resources to make up these shortfalls, so its people will expect more. In turn, they will become more like the rest of the world.

The Japanese government *Gaimusho* — the Ministry of Foreign Affairs — needs a major overhaul and strengthening in terms of its pigmy-like status when compared with, say, the Ministry of Finance and the Ministry of International Trade and Industry, which have both long dominated bureaucratic affairs in Japan and abroad. The *Gaimusho*'s perception of itself must change, as must the perception of the public and, in particular, the politicians who are more insular and provincial than in any other OECD country. In the new world order where Japan needs leadership skills, the *Gaimusho* must play an important role. It must be more proactive, rather than reactive, i.e. waiting for usually conflicting cues from the politicians and the heavy, self-interested nudging from the other ministries. A touch of confident Machiavellianism would not go amiss, especially as in this new world order it is only really the *Gaimusho* who can orchestrate Japan's foreign initiatives and its responses to foreign events. To paraphrase Machiavelli, 'a leader who is passive or irresolute comes to be seen as a useless friend and a despicable enemy, after which he will find himself hopelessly lost.' The *Gaimusho* has the people: experienced, multilingual, and impressive; they now need to be bold, to take initiative, and to be used and supported properly by Japan.

Similarly, Japan's business (and government) communities must take more individual, personal initiatives to 'network' (to use that rather efficient American term) cross-culturally. This concept has been applied in all cultures, since time began. However, outside their own culture, the Japanese have generally found it difficult to network and develop close personal friends, in the Western or Asian individualistic monkey culture sense of the word. Likewise, non-Japanese have found it almost impossible to network into Japan. On a more general note, as the middle and older generations of Japanese leadership are particularly weak in this area, it is thus important that establishment members from Japan develop close personal friendships on an individual basis with their opposite numbers in Asia Pacific and in the West. This will facilitate better communication and understanding, as well as the ability to resolve problems and to effect mutually desired objectives in a more efficient and personally rewarding manner.

Unfortunately, at meetings between individuals from the establishments of the Japanese and the other Asia Pacific and Western cultures, the general interpersonal communication environment is often prejudiced by both sides having a corporate or government agenda which obliges them to meet in a formal, institutional, and often politely confrontational manner. It is therefore also important that these relationships are based on a personal respect and liking for the other individual, rather than on the corporate or government affiliation of each individual. Businessmen such as Hideo Ishihara of IBJ Leasing, Kazuo Wada of Yaohan International, Shigekuni Kawamura of Dai Nippon Ink & Chemicals, Dr Reinosuke Hara of Seiko Denshi Kogyo, Minoru Akimoto of Time-Warner Japan, Inc., Minoru Murofushi of Itochu Corporation, Reiichi Shimamoto of the Japan Research Institute, Akio Morita of Sony, Diet Members Yuji Tsushima and Koji Kakizawa, and many others, have the individual vision that has enabled them to throw off many of the traditional Japanese cultural inhibitions — they have many non-Japanese friends, they network actively and, in so doing, they bring Japan closer to the rest of Asia and the world. They and others have started this process, the younger generation is continuing it, but many more Japanese individuals need to become involved in this process.

Japan's responses to its relationship with the region are still relatively unchanged. More specifically, the various Japanese group advocates to date of regional co-operation have, in traditional Japanese style, had their own different and competing independent agendas. For example, there are some who have advocated domination of regional forums in order to compensate for their frustration at not being able to play a leading role in global forums, such as Japan's role in the Asian Development Bank. There are also those who wish to create and support new forums because of their domestic institutional inability to participate in international forums. For example, the Ministry of International Trade and Industry, which cannot either participate in the G7 meetings (because this is the Ministry of Finance's territory) or participate as observers at some of the ASEAN deliberations (because this is the Foreign Ministry's territory), was a major behind-the-scenes promoter of APEC and Japan's role in APEC. Then there are those who, on a more emotional and somewhat more primitive basis, want to counteract the Japan-bashers in the United States by actively promoting Japan's ties with Asia Pacific. As all these cases have ulterior motives, it is not surprising that the recipients often not only recognise such ulterior motives but that they are suspicious of Japan's general motives as a result. Even if they cannot recognise these motives, it is ultimately the very alien, ongoing Japanese response to these situations that leads to confusion and suspicion as to what, exactly, the Japanese are trying to achieve.

Japan must also realise that it cannot continue to enjoy such massive trade surpluses, such as its estimated surplus of more than US$100 billion in 1992 and its likely surplus of more than US$150 billion in 1993. This contrasts with the G7 group of countries (including Japan), which ran a current account deficit of US$140 billion in 1992. Japan is thus in a position to deal more effectively with its recessionary problems, which causes its less fortunate Western G7 member countries considerable envy and resentment. Japan must therefore recognise that, irrespective of the rights and wrongs of how all the parties arrived at the global recession of the early 1990s, it must make more of an effort to take a larger share of the responsibility for eliminating the 1993 deflation of the world economy. Unless Japan is able to reverse its cycle of building larger and larger surpluses, the tensions between it and its G7 partners could lead ultimately to a breakdown of the world's financial and trading markets. On a smaller, regional scale, the same principles apply between Japan and its neighbours. Furthermore, any rupture between Japan and the West will have an immediate knock-on effect on its regional neighbours.

Japan's strategy must extend beyond paying for friends. Japan needs to approach the world on several different fronts. In trade, it should change and be more sympathetic to the effect it is having on its trading partners. In other arenas, such as politics, diplomacy, and individual human relationships, it should develop radically new approaches. Most importantly, it must accept a common higher value system. In this context, one of the most important examples of the challenges facing Japan's leadership establishment, most of whom are from the pre-World War II generation, in developing a different value system is the question of whether or not it should give full, public recognition to Japan's military behaviour *vis-à-vis* Asia during the period from the late 1800s to the close of World War II. Japan's official resistance to recognising its behaviour in its own history books relating to this period is a source of bemusement to the West and, more importantly, a source of extreme frustration and, in some cases, outright anger to the countries of Asia Pacific. The constant question is, 'Why can't Japan simply acknowledge what it did and express genuine remorse? We all know that the circumstances were different then and that Japan has since changed. We all want to put the whole matter behind us and get on with the future!' However, by Japan refusing to make a clean breast of it all and wholeheartedly throwing itself into developing its new relationships within the region, there remains the lingering suspicion that Japan may not really have changed and that it could revert to its old behaviour patterns. This attitude highlights my earlier comment that too many Japanese don't feel and understand guilt in the way the rest of the world appears to do. They don't subscribe to a higher moral value system that transcends what is politically expedient, what could be deemed to cause national shame. In national terms, many countries have gone through this cathartic experience of expressing publicly their remorse about past actions — the Germans in recognising the awfulness of Nazi Germany and of the recent rise of Neo-Nazism, the Chinese in their recognition of the appalling effects of their Cultural Revolution as the 'Ten Years of Chaos', and others.

Perhaps the Japanese reaction stems, at least in part, from its old attitudes that if society deemed an individual to be in the wrong, the only honourable form of accepting guilt and offering an apology was by committing ritual suicide, as the shame was too great to live with. A related example was the case of Japanese soldiers who, when likely to face defeat, committed suicide rather than endure the shame of living with such defeat

thereafter. This reaction can be compared with captured Japanese soldiers' readiness to do whatever their captors asked of them — as if they had
effectively died by being captured and therefore nothing thereafter
mattered. This is quite a different reaction to that of, say, a captured
Chinese or Australian soldier, who would generally volunteer nothing and
do everything possible to escape, all the while feeling little, if any, shame
at being captured. In this national trait, perhaps, lies Japan's enormous
reluctance to officially acknowledge its past actions. Furthermore, there
is the absurdity of the phenomenon that occurs so frequently in Japanese
life, namely when everyone knows that something unacceptable has
happened, yet if it isn't officially recognised, it somehow didn't really
happen. It must be seen that such a system is pointless, particularly when
subject to international scrutiny.

One example of this behaviour, which will simply not go away and
which the Japanese establishment would do well to recognise officially,
express full remorse about, make compensation for, and put behind them,
is the fact that the Japanese military effectively seized, enslaved, and
turned into 'Comfort Women' some 80,000 Asian women (including
some Dutch women from Indonesia) to provide sexual services to
Japanese soldiers while the army advanced through Asia. This system was
apparently put in place in order to prevent a repeat of the excesses of rape
and brutality committed by Japanese soldiers in Shanghai in 1932 and
subsequently in Nanjing. This system had a positive effect in reducing the
number of reported rapes — but at what cost to the unfortunate women,
most of whose lives were ruined as a result. It is largely due to history
professor Yoshiaki Yoshimi of Chuo University, Japan, who has specialised
in researching some of Japan's less than admirable past military activities
and who discovered not only clear evidence of the military's development
and implementation of the Comfort Women plan but also of the military
using Chinese civilians as guinea pigs for the testing of bacteriological
weapons, that this former matter was published in Japan's left-leaning
paper, *Asahi Shimbun*, in January 1993. It was only then that there was
reluctant official acknowledgement of the military being somehow involved and official remorse expressed. Japan must understand that the rest
of the world demands their recognition of these and other historical facts.
Further, they must realise that these sadly brutalised and psychologically

scarred women living in today's more democratic, people-power driven Asia have the moral support of their governments, and that they will collectively demand that Japan responds officially. If Japan doesn't take positive steps to deal with this specific subject and the general subject of writing objective accounts of its past history, it will be making a major tactical—and strategic—error with regard to its Asia Pacific neighbour relations just as they are showing real signs of fundamental improvement.

A further example is that Japan continues to show a scant regard for the environment, such as in its logging practices, its use of tuna nets that kill dolphins, and its continuing maintenance of whaling fleets. Such policies harm Japan's image abroad. Japan should lead by example. If it wants foreign markets to remain open, it should open its own markets. If the Japanese want to be accepted by the rest of the world, then their expatriate or travelling businessmen should stop living and socialising only with each other. Rather than always going its own way on aid policy, Japan must learn to be a partner, to pass on technology to Third World countries, to become a true multi-polar leader by, for example, working with other world leaders to develop a common strategy for helping Eastern Europe, the Third World, and the world environment.

However, it should also be said that the other global multi-polar leaders in the West are reticent about, if not against, inviting Japan into their innermost councils. Without change on their part, it is not reasonable to lay all the blame at Japan's door.

Japan's real front line of defence lies, therefore, not on any military perimeter but in the maintenance of growing global free trade and international co-operation. One aspect would be for it to fully accept its regional OECD status in substance, as well as in form. Like the United States and Britain (who had, and hopefully still have, a more global vision of unity), it must be prepared to open its borders , i.e. its economy and its culture, particularly to the countries of Asia Pacific, with the concomitant risk and cost that such an action will involve. The great challenge for Japan is to develop multi-dimensional leadership skills and individual accountability. The great challenge for the rest of the world is to help Japan get through this period. Asia Pacific needs Japan, but given Japan's past imperial adventures, it is wary. Only with the development of proper leaders, a regional and global vision, and individual ties of friendship can Japan persuade the other nations of Asia Pacific that regional co-operation is in the best interests of all concerned. Such co-operation should include Japan's participation in regional peace-keeping initiatives, with the possibility of it helping the other countries of the region to develop an Asia Pacific equivalent of the North Atlantic Treaty Organization (NATO).

Even if a trade war can be averted, Japan is still becoming more isolated from the United States and Europe. The United States is turning inward to confront its many domestic problems and its new involvement in NAFTA. With economic unification of the EC countries, with the trauma surrounding the Maastricht Treaty, and with the changes in the erstwhile Soviet bloc offering the prospect of a 'Greater Europe', Europe is also becoming more inwardly focused, albeit at present in a more confused way — no doubt because of the huge challenges to be faced.

With the real risk of alienation from the West, Japan simply cannot afford to risk cutting itself off from Asia Pacific. In this environment, for both Japan and the rest of Asia Pacific, a new regional community based on mutual interdependence and support is the only realistic strategy. If they don't co-operate, the individual nations of Asia Pacific — including Japan — will be at an increasing disadvantage.

Only with the support of Asia Pacific will Japan find its place in the world. In return, the rest of the world, and particularly Asia Pacific, should accept that they can all learn a great deal from Japan and its culture. Asia Pacific needs Japan for its global clout, its capital, its technology, its industry, its financial muscle, and its markets. Further, as many countries in Asia Pacific have already acknowledged, they need Japan if they are to be able to negotiate in the future as a region bilaterally with both the EC and NAFTA. With the likelihood of increasing imbalances of trade with the EC and the United States, Japan must seize this opportunity to join the rest of Asia Pacific as a neighbour, friend, and co-leader. If it waits too long, Greater China and/or the other countries of the region may develop to the point where they believe that they no longer really need Japan. Further, if Japan continues to pursue its own alien goals, it will then only exist more or less at the whim of the rest of the world — shut out and without any real friends.

GREATER CHINA
The Most Powerful Regional and
Global Force in the Making?

THE PEOPLE'S REPUBLIC OF CHINA
HONG KONG
TAIWAN
THE CHINESE DIASPORA

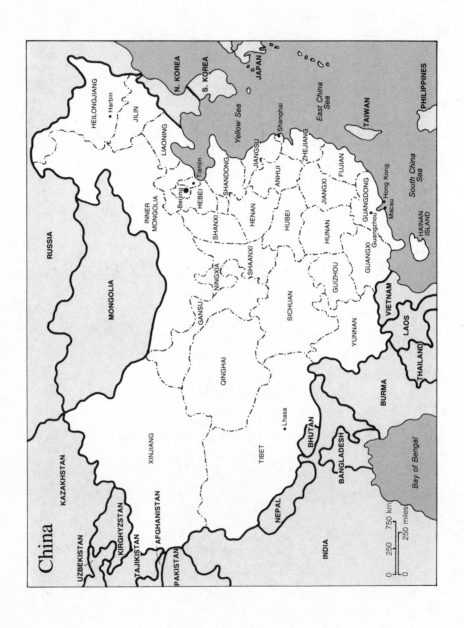

THE PEOPLE'S REPUBLIC OF CHINA
Balancing on the Knife Edge of Order and Chaos

In recent years, the most widely-held belief of amateur China-watchers has been that democracy should and must now come to the People's Republic. This is nonsense. The world would be foolish and naïve to try to impose Western-style democracy on China. Pluralistic, representative government would not help the some 1.2 billion Chinese in the near future. In fact, it would be more likely to cause them great harm.

Such democracy will only divide the country. China is, and always has been, threatened by anarchy. Autocratic, centralised governments have ruled China for thousands of years. But this tradition of authoritarian rule has been countered by an equally powerful tradition of provincial insubordination. In imperial China, especially in the nineteenth century, provincial warlords challenged the authority of the emperor. In today's Communist China, a new breed of 'economic warlords' in the provinces are beginning to flout the authority of the bureaucrats in Beijing. Give each person a vote today, or even in the next five to ten years, and the nation could easily disintegrate into warring economic factions with provincial economic warlords vying for power in the midst of chaos. Alternatively, using the pretext of preventing the country from sliding into chaos, the army could step in and impose authoritarian order.

When the Chinese government ordered the army to fire on demonstrators in Beijing in June 1989, the world reacted with naïve, and in some cases hypocritical, horror. This event became known around the world as the Tiananmen Square incident. Virtually no one seemed to realise that China's leaders were trying as best they could to control the divisive forces that, if left unchecked, risked splintering their country. Vigilance against anarchy has been an absolute throughout Chinese history. This is largely because of the traditional schism between city and country, between the ruler and the ruled. China's emperors, and communist cadres after them, built a state structure on the backs of peasants. The state, requiring order and a monopoly on ideology, made a deliberate break between the government and the citizens. Bonds of obligation never formed between the governors and the governed; the government exploited the people, and the people tried to protect themselves, sometimes by evasion or corruption. In the last resort, they used revolution.

It is a folly to assume that outside standards or concepts can be applied wholesale to Chinese problems. For their part, the Chinese are certain they have the right way to do everything — whether it be a way to cut onions, a way to wash feet, or a way to negotiate contracts. China's history has moulded a people whose confidence is difficult to overstate, a nation whose emperor in 1793 proclaimed to a British envoy that since his 'celestial empire' had all things in prolific abundance, he had no need for 'the manufactures of outside barbarians'.

The Chinese claim to have invented everything from gunpowder to paper, some say even pasta. Outsiders conclude that the Chinese are arrogant. Possibly they are. However, things just look different when you have five thousand years of recorded history.

This long history, and China's early technological advances, have not saved the country from the past two centuries of humiliation by the Western barbarians and from general turmoil. Yet China's unspoken conviction that the rest of the world is essentially barbaric lives on. The Chinese name for their country is still the Middle Kingdom — between heaven and earth, the centre of everything. Their confidence, or arrogance, outshines that of even the British and the French. In the face of China's underdeveloped country status this seems almost inexplicable.

Despite the almost frightening pace of change in China in recent years, the country is still underdeveloped in a way almost impossible to communicate to the rest of the world. China is medieval in many senses. It has only a very patchy, thin veneer of the twentieth century. While the nation boasts laser laboratories and satellite launch pads, these are the exception, not quite yet the rule. Even in Beijing, morning comes with sounds from another era: the clop-rattle of horses pulling cartloads of coal to furnaces which belch forth the sulphurous clouds that hang over the city; the scratching of construction workers excavating foundations by hand; the ringing of bicycle bells as millions of commuters glide eerily through the streets. However, all this is now changing at an astonishing pace — soon, no doubt, traffic jams, with hooting, irate drivers, will become the norm.

Approximately 700 million Chinese are semi-literate peasants. Almost 200 million are totally illiterate — in the early 1990s, the illiteracy rate amongst the adult population was 27 per cent. While China has only one major language, i.e. written Chinese, it is confusing in that there are 57 spoken dialects, many of them unintelligible to the speakers of other dialects. For example, someone who only speaks Shanghainese will not be able to understand someone who speaks Hakka. This problem is further compounded by the fact that there are some 50 minority groups each with its own language. However, the government has made major efforts since 1956 to impose Mandarin as the country's 'national language', with considerable success in the major cities.

In most places, the People's Republic of China doesn't meet the efficiency standards of even the erstwhile Soviet Union. Breaks in the electricity supply and water-stoppages regularly shut down Chinese cities. No major road exists between the capital, Beijing, and Shanghai, the country's major industrial city; nor between Shanghai and the modern trading city of Guangzhou. China can launch space satellites while being the last major country to manufacture steam locomotives. In many cities, goods travel to market on donkey carts. In most fields, human excrement — collected from the cities in oil drums — is used as a fertiliser. Manufacturing standards have little meaning in the Middle Kingdom. There is neither an accounting system, nor a real legal system upon which foreign businessmen can rely. Chinese enterprises must survive on patronage and/or corruption. Policemen and officials create laws and policies according to whim. Corruption affects not only large enterprises and big-time politics, but also everyday actions as simple as getting a train ticket. Often large blocks of train tickets are set aside for the well-connected. In certain circumstances, it can be almost impossible to get on a train without buying a ticket on the black market.

Against this backdrop, the only efficient unit of organisation for progress, economic or otherwise, is the family group. It is only with their family and their immediate friends that the Chinese feel any sense of loyalty and obligation. This is one of the primary reasons why successful

Chinese businesses start small and generally stay small. Once they expand outside the family group, the internal loyalties which bind any organisation together become lost. Factions develop, and chaos ensues.

The family has been stressed as the most important link since time immemorial. When Confucius defined the five most important relationships between people, one exhorted the subjects to obey their emperor as long as he provided a fair, strong framework of government. The remaining four relationships dealt with the family. All too often these family ties took precedence if the government representing the emperor was weak. This was, and remains today, what I call the 'chaos factor'.

Most foreigners discount the dominant role anarchy has played in Chinese history, assuming that anarchy is a modern development brought about by the irrationalities of communism. It is not unreasonable to presume that China's civilisation enjoyed continuity for at least five thousand years. Legends tell of celestial emperors who ruled for tens of thousands of years before the reigns of the 'Five Sovereigns' who were credited with inventing writing, establishing the social structure, and teaching the people how to farm and fish. But although Chinese history has been long, it has not been static.

Two dynasties after the legendary sovereigns, in the eleventh century BC, the Zhou dynasty established some of the most enduring Chinese ideas — ideas which would bestow a legacy of turmoil. As justification for overthrowing the tyrannical king who preceded them, the Zhou claimed that heaven bestowed a 'mandate' on virtuous rulers. As long as the kingdom was peaceful, the emperor retained the mandate. War and chaos signalled that the mandate had fallen from the ruler's hands. This tradition also dictated that when the mandate was lost, the people not only had the right, but a duty, to rebel. Although autocratic governments have ruled China for its entire history, the populace traditionally has had access to this court of last resort. The mandate-of-heaven concept survives under communist rule today.

The Zhou dynasty went into decline in 700 BC and China slipped into three hundred years of disunity. Divided into small kingdoms, it became known as the 'Warring States' period. One of the other enduring influences on Chinese culture — Confucianism — had its birth in such chaos. The strife and troubles inspired Confucius to write about virtuous government. But the wars did not end until the state of Qin (or Chin — hence the Western name 'China') defeated the other kingdoms in 221 BC.

The Qin ruler is generally remembered for his cruelty. But despite his book-burning and the slave labour into which he forced the peasants, this emperor standardised the transportation system, writing, weights, and coinage. All these developments laid the foundation for a large and unified Chinese empire.

A large empire required a large administration. The Han dynasty, following the Qin dynasty in 207 BC, created the elaborate system of Chinese bureaucracy which survives even in today's communist government. The Han established twenty grades of administrators — the mandarins — and started the examination system which opened the doors of bureaucracy to any scholar with a good memory and a talent for interpreting the works of Confucius. Confucianism — much like communism in modern China — became an orthodox foundation of education, and thus the key to government, power, and prestige.

In the sixteen centuries of Chinese history which followed the Han dynasty, China would build the dominant civilisation in East Asia. During the T'ang dynasty of the seventh and eighth centuries AD, China's walled capital at Chang'an was the world's largest and most brilliantly cosmopolitan city. It was a Mecca to which traders, diplomats, and artists travelled from Japan, Korean, Central Asia, Vietnam, and the South China Sea. Chang'an's gates also welcomed Arabs, Persians, Jews, and Christians from the Mediterranean basin.

The T'ang finally fell in the early ninth century, and China split again into a number of independent states plagued by war. The Song dynasty, beginning in 960, was a period of considerable creativity, although it remained weak and divided. Gradually, central government was restored and there was vigorous intra-regional trade. By the time Marco Polo arrived in the thirteenth century, when China was ruled by the Mongol Yuan dynasty, he found huge and prosperous Chinese cities on a scale quite unlike anything in Europe.

Periodically throughout Chinese history, the Mongols had gone to war with the Chinese, just as Germanic tribes had periodically invaded southern Europe. The Mongols, despised by the Chinese for their rough ways and ignorance, had always been defeated. But when Genghis Khan united the Central Asian tribes in the thirteenth century, he swept into China, breaching the Great Wall and conquering the northern half of the country. He left the conquest of southern China to his grandson, Kublai Khan. Marco Polo returned to Europe with stories of a great and advanced civilisation, forming a Western vision of China which more or less survives to this day.

In 1368, the Mongols were expelled by the first of the native Ming dynasty emperors, who expanded the empire. Ultimately, the Ming dynasty left China as a totalitarian state, which sapped the efficiency and integrity of its early bureaucracy. The Ming dynasty's successors, the Manchu Qing dynasty rulers, also concentrated power in their own hands, isolating themselves from the general population. These rulers continued the Ming dynasty's moribund isolationism and intellectual conservatism.

When Western traders came to Asia in the sixteenth century, it signalled the beginning of the end for the Chinese empire. While many European emissaries were forced to kowtow before the emperor, they submitted only symbolically. They went on to wreak havoc upon a China unprepared for the challenge.

China was unfortunate enough to produce something the British wanted, and soon grew to need: tea. Before long the British were 'addicted', importing so much tea that they created a trade deficit with China, which claimed only silver or gold in return. This was a drain on Western treasuries. By the eighteenth century, the 'Western barbarians' had devised a solution to their trade problem, exchanging one addiction for another. They smuggled opium into China, creating a population of real addicts. By the nineteenth century, other Western countries had joined in the lucrative drug trade. Foreigners divided up China's major port cities among themselves, controlling the trade routes and challenging traditional philosophies and processes. Twice the Chinese went to war to stop the Western drug barons, but each time they were soundly defeated.

The Celestial Empire was made to pay huge war reparations, reduce customs tariffs on imported goods, and permit Westerners to take up residence in the treaty ports, where they insisted on immunity from

Chinese law. China also had to allow freedom of movement for foreign missionaries. The foreign powers seized Chinese territory or territory controlled by China: the French took Indochina; the British took Burma; and when the declining Qing lost a war with Japan they had to give up Taiwan. When a messianic Chinese tried to lead what was called the Boxer Rebellion, the Chinese government could restore order only with the help of British soldiers. In effect, during the second half of the nineteenth century, foreigners did as they pleased in China. This experience exacerbated the already xenophobic nature of the Chinese.

In 1911 revolution broke out. The infant Qing emperor was deposed by nationalist forces and a new Nationalist Party was formed, led by Sun Yat-sen. Sun was an idealistic Chinese doctor, educated in Hawaii and Hong Kong, who returned to the mainland at the beginning of the century with a philosophy popularly known as the 'Three Principles of the People': nationalism, democracy, and economic socialism. Sun formed the Kuomintang (KMT), or Nationalist Party, in 1914. Nationalism was an important concept for a nation which had been humiliated and brought to ruin by foreign opium traders and corrupt native bureaucrats. Democracy did not mean representative government so much as the need for every Chinese to read and write. Sun's socialism was simple: those that tilled the land should own it, and the government should oversee industrialisation. He was able to put money behind the nationalistic yearnings of his countrymen, partly through the fabulous wealth of his father-in-law, the industrialist Charles Soong, and partly through dealings with the Soviets.

In 1924, the KMT and the Chinese Communist Party put aside their ideological differences and joined forces to expel the foreigners, who had made fortunes by extracting trade concessions from the Chinese government. The KMT adopted a policy of 'Co-operating with Russia and absorbing the Communists'. In 1925, Sun died of liver cancer. Chiang Kai-shek, the head of the Whampoa Military Academy until Sun's death and 'generalissimo' of the KMT, had retained violently anti-communist feelings gained during four months of study in the Soviet Union. When Chiang took over after Sun's death, the alliance between the Nationalists and the Communists quickly fell apart. At that time Chiang had more money and firepower than the Communists, and he used it. Then the

KMT massacred the Communists in Shanghai in 1927. They went on to purge the Communists from the other major cities, and drove them into the countryside, where in 1934 they undertook their fabled six thousand-mile 'Long March' and regrouped in northwest China. Chiang focused on a revival of Confucianism and followed the example of emperors before him, concentrating on internal intrigue and the enemy within. Then, in 1936, the warlord Zhang Xueliang, believing the Japanese to be a more important threat, kidnapped the generalissimo to prove the point. Ironically, the Communists came to Chiang's rescue, on the condition he leave them alone and concentrate on fighting the Japanese.

Throughout World War II, the KMT were split over the question of which enemy was more important, the Communists or the Japanese. The Japanese had taken over Manchuria; the Communists had fortified a redoubt in Yenan in northwest China. Chiang had first established a government at Nanjing in central China, but in 1937 he was driven inland by the Japanese. His government moved to Chungking (now Chongqing) on the Yangtze River in southern central China. But neither the Communists nor the Nationalists had much success in ousting the Japanese, until American atom bombs settled the issue.

Japan's surrender did not bring peace to China. When World War II ended, the Communists and the KMT went back to their internal dispute and began to fight in earnest, racing each other to claim territory and arms left by the retreating Japanese. Before long the country had been divided into two camps. Both sides claimed victories. The Communists, led by Mao Zedong, won control of the north. After several thousand years of hierarchy and exploitation by the ruling classes, followed by 150 years of deprivation and chaos, it was almost inevitable that the Chinese peasants and students would be seduced by the egalitarian ideals of communism. Young Chinese intellectuals and would-be revolutionaries, reading Marx on nineteenth-century Europe, recognised a description of China in their own time: child and female slave labour, starvation wages for overworked labourers, no protection against sickness, injury, unemployment, and old age, and no bargaining power for better conditions.

The Communists came to champion the poor peasants. They promised the masses land and relief from ruinous taxes, usury, and starvation. In the areas they controlled, they enforced 'class struggle' and eliminated the landlord-gentry class. After gaining the allegiance of the peasantry, Mao started to move into the cities, previously KMT territory. In 1948, the tide began to turn against the KMT. They suffered large-scale defeats brought on by low morale and an inefficient, autocratic leadership. Corruption and ineptitude had sapped their strength and their ideals. In Manchuria alone, the KMT lost 200,000 men to the well-organised and popular communist Red Army. The final blow came between November 1948 and January 1949, when the KMT lost Peking, half a million men, and their equipment. As 1949 ground to an end, the Communists mopped up the rest of the country.

Chiang and two million of his followers fled to Taiwan, taking with them most of the antique treasures from the imperial Forbidden City. On the mainland, the Communist Party declared a new regime, establishing the People's Republic of China on 1 October 1949. Mao's victory surprised even the Soviet Union, which had insisted that according to Marxist dogma, revolution must start in the cities. As the Soviet Union started to aid its new, enormous ally, Mao tried to form a viable government. He led the country through successive upheavals and reform campaigns until, in 1960, after many disagreements on the best way to achieve communism, the Soviet Union withdrew its aid. This caused more upheaval and famine, and the rift between the world's two largest communist states was not mended officially until President Gorbachev's state visit to Beijing in May 1989, by which time the Soviet Union was beginning to abandon Marxist-Leninist orthodoxy.

In the years that followed the 1960 break between Moscow and Beijing, moderates like Deng Xiaoping began to push pragmatic economics before class struggle, production before ideology. Others wanted to resurrect the Soviet-Chinese alliance as a protection against American aggression. Mao, sensitive to the damage China had suffered at the hands of outsiders, did not want help from any barbarians. Sensing that China was slipping away from the revolutionary spirit, he started the reform campaign which would try to destroy Chinese traditions developed over several thousand years.

In August 1966, Mao launched the Cultural Revolution in order to purge the Party of the bourgeoisie who he claimed were attempting to stage a comeback using old ideas, culture, customs, and habits of the exploiting class to corrupt the masses and capture their minds. The aim of the Cultural Revolution was to struggle against, and crush, those persons in authority who were taking the capitalist road, and to criticise and repudiate the reactionary bourgeois academic authorities and the ideology of the bourgeoisie and all other exploiting classes.

The Revolution rapidly turned into political mayhem, personally orchestrated by Mao and his wife, Jiang Qing. Backed by his supporters in the army and by the Socialist Education Movement, Mao was able to purge dissenting officials in the Party and eviscerate the bureaucracy of his rival, the state president Liu Shaoqi. Reformers like Deng Xiaoping were exiled to the provinces.

For the next ten years, China's youth — the Red Guards — rooted out alleged rightists. They closed schools and factories, burned books, and pitted children against parents, students against teachers. Members of almost every Chinese family were negatively affected in some way or another — many were persecuted, imprisoned, or killed. The state tried to dispose of the Confucian tradition of honouring parents and authority, an action as drastic as attempting to destroy the American icons of motherhood and apple pie. They tried to undermine the family unit, arguing that the state was the family and the paramount authority. Anything that was a physical reminder of China's past — usually revered in the Middle Kingdom — was ordered to be smashed. Temples, monuments, and works of art disappeared or were destroyed. Propaganda and fear governed every aspect of daily life. Workers, instead of working, spent endless hours in Marxist philosophy study sessions or in persecuting those judged to have strayed from the Party line.

Jiang Qing, a former B-grade Shanghai film actress, effectively directed the purging process. As the country's cultural empress, she watched American movies in her private cinema while allowing the people to see only a handful of 'Revolutionary Model Operas' with such titles as *Taking Tiger Mountain by Strategy* or *The White-Haired Girl* (in which the heroine's hair turned white when she was chased by the KMT). Musical connoisseurs could enjoy pieces like *The Production Brigade Celebrates the Arrival in the Hills of the Manure Collectors* and *The People of Taiwan Long for Liberation*. The Cultural Revolution — or 'The Ten Years of Chaos', as it is now known — ended when Mao died in 1976. By then

China had undergone the twentieth-century equivalent of Europe's 'Dark Ages', when similar excesses were perpetrated on the population.

Deng Xiaoping became head of the new Party Advisory Commission and went on to become the country's paramount leader. When Deng came to power, the relationship between the Chinese government and the people had changed little since imperial times. In Communist China it was still everybody against the central government, while regional rivalries remained intense. Ventures in Shanghai would not help ventures in Beijing or Guangzhou. Peasants were concerned only with their crops and their families. As Deng's government cautiously lessened the rigidity of central Party control, rival Party factions and bureaucrats began to vie for power. Everyone rushed in to take advantage of the new freedom.

However, Deng allowed only as much freedom as he thought was needed to start reforming the economy. He had been forced to conclude that Mao's isolationist policies and rigid central planning were holding China back. For the first time since the 1960s, peasants were encouraged to take jobs in urban areas. The country enjoyed a record harvest, double-digit industrial growth, and a 20 per cent jump in foreign trade as, for the first time, China began to open itself voluntarily to the outside world. But although Deng's reforms increased foreign trade and the peasants' real income, the economy suffered from overheated growth, excessive imports, and increased corruption. Industrial growth began to outstrip the energy and transportation networks that supported it. Despite progress, China laboured under a nineteenth-century infrastructure.

Political changes were necessary to allow the economic reforms. In 1981, Deng and his lieutenants formally declared the Cultural Revolution a catastrophe, and urged the army to re-examine its actions during it, such as dressing up professors in dunce costumes, and torturing officials in front of stadium crowds. Intellectuals who had suffered during the Cultural Revolution were sought out and 'rehabilitated'.

In 1985 Deng orchestrated the resignation of sixty-four ageing or infirm Central Committee members, including ten members of the Politburo. The resignations allowed China's leader to install younger cadres more open to his policies. Deng also announced that the 4 million-strong People's Liberation Army would be cut by 25 per cent, and that the country's educational system would be reformed. On the international front, Deng tried to play off the two superpowers against each other, holding out China as the third factor in the global defence equation.

Outsiders naïvely concluded that Deng's changes were leading towards capitalism and democracy. In 1986, the American magazine *Newsweek* breathlessly proclaimed on its front cover, 'China Goes Capitalist'. Chinese students were also naïvely optimistic about the Party's liberal line and held demonstrations in late 1986 and early 1987. But the students' rhetoric about democracy gave the Party's hard-line conservatives the opening they needed in order to engineer the ousting of Hu Yaobang, the liberal Party General Secretary and the then heir-apparent to Deng. The more conservative Zhao Ziyang, although still a reformist, took Hu's place. An unseen power struggle began. On one side were those promoting the growth of market forces and economic openness and ignoring the fundamental lesson of Chinese history, that too much freedom leads to anarchy. On the other side of the struggle were Mao's old lieutenants and their protégés who wanted to maintain political control at any cost. While both sides in the dispute agreed on the goal of modernising China, the fundamental dispute was over the pace and method of reform.

Although he was more or less above the fray, Deng Xiaoping tended to side with the economic reformers. In 1987, over strong conservative objections, he managed to introduce a system to replace the centralised economy. Under the new system, factory managers were supposed to borrow their capital from banks, obtain their own materials, hire and fire workers, and go bankrupt if they couldn't pay their bills. Beijing was supposed to lift the freeze on many prices which had long been fixed to prop up industry.

However, under pressure from the conservatives, the ruling faction backpedalled on some of the more controversial measures. The lid on prices was only partially lifted, owing to widespread fear of inflation. The *apparatchik* factory managers were uncomfortable with Deng's changes because they meant more scrutiny and much less security. As an indication of how little had changed by the late 1980s, the number of state-owned enterprises operating at a loss was still 20 per cent, down only 5 percentage points since the changes had first begun in 1979.

Inflation, a bad harvest, and a budget deficit further plagued the reformers. In contrast to the relatively smooth rural reforms, urban reform created large external trade deficits. Officials did not stick to their budgets. The rate of wage increases outstripped productivity. Rising expectations, increased incomes, and easy credit created a feeding frenzy for an inadequate supply of goods. As relations with the United States improved in 1988, China also laid the groundwork for a summit with the Soviet Union. But China's economy, under the dual pressures of the market and the central planners, seemed to be coming unglued.

The rate of inflation spiralled and panic-buying erupted in the cities as rumours circulated that all price controls would be removed that September. The economic chaos was exacerbated by the country's underdeveloped political and legal systems. The lack of laws and standards allowed corruption to flourish as never before during the communist regime. It became impossible to buy a bicycle, or rent an apartment, or buy factory materials without paying off somebody. Public confidence ebbed with each rise in prices and the mounting resentment over official corruption.

When the ousted Hu Yaobang died in April 1989, two thousand students in Beijing marched from the university district to Tiananmen Square, near the government headquarters, to mourn the former leader. Many believed Hu had been more sincere in his attempts at reform than the coalition which had followed him. The student demonstrators presented the government with a list of demands which ranged from guaranteed freedom of speech and the press to the open publication of private bank accounts belonging to the top leaders and their families. Their primary goal was to get rid of nepotism and corruption. They also favoured some modest political reforms to match the economic changes. Despite a ban on further demonstrations, students used Hu's death as a cloak of legitimacy, and started to gather support from the public. The next day, one hundred thousand of them marched to Tiananmen Square.

Soon, the movement took on a life of its own. A month later, one million demonstrators — not only students, but workers, shopkeepers, and housewives — crowded into Tiananmen Square to support three thousand students who refused to eat until the government made moves to reform.

While public support was widespread, it was the student leaders who organised the movement and negotiated with the government. As they did so, the demonstrators caught the world's imagination. Foreign observers began to predict an emergent democracy in China, and the students started to believe this misguided interpretation of their actions.

Without the outside world's naïve and romantic exhortations to press for democracy, the students might have been satisfied with their already considerable victory. This was the first time the communist government had ever negotiated peacefully with dissenters — it was probably the first time in China's history that any government, imperial or otherwise, had done so. But instead, they stayed on. No doubt they had many motives for doing so. However, without question, one of the main reasons was the attention given them by the international media; financial and moral support left the students with a perceived obligation to achieve what they thought the people of Hong Kong and the West wanted them to achieve — democracy — something of which they had no practical knowledge and which the government could not possibly give them.

It also forced them into an artificial ideological position: continued independent dissent in the Western style, rather than an alliance with a sympathetic Party faction in the traditional Chinese style. This meant that the Tiananmen Square demonstrators had no reformist allies to plead their cause when the Party's conservative wing began to prevail.

After four or five weeks of demonstrations reported in media and television broadcasts all over the world, the government leaders had their backs against the wall. Despite their genuine initial efforts at negotiation, they had not been able to resolve the student crisis before the first state visit of the Soviet head of state in thirty years. Mikhail Gorbachev arrived in Beijing while demonstrators still occupied the square. Chinese officials had to sneak the Soviet leader in through a side door of the Great Hall of the People. It was an extreme loss of face, particularly since Deng wanted to restore good relations with the Soviet Union, just as Mao had done with the United States. Much more importantly and alarmingly, people also began to demonstrate in provincial capitals all over the country.

As time went by, many students and other demonstrators gave up, dirty, tired, and discouraged after weeks of living at the protest sites. On 4 June 1989, only a few thousand die-hard students remained in Tiananmen Square. But no matter how few remained, by then the conservatives had decided it was necessary to reassert control. The country had no previous tradition of loyal opposition, and Beijing's hard-liners felt that dissent should be eliminated. With no experience in dispersing protesters without violence, they had none of the equipment to do so, no water cannons, no shields, no tear gas. So they sent tanks and troops to put down the students and clear the square. The exact number of casualties still remains controversial. It is generally believed that about a thousand people were killed, with hundreds being wounded. However, knowledgeable commentators believe that only about forty students were killed. This small number makes sense in that the students represented the flower of Chinese youth and many of them were the children or grandchildren of the Party's leaders at all levels.

After the 4 June crackdown, real power reverted to a group of veteran conservative leaders, proponents of the traditional Chinese view of government. They had been Deng's allies when he was an outsider struggling against Mao during the Cultural Revolution, but increasingly had become rivals creating obstacles to Deng's reforms and to his plans for succession. Reformist party leader Zhao Ziyang was dismissed and replaced by Jiang Zemin, with the more hard-line Li Peng remaining as prime minister. By October 1989, hopes had faded that surviving liberals and moderates within the leadership would be able to blunt the resurgence of the conservatives. Mass arrests, executions of student leaders, denunciations of foreign governments, and the intensely anti-foreign tone of some Chinese press reports caused unease among observers of the Middle Kingdom.

For all the wrong reasons, the Chinese people, and those of the outside world, felt betrayed. The Chinese intellectuals and students felt they had been denied their version of democracy, which they simplistically conceived to be wealth, fairness, and freedom. They had no conception of the wrenching process of trial and error that each Western democratic country has been through over a period of hundreds of years in order to develop its own version of democracy. They also had no conception of the complex system of checks and balances that have to be put in place in order to keep a democracy democratic.

The West, in a fit of moral outrage, conveniently forgot about other examples of violent response to civil unrest which had taken place even in the United States, one of the bastions of democracy. In 1970, the American government called in the National Guard to put down a demonstration at Kent State University in Ohio; they shot into the crowd, wounding many and killing four students. Yet then, the world didn't cry out in outrage, since similar incidents had occurred in other Western nations. In 1968, for example, the French government had violently put down students and other members of the public demonstrating in Paris. In the same year, Catholic civil rights demonstrations in Northern Ireland were broken up with savage force — this marking the start of the modern 'troubles' in Ireland. Given the vast scale of China's problems and the real progress that Deng's regime had made, it was naïve in the extreme for so many to expect China to produce democracy like a rabbit out of a hat. It was also highly inappropriate for so many to cry out against the 'brutality' of the government's suppression of the demonstrators, as the government had little choice if it wanted to survive and so ensure China's survival as a whole.

Almost without exception, the nations of the Western world condemned the Chinese government crackdown. Those Asian countries that made any comment, only paid lip service to the strident cries of the rest of the world. Yet foreign interference had prolonged the demonstrations to the point where the government had seen no alternative. China had made a serious attempt at reform, and at having a serious and prolonged dialogue with the demonstrators. This is the ultimate irony of the Tiananmen Square-related massacre: the foreigners, as well as the people of Hong Kong, helped to create the tragedy and then blamed the Chinese government.

Relations with both East and West became tense. Many of the gains of earlier economic reforms were lost. As the economy contracted, the balance of payments deteriorated. Capital ebbed away from Beijing. But the Tiananmen Square incident did not stop nations from dealing with the country for long. Japan reopened trade relations within months. The United States began to deliver again on contracts for aircraft and communication satellites, and later renewed China's 'Most Favoured Nation' trading status. President Bush declined to legislate amnesty for Chinese foreign students in America, although he did protect them with administrative action. Within six months the United States had secretly sent its National Security Adviser and a Deputy Secretary of State to China. Almost a year after the crackdown, a 'democracy ship', which was to broadcast news and dissident opinion to the Chinese mainland, had to be scrapped because no nearby Asian nation would let it drop anchor. Even Taiwan, which publicly denounces the Beijing leaders as 'rebellious usurpers', declined to give the ship the necessary support.

Commentators, politicians, academics, and China-watchers of all stripes have roundly condemned nations, especially the United States, for dealing with the repressive regime in Beijing. These observers claim that it makes no sense to deal with the current Chinese leadership because they don't represent China's future. They point out that conciliation hasn't softened China's leaders, who continue to arrest and execute people with only a cursory trial, to muzzle foreign correspondents, and to interfere with 'Voice of America' radio broadcasts. Until the early 1990s, China still continued to give US$100 million a year to Cambodia's Khmers, according to US intelligence estimates. Most of all, the critics charge, those who fail to mete out harsh sanctions to the People's Republic are not only betraying the Chinese people, but also the sacred principle of democracy. Nothing could be more absurd.

About 75 per cent of the Chinese people live in small, scattered peasant villages. For all their cultural pride, they have only a vague sense of sharing in the larger Chinese nation. It is understandably difficult for them to feel loyal to over a billion fellow countrymen, particularly since they have little exposure to, or experience of, the world outside their village and the nearest market town. China has none of the systems that modern societies take for granted. Although the Chinese share a common written language, they speak dozens of often mutually unintelligible dialects. And while tens of thousands of local periodicals are published, only a few dozen have a national circulation. These are almost entirely filled with turgid discourses on the nuances of Marxism, 'educational' propaganda, and lurid tales of freaks or the horrors of the outside world — hardly the way to give China's hundreds of millions of families a sense of national unity and purpose. With comparatively few telephones or workable roads and no opportunity for an efficient, national opposition to develop, the country's only unifying factor is the Communist Party and its highly developed political infra-structure.

Many of the countries which have been conciliatory to the Beijing leaders who ordered the crackdown on the student demonstrators have, at the same time, applauded and encouraged the protest movements in the former Soviet Union and Eastern Europe. Their stance has been criticised as hypocritical. But the situation in China is fundamentally different from that which existed in the Soviet bloc. Without losing or even jeopardising its central political control, China pioneered economic reforms before the Soviet Union did. Its shops and free markets are as bountiful as those of the former Soviet Union were (and are now still) bare; lavish joint-venture hotels and international direct-dial telephones are found in the major cities; agriculture has been decollectivised; and the state sector's share of industry has fallen to about 60 per cent.

On the international front, China has not had the huge overseas commitments of the Soviet Union. Although China has been supporting conflict in Indochina and funding military stand-offs across its borders with India and the Soviet Union, it has no client states such as Cuba or North Korea to subsidise, as the Soviet Union had until only recently. The Soviet Union was effectively bankrupted into making political changes before being able to tackle economic reform. Conversely, as China makes steady economic reforms using its existing Communist Party political structure, it is still able, more or less, to grow gradually towards political change. This could be more than fortunate, given the chaos that now prevails in most of the countries of the erstwhile Eastern bloc, and its now destabilising effect on the rest of the world.

Equally important, the scale of China's problems overwhelms that of the ex-Soviet Union. China is still a largely agrarian society. The stubborn loyalty of generations of peasants to their ancestral homes has helped the communist government to keep the country and the city sharply sepa-rated. The separation has also kept the relative wealth of the cities from filtering down to the villages. With the exception of Hong Kong's neighbouring Guangdong province, this has left most of the peasants without many of the basics, such as electricity or adequate water supplies. Yet, at the other end of the scale, modern appliances like washing machines have become standard in the homes of the urban élite.

Chinese communism focused first on the peasant, not on the factory worker, as in the Soviet Union. The same is true of China's economic reform, which started in the rice paddies and has enjoyed great success. Grain production leapt from 305 million tonnes in 1978 to 407 million tonnes in 1984, an increase equal to the total gain from 1949 to 1977. It then rose to 435 million tonnes in 1991.

By the late 1980s, industry was growing faster than agriculture, but China has not nearly reached the levels of industrialisation of the former Soviet Union. Despite Mao's attempt to introduce steel smelting to the villages during the 1950s, industry is still largely confined to urban areas. A year-long clampdown on construction at the end of the decade sent millions of peasant factory workers home from the cities; since then, some villages have started factories. These small enterprises, operating in a homogeneous family-type environment, have flourished and their numbers have grown by more than 30 per cent a year since 1985. But village factories have only just begun to shrink the huge gap between rural and city life.

For China's peasants, development has not necessarily meant more education or more leisure time to contemplate politics. In the villages, reforms have meant that families can make more money if they keep their children in the fields. And under Deng Xiaoping, China has moved away from Mao's egalitarian ideal of universal education. Mao's system produced a large number of students and helped to reduce illiteracy. But, as the Chinese authorities admitted in the late 1980s, a significant percentage received only a second-rate education.

In a return to a more traditional, élitist approach to education, Deng decided it was more efficient to educate a few well, rather than many badly. Accordingly, the number of high school graduates dropped from 7.2 million in 1979 to 1.96 million in 1985. In the same period, the number of high schools declined from 192,000 to 93,000. Many provincial schools lack books and even paper. The 1982 census found that an estimated 25 per cent of pupils older than twelve years were illiterate. More recent estimates put the figure higher.

The Soviet people may not relish the idea of a transition to multi-party democracy, but they are considerably better prepared than the Chinese. Most Chinese still live in a traditional, feudal world where children are used as collateral for loans and, although admittedly now rare, some parents spend hundreds of dollars marrying their dead children to other dead children so that they won't lack for company in the spirit world. Despite all its problems, socialism in the Soviet Union and Eastern Europe still managed to create a large, literate middle class. There was until very recently no middle class to speak of in China.

Amongst other factors, such as foreign investment, the communications revolution is gradually changing things. Chinese in the rural areas can now glimpse life in the developed world through television images. In the cities, communications have taken a quantum leap. It is not uncommon for intellectuals in major cities to have telephones and fax machines — rarities in the mid-1980s. Students in Europe and the United States can communicate regularly with colleagues and friends in China by using electronic computer mail. Ideas are cross-fertilising. People in China are not content to remain underprivileged and undereducated. More than anything else, they are increasingly concerned about fiscal matters. In his book *Tell the World* (1989), Liu Binyan describes how peasants in several areas have refused to pay taxes in protest against the Communist Party's ineptitude. In one provincial county, angry peasants took over the county government buildings for seven months. The Party had told them to grow green onions, creating a surplus which it then declined to buy. But when the people rise up in this way to challenge their government, they are not necessarily calling for democracy. They are calling for changes that will improve their economic lot.

It is unrealistic to think that the successor to Deng Xiaoping will come from outside the Party, while the Party is the only common denominator. In the Soviet Union, political reforms gave dissenting groups time to organise. Even so, Boris Yeltsin is an apostate Communist Party official. In China, the Party's monopoly on power is far stronger. There is no organisation, not even a student organisation, to compete with the unifying force of the Party. Repression still works in China. The reality of Chinese politics is that decisions are made by a group of 'Superior Men' for the masses of 'Little People'. The 'Gang of the Old' are not likely to be replaced by student leaders now in exile. The dissidents-in-exile have already degenerated into bickering factions. Within the Party, even the reformers are sceptical of too much political freedom, just as they are disdainful of international kibitzing. It must, however, be acknowledged that there is as yet no likely successor to Deng within the Party. Furthermore, after his departure, a stalemate, a military takeover, or even complete anarchy, could ensue, as I will discuss later in this chapter.

While it is unlikely that, in the short and medium term, any outside country will be able to convince the Chinese to become fundamentally more humanitarian, let alone democratic, it is entirely possible to encourage the Chinese tendency to xenophobia. The Chinese today face a situation very similar to that faced by Japan's Tokugawa shogunate. In feudal Japan, as in modern China, rival provincial powers threatened to tear the country apart. The Tokugawa imposed tight controls over the developing merchant class and threw out the foreigners, having concluded that they could better keep control through feudalism. China's modern leaders could make the same conclusion, although, after Deng Xiaoping's reforms and particularly after the October 1992 Communist Party Congress (held every five years), this appears to be very unlikely.

During the Cultural Revolution, China's leaders managed to convince themselves that 'nobody understands'. With few balancing forces, they slid into an extremism that nearly destroyed the country. Today, the leadership is an uneasy coalition of potential rivals. They are held together by their fear of another bout of chaos and by their connections with the country's elderly senior leader, Deng Xiaoping. In such a situation, moderation in tone is better than moralism; the best policy is one that singes selectively without burning wholesale, again as demonstrated by the results of the 1992 Communist Party Congress.

The necessity of economic development has provided, and will continue to provide, the world with more and more influence over China. The leaders responsible for the Tiananmen Square massacre have continued to emphasise that they still want economic reform — if gradually, and largely on their terms. China's leaders are united in their desire to rationalise the economy while retaining Communist Party control. Li Peng, hated for his role in the crackdown, is willing to make some use of market forces and sincerely wants more foreign investment. The best way to encourage this is by continued economic communication. President Bush's unpopular initiatives with China, such as renewing its 'Most Favoured Nation' trading status, were generally opposed by the US Congress. However, they represented a shrewd recognition that industrial development in the People's Republic will eventually lead to political reform, while hopefully avoiding the chaos of the break-up of the Soviet Union.

It is to be hoped that the events of 1989 will have convinced foreign investors to become more realistic about what it is possible to accomplish in China. For more than a century, foreigners have been seduced by variations on Britain's dream during the Industrial Revolution: 'If we could only persuade every person in China to lengthen his shirttail by a foot, we could keep the mills of Lancashire working round the clock.' But the dreams have taken until the early 1990s to begin to be translated into reality.

The most recent dreams began in December 1978 when, at a meeting of the Chinese Communist Party, the then General Secretary Zhao Ziyang announced a strategy of encouraging joint ventures with foreign companies. In the early 1980s, the Beijing Hotel began to look like a colonial watering hole, as foreigners, including Overseas Chinese, Western executives, and entrepreneurs, crowded into its lobby and gathered at its bar. Dozens of world business leaders made the pilgrimage to the Chinese capital: Armand Hammer of Occidental Petroleum, Marvin Traub of Bloomingdale's, Donald Regan, then chairman of Merrill Lynch & Co., Carl H. Hahn of Volkswagen. Tens of thousands of other businessmen came too. Some came to buy cheap products. But the overwhelming majority came with one of two dreams: either to sell to the vast Chinese market or to exploit what they thought — based on their experience in Taiwan, Hong Kong, and Singapore — was a cheap, educated, and industrious pool of labour. They were gripped by the idea that, even if it cost a lot to set up shop and even if they couldn't do the sort of business they wanted to do immediately, it made sense to establish a foothold, to do anything to get started. However, at the time, they couldn't have been more wrong.

China does have a lot of people (one-quarter of the world's population). But a World Bank study estimated that in the mid-1980s, the amount available for consumer spending was less than US$100 a year for each person in China. China's optimistic goal for the year 2000 — a per capita GNP of US$800 — would bring it only to the level that Nicaragua or South Yemen reached in 1985. In 1990, per capita GNP in China was about 5 per cent of Taiwan's, and an even smaller percentage of those of Singapore and Hong Kong.

Those expecting a cheap, educated, and industrious workforce found themselves saddled with thousands of truculent, inefficient, and uneducated workers. The workforce was accustomed to three-hour lunches, mid-afternoon rest breaks, and even sleeping on the job. While foreign businessmen expected Chinese factories to operate pretty much like factories everywhere, they soon learned that Chinese factories operated more like a nightmarish municipal government. Even worse from the standpoint of the bottom line, they operated like a nightmarish communist municipal government. Workers expected their employers to provide them with a full plate of social services: housing, day care, schools, and medical care.

At the height of this absurdity, the costs of doing business were sky-high — higher, in some instances, than in Paris or Tokyo. The government agency that supplied foreign representatives with office staff might charge four or five times the amount that actually made it into the workers' pockets. In a matter of weeks during 1980, the cost of installing a telephone rocketed from US$20 to US$1,400, the price of a telex line from US$100 to US$2,800. Between 1981 and 1984, rents at the Beijing Hotel more than doubled to about US$3,000 a month for a two-room suite. At the Great Wall Hotel, rent for a family could run to more than US$125,000 a year, while monthly laundry bills could be as high as US$400. And in 1985, import duties on automobiles had risen to 260 per cent; a small Japanese car might cost as much as a Mercedes sedan in the West after all the duties had been assessed.

To make matters worse, China was not so much a national market as a crazy quilt of overlapping local, provincial, and regional markets. In each one, government bureaucrats tried to protect their regional and functional territory by excluding other bureaucrats. In Beijing, for example, the electric company would fight the water company, so that some new buildings would have power but no water and others would have water but no power. Often, businesses would be started without the foreign investor realising that a permit was necessary. Officials seldom guaranteed that after setting up a business, a foreigner could actually sell his product in China. All these facts caused a certain amount of consternation as they became known in international headquarters around the world. CEOs began to doubt the sanity of their representatives in China. In time, as problems multiplied beyond any reasonable person's expectations, they began to doubt their own sanity in agreeing to invest in China in the first place.

If a foreign investor became embroiled in a dispute, he could not rely on a contract to set agreed-upon limits. Laws in China did not form a framework for business, but instead were a trap of quicksand into which everyone sank, the Chinese included. In China, a contract is seen as merely a symbol of harmonious relations between two parties. Companies initially enthusiastic about investment in China found themselves renegotiating for the eighteenth time contracts they had thought were final. And those who had built factories in China with an eye to selling to the Chinese, found themselves dramatically reducing anticipated production volumes, as the Chinese could not afford their products.

When there was a reasonable objection to the quality of Chinese workmanship — a frequent occurrence — the government could add a new dimension to the risks of contractual disputes by preventing dissenting foreign businesspeople from leaving China. In November 1989, the director of a Hong Kong picture-frame company was held in Guangzhou and denied an exit visa for more than three weeks because she refused to pay for ordered goods which she considered substandard. Another executive, who refused to agree to irrational terms set by a concern in northeast China, was not allowed to leave for six months. Such stories were not uncommon.

Finally, during this period, foreign exchange was also a problem. China runs on a two-currency system. *Renminbi*, or 'people's money', is used inside China and cannot be exchanged for other currencies. All foreign currency has to be converted into foreign exchange certificates (FECs). Foreigners have to pay their rent, staff, and all expenses in FECs. But if they want to sell to the mythical Chinese market, they receive *Renminbi*, unless the Chinese government makes a special exception.

In the end, it became unclear whether foreign companies were making any money at all. After fierce international competition to build China's first nuclear power plant at Daya Bay near Hong Kong, a French company won the contract. But the Chinese had negotiated such a low price that the French later claimed it was impossible for them to make a profit. Beatrice Companies, Inc., an American food giant, formed Guangmei Foods Corporation to produce soft drinks, ice cream, and other snack foods both for sale inside China and, it was hoped, for export. But the company had trouble getting enough electricity to run its Guangzhou plant. And the bottles which it had to buy from domestic Chinese suppliers suffered from some rather alarming quality problems — when filled and capped, they tended to explode at random.

In 1986, the amount of foreign investment China obtained in new contracts slumped to US$1.24 billion, a drop of about 20 per cent from the previous year. That same year, it became clear that China's oil fields — expected to hold huge reserves — were modest at best. So beginning in the mid-year, the Chinese regime launched a drive to reassure Western businesses of both the wisdom and safety of putting money into China. Zhao and Deng began greeting delegations of foreign businessmen. Some business rules were also changed. New tax benefits and lower land-use fees were approved. Ventures could get priority loans from the Bank of China. But whatever money foreign ventures earned from sales in China was still in nontransferable Chinese currency. The changes failed to bring any improvement. By the end of 1986, new investment had dropped by nearly 50 per cent, and the violent government suppression of the Tiananmen Square demonstrators brought a further 30 per cent drop. United Airlines and Northwest Airlines cut flights to one a week because of slack demand.

The Chinese, for their part, intensified an austerity programme which had begun in the summer of 1988, tightening credit and slashing imports by cutting off funds to many government entities and industrial enterprises that would have otherwise purchased foreign products.

One of Deng's early reforms, namely his government giving up its monopoly over foreign trade and creating an 'open-door policy' by setting up, in the early 1980s, four experimental 'special economic zones' (three in Guangdong province, i.e. Zhuhai, Shantou, and Shenzhen, and one in Fujian province, i.e. Xiamen, across the strait from Taiwan), provided the vital catalyst for China to at last launch itself on the road to 'capitalism'. By the end of 1992, there were still only the original four official special economic zones, but to these had been added fourteen designated 'coastal cities', each with its own economic and technology zone. Since then, numerous other towns and cities have set up their own, often not 'official', 'economic zones' which offer various incentives to foreign investors.

The first businessman to set up shop in China after the Tiananmen Square crackdown — an Australian planning to sell pieces of the Great Wall as souvenirs, in the Berlin Wall tradition — ran into the usual Chinese problems. He found that his twenty-three members of staff were almost all friends and relatives of his local partners. When the new company remodelled an old factory building, neighbours stole the windows. But after the investor threatened to pull out in the summer of 1990, the government gave him management control, something previous investors had never enjoyed.

During the immediate post-June 1989 period, more and more companies were evaluating their China operations for what they *were* rather than for what they could *become*. Companies were counting costs, driving harder bargains, and picking partners carefully. International clothing companies were beginning to diversify their supply sources. China was still a good source, but not the only source. While the Chinese pushed for short-term ventures and fast returns, Western companies were now pushing for longer-term agreements. Rather than go misty-eyed about the potential of the Chinese consumer, companies were beginning to view China not only as a market but also as a factory.

The first casualties of this new realism were the big projects which got so much fanfare in the 1980s. Car plants, oil refineries, and coal mines needed foreign-made parts, which means they needed foreign exchange. China, with US$46 billion in foreign debt in 1989, did not have the money. No one made any, let alone huge, profits on Chinese mega-projects during the period. However, now that the Deng reforms seem well entrenched, the dream of huge new projects has risen once again, but whether they will prove to be another El Dorado only time will tell.

Since the 1989 crackdown, foreign investors have tended to invest in smaller amounts: in the first quarter of 1990, investments in each new project averaged US$700,000. A form of 'grass-roots' investment focus has replaced the large projects, which involved multiple bureaucracies, at the local, regional, and national level; for the private-sector investor, this has proven to be by far the best strategy for the time being. The Japanese have yet to learn this — they are conditioned to believe that large projects with large, state-owned companies or government agencies are best. In the ant world they are right, but in the monkey world it is asking for trouble at best, and chaos at worst. Investors in China who have been involved in such small projects have been the most successful. The main engines of China's almost 9 per cent average annual growth since 1978 were the dramatic increases in farm production and in the number of township and village enterprises that sprouted in the coastal areas. More flexible and tuned to the markets, the farmers increased grain output by 33 per cent from 1978 to 1983, cotton by 300 per cent, oil-bearing crops by more than 100 per cent, and fruit production by 50 per cent, according to 'China Survey', published in *The Economist* on 28 November 1992. Similarly market-oriented and flexible, unlike the state-run behemoths, thousands of small business enterprises in the provinces are producing a range of goods including sweaters, plastic flowers, shoes, and simple electronic goods. These 'township and village enterprises', or TVEs, are too small to merit much bureaucratic interest and in-fighting, and are often funded by foreign businessmen (mostly Chinese living abroad, including investors from Hong Kong who are estimated to have provided between 75 and 85 per cent of all foreign investment since 1978). Collectively, the farmers and small businessmen are transforming the economy. After all, such a strategy, accompanied by a strong government framework, has led to Taiwan's extraordinary economic success. By 1990, this trend resulted in these TVEs, both with and without foreign investors, capturing some 45 per cent of China's industrial output, from 12 per cent in 1978. If agriculture and services are taken into account, *The Economist* estimates that Chinese state-owned entities now account for no more than 25 per cent of the country's output — already better than in a number of Western countries!

China cannot close the door again without provoking chaos. Even the intransigent left wing realises that the near revolution in 1989 was not so much about a form of government, as it was about the massive failure of the Communist Party, after so many years, to improve the material comfort of the ordinary Chinese. Although China has enjoyed high GNP growth rates, it lags seriously behind almost all other Asian countries. The Chinese people know it. Those people in power know it. The only way they can change this situation is by becoming a bigger trading nation and by importing foreign capital. Neither can be done behind a closed door.

Since 1991, everything has changed dramatically, with the exception of the political party structure, although it too has undergone considerable change. What has been achieved in 1991 and 1992 in terms of small-scale economic and trade development fuelled by foreign investment, particularly in the south of China, which has almost become an extension of Hong Kong, is extraordinary. By the end of 1991, the Chinese government estimated that there were some 82,000 foreign ventures in China involving an aggregate foreign investment of some US$22 billion. This included new investment in 1991 of some US$3.5 billion, according to *The Economist*. In order to encourage more capitalist-oriented growth, Deng's benign 'walkabouts' in southern China in January 1992 provided a clear signal that his pragmatic government favours the non-state, market-oriented private business sector, which in 1992 provided some 50 per cent of China's output. Estimates by *The Economist* put investment during the first nine months of 1992 at US$6.6 billion. Deng has even influenced the powerful Chinese military, the People's Liberation Army, to go capitalist and keep their foreign exchange earnings — they now manufacture and export everything from radios and motorcycles to refrigerators and arms. They have even put their firing ranges to use, where for a range of prices, in US dollars, anyone can go along and fire anything from a pistol to a missile! Even China's schools and universities have become infected with the national obsession with making money. Many are becoming active capitalists by setting up shops or factories within school or university premises — hardly in accordance with traditional Confucian views on teaching versus commerce. However, there are many benefits in that, if profitable, the institution is able to fund, and thus provide, much better facilities than can be funded from government sources. Thus they are able to attract a higher level of student interest. If unprofitable, they tend to switch products and try again.

It is also estimated that, in 1992, of the total foreign investment in the poor countries of Asia and in poor countries worldwide (there are twenty-five 'poor countries' as defined by the World Bank), China received 25 per cent and 15 per cent respectively of such investment. Additionally, it is estimated that it received the equivalent of 40–50 per cent and 400–500 per cent more, respectively, of all the foreign direct investment in the United States and Japan. The country's trade has leapt from some US$30 billion in 1980 to over an estimated US$135 billion in 1992. It is also estimated that it had some US$50 billion in foreign exchange reserves at the end of 1992.

Shenzhen and Guangzhou are already becoming clones of Hong Kong. Also, given the frenetic pace of change taking place in Shanghai, its geographical location, and the nature of the Shanghai people, I believe it is reasonable to imagine it overtaking Hong Kong in importance within the next, say, fifteen to twenty-five years. By building a strong and broad coalition of different interest groups, Deng's reforms have taken root and are producing results, all without the drama and futility of Russia's efforts where traumatic political reform has led to a collapsed economy. By putting economic reform ahead of political reform, as was the case with South Korea, Taiwan, and Singapore, the population is likely to be given the opportunity to experience its benefits and to grow while the process of political reform takes place gradually.

To put China's past, current, and likely future economic prospects in perspective *vis-à-vis* the rest of Asia and the world as a whole, it is quite possible that China's economy in 1994 will be four times larger than it was in 1978 when Deng's reforms began. Further, if China achieves its reasonable targets in 2002, its economy could be eight times that of 1978. Put another way, China's foreign investment would have grown to around US$170 billion in 1992, in the midst of a world recession, from US$135 billion in 1991 and from US$21 billion in 1978. What many people may not realise is that China is now the world's fourth, if not third, largest economy after the United States, Japan, and Germany. It has achieved the same level of growth as did Japan, South Korea, and Taiwan in their respective fastest twenty-five years of growth.

Despite China's officially estimated 1992 GNP per capita of US$370 and its official status as one of the world's twenty-five poorest countries, i.e. a 'low income economy', many economists believe this figure is highly misleading and that, in fact, on the basis of many comparisons such as life expectancy, adult illiteracy, calorie intake, and so on, China is much more like 'middle income economy' countries with US dollar GNPs five times that of China. These official US dollar-based figures are considerably distorted by the fall in value of China's currency, the *yuan*, from the official 1.7 *yuan* to US$1.00 in rate 1978 to the March 1993 official rate of 5.9 *yuan* (or the 8.2 *yuan* rate in the semi-official foreign exchange centres). This devaluation of the *yuan* has in effect more than off-set China's real economic growth over this period. Lawrence Summers, chief economist with the World Bank, believes that if one uses figures based on 'purchasing-power parities' (PPP) against actual cost-of-living standards, China's PPP in 1992 would be around 45 per cent of that of the United States. Some others estimate that it could be considerably higher. According to *The Economist*, 'Each year, on average, for the past 14 years China's real GNP has grown 6.5 percentage points faster than America's. If that difference persists, a little after 2010, China will have the world's biggest economy. ... Can China's economy go on doing what it has done ever since Deng Xiaoping began unshackling it in 1978? If it does the world is in for the biggest change since the Industrial Revolution.'

However, before one becomes too euphoric, there will no doubt be many a slip 'twixt cup and lip. Prime Minister Li Peng in late December 1992 conceded publicly that the economy was again growing too fast. He advised that his stated target of 6 per cent annual growth for the period 1991–1995 was probably not achievable, but he urged that all efforts be made to keep it under 10 per cent. The Party newspaper, the *People's Daily*, stated at around the same time that the government should take an important first step by making the *yuan* freely convertible by replacing separate official and unofficial exchange rates with a single rate.

Self-interest demands that China reaches out to Asia Pacific and accepts a broader, common community set of goals. China cannot rely on free entry to Western markets, as Japan did during the early years of its post-World War II reconstruction. Asia Pacific, on the other hand, should be motivated to welcome China's overtures. Unlike the United States and Europe, such countries as India, Australia, and Korea must always face the threat of the Chinese dragon on their doorstep. To isolate China is not only short-sighted; it is dangerous. Theoretical as it may seem, a China faced with anarchy and no perceived solution may determine that the only way to give its people a sense of focus and purpose is to take over its neighbours. It is a policy that has been employed by the Chinese many times before, during the Han, T'ang, Yuan, and Ming dynasties — and by Mao in the case of Tibet.

Like the leaders of the former Soviet Union, China's leaders have faced the fact that the Marxist ideology on which their power has been based must be modified if their country is to survive, let alone evolve. However, they have modified their system in a totally different way. At the opening in October 1992 of the first party congress since 1987, which congress will, in principle, set the tone for the next five years, the Communist Party's chairman, Jiang Zemin, stated in his opening address, 'Where market forces have been given full play, the economy has been vigorous and has developed in a sound way.' He made it clear that, unlike the former Soviet Union, there could be no alternative to the Communist Party retaining political power, so as to ensure that social stability was maintained and the economy continued to thrive. But he acknowledged that China needs to focus on change and 'not get bogged down in what is socialist and what is capitalist'. China, in its own inimitable, pragmatic way, has adapted to both a market economy and a non-ideological approach to reforms that it hopes will bring about a top-to-bottom restructuring. It has also begun to play the role of 'statesman' — in October 1992, its support of Japan's participation in the region's security issues and its welcome to Emperor Akihito on Japan's first ever imperial state visit to China gave some evidence of this gradual change in attitude — despite the pragmatic economic reasons underlying these actions.

The question that many will ask is, can economic decentralisation proceed without political decentralisation? The answer is probably that economic decentralisation is already taking place, without necessarily the backing of Beijing. However, it is a sensitive balancing act in that strong, overt Beijing government resistance to such a trend could lead to severe economic warlordism, which Beijing probably could not effectively handle, and, as a result, real conflict. Hence the fragile equation. Furthermore, in a country the size of China and in its current state of development, political decentralisation would only exacerbate the evolution of economic warlordism and, furthermore, it could possibly lead to a break-up of the current Chinese state.

China's future behaviour will naturally affect one of its frequently stated, priority goals: specifically, to bring Taiwan, some way or another, back into the fold — the most likely way being in a confederal sense. But the process will take an inordinate length of time. In this regard, there are interesting indications that an official dialogue between the PRC and Taiwan may at least take place in 1993. It will obviously not achieve some form of union with Taiwan in the same way it assumes control of Hong Kong in 1997, but certainly the way it takes over Hong Kong will have a direct bearing on any future relationship it might have with Taiwan. In a parallel process, the way in which it deals with the rest of Asia and the rest of the world will also have a major influence on how its relationship with Taiwan evolves. Taiwan, which sees its future as being definitely linked to the global community and particularly to the Asia Pacific regional one, will need to be convinced that China subscribes more or less to the general principles governing international relationships.

Politically there is obviously considerably more cause for concern — to state the obvious, Deng cannot go on forever. While he has clearly been attempting to prepare the way for his departure by removing those senior figures he deems to be dangerous to the reforms he has set in motion, as of the end of 1992 he appeared to have no clear successor. Could there be another cycle of chaos following order? It is difficult to tell. On the one hand, there is the Communist Party with some 50 million members, which is a good thing, despite the probable, liberal knee-jerk reaction of horror in today's democratic world to this statement. It is the only machine in place for control which is highly organised, centralised, and which reaches every corner of the country, however remote. The structure works, and it is essential in guiding China through the extraordinary changes taking place. Further, there is no other organised political alternative. Its main job, like that of China's emperors in the past, is to keep power. It appears that Deng Xiaoping appears to follow, more or less, the same Confucian principles as imperial China, where if the ruler could not keep order, he could expect to be legitimately deposed. He seems to recognise that his and the Party's job is to keep order by reforming the economy and bettering everyone's lot. This view seems to have pervaded the entire Party, whose members not only oversee and implement the process, but also enthusiastically join in.

It is appropriate to note that China's approach, of maintaining its government structure while tackling its economic reforms, was and is far more intelligent than that of Russia, which allowed events to cause the dismantling of its government before reforming its economy. The result: great success as opposed to abysmal chaos, although China did have the advantage of watching the Soviet Union slide into chaos before it implemented its recent reforms.

That is the good news; however, the potential for chaos is still there. Too many riches too soon will exacerbate the potential for uncontrollable corruption and for the parallel development of economic warlordism. In addition, the new primary focus of central and local government ministeries and municipalities on developing, and running, their own businesses, instead of providing the impartial mechanisms for the implementation of government policy, seriously calls into question the Chinese government's ability to govern effectively in the future. Furthermore, with a weak, or confused, succession leadership to Deng being coupled with the 'family-village-province first' nature of each individual Chinese, it is not unthinkable that these collective trends could, in fact, cause China to break up by the middle of the next century, or at least suffer massive chaos, followed by repression. A population by the year 2050 of, say, 1.3 to 1.4 billion people, all vigorously competing with one another, all seeing the fate of other Chinese (i.e. those outside their family, village, and province) as not really being their affair (particularly now that the Communist Party's political ideology is quietly vanishing to be replaced by economic bottom line reality), presents an awesome control equation.

If the Western world applies aggressive pressure on China to become more democratic, if not fully democratic — despite the foolishness of this notion being amply demonstrated by the current state of chaos in the former Soviet Union — for the above reasons, the Party's currently fragile ability to maintain control could be considerably and dangerously weakened. For example, the removal by the US Congress of China's 'Most Favoured Nation' trading status could increase dramatically the possibility of such a result. By extension, it is also possible that, if China's economy keeps growing exponentially (comparatively speaking), then in any post-Deng confusion or anarchy, this additional pressure could lead some group or other to try and seize control under a territorially expansionist banner in order to acquire more territory, more wealth and, at last, eliminate the influence of the Western barbarians — although somewhat far-fetched, this is hardly a welcome thought! One can also imagine the region's response.

There is also a major, as yet largely unrecognised, 'joker factor' quietly evolving. Specifically, the Chinese government's policy of one family one child, if successful, will no doubt over the next two to four generations have a material impact on the social structure of the Chinese family. There will no longer be the numerous brothers, sisters, uncles, aunts, and cousins of the extended family. At the very least, this change will cause considerable destabilisation of existing social patterns of behaviour and it is likely that this will add to the potential for chaos. Conversely, it is also possible that it will cause the individual Chinese to view more positively the concept of giving more allegiance to China as a nation state. However, it is much too early to determine whether this birth control policy in the newly economically driven China will continue to be pursued, monitored, and implemented in such a draconian fashion and, if so, how it will impact on China's future. It is also reasonably likely that, with the new wealth being generated in China, many will simply ignore or 'buy' exemption from this regulation—thus, in turn, creating the potential for more chaos by sharply dividing Chinese society into the big families and the one-child families. In turn, if this policy is ignored on a large scale, the sharp increase in population will also add to the potential for more chaos.

I strongly believe that insufficient attention is paid to this question of China's population size and the considerable dearth of 'nation state' binding influences of any material kind across this huge country. It is possible to say that parts of China are much closer to their tribally related pockets of Overseas Chinese than they are to the Chinese from the next province, let alone to the nation state as a whole. With the EC's population of only 360 million, it is curious that, despite the clear example to any observer of the confusion and conflicts of interest that reign in the Community whenever it tries to develop or implement some major new initiative or other, so few observers of China have made the natural extrapolation that China, with almost four times the population size and, in a number of ways, more diverse conditions, will not be infinitely more difficult to manage — for all the reasons set out above. Even the example of the world's most democratic and largest multi-racial society, the United States, with its population of under 300 million, hardly gives the objective observer much comfort that it, too, is not riven with competing economic, political, regional, and ethnic prejudices — I would even argue that the United States, too, is likely to break up in the next century. Maybe, in the future, it will be taking lessons from its Asian neighbours!

Cries from the US Congress to remove China's 'Most Favoured Nation' status would only create a polarisation and could risk re-introducing a new form of superpower confrontation: China/Asia versus the West. In this process of working with China, while China has been lectured *ad nauseam* on what the rest of the world requires of it, it might also be helpful if the rest of the world understood what China requires in order for it to be understood. Everyone has heard of 'face' and its importance in Asia, particularly to the Chinese. However, the substance underlying the concept of 'face' is not necessarily widely understood outside Asia. Superficial respect for this concept is, in a way, more insulting than no recognition at all. What the Chinese require is neither endless public dialogue (which usually becomes confrontational), nor endless contracts and treaties. What they require is respect in the form of private consultation first, so that a more or less mutually agreeable public position can be taken and, more fundamentally, the acceptance of a mutual contract of trust based on mature, broad medium- and long-term considerations, not on narrowly focused, immediate considerations. In 1992 and early 1993, Hong Kong's governor, Chris Patten, could have usefully followed such a policy without necessarily materially prejudicing his subsequent position, and in doing so, he might have ensured a lot less confrontation in his relationship with Beijing.

It should also be noted that a new, as yet incipient, Asian nationalism is developing, with Greater China, through its various parts (particularly including the Overseas Chinese), possibly providing the catalyst. Such a sentiment is a natural extension from being a collection of ancient cultures, from being abused by the Western colonial powers, and from the aftermath of World War II, to being arguably the most vigorous, active, and successful part of the current world economy. To counter this, China must be made to feel that it is part of the world community. To do this, it needs to be convinced of the value of the real benefit it already enjoys by being linked to the regional and global communities.

What China must also be made to appreciate is that it has had a 'free ride' in the international community for too long. This is particularly so since China replaced Taipei in 1971 in the UN and at the same time gained China's permanent seat on the UN Security Council. Traditionally, its view has been, what can the rest of the world do for China, with barely a thought for what China might do for the rest of the world. China's current position on the UN Security Council is a historical anomaly, earned as a result of Western political expediency, not because it was intrinsically worthy of such a position. Today, China has a major role to play in the region's, and the world's, affairs. To achieve this, it must give up its traditional, and now thoroughly irrelevant, view that each country is an island unto itself. This is simply no longer true, as today's world is interdependent on many levels. Surely the evidence of this is staring the Beijing leadership in the face: its US 'Most Favoured Nation' status, its export reach to the world at large, the investment funds it receives daily, the recognition and support it receives from its regional neighbours, and the general respect and attention it receives from the rest of the world. It is time it became more proactive: it should participate in UN peacekeeping initiatives instead of reacting in a traditional, knee-jerk manner and abstaining from UN Security Council resolutions to send such forces to hot-spots around the world. China should have the courage of its conviction in its five thousand-year-old culture and be prepared to be a true co-leader and teacher in the Confucian sense, without always looking at the immediate risk/profit ratio. It has made certain strides in this direction, as it has joined the Nuclear Non-Proliferation Treaty (NPT) and signed the multilateral convention to ban chemical weapons. As an extension of these steps, it should also join the Strategic Arms Reductions Talks and sign the Limited Nuclear Test Ban Treaty. Ultimately, China must persuade itself that all this is necessary.

Hopefully, through strong and essential interaction with the world economy, which phenomenon itself is enabling China and Asia to take such dramatic strides, China will begin to feel not only that it is a part of the regional and world communities, but that it also has concomitant responsibilities to these communities. The other countries of Asia Pacific should make every effort to involve China in the region's affairs, as an independent China with its own agenda could seriously destabilise the region. They must also make every effort to persuade China that time is on its side and that, if Taiwan were to decide to become an independent country, China should withdraw from its previously stated belligerent and absurd position of threatening military intervention to prevent such a thing from happening. After all, giving face works both ways.

A careful balance must be struck. If China's neighbours, and the rest of the world, concede too much in accepting China's requirements, it could lead to China assuming that it is still at the centre of the universe, the 'middle kingdom between heaven and earth', and that it can bully its people, its neighbours, and the rest of the world into allowing it to create its own set of rules, which will, in turn, allow it to continue to play the various countries, particularly the United States and Japan, off against one another. This careful balance is essential as, before China grows too strong, the rest of the world must persuade it that there are general limits beyond which it should not go and that it can only survive and prosper if it grows towards being a co-operative member of the regional and global communities. As stated above, it has already begun to demonstrate this by its membership in the NPT and its participation in other global conventions. It has given a further demonstration of this new attitude by stating in early 1993 that it would support the results of the 1993 Cambodian general elections, even if its former ally, the Khmer Rouge, boycotts them. It subsequently advised its long-standing friend and ally, North Korea, to work within the structure of the NPT rather than withdraw, as North Korea announced it would do in March 1993 in response to demands for further nuclear site inspections. These are positive signs.

In the meantime, the outside world, while keeping up specific pressure on these issues and others such as China's human rights record and, particularly, its arms build-up and sales, must give more than lip-service to the question of 'face' in dealing with the Chinese. It must also allow China a reasonable latitude to reform largely at its own pace and in its own way. Any other policy of either aggressive confrontation or outright appeasement is not only naïve and foolish, but doomed to failure and could, if prosecuted too vigorously in either direction, have catastrophic consequences for the rest of Asia Pacific.

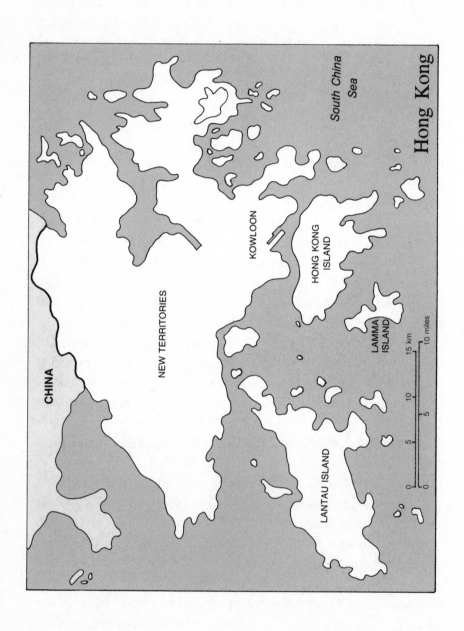

Hong Kong

South China Sea

CHINA

NEW TERRITORIES

KOWLOON

HONG KONG ISLAND

LANTAU ISLAND

LAMMA ISLAND

15 km

10

5

0

10 miles

5

0

HONG KONG

Acute Schizophrenia — Western Democracy versus
Chinese Political and Cultural Absolutes

While the Chinese people of Hong Kong could be defined as being Overseas Chinese, given the fact that Hong Kong, for better or worse, will revert to China in 1997, for the purposes of this book, I have treated Hong Kong as a separate entity with its own unique characteristics.

What is now the British colonial territory of Hong Kong consists of three parts: Hong Kong Island and Kowloon, which were ceded to Britain in perpetuity, and the New Territories, which were leased to Britain until 1997. When the two countries began to discuss the termination of the lease in the early 1980s, it became clear that Britain would have no realistic choice but to give all three parts back, as Hong Kong Island and Kowloon, comprising only 10 per cent of the overall territory, would be unviable on their own.

At that time, the West was enthralled with China's economic reforms. Britain, with its own economic and political problems, was not averse to divesting itself of one of its last imperial possessions. The only other option Britain had was to hold on to Hong Kong Island and Kowloon, though they would be useless without the New Territories, thereby enraging the Chinese, and also ruining an opportunity for Hong Kong to play a role in China's development. It was not really an alternative. In September 1984, the British and the Chinese signed a Joint Declaration under which terms the British agreed to hand back the entire colony, skyscrapers and all, to China on 1 July 1997, on condition that there would be 'one country, two systems' for another fifty years and that the new 'Special Administrative Region' (of Hong Kong) would be directly administered by Beijing — and not by Guangzhou.

The territories which make up Hong Kong were carved out of China after the British Empire humiliated the Chinese in the Opium Wars of the nineteenth century. When Mao proclaimed a new China in 1949, there was little he could do about Hong Kong immediately. The colony remained as it had for more than a hundred years — a thorn pricking China in the flank.

The pain has been doubly acute since the craggy, malarial colony turned itself into such a success. The official World Bank figure for Hong Kong's GDP per capita in 1990 was US$11,490, an average increase of almost 6.2 per cent per annum since 1965. In stark contrast, the figure for China's GNP per capita in 1990 was only US$370. Thus Hong Kong was not only a symbol of imperial China's fall before the onslaughts of the Western barbarians but also of the current Chinese regime's inability to create a robust economy. Since 1990, of course, China's economic affairs have undergone a burst of hyperactivity, due largely to Hong Kong's, and other Overseas Chinese, investments in the mainland.

From almost the beginning, Hong Kong was the West's gateway to China. From the 1840s to the 1950s, excluding the period of Japanese occupation during World War II, Hong Kong was the staging post and transshipment centre for trade with China. When the Korean War and the UN embargo on the export of goods to China cut off most of this trade, Hong Kong set itself up as a manufacturing centre. When the factories brought exploding growth, the city became both a major commercial services centre and the world's fourth largest financial centre after New York, London, and Tokyo. In 1990, 134 foreign banks had operations in Hong Kong.

Hong Kong is probably the most absolutely capitalist place in the world. It runs a duty-free port where everyone is making a deal, where even the McDonald's commercials have a stock-market theme and where yuppies and even teenagers carry cellular phones just in case their 'big deal' comes through. The colonial masters have run the business of the territory in classic English *laissez-faire* style. Yet, at the same time, they have poured vast sums into social services and provided the strong governmental framework of law and order that the Chinese need in order to prosper. This has given Hong Kong stability and an ideal business climate. There are virtually no restrictions, limitations, or guidelines inhibiting legitimate business. The territory has a freely convertible currency. Taxation is light — a maximum of 15 per cent for individuals — and company law is based on familiar English principles. Western accounting procedures are the norm for all companies listed on the thriving Hong Kong Stock Exchange, which attracts substantial interest from foreign investors worldwide. And, most importantly, Hong Kong has a long tradition of endless adaptability to changing circumstances.

Hong Kong is Asia's number one tourist destination. Visitors spent US$5 billion in the territory in 1990. With no resources save skilled labour, an excellent infrastructure, and a geographically strategic location, Hong Kong has become so useful that people have quipped, 'If Hong Kong didn't exist it would be necessary to invent it.' It has been an unsinkable aircraft carrier for all sorts of corporations operating under sometimes risky or difficult conditions elsewhere in Asia.

Theoretically, the Sino-British Joint Declaration will allow Hong Kong to retain its present social, economic, and legal systems for at least fifty years after 1997, with Hong Kong becoming a Chinese Special Administrative Region (SAR). But by most accounts, Hong Kong's 96 per cent Chinese population look on 1997 with a mixture of pride and concern — pride in their Chinese civilisation, combined with concern about, or even fear of, the regime that will take over Hong Kong's affairs.

The Hong Kong Chinese today enjoy probably more freedom (in many different forms — such as low taxes, travel, and minimal violence and crime) than the residents of any other major city in the world. They have become far removed from the traditional Chinese constants of chaos and authoritarian rule. Neither have they had to fight the hostility of intermittently inhospitable host cultures, as have the Overseas Chinese in Malaysia and Indonesia. Fear of losing their freedom had already created an emotionally-charged environment when the 'democracy' demonstrators took over Beijing's Tiananmen Square in 1989. When the troops fired on the demonstrators, the Hong Kong stock market fell 22 per cent in one day. A number of Hong Kong's leading Chinese leapt into an emotional activism, which was even more unrealistic and misguided than the reactions of the West. More than a million people from all walks of life subsequently took to Hong Kong's streets to protest against the crackdown and insist on 'democracy' for China.

The territory's slightly less than 6 million people have a not unjustifiable reputation for being concerned primarily with making money. But after the Sino-British agreement was signed in 1984, many became interested in politics, democracy, and — just in case — in getting out. Immediately after the Declaration was signed, Jardine-Matheson, one of the oldest British commercial houses in the territory, announced it was moving its world headquarters to Bermuda. At that time, more than half of the forty-nine multinationals responding to a survey said they might move their regional offices from Hong Kong. Although this did not in fact happen, by July 1990 a thousand people a week were emigrating from the territory.

Investing a couple of hundred thousand dollars in a business will open the borders of Australia and Canada to emigrés. Some countries are selling their passports to Hong Kong citizens. Those desperate to have a fall-back plan for post-1997 could become instant Tongans for US$45,000, or Paraguayans for US$50,000. But most who have left Hong Kong have emigrated to Canada, the United States, and Australia.

Beijing has not helped itself in the face of this hysteria. It vetoed a referendum that would have allowed Hong Kong people to express their opinions on the Basic Law, the constitution for the new Hong Kong SAR. As the final touches were put to the Basic Law in early 1990, China also made it clear that it would brook no dissent from the territory after 1997. A few months later, Beijing announced it would not recognise the British passports of ethnic Chinese in Hong Kong who received such passports under the UK government's 1990 British nationality scheme for 50,000 qualifying Hong Kong residents. This position, if enforced, will see such residents, who might have stayed, emigrating before July 1997. As early as July 1990, the territory had 200,000 job vacancies.

Investor confidence, while shaken, has not deserted Hong Kong. Many businesses which were thought likely to move after the Sino-British Declaration have not done so. After the Tiananmen Square crackdown on 4 June 1989, Willie Purves, chairman of HSBC Holdings plc, said that its subsidiary, HongkongBank, the colony's leading bank, will continue to invest in the territory. However, HSBC's subsequent acquisition of

Britain's Midland Bank will no doubt provide it with some insurance if matters become difficult in the future. More recently, in May 1992, the last major prime site in the Central business district was sold for US$269 million. Many foreign firms have also moved their regional headquarters to Hong Kong from Tokyo, to avoid the high cost of living and of employing staff in the Japanese capital.

If foreign companies continue to invest in the territory, some emigrants and companies that have left may return. Many Hong Kong Chinese who have left with foreign passports have not found it easy to integrate. According to the Hong Kong Trade and Economic Office in the United States, many immigrants have become frustrated at the low pay and slow career advancement in their adopted country. Once they have their foreign passports, many plan to return to Hong Kong. Because of Hong Kong's and neighbouring south China's hyperactive economies, they believe they can make more money before 1997 than is possible abroad. This will leave them even more options after 1997.

Hong Kong may not be the same after 1997, but barring any major political upheaval on the mainland, it is unlikely that the former colony will be ruined. Hong Kong's most important defence is that the territory and the mainland need each other. Hong Kong needs China's space and labour, and China needs Hong Kong's capital, expertise, and strategic physical location. Collectively, these provide potential investors in China with an ideal jumping-off point. If a foreign investor has to travel directly to Guangzhou, Shanghai, or Beijing, he will find it considerably more difficult to get his business accomplished. Post-1997 Hong Kong, if left to function as it always has, could continue to offer one of the world's most efficient service centres for these investors. If China changes the nature of Hong Kong and ruins this remarkable economic staging post for the mainland, it risks losing a considerable percentage of the investment which might otherwise come its way. Hong Kong's importance as a financial, legal, accounting, and management centre servicing investments in China cannot be emphasised enough, and therefore, in the short term at least, China needs a prosperous Hong Kong. During this period, Hong Kong should take full advantage of this opportunity. It should ensure that it becomes the prime gateway to China, that it leads China's economic grass-roots development, and that it becomes an integral, if not pivotal, part of China's future economic development. In 1991 and 1992, it demonstrated this theory with a practical vengeance.

During this process, Hong Kong could have great influence on how China evolves after 1997, providing it doesn't become a political lightning rod before then. Thus, for both countries to mutually benefit from each other, Hong Kong should aim to become Beijing's Manhattan and subsequently accept Beijing as its Washington D.C., but with responsibility for all the consequences which such a position entails.

Arguably, one practical means of assisting this possibility in a physical sense is the new Port and Airport Development Strategy project (PADS) devised by the Hong Kong government in the late 1980s. This project will provide major new transportation facilities and an associated urban infrastructure, which could collectively tie Hong Kong successfully in with the rapidly urbanising axis between Hong Kong and Guangzhou. The PADS project should also ensure a pivotal role for Hong Kong in a wider regional sense. However, because of the problems between the governments of Hong Kong and Beijing in late 1992 and early 1993, the whole project is mired in uncertainty. Hopefully, PADS will be developed as originally planned.

There is one major risk remaining to be resolved. It is in the nature of the extraordinary 'freedoms without responsibility' which the people of Hong Kong have enjoyed under British colonial rule and which are mixed together with the alien, and quintessentially Western, democratic ideals manifested by Governor Chris Patten and the British government's democratic reform initiatives in October 1992. This gift of freedom without responsibility has led to two fundamental problems.

The first problem is that the Hong Kong population of slightly less than 6 million has led a terribly spoilt existence by even Western standards, let alone by other Asian countries' standards. The Chinese residents of Hong Kong have not had to go through the tortured, often chaotic, and usually pain-wracked experience of earning their current 'system' — instead, it has been a gift by the succession of British government-led local governments. For a small but vocal minority of them now to clamour and agitate for more democratic structures to be put in place before 1997, against strong Beijing opposition, is the height of folly. It looks very like a replay of the initial efforts of the students of Tiananmen Square — hopefully not a dress rehearsal for a post-1997 event. In theory their actions are laudable, as democratic representation should be everyone's inalienable right. And there is a trend throughout most of Asia in this direction. However, in reality, by unduly rushing the process, this small minority is charting a dangerous course. Neither they nor their British mentors have ever had direct experience of a repressive government acting in the strong and valid belief that its actions are for the good of the greater whole. These matters in China are on a scale that is incomprehensible to the spoilt, democratic extremists of Hong Kong. In response, they could exclaim, 'Ah, but we suffered the riots of the 1960s'. In fact, those riots, linked to the unrest generated by the Cultural Revolution across the border, were largely a hollow drama, with very little in the way of absolute violence and pain — other than financial pain, and a lot of noise and stress.

Technically, it should be noted that, out of the total Hong Kong population, there are some 34 per cent who are Chinese and only have Hong Kong re-entry permits. A further 59.6 per cent are Chinese citizens of Hong Kong who have the right to a Hong Kong passport, which gives them the right to travel abroad. Of the remaining 6.4 per cent, 2.1 per cent are Chinese with foreign passports and the balance of 4.3 per cent are non-Chinese.

The second problem revolves around Governor Patten, who is generally considered to be a thoughtful, intelligent, and decent man, albeit young by Asian standards. One interpretation of his recent actions is that he and his colleagues are driven by reasonable, but overly naïve, principles of fair play and British democracy. In addition, they may possibly feel that they should redress what many have called the 'sell-out' by the Thatcher government on the Joint Declaration. What is not appreciated is that, in negotiating this agreement, former British prime minister Margaret Thatcher, former Hong Kong governor Lord Wilson, and former British ambassador to Beijing, Sir Alan Donald, were all realists, and both of the latter two having a broad knowledge of China. All three had strongly supported the interests of Hong Kong, despite many views to the contrary, but they did so within the realistic framework of what would be acceptable to Beijing in terms of a reasonable compromise — something Patten and his advisers appear not to have taken into account.

Many have also made the interesting criticism that the British government has had over a hundred years to implement a democratic system in Hong Kong. Why, they ask, did the government wait until five minutes to midnight to introduce the current democratic reforms? They also ask why it is that the British government — which didn't institute such reforms before because no doubt it was easier to run Hong Kong without the proposed democratic system in place — believes that the Chinese government would accept such reforms when they take over in 1997.

The Hong Kong Chinese need look no further than the rest of Asia to appreciate their own extraordinary benefits. They, the UK government, and the Hong Kong government should look to recent events both around the world and closer to home, to gain comfort that these events, in a philosophical and Darwinian sense, are leading inexorably towards the results the Hong Kong democratic extremists so short-sightedly require now. To pursue Patten's October 1992 policy 'changes' to the Joint Declaration — certainly, China and many of Patten's supporters privately interpret some of his initiatives as changes — could not only jeopardise the smooth transition of Hong Kong from a British colony to being part of China, but they could also put unnecessary pressure and strain on the Beijing government's extraordinarily complex task of managing mainland China's own economic and political transition.

Hong Kong should appreciate that in Asia in general, and certainly in China, if the government is presented with too excessive a confrontational position, its last resort is usually to bring out the traditional Chinese authoritarian fly-swatter, with often tragic consequences. During his October 1992 visit to Beijing, Patten's initiatives elicited a series of snubs and a number of strong subsequent statements by Lu Ping, the Chinese government official responsible for Hong Kong affairs. He threatened that if Patten enacted the proposed policy changes, Beijing would replace the colony's government legislature and judiciary. Further, that if Hong Kong proceeded with its new airport (as part of the PADS project), China would neither permit planes flying to, or from, the airport to use Chinese air space, nor be responsible for any financial obligations relating to the airport which fall due after 1997. This is strong stuff and not to be dismissed lightly as just more Beijing rhetoric. It is clear that the Hong Kong Chinese business community is also beginning to become increasingly vocal about its concern over the way these matters are evolving. The Hong Kong stock market, too, reacted negatively; from its high in early November 1992, the exchange's Hang Seng index dropped 23 per cent by early December. It has since recovered, but this type of volatility underscores the instant knee-jerk reaction of the Hong Kong stock market to bad (or, for that matter, good) news from Beijing.

The *South China Morning Post* report of 1 November 1992 on its survey by telephone of 456 residents in Shenzhen and Guangzhou, the two mainland Chinese cities closest to Hong Kong, showed a high proportion in favour of Patten's actions. This reaction provides further evidence of the dangers of Patten's initiatives. Obviously, the Beijing government will become even more concerned, and hostile, if Patten's actions cause the spread of more people-power — or, even worse, democracy — in southern China. This will increase what I call the 'Tiananmen factor', namely Beijing's constant paranoid concern as to its ability to continue to retain control over this part of China, as well as of China as a whole. To give an economic indicator of these potential tensions, the population of the 'special economic zones' along the coast of China are estimated by many to have a GNP per capita in 1991 of some US$1,200 (some say as high as US$2,500), which was 400 per cent more than for the rest of China. Shenzhen on its own is likely to be competing with Asia's four 'Little Dragon' economies within five years. It will require great skill by Beijing to manage this disparity, let alone all the other obvious problems facing it.

Originally, there was considerable concern that the new Hong Kong government would attempt, under the guise of the human rights issue, to involve the Clinton administration in the United States in threatening to revoke China's 'Most Favoured Nation' status in order to put further pressure on Beijing to concede to its demands. In fact, Patten's government very sensibly lobbied for the United States, in particular the US Congress, to be more patient, to give China more time to make the transition, and for it not to involve itself in taking a stand on Patten's initiatives.

The people of Hong Kong as a whole must speak out and demonstrate to the Hong Kong government that the democratic extremists are not truly representative. In doing so, they must also persuade their government that it must give Beijing more 'face' in its dealings with China, as well as more sympathy and time with regard to its problems of maintaining overall control. If they do so, there is a real chance that, come 1997, Hong Kong and China together will pull off a smooth transition. The people of Hong Kong have not become so spoilt or so Westernised that they cannot appreciate the extraordinary, almost impossible, task already facing the Beijing government in bringing China as a whole safely into not only the twentieth century, but into the new world order. Why, then, are they not more forceful about their views, and why do they allow the vocal extremist tail to so vigorously wag the dog!

The frustrating aspect of the late 1992 Patten-led democratic feeding frenzy is that the activists and their supporters probably only represent a very small percentage of Hong Kong's population — as opposed to representing a large proportion of those who are politically active. Hong Kong, along with the rest of Asia, needs to evolve at its own pace, taking into account its own individual, cultural, and economic circumstances, albeit with some reasonable and thoughtful help from its Western and other foreign friends.

When all is said and done, there are probably only three meaningful interpretations of the cause of these initiatives. One is the possibility that they were ill-conceived and that they represented a mixture of incompetence, inexperience, and a general misreading of the situation — on the same scale as the Prime Minister Major/Minister Heseltine UK coal mine closure debacle in late 1992. The second interpretation, for those inclined to a Machiavellian view, is that the British government, with Patten as its vehicle, took this political stance in order to prove to the people of Hong Kong, and the world at large, that it would make every possible effort to provide Hong Kong with the best possible democratic structure before it is relieved of its responsibilities on 1 July 1997 by Beijing. In this equation there are certain key factors, namely Britain's long dealings with China and its natural desire to maintain cordial relations with China after 1997, certainly from a trading and economic point of view. It must have been clear to the British government that China would angrily resist the proposed reforms. It must have been equally clear that there would be the strong possibility that the overall Hong Kong Chinese population's reaction would likely be one of suspicion concerning the UK/Patten governments' intentions, and thus that the Hong Kong people would not want to be an unwitting pawn in some superior, unseen political chess game between Britain and China. Finally, there can have been no doubt that the Hong Kong population would become more nervous about China's current threats in relation to China's post-1997 sovereign control over Hong Kong.

The vast majority of the people of Hong Kong remain fundamentally Chinese in character and, being a pragmatic race, what they ultimately want is stability. In view of these facts, the UK team could have concluded that the Hong Kong population, while initially sympathetic, would ultimately be negative concerning the UK/Patten governments' democractic initiatives because peace and stability *vis-à-vis* the Beijing government would be more important to them. This could then force the UK government to withdraw gracefully, saying that they had behaved honourably in trying both to redress previous grievances concerning the Joint Declaration and the subsequent Basic Law Agreement and to put in place a stronger democratic structure before China's takeover. It is further interpreted that this possibly planned result will enable the UK government to be free to get on with its own agenda, which is to build a strong, new UK/China relationship relatively unhindered by vexing Hong Kong issues. And from Patten's point of view, if he remains as governor until the handover in 1997, it will be too late for him to enter the next UK elections which must take place before mid-April 1997. Therefore, if this interpretation is correct and the Hong Kong people request Patten and the UK government to withdraw the October 1992 initiatives and maintain the *status quo*, the UK government could quite reasonably ask Patten to return to Britain and replace him with a new governor to oversee the handover. Any likely successor would have considerable experience in Chinese affairs, be realistic as to how best to marry effectively the interests of all parties, and have the best interests of all the Hong Kong people at heart. Patten could then return to Britain, with considerable honour for having tried his best and with considerable positive international exposure. He could then set about the process of positioning himself for the next UK general elections. However, I must confess that, while this interpretation is fascinating, it is somewhat far-fetched! Also, despite the view that he has been very misguided in the way he has approached this issue, I for one do not doubt the basic sincerity of his position.

The third, more likely, interpretation is a mixture of the first two. It is alleged that prior to Patten determining and then announcing his 'democracy' initiatives, he was not made privy to the highly relevant exchange of confidential letters between Foreign Secretary Hurd and Foreign Minister Qian Qichen concerning the UK and Chinese governments' 'understanding' as to the future evolution of Hong Kong. Had he had foreknowledge of both the intent and content of these letters, Patten might have behaved differently. However, Patten certainly was too precipitous and gave Beijing little, if any, 'face' in his determination of what needed to be done and how to do it. Nevertheless, it is necessary to give full credit to Patten on one important issue. As his reform initiative has achieved worldwide recognition and support, in the process, he has reminded the Chinese government that there are certain global standards which have such recognition and support. Further, no matter how that particular game is played out, and whether Patten was right or wrong at this particular point in time, and on this particular issue and how he handled it, China must recognise that as time goes on there will be increasing pressure on it, from both its own people and the outside world, to institute over time a more democratic form of government in China. Furthermore, China must accept over time that it should subscribe to a set of universally accepted, common rules of behaviour.

Whatever the underlying reasons, the only really relevant net result is the impact these shenanigans will have on the people of Hong Kong. Even the most charitable or optimistic assessment provides little doubt that they have been negatively affected, at least in the short term — to what extent in the medium and long term, only time will tell. Yet for all the air of antagonism, both within Hong Kong and between Hong Kong and China, the future need not be black for the territory. Britain and China are likely to agree to a new general round of talks — no doubt a face-saving solution will be found.

It should not be forgotten that throughout the most tumultuous, anti-capitalist periods of the People's

Republic's short history, the communist regime has left Hong Kong alone, never attempting a forceful takeover. Even without force, the Chinese could have simply cut off the food and water which nourish Hong Kong's factory workers and stockbrokers alike. Or they could have ripped down the fence along the border and let would-be refugees peacefully inundate Hong Kong territory. In 1962, China actually staged what looked like a trial run of this plan and allowed 70,000 people across the border over a period of a couple of weeks. In 1967, radical Red Guards on the mainland inspired riots in the colony. Many bombs exploded, though little damage resulted. In July of that year, a militia of approximately three hundred Chinese soldiers crossed the border with automatic rifles, killed five policemen, and advanced three kilometres into the New Territories before pulling back. As a result, property values in Hong Kong fell dramatically, and trade and tourism ground to a halt, along with China's foreign exchange earnings. Perhaps the loss of the then sorely needed foreign exchange helped to sober China. In any event, by the end of 1967, order was restored to the territory.

China's fortunes have, over the years, become ever more closely linked with Hong Kong. Many major new investments into Hong Kong in the late 1980s and early 1990s have been made by mainland entities, such as China International Trust and Investment Corporation and China Resources. Although, in the past, much of Hong Kong's business was run by British and other Western firms or individuals, from the mid-1980s this changed. Chinese businessmen now manage most of the territory's big enterprises, with the exception of the few remaining traditional British firms like Swire's and Jardine-Matheson. Hong Kong Chinese officials now administer the majority of government departments, and a 'local' Chief Secretary is expected to be appointed in 1994. The vast majority of mainland China's trade is unloaded and repacked in Hong Kong. In 1991, Hong Kong's merchandise re-exports totalled US$69 billion, most of it coming from China, while exports totalled US$30 billion. For the period 1981–1990, the value of Hong Kong's re-exports from and to China increased about 22 times. Approximately one-third of Hong Kong's total trade was China-related trade, compared to less than 10 per cent in the late 1970s. In 1991, almost half of all China's exports were directed to or through Hong Kong, making them each other's main trading partner,

according to the Hong Kong government's Economic Services department. Furthermore, China does not have any port that can compete with
Hong Kong's for speed and efficiency.

A survey in 1992 by the Hong Kong Trade Development Council
indicated that more than 80 per cent of Hong Kong's manufacturers have
transferred most of their land- and labour-intensive operations to the
Pearl River Delta area of southern China's Guangdong province. These
and other Hong Kong companies own or operate more than 16,000
factories, many with other overseas investors, and employ some 3 million
mainland workers, compared with Hong Kong's total manufacturing
labour force of some 700,000. All this activity results from, and/or is
reinforced by, the close family and ethnic ties, the common dialect, and
the geographic proximity of the Pearl River Delta to Hong Kong. The
People's Republic itself has many lucrative investments in the colony, such
as the Bank of China building which rises, triangle upon triangle, to be the
territory's second tallest skyscraper after Central Plaza. Other investments
include hotels, banks, department stores, shipping companies, and real
estate. It is highly likely that China's political and business leadership will
want a *pied à terre* in Hong Kong, if not a business as well. After all, Hong
Kong can provide all the comfort, services, and other support functions
that are in short supply in China. This in itself should be sufficient to
ensure a strong real estate market over the medium and long term, which
in the past has been subject to wild fluctuations due to political uncertainties.

The leadership in China will have an incentive to leave Hong Kong
more or less as it is. Why kill the goose that lays so many golden eggs?
However, it should be realised that the Beijing government may do so if
pushed too far — the golden goose analogy carries only limited weight in
the infinitely more important political equation. Put another way, Hong
Kong's economy is said to add only some US$5 to China's US$370 GNP
per capita. Additionally, given the economic momentum that already
exists in Guangdong province and in Shanghai, they could over time take
over from where Hong Kong could be obliged by a future Beijing
crackdown to leave off.

Hong Kong also suffers from the same China 'order versus chaos' syndrome, except that its cycles are of a much shorter duration. No doubt it is a reflection of the behaviour patterns of its giant neighbour to the north. After the late 1992/early 1993 bout of Patten-led mini-chaos, the more important question is what is likely to happen to Hong Kong after 1997. It behooves all observers of, as well as participants in, the affairs of Hong Kong to remember the words of the writer Dick Wilson, 'The heroic vision of the liberal democrats of tiny Hong Kong valiantly keeping China's dark forces at bay through pure democracy is a suicidal illusion' (*Hong Kong Business*, September 1992). It is essential, amongst other things, to be realistic about Hong Kong's relationship with China. In this context, I essentially agree with Helmut Sohmen's remarks, made in a speech given in Hong Kong in September 1992. To paraphrase his views and include some of my own at the same time, there are basically three factors which will come into play. The first will be the natural reaction after 1997, or most likely even before, for the people of Hong Kong to re-identify with, or reinforce, their 'Chineseness'. This could take many forms, including more focus on speaking Chinese rather than English and with English receiving less attention in the educational system and the media, and following the Chinese way of *guanxi* — connections — rather than relying on more open and abstract Western notions, such as fair play and full disclosure. The Hong Kong Chinese could also wish simply to be seen to be more Chinese rather than international and thus they could evince a greater degree of arrogance on the basis of China's historical attitude to foreigners — namely, that to be Chinese is to be superior.

The second factor is that, once the border between the separate states of China and Hong Kong disappears, it is natural that many in Hong Kong will quickly wish or feel obliged to adapt to the ways of their new cousins across the old border. This will materially erode many of the value systems so laboriously built up under British rule. As Sohmen says, these attitudes will probably no doubt have a strong effect on the Hong Kong judicial system. Chinese is likely to become the language of the courts, the existing foreign judges are not likely to remain in place for long, and the relationship with common law countries and their legal developments will weaken. Will Chinese judges provide the same degree of judicial independence in a rapidly evolving mainland Chinese-oriented economic and social environment? Will foreign businessmen continue to feel comfortable with such a changing judicial system? Might they not feel more comfortable in going direct to, say, Shanghai and tackling the 'real' Chinese head-on, rather than dealing with the uncertainties of a chameleon hybrid which Hong Kong is bound to be until it finds its feet in the new environment?

This leads to the third factor: namely, will the people of Hong Kong continue to demonstrate the great commercial vision which has characterised British-ruled Hong Kong? It is unlikely, again at least in the short term. There is bound to be considerable self-induced, and Beijing-induced, pressure to conform. Self-censorship to ensure that one's future actions will be deemed politically and culturally correct will become an instinctive reaction. The same phenomenon will no doubt apply to Hong Kong's currently free-wheeling media, with the English-language press also suffering from a diminution of support and increased competition from the national Chinese press and other media forms. Finally, corruption, endemic in China proper, will no doubt spill over and have its human effect. This would be tragic after all of Hong Kong's efforts to create a corruption-free, level playing field for its affairs.

All of these factors may appear very negative, but in realistic terms they should be seen as a natural result of a complex transition period. All need not necessarily be lost. Hong Kong and its people are not likely to lose their old habits overnight, or to switch wholeheartedly to the 'new rules', which will in any event not be very clearly defined. The challenge for both Hong Kong and China will be that, barring any more periods of 'chaos', while Hong Kong is adjusting to the new Chinese rules, China will simultaneously be obliged to take greater note of the international rules that govern the global marketplace. It will also have to adjust to the Asian world's general evolution towards the application of democratic processes of government. In this connection, Hong Kong can continue to serve China as a recognisable role model, more or less, for an international rules player. This should assist China in pushing through its reforms.

Over time, hopefully well before the fifty-year time period governing the Joint Declaration's 'one country, two systems', and as long as all parties, including the rest of the world, do not impose unrealistic expectations on the two players, particularly on China, this convergence should be achievable. Finally, I fully agree with Sohmen's concluding statement, that 'Hong Kong will occupy a place of honour in the Chinese order of things in having been the catalyst and the promoter, and the dynamo which got the whole country sparked up, and which — hopefully for China and for the rest of us — continues to do more than its fair share to keep it [China] moving along. The British legacy will no longer be very visible but will remain (from the perspective of history) as a monument to an incredible achievement.'

Taiwan, Korea, and Thailand have, for example, shown that, with the development of a strong economy, the concomitant generation of an affluent, articulate, and demanding middle class has given rise to more democratic governments being voted into power. Thus, in the end, the more that China, including pre- and post-1997 Hong Kong, is encouraged to become an active partner in a new Asia Pacific community, the more likely it is that common sense and the increasingly active economic participation of all the Chinese people in Greater China will ensure the peaceful evolution towards at least some form of 'democracy'. Surely this is all that the people of Hong Kong and the People's Republic of China and, for that matter, the rest of the world, can reasonably want and expect.

Conversely, it would not be in the best interests of the rest of the world, let alone the region, if China began to implode in the same manner as the former Soviet bloc. The world needs a stable, evolving China, including Hong Kong, even if some of its current practices may, by Western standards, be unacceptable. Surely it is a question of degree, of what is realistically possible. Does the world really want a Chinese version of the tragic break-up of Yugoslavia, or another huge and frighteningly unstable political, economic, and military time bomb along the lines of Russia? If China were to slide or be pushed into a state similar to that of the former Soviet Union, a world state of previously unparalleled volatile instability could result.

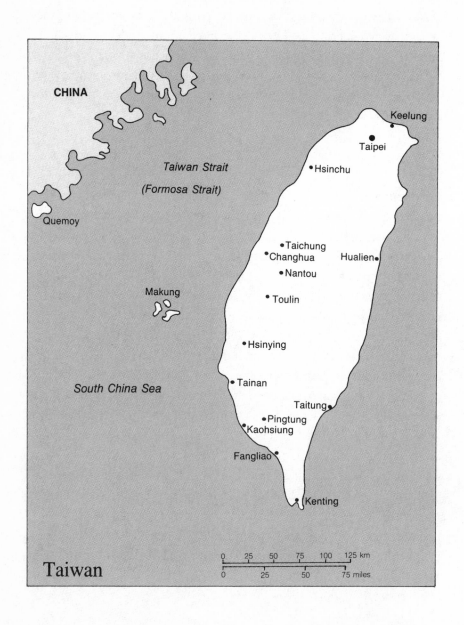

CHINA

Taiwan Strait

(Formosa Strait)

Quemoy

Keelung

Taipei

Hsinchu

Taichung
Changhua   Hualien
Nantou

Makung

Toulin

Hsinying

South China Sea

Tainan

Taitung

Pingtung
Kaohsiung

Fangliao

Kenting

0   25   50   75   100   125 km

0   25   50   75 miles

Taiwan

TAIWAN

From a Financial Wild West Show to the
First Representative Chinese Democracy

The dispute between Taiwan and China often has the quality of a conversation from *Alice in Wonderland*: it is based on illusion, backed by posturing, and treated with utter seriousness. Both know that Taiwan is the holdout for China's Nationalist Party, or Kuomintang (KMT), and that the mainland and the island are separate. But neither will say so out loud. If one defines Taiwan as a country in its own right, one will enrage both Chinas — the Republic of China (or Taiwan) and the People's Republic of China. Taiwan fortifies a number of small islands between itself and the mainland but claims to rule China all the way to Mongolia and Tibet. China claims that Taiwan does not exist, while at the same time trying to cash in on Taiwan's economic success.

It is impossible to understand Taiwan without understanding its links to the mainland. The history of the island — named Formosa, meaning 'the beautiful', by the Portuguese in the sixteenth century — begins with the mainland. Aboriginal tribes arrived there first, settling in the island's mountains where they still live. Then Chinese Hoklos from the mainland's Fujian province arrived, followed by Hakka people from Guangdong. For centuries they farmed on an island apart, unbothered and unnoticed by the rest of Asia Pacific. Only when trade between Japan and China flourished in the fifteenth and sixteenth centuries did Formosa come to prominence — as a pirates' hideout. Pirates could raid the ships using the nearby sea lanes and then slip into one of Formosa's protected inlets. The Japanese tried to put a stop to this but failed. The Dutch, anxious to protect their new holdings in the spice islands of what is now Indonesia, in the early seventeenth century, finally established a beach-head settlement, with forts and churches.

By the mid-seventeenth century, changing tides on the mainland had engulfed Formosa. The Ming dynasty, which had held the Chinese throne for 250 years, was falling to the invading Manchus from Manchuria. As part of their last-ditch effort to hold the country, the Ming ordered a swashbuckling sailor named Koxinga to keep the waves of invading Manchus from flooding south China. Foreshadowing the experience of Chiang Kai-shek's armies in similar circumstances three centuries later, Koxinga failed to push back the invaders and sought refuge on Formosa, having decided that if he could not be part of the Chinese ruling class, he would rule the island instead. He threw out the Dutch, took over their forts, and installed himself on a throne. Again foreshadowing Chiang Kai-shek, Koxinga used Formosa to oppose Manchu rule on the mainland. But unlike the current regime, Koxinga's dynasty did not last long. He died soon after taking the throne he had created, and although the crown passed to his son, and then to his grandson, the island was back in the mainland Chinese fold within forty years. Formosa slipped back into obscurity as a minor part of a large empire.

Two centuries later, in the late nineteenth century, when the Manchu Qing dynasty was struggling in its death throes, the Japanese sent a military expedition to Formosa. They stayed until the Chinese emperor paid them to leave. But visions of an empire were beginning to dance in the heads of Japan's rulers. In 1894, Japan invaded Korea, another Chinese satellite. This time the Japanese would not take money. They refused to leave the Korean peninsula until they had obtained some territory for their trouble. The Chinese gave them Formosa.

The Japanese ruled with a relatively light hand for half a century. They looked upon Formosa as part of China, Japan's elder brother, and perhaps out of unconscious respect, they did not force its inhabitants to survive on rice and bean husks as they had forced the Koreans to do. Formosa came into the modern age under the Rising Sun. The Japanese built roads, hospitals, schools, and industrial plants. The people were required to speak Japanese and to trade their Chinese names for Japanese names, but the Chinese on Formosa never resented the Japanese with the fervour of other peoples later colonised by Japan. The island waived war reparations when Japan surrendered in World War II. Japanese investment there was considered compensation enough. Still, Formosa was never really centre stage during World War II. That would have to wait until December

1949, when the Kuomintang came barrelling on to the island's beaches, in retreat from the Red Army.

In pursuit of Chiang and his nationalist followers, Mao's communist troops launched a furious assault on the small islands of Quemoy and Matsu, just a mile off the mainland coast and the first line of defence for Formosa. But when the smoke cleared, the KMT had not budged. Since then, Formosa — renamed Taiwan — has been at the centre of a legitimacy dispute.

Although in a minority — the Nationalists and their descendants represent only 15–20 per cent of Taiwan's population — the KMT shaped life on the island. Because vigilance was needed against the communist threat, the army controlled most areas. Taiwan, an island with 20 million people, maintains a disproportionately large army of around 360,000 troops (one-fifth more than Indonesia with its 180 million people). Political dissent was ruthlessly repressed. Dissident magazines were closed with regularity, and some political opponents were assassinated.

As the Cold War began, Taiwan, like South Korea and West Germany, became one of the world's ideological border states. Taiwan then had friends throughout the communist-hating world. The United States, stunned at losing the mainland and united in its hatred of Red China, became Taiwan's closest friend. During the Korean War, the United States stationed the Seventh Fleet between the two Chinas and increased military and economic aid to Taiwan. A loosely-knit right-wing lobby in the United States, initially led by Henry Luce's *Time* magazine, kept up the pressure on the American government to isolate the mainland and to maintain the façade that Chiang and the KMT would eventually return there. In 1960, the mainland's daily bombardment of Taiwan-controlled Quemoy became a major campaign issue between presidential candidates Kennedy and Nixon.

For its part, Taiwan blackballed those countries who refused to support the anti-communist line. In 1950, the government in Taipei broke off diplomatic ties with Britain after London had recognised the People's Republic. In 1956, it was Egypt's turn; in 1960, Cuba's. Like the Formosan pirates of old, many of the new Taiwanese turned to commercial piracy, ignoring patents and copyrights enforced everywhere else in the West. To be fair, the same could be said of most Asian economies in their initial emerging years, and of China today. This helped to fuel an economic miracle as impressive as, if not more so than, any other in Asia.

The years passed, and although Taiwan remained under martial law, the shelling of coastal islands faded into a propaganda war. Taiwan resorted to knick-knack bombardment, sending thousands of balloons filled with pens, can openers, bright T-shirts, and other cheap items to float over the mainland where they would pop and shower the mainland with the flotsam of capitalism. Authorities offered a million dollars in gold to any Chinese pilot who flew a plane to Taiwan, and so lured a few defectors.

Yet the more Taiwan succeeded economically, the less likely it seemed it would ever take over the 'other China'. Mao's communist regime had consolidated its rule over the mainland, resulting in more unity than the country had enjoyed in almost a century. Taiwan may have had money, but it did not have the manpower to launch an invasion and it could not count on support from its allies to do so. The rest of the world began to realise that, however crazy politics were on the mainland, a country the size of the continental United States with more than one-quarter of the world's population could not be ignored. Strategically, China could be a counterweight to the Soviet Union. Taiwan was not big enough to compete. Economically, China was an enormous potential market, with a population fifty times that of Taiwan. Left out of the UN, China had little reason to be influenced by most nations. Yet China had the potential to cause dramatic changes in the world.

The diplomatic tide began to turn in 1971, when the Republic of China on Taiwan was expelled from the UN and replaced by the People's Republic. Many nations subsequently changed their allegiances from Taipei to Beijing. However, the defection that had the most damaging effect was American Secretary of State Henry Kissinger's overtures to mainland China, details of which were revealed after Taiwan's expulsion from the UN. As the United States courted Beijing, Taiwan could do nothing but watch in dismay. Finally, on 15 December 1978, US President Carter announced that his country was opening diplomatic relations with mainland China. The American embassy would henceforth be in Beijing, not Taipei.

Although the world was turning against it, the Taiwanese government refused to modify its stance towards the mainland. Whatever the price, Taiwan continued to insist that Chinese relations were an either-or proposition: it was either the People's Republic of China or the Republic of China, but never both. When Deng Xiaoping came to power on the mainland in the late 1970s he began a 'smile campaign' towards the former — and, Beijing hoped, future — province. In 1979, Marshal Ye Jianying made a nine-point proposal for reunification, dangling such incentives as a promise that Taiwan could retain its armed forces and a large degree of autonomy. Taiwan spurned such advances. Later, China's agreement with Britain to take back Hong Kong inspired Deng to offer Taiwan the same 'one country-two systems' solution. He promised an even better deal for Taiwan: it could keep its military, its foreign policy, and its capitalist political and social systems. Again, Taiwan said no.

The longtime policy of the KMT has been to refuse dual membership with China in any inter-governmental organisation and to insist on using the name 'Republic of China'. The same standard holds for diplomatic recognition by individual governments. If Taiwan acquiesced while countries recognised the People's Republic, how could Taipei insist that the officials in Beijing were running a 'rebel government'? Country after country has had to choose between Beijing and Taipei. Most have sided with the larger, if poorer, People's Republic, increasing Taiwan's isolation from the international community. Whichever way the KMT has sought to advance, in the United States, in Hong Kong, Europe, and South Korea, the Communists have been there to thwart them. China has also maintained its efforts to block access to international groups. In the late 1980s, Taiwan was a member of only ten international bodies, most of which, like the Asian Productivity Organization and the Afro-Asian Rural Reconstruction Organization, were neither well known nor relevant.

By the late 1980s, the list of Taiwan's diplomatic partners had shrunk to around twenty, including South Africa, South Korea, Saudi Arabia, and a collection of South Pacific island nations. As mainland China's image improved during the mid-1980s, even South Korea, a virulently anti-communist government and Taiwan's last Asian diplomatic partner, began to court Beijing. In 1984, a mutiny on a Chinese torpedo boat ended as the boat floated into South Korean waters, with two sailors and their six dead comrades on board. In similar situations previously, the

South Korean authorities had always allowed 'freedom seekers' to go to Taiwan. But in this instance, the Koreans, overriding Taiwanese objections, returned to China both the boat and its entire crew, including the two sailors who had murdered their colleagues in an apparent defection attempt. This gradual *rapprochement* between South Korea and the People's Republic finally culminated, to Taiwan's angry dismay, in the two countries formally recognising each other in September 1992.

In the late 1980s, Taiwanese leaders made official trips to Latin America, where Taiwan still has considerable influence. Despite these efforts, even Bolivia switched to Beijing's camp. Furthermore, despite the aftermath of the Tiananmen Square incident, Taiwan only won a few new friends. In July 1989, Grenada recognised Taiwan and then, in October, Liberia and Belize followed suit. However, so far, Taiwan has managed to overcome its diplomatic isolation almost by ignoring the problem. For while diplomacy has been a disappointment, business has been booming. Most countries that have embassies in Beijing keep quasi-diplomatic trade offices in Taipei. A country with more than US$85 billion in foreign exchange reserves in 1992 commands at least that much respect.

Nationalist Taipei is a city geared to businessmen, not tourists. Even the city guides placed in hotel bedrooms include catalogues of items that can be bought for export. Of prime importance to Taiwan has been a series of four-year economic plans begun in 1953, including a 'land to the tiller' programme of land reform first suggested by Sun Yat-sen as a way of breaking up the land baronies on the mainland. The impact went well beyond redressing rural inequalities. The dispossessed landlords no longer had an interest in local politicking; instead, they had incentives to enter business. Former landlords became small businessmen.

In the early days, Taiwan was almost entirely dependent on the United States for raw materials. In the 1950s, therefore, the government encouraged agriculture and domestic production in an effort to reduce reliance on imports. But since the KMT was still sure that its stay on Taiwan would be only temporary, the idea was to be self-supporting for just long enough to launch a counter-assault.

By the early 1960s, planners had to prepare for the end of American aid, scheduled for 1965. The government gave less support to the farmers and encouraged aggressive exporters. Textiles led the way, as Taiwan began to provide a cheap source of labour for quality goods. Other factories began to make more complicated items such as bicycles and televisions. And Taiwanese firms stayed small. Unlike the Japanese and Korean economies, which are dominated by huge industrial groupings and conglomerates respectively, Taiwan's success has been built by thousands of small companies, some consisting of only a telex machine to receive orders and a telephone to tell the manufacturer how many pieces to make. Between 1966 and 1976, the number of manufacturing firms in Taiwan increased by 150 per cent, while the size of the average enterprise increased by only a third — around 90 per cent of all Taiwanese companies were said to employ twenty people or fewer.

During the 1970s, the government linked these constellations of small industries together with a modern infrastructure of roads, telecommunications, and ports. Meanwhile, the state set up capital-intensive industries too large to be run by all but a few family firms. Petrochemicals, heavy machinery factories, and the like were built to serve the rest of the economy.

Then, in the mid-1980s, surging growth in the United States served as a locomotive that pulled this emerging Taiwanese economy into a boom. In 1986, declining oil prices cut costs for Taiwan, which imports most of its oil. Meanwhile, the rising Japanese yen made Japanese goods considerably more expensive. As American importers looked for cheaper sources of VCRs and other consumer goods, Taiwanese exporters were able to slip into the cheap consumer goods niche formerly held by the Japanese. Exports boomed. Taiwan, which was able to adapt quickly and to get access to cheap financing, was perfectly suited to the situation.

Taiwan's legions of small companies are able to react quickly to market changes and last-minute orders. In the coffee shops of downtown Taipei's hotels, where the deals are made, a client might ask a running shoe company representative where to obtain 50,000 pairs of sandals and get the answer that the running shoe company will go into sandal-making!

And Taiwanese savings habits also helped to provide companies with capital. An attitude that the current political situation is transient has pervaded Taiwan since 1949. One can't take a cement plant back to the mainland, but cash is portable. So collectively the nation has continued to stuff money into the mattress. At around 40 per cent of GNP in 1988, the national savings rate was one of the world's highest.

By 1989, Taiwan was overwhelmed by a financial gold rush. More than US$70 billion in cash reserves backed its economy. This represented the world's second largest reserves after Japan. There was so much money that the government started buying gold bullion by the planeload — US$340 million worth in 1988. This made the government's books look less embarrassingly good and got rid of the excess cash that could fuel inflation. The government billed the 1980s as the years of industrial fulfilment: more efficient use of energy, automated production methods, and the move upmarket from sweaty labour-intensive products to high tech. But as the plan moved into practice, it was held back by the financial 'cattle-rustling', which became the national pastime.

By the late 1980s, the Taipei financial scene had gone wild. Anything could happen. Almost anything could be considered a company. A typical story on the street in Taiwan during this period went something like this: 'Company X has no sales, no earnings, no executives, no assets, and no prospects. No matter. People are willing to invest in the venture, and the stock is trading at just over US$1 a share.' One broker says he doesn't like it, as the stock price is too high compared with earnings, but the other broker says he's sticking with it since 'there are rumours that this company may be taken over'. In a climate where anything could be a business, small companies popped up everywhere. Another story making the rounds during this period was that when a sign fell on four people on a Taipei sidewalk, it hit a company chairman, two company presidents, and a major shareholder of a fourth company.

Although these were popular jokes, they were not far from the truth. Taiwan became home to legions of fly-by-night companies. Many of them didn't have any earnings. Company presidents became almost as common as mail-room workers. Investors called it the 'go-go atmosphere'. Even government officials were said to refer to their country occasionally as 'The Republic of Casino'. The average share was traded thirty-five times in a single year. By 1988, more than 1.5 per cent of Taiwan's GNP was passing through the stock market each day. Stock values rose to breath-taking levels, ludicrously far above the real value of the companies they represented. In 1988, International Commercial Bank of China, a Taiwanese bank, had a stock-market valuation of US$11.3 billion, more than America's biggest bank, Citicorp.

In Taiwan's financial rodeo, there was quick money to be made. Housewives could, and did, invest their life savings and double them. There was risk. Companies, and fortunes, rose and disappeared. There was mystery. Dozens of unlicensed investment houses took investors' money, promising anything from a 40 per cent to an outlandish 70 per cent return. Sometimes the companies disappeared into the night. But often, almost unbelievably, they made good on their promises. And there was fame and fortune. During this period, eight to ten investors, who were openly called 'the Big Hands', were rumoured to be manipulating the market. They achieved the status of cult figures, with a mass of followers who tried to emulate their financial derring-do. And, of course, there was dishonesty — not just commonplace insider trading, but big-stakes scandals. In February 1985, the first of the big financial debacles rocked the island. The government suspended lending operations at the Taipei Tenth Credit Corporation, part of the second largest business empire on the island. The news precipitated runs on two financial institutions controlled by the group. Two cabinet ministers and the KMT general secretary resigned in the aftermath. The chairman of the group was convicted of writing bad cheques, and was tried for fraud and forgery involving improper loans from his banks. This major upheaval was followed by a battery of smaller scandals throughout the second half of the 1980s, contributing to the general atmosphere of lawlessness.

The boom brought chaos. The market rose tenfold between 1987 and 1989. In 1989, only 186 stocks were officially traded on the Taipei Stock Exchange, compared with 2,241 in New York. But in reality, the stocks of hundreds of other companies were traded on Taiwan's shadow exchange. Taiwan had previously concentrated on the brick and mortar economy, not on building financial companies to manage the money once it had been made. The country's money had to go somewhere. It went to the confidence men and speculators who ran the shadow economy.

The money that did not go into stocks flooded the real estate market, causing property prices to skyrocket like stock prices. High rent made it more expensive for small and medium-sized companies to operate. Other prices went out of control. By the end of 1989, a rib-eye steak in Taipei cost US$23, a cup of coffee US$4.50. A 100-square-metre apartment cost the equivalent of forty years' wages for the average factory worker.

With prices so high and the lure of so much money to be made in the soaring stock market, it made sense to many owners and managers to close down shop and play the stocks. With easy fortunes to be made, housewives and factory and office workers joined the professionals on the stock market. These amateurs discovered they could buy a stock one day, sell it the next, and make as much money as they would in a day at the office or the factory. Talk of stocks became common at aerobics classes and around the dinner table. In August 1988 alone, 105,000 new accounts were opened at brokerage houses. Tales of taxi drivers and bar-girls mortgaging their houses and apartments to play the market were not exaggerated. Analysts estimated that 4 million people played the market, out of a total population of 20 million. By the end of 1989, some 60,000 workers had been lost to the ranks of speculators, and young graduates had stopped pounding on the doors of manufacturing companies as they had done before the boom. In a nation with only 1.5 per cent unemployment and an economy that is still growing, a labour shortage could become a real problem. The get-rich-quick fever could undermine the work ethic that made Taiwan such a success in the first place.

By early 1989, brokers enthusiastically estimated that an investment on Taipei's exchange could earn triple the money it would make in Tokyo, fifteen times what it would get on New York's Wall Street, and sixteen times the return in the City of London. Turnover on the exchange reached a peak of nearly US$8 billion one day in August 1989, outpacing even the New York Stock Exchange on that date.

Clearly, the Taiwanese government needed to slow the economic boom before it went bust. But when it had earlier made attempts to cool down the economy's hyperactivity, it brought howls of protest from all sectors. At the end of September 1988, the Finance Minister announced plans to impose a capital gains tax on stock-market sales exceeding US$107,000 a year from January 1989; the move triggered a wave of panic selling and mass protest. Riot police were called in to keep demonstrators from storming the Ministry of Finance. Each time the market plunged, demonstrators took to the streets.

The government was caught in a Catch-22 situation. If it didn't introduce some badly needed regulations to control the speculators, they could bring the whole Taiwanese economy tumbling down. Yet if the government brought order to town, it would hurt not only the big financiers, but also the ordinary members of the public who had poured their savings into the market. The 'Wild West' needed to be tamed, but things had to get worse before they got better. Then, between February and July 1990, the Taipei exchange lost 60 per cent of its value. A tighter monetary policy and a crackdown on kerb market activities caused the asset bubble to burst.

There is irony in Taiwan's present situation. For four decades the government of Taiwan has been sustained by the dream of eventual reunification with the mainland on Taiwan's terms. For this dream to be realised, Taiwan would need militaristic discipline in politics, economics, and diplomacy. In pursuing these goals, the Taiwanese government has been fairly successful. And yet success has slowly made the original goals irrelevant. Iron political discipline and repressed political and human rights had created the stability necessary for a developing economy and the rise of a middle class. This middle class now clamours for more political rights. Economic control was necessary at first to manage the wildcat tendencies of Taiwanese businessmen. But strict economic policies created the widespread wealth which made the shadow economy flourish. Severe political and general economic restraints were necessary to maintain the survival of the KMT government in Taiwan. But Taiwan has survived so long and so well that it has begun to evolve into its own entity. The disputes of forty years ago have lost their urgency, if not their meaning. A whole generation of children has grown up without ever visiting the mainland. They are now adults with concerns and interests which don't revolve solely around Beijing.

While Chiang Kai-shek was alive, this could never have happened. Chiang had once considered himself China's emperor. When he lost his empire, the generalissimo was so stunned he did not speak for several hours. Chiang made sure that his son, Chiang Ching-kuo, would succeed him, to carry on the family tradition of struggle against the communist mainland. But Chiang the younger had the imagination to see that Taiwan needed to adjust. He had no wish to be seen as a tyrant by future generations. The downfall of President Marcos in the Philippines and the discrediting of President Chun Doo-Hwan in South Korea were powerful regional demonstrations that no leader is immune to popular will. Some safety valves had to be opened to prevent domestic pressures from rising, especially among frustrated Taiwan-born young people. Although Chiang Ching-kuo's liberalising vision disturbed many of his supporters, he had the family name, the public support, and the political savvy to make the uncertain come around to his way of thinking.

Many of the doubters were in the National Assembly. The National Assembly last had full elections in 1947, when its mainland constituencies chose 2,961 assembly members. Natural attrition has reduced their numbers by about 2,000. Those who remain cling to the fiction that they represent the mainland but cannot face their electorate again until the communist 'rebellion' is over. In reality, the Assembly is the last bastion of a KMT old guard with jobs for life, an average age of well over seventy, and a tendency to block any creative discussion of Taiwan's future.

The reforming Chiang gradually allowed an opposition party to develop. In 1986, the authorities allowed Yao Chia-wen, a tall, fifty-year-old Taiwanese who once studied at Berkeley University across the bay from San Francisco, to form the Democratic Progressive Party (DPP), even though opposition parties remained technically illegal under martial law. Three months later, the DPP was allowed to campaign in the partial elections to the Legislative Yuan and the National Assembly, winning a quarter of the vote. Both rival parties shared the belief that Taiwan should ultimately proclaim itself an independent country. This idea — completely taboo in Taiwan for years — became openly discussed. A group of twenty candidates from an opposition party even proclaimed full independence from China as part of their electoral platform.

In September 1987, a thirty-two-year-old DPP leader, Ju Gau Jheng, created the most celebrated local political incident in many years when he jumped on desks inside the National Assembly chamber, kicked aside the papers of old KMT legislators, and shouted, 'Who do you represent? Where are your voters? You were elected on the mainland four decades ago, but we have no mainland. You are irrelevant.'

Political outbursts were not unknown in the past. What is significant is that this time there were no reprisals against the desk-stomping Ju or other demonstrators. This signalled more liberalisation to follow. The younger Chiang, in precarious health, paved the way for the succession of Vice President Lee Teng-hui, a technocrat and the first Taiwanese to rise to such prominence in the mainland-dominated government. Martial law — one of the symbols of KMT power — was lifted in 1987, after thirty-eight years of curfews and summary arrests. Taiwan's thirty-one newspapers were allowed to double in size to twenty-four pages, and other newspapers were set up in competition. In 1987, there were some 1,800 street demonstrations, almost all ignored by a police force grown suddenly tolerant.

There is not yet complete freedom. Martial law has been replaced by a 'national security law', which still bans any call for either communism or independence. Taiwan's men over the age of fifteen cannot leave the island until after they have completed their military service. The KMT still monopolises the broadcast media.

But the reforms are striking nevertheless. When Lee took the presidency after Chiang's death in January 1988, most considered the new president a transitional figure. Lee cautiously continued his patron's political reforms, pressed to do more by the street demonstrations of the middle class and students who were calling for an end to the KMT monopoly on power. But after his re-election to a full six-year term he became more aggressive, announcing plans for sweeping democratic reform and expressing hope that Taipei and Beijing would ultimately open talks on reunification of the island with the Chinese mainland. In his inaugural address in the spring of 1990, Lee also announced that he would end the four-decade-old 'Period of Mobilisation for the Suppression of the Communist Rebellion'. This action undercut the current legal basis for KMT rule and required extensive constitutional revisions of procedures of parliamentary and presidential elections. Lee called for 'a great model of political democracy' to be completed within two years and bought a respite from demonstrations by holding a National Affairs Conference in the summer of 1990. Reform was on the agenda, but not reunification. In fact, the conference failed to reach a consensus, being deadlocked between reformers and KMT diehards. The attitude of the latter was summed up by Vice-Premier Shih Chi-Yang: 'We don't rule out the possibility of a new constitution,' he said, 'but why tear a house down just because the roof is leaky?'

Changes are also being forced in the economy. In 1988, there were thirty-three foreign banks in Taiwan, but they were restricted to one branch in Taipei and one in Kaohsiung, the country's other major city. They could not engage in credit card operations, nor could they undertake trust business which would allow them to invest in equities and to deal profitably in commercial paper securities. Because the government still cramped the movement of capital, much of it lay around unproductively in the system.

However, in a new banking law, the government has relaxed regulations allowing foreign banks in and private banks to be set up. This new banking law paves the way for the privatisation of the three large commercial banks, government institutions which formerly dominated the island's economy. The law allows foreign banks to expand their scope by offering savings, trust, and underwriting services. Newly-rich Taiwanese will no longer have to turn to black market banks to manage their affairs; in fact, the new banking laws have also been amended to curb the underground investments that caused rampant speculation. For the first time, the legal light has been shone on Taiwan's large underground, deposit-taking companies. Where formerly they operated freely in a grey area of the law, these companies are now banned from taking deposits. The central bank has also responded to pressures to liberalise the foreign exchange market, allowing it to be determined by market forces. From 1986 to the end of 1992, Taiwan's currency appreciated by approximately 40 per cent against the US dollar, reflecting Taiwan's growing trade surpluses with the United States.

As the government has begun to rein in its domestic economy, it has also begun to address the issues which have enraged its trading partners. Because almost the entire Taiwanese economy is geared to export, the country's pool of excess cash has fuelled business ventures that are largely in the export sector. The more Taiwan exports, the more it runs up its trade surplus with trading partners, in particular the United States. Taiwan and the United States have sparred over trading issues for most of the

1980s. The United States wants to limit the import of Taiwanese textiles, machine tools, and other products, and it has, over the past few years, launched two 'unfair trading practice' actions against Taiwan. The first came when Taiwan used a customs valuation table that the United States said violated agreements. The second came when Taiwan failed to reach an acceptable formula for implementing its promise to open its market to imports of American wine, beer, and cigarettes. Now the tariffs and duties that have sheltered Taiwan's domestic market are being reviewed. Import tariffs on thousands of items, from turkey to chocolates, have been lowered.

In the mid-1980s, Taiwan also took action to clear its reputation as a haven for commercial pirates. Because of the plethora of small and medium-sized family firms, there had never been much capital for research and development in design and marketing. Buyers in the United States wanted cheap copies, and Taiwanese businessmen were able to produce a product quickly and find a market by riding the wave of a fad. The government's Legislative Yuan passed a bill substantially stiffening penalties against copyright infringement, and for the first time explicitly protected computer software. As a consequence, the government has also tried to encourage domestic research and development by setting up research clusters around the country.

As reforms take hold, Taiwan is likely to have a less impressive economic performance. The official growth target for the 1990s is 6.5 per cent per year, which may seem lukewarm compared with the average 9 per cent growth between 1983 and 1988. But like any economy entering a more mature phase, Taiwan needs slower, sustained, non-inflationary growth. With labour costs rising, companies will have to move into more high-tech fields. In October 1989, the Taipei government named five 'star' industries it would encourage with government grants and tax incentives: information, consumer electronics, telecommunications, automation systems, and advanced materials, such as titanium. It will be tough for Taiwanese companies to evolve from economic guerrillas and patent pirates to financial generals presiding over long-term growth. But such a development will only increase Taiwan's leverage in resolving what remains its most important concern: its dispute with the mainland.

With little recourse to official diplomacy, Taiwan hopes that its economic success will serve as a model for China, and as a means to broaden and deepen its relations with the rest of the world. Taiwan has commercial links with 150 countries. Taipei and the capitals of its trading partners are dotted with quasi-embassy 'trade missions' and 'cultural centres' which will grant a visa and publicise a contract. In 1989, for example, the Taiwanese cabinet approved preferential tariffs for East Germany, Hungary, and Yugoslavia. Direct trade is planned with Vietnam, Cambodia, Laos, and Cuba, despite their communist governments. Taiwan trade missions even made trips to the old Soviet Union, parts of which are now significant partners in Taiwan's burgeoning Eastern European trade. The question is whether Taiwan can win more friends by providing investment and aid.

The island has become too rich to remain insular. With only 20 million people, it has become the world's thirteenth largest trading nation. The Ministry of Economic Affairs said in 1988 that it had approved overseas investment of US$218 million, of which US$123 million went to forty-two projects in the United States. *The Economist* judged this a huge underestimate. It reported that in 1988, Thailand alone had approved Taiwan investments of US$2.1 billion, ten times the alleged total. In the same year, the Philippines and Malaysia each approved investments thought to have topped US$500 million. The confusion stems from the Taiwanese businessman's contempt for transparent accounting (i.e. accounts that have been audited by an international accounting firm) and a Taiwanese law which says firms may not invest more than 40 per cent of their paid-up capital abroad. Taiwan is building bridges to the rest of the world with billions of US dollars in investments. In the meantime, businessmen from Taiwan are spreading out over the Asia Pacific region, exporting capital, expertise, and trade links everywhere. Forced by the Taiwanese dollar appreciating by some 40 per cent against the US dollar and the rising cost of land and labour at home, it is estimated that, since 1987, some 4,000 Taiwanese companies have invested around US$12 billion in setting up their operation elsewhere in the region (excluding China). There are also some tens of thousands of Southeast Asians trained in Taiwan who are assisting in building the Taiwanese business network throughout Asia. Taiwan is certainly in the vanguard of the recognition that there is a need for regional co-operation in order to face competitive pressures from the West. This aggressive, industrial grass-roots proselytisation of the region's markets, from Australia to the Philippines to Vietnam, is helping to bring the region together.

Taiwan also has a US$1 billion aid package to distribute to friendly countries. However, the battle to win hearts is an uphill struggle, not least because Beijing invariably severs relations with any country or international body that links with Taipei in this way. The Philippines has been caught in this dilemma. Taiwan invested in several petrochemical plants, for which it asked investment guarantees. Beijing retaliated and put the Philippines in the awkward position of having to decide between needed economic aid from Taiwan and needed political links with Beijing.

In a sense, all Taiwan's relations come back to the essential conundrum of its relationship to the People's Republic; namely, the long-standing, former Taiwan's 'Three No's' (no compromise, no negotiation, and no contact with the communist mainland) face off against the mainland's long-standing, former 'Four Cardinal Principles' (leadership of the Communist Party, the socialist road, the dictatorship of the proletariat, and Marxism-Leninism-Mao Zedong Thought) as the basis for reunification. However, even on the emotional side of the 'civil war', Taiwan has shown signs of bending. In October 1987, Taiwanese mainlanders and their descendants were allowed to visit, by way of Hong Kong or Japan, the families they left behind in the People's Republic. And in 1988, the Taipei government's chief policy researcher floated the idea of 'dual recognition' in international bodies. His suggestion implied that Taiwan may have to establish diplomatic relations with countries which simultaneously recognise Beijing, if only to keep growing as a major economic power in the region.

Dual recognition had a scant chance of succeeding given China's strong objections. However, when the Asian Development Bank allowed the People's Republic of China to join, and renamed the Republic of China 'Taipei, China', the Taiwanese delegate did not pick up his briefcase and leave in a huff as he would have done in Chiang Kai-shek's day. In fact, in 1989, Mrs Shirley Kuo, the then Minister of Finance, led a delegation to Beijing for the Bank's annual meeting. She was the first official of the KMT government to set foot on the mainland since 1949. And in the same year there was another first: athletes from Taiwan went to Beijing for a gymnastics competition. They went again in 1990 for the Asian Games.

Hundreds of thousands from Taiwan now visit the mainland. Despite the Tiananmen Square crackdown, China's main tourist agency reported that 540,000 Taiwan citizens — 2.7 per cent of the population — travelled to China through Hong Kong in 1989; in 1991, it is estimated that this number had risen to some 1.4 million. Trade with the mainland, done indirectly through Hong Kong, was worth more than US$1 billion a year in 1990, with the balance running heavily in Taiwan's favour. This cumulative balance, in 1992, rose to some US$7.3 billion. Large numbers of Taiwanese businessmen, like their Hong Kong counterparts, have even moved factories, particularly labour-intensive ones, to the mainland to take advantage of lower costs. It is estimated that an astonishing 7,000 Taiwanese companies have set up operations in mainland China. It is further estimated that the official and unofficial totals of Taiwanese investment in China for 1992 itself reached some US$5 billion and US$10 billion respectively.

Since 1990, a *de facto* recognition between the two Chinas has evolved. An example of this economic reality is the setting up by the Beijing government of a 'special economic zone' in Fujian province, immediately across the strait from Taiwan. Additionally, China's Pintang Island, a kilometre or so off the coast of Fujian, has been designated a special investment area for Taiwan. This is of great interest to Taiwan. All other things being equal, it is quite likely that China and Taiwan will soon agree to direct transport and business access between Fujian and Taiwan. This could lead rapidly to Fujian being a serious competitor to such areas as Guangdong and Greater Shanghai.

More generally, there is the strong likelihood that Beijing and Taipei will soon officially sanction direct transportation, telecommunication, and economic links between the two countries. More importantly, this could also soon lead to direct talks between the two governments. The last major step, albeit some time in the future, would be political association on some sort of federal, or confederal, basis. Should these initial sorts of accommodation become established, Taiwan could provide much of the capital and management to fuel the Chinese manufacturing engine, producing goods both for the enormous Chinese market itself and for export. China would benefit from Taiwan's expertise. In turn, these results would accelerate the evolution of Taiwan becoming part of a Greater China, thus helping to bring China into the Asia Pacific community.

What China and the rest of the world must realise is that, as the editorial in the *Far Eastern Economic Review* of 29 October 1992 stated so succinctly and accurately, 'Less well known, and completely unpredicted by most of the world's China "experts", has been a political revolution of historic proportions: the transformation of Taiwan into the world's first real Chinese democracy. Although the growing pains have not always been an edifying sight — chair throwing appears to be a parliamentary privilege in the legislature — they compare most favourably to the spectre of tanks rumbling through Tiananmen Square. Unfortunately, Taiwan's splendid achievements have thus far gone largely unnoted and unrewarded. Taiwan's key place in the world economy has minimised the importance of its diplomatic non-recognition, but its neighbours continue to create difficulties in trade. While it is natural that other nations in the region see Taiwan as a competitor, many have yet to recognise that trade is not a zero sum game and that a secure (and democratic) Taiwan is essential to the region's future prosperity and security.' The question is, of course, whether, despite the considerable polarisation and confusion that is already evident, Taiwan can sustain its new democratic system. Certainly the February 1993 resignation of Premier Hau Pei-tsun has weakened the KMT's pro-China faction *vis-à-vis* the increasingly powerful Taiwanese majority. This has resulted in President Lee Teng-hai, a native Taiwanese, gaining control of key government and party posts and pushing for party reform and a more democratic government. This would give potentially more support to the native Taiwanese desire to throw out the hoary old KMT desire to reunite (on their terms) with the Chinese mainland, and instead to declare Taiwan an independent country.

Will the age-old Chinese 'order versus chaos' factor once again come into play? The KMT are certainly not yet resigned to political obscurity. This new development has been made even more complex by China's repeated promise that, if Taiwan were to declare itself an independent country, it would intervene militarily. If China should do so, there would presumably be a justifiable international outcry, sanctions would most likely be imposed, and, in reaction to all this, China could decide to go it alone — causing at the very least massive confusion around the world, particularly as China is a permanent member of the UN Security Council. However, hopefully this is only hypothetical, as there is every reason to believe that China's leadership would not in fact wish to put at real risk everything they have achieved for what, in effect, would be a pointless face-saving exercise.

Taiwan and China must become more flexible on the question of their relations with each other, not only because their peoples demand this for economic, trade, and family reasons, but because the two Chinas must, sooner or later, come to terms with each other. The mainland, in the short to medium term, will need Taiwan more than Taiwan needs it. Taiwan should therefore swallow hard and be more proactive, concentrating on building trust and, during this process, concentrating less on the detail. Later, in the longer term, China will, if it continues at its current rate of economic and political growth, not need Taiwan at all. Conversely, with the rest of the world possibly evolving rapidly in different directions, Taiwan could then begin desperately to need the relationship with and resources of China.

If a direct, defined relationship between the two is to evolve, it is likely to be a confederational one at best, failing which it is most likely to be achieved through the evolution of a regional community. The other countries of Asia Pacific must do all they can to help this process, as with Taiwan's economic muscle and freedoms, and China's immense size, political strength, and vast economic potential, both are needed to ensure intra-regional co-operation and the evolution of a balanced regional community.

THE CHINESE DIASPORA
Will They and Their Hosts Know How to Behave?

While there are many Chinese dispersed to countries all around the world, where they have created thriving communities and achieved great individual success, for the purposes of this book, I have concentrated only on those Chinese who have left China to settle elsewhere in the Asia Pacific region and who, in any event, represent by far the majority of such Chinese.

Driven out of their homeland by abject poverty and starvation, the Chinese emigrants who sailed for the shores of Southeast Asia were to become, in a generation or two, the region's economic backbone, and some of its richest men. They left China in droves from the middle of the nineteenth century. The long period of peace preceding the exodus had led to a population explosion. The weakening imperial rulers of the Qing dynasty could not cope. More than 2 million people died during the major famines of 1846, 1849, and 1877. Another 60 million were estimated to have died subsequently, during rebellions that spanned two decades.

These emigrants were called *Nanyang hua ch'iao*, or 'Overseas Chinese' as they are now generally referred to. '*Nanyang*' means 'South China Sea', and most emigrants settled in the surrounding region, specifically in Thailand, the Malay peninsula, Indonesia, Singapore, Indochina, the Philippines, and Borneo. They also emigrated north to Manchuria, east across the Pacific to California, and further south to Australia and Melanesia. Trade links had already been established with countries scattered throughout the South China Sea: porcelain, silk, and tea from China were exchanged for the region's spices. These places were also easy to reach and the climate was kind. '*Hua ch'iao*', meaning 'sojourning Chinese', implies that these Chinese are only temporarily out of the country and will some day return to China. This was indeed the case for many of the first-generation emigrants. Out of dire necessity, they worked hard in the countries in which they had landed, squirrelling away their money. They sent back money and parcels of clothing to their destitute families in China, a practice which continues today. Their dream was to return wealthy enough to retire comfortably in China. If not, then it was enough if they could return to die and be buried in Chinese soil. Even today, many emigrants remain spiritually, if not physically, close to mainland China.

The *Nanyang hua ch'iao* were attracted by economic opportunities — to trade, mine, or plant sugar or pepper. They were attracted, for example, by the tin and rubber in the Malay peninsula and by the gold to be found in western Borneo, where a Chinese mining community was established. The early days were characterised by hard, unremitting work, often under appalling conditions. But the Overseas Chinese thrived, and quickly became the economic dynamos of the communities in which they lived. As the Chinese prospered, so did the cities. Sarawak's Kuching, for example, has traditionally depended for its prosperity on the skills and industry of its immigrants from Teochiu, a county in Guangdong, and Fujian — both provinces of China.

S. Gordon Redding, Dean of the business school of Hong Kong University, has estimated that in 1990 the Overseas Chinese totalled some 43 million in the region, and controlled a disproportionately large share of the region's economy. For example, the Chinese in Indonesia make up only 2–4 per cent of the population, but own about 75 per cent of its private capital. In the Philippines, only 1–2 per cent of the population are Chinese, yet this group controls nearly 60 per cent of the economy. In Australia and New Zealand, too, Chinese communities are also achieving business success.

Almost the entire merchant class of many Southeast Asian countries is comprised of Chinese, or partly of Chinese. A league table of the region's millionaires would be dominated by this race. *Fortune* magazine's list of richest men in the world contains names such as Liem Sioe Liong, Chairman of Bank Central Asia, Jakarta, and head of the Salim Group. Liem, whose Indonesian name is Sudono Salim, was born in 1916 to Chinese peasants in Fujian province. His first business venture was a noodle shop in his home village. In 1991, his wealth was estimated at US$2 billion.

The Overseas Chinese have a remarkable talent for making money, in spite of obstacles put in their way by the governments of many of their adopted countries, notably Indonesia, Malaysia, and the Philippines. The economic success of the Chinese in these countries has often earned them the hostility of the indigenous people, and the governments there have felt it necessary to discriminate in favour of the native people by restricting Chinese commerce. Strong anti-Chinese feeling in Indonesia came to a head under Sukarno in the 1960s, resulting in violent race riots. Ninety thousand Chinese fled Indonesia in the first three months of 1960. Five years later, the army launched a purge of Communists that left tens of thousands dead. Many took the bloodletting as an excuse to get even with the Chinese community. The Chinese merchants enjoy somewhat better days under Suharto, although many Indonesian Chinese, even billionaire Liem, feel the need to keep a low profile.

Overall, the Indonesian government has eschewed policy prescriptions and has instead sought less formal ways of redistributing wealth. The 1950 Benteng Programme reserved certain categories of imports for the indigenous population who qualified for government handouts. The Chinese businessman was not put off so easily, however. He would engage an ethnic Indonesian, or *pribumi*, to obtain the licence or to act as the front-man for his Chinese-owned company. The *pribumi* would then either sell the licence to the Chinese businessman at a higher price, or remain a sleeping partner and take a cut of the profits. However, constant complaints from the *pribumis* are increasingly leading ethnic Chinese to invest profits in China instead of back into Indonesia.

The Malaysian government, under Prime Minister Dr Mahathir Mohamad, went much further. It tried to engineer a more equitable distribution of wealth, income, and jobs between the Chinese and the ethnic Malays, or *bumiputras*, through the so-called New Economic Policy, which was established in 1971. At that time, foreigners owned 62 per cent of the economy, ethnic Chinese and Indians 34 per cent, and the *bumiputras* 4 per cent. The aim of the policy was to give the *bumiputras* control of at least 30 per cent of the economy, leaving the rest to be carved out between the Chinese, Indians, and other foreigners. This far-reaching measure was introduced after bloody racial riots swept through Kuala Lumpur in 1969. The trigger was a minor incident, but the underlying cause was the resentment felt by the Malays at being the largest racial group, while holding only a small proportion of national assets. The government in Malaysia was rather more successful than the Indonesian government. *Bumiputra* control of the economy has risen to over 20 per cent, although there are no estimates of how many of these are merely enterprises with *bumiputras* as frontmen. While the *bumiputras* have been successful in the plantation and banking sectors where government influence is strong, they have still not been able to take on the Chinese and Indians in commerce and manufacturing.

In Malaysia, where the Chinese make up about one-third of the 14 million population, the government has also felt it necessary to bottle up the Chinese culture. For example, it is only at the primary school level that Chinese children can study in Mandarin-language schools. From there, nine out of ten of them have to switch to secondary schools where lessons are taught in the Malay language, known as Bahasa Malaysia. Within Southeast Asia the Malaysian Chinese have assimilated least well. They have retained their Chinese names, whereas even in Indonesia they have taken local names. The New Economic Policy, abolished at the end of 1990, institutionalised positive discrimination and made many Chinese feel put upon. Malaysia's subsequent New Development Policy, launched in June 1991, also offered certain incentives and benefits to the *bumiputras*.

Much the same approach had been adopted by the Philippines. The government under Ferdinand Marcos tried to stunt the growth of Chinese merchants by keeping certain sectors of the economy out of the hands of Chinese who were not citizens of the country. This conveniently meant most of the Chinese population, because it was only in the mid-1970s that the Chinese were allowed to become citizens, following the establishment of diplomatic relations between the Philippines and the People's Republic of China. The Marcos administration also tried to kill off 'Chineseness' in the schools. Shortly before the mass naturalisation of the Philippine Chinese, Marcos ordered all Chinese schools to be phased out in four years, and limited Chinese-language teaching to just a couple of hours a day.

By contrast, the Chinese have found a warmer welcome in Cambodia and Thailand, and so have integrated better with the local people. Cambodia was probably the best example of successful assimilation on the part of the Chinese, until the murderous Khmer Rouge took over in 1975. In Vietnam, despite the traditional enmity between the Vietnamese and the Chinese, Chinese immigration was encouraged by the French colonialists in the late 1850s. They wanted the Chinese to play a specific commercial role in Vietnam, a role in which neither the French nor the local Vietnamese were particularly interested. But the French subjected them to stiff immigration requirements, as well as subsequently to heavy taxation.

The Vietnamese Chinese grew wealthy, but assimilated less well than in Cambodia. Cholon, the Saigon Chinatown, was a symbol of the community's separateness. When the Communists took over South Vietnam in 1975, new restrictions on both the acquisition of Vietnamese nationality and on their participation in certain business sectors, had a serious negative impact on those Chinese who remained behind. Thus, the ethnic Chinese formed a disproportionate share of the people who fled the country, many of them taking to the dangerous seas that washed them up, unwanted, on the shores of neighbouring countries. In the early 1990s, all these attitudes were reversed as the Vietnamese needed Chinese investment and Chinese business skills.

In Thailand, the Chinese have adopted Thai nationality and Thai names (for example, the Chinese surname Ma becomes Mingwatanabul) and, most importantly, tend to feel now a sense of belonging to the country. The Chinese merchant and Thai upper classes are inextricably linked, by tradition and by marriage. The relationship was moulded through trade, first between China and the Thai court, and later when Thailand was opened to Western trade by the Bowring Treaty of 1855. The Chinese found a cosy niche for themselves as the middlemen between foreign interests and the local economy. But political power lay in Siamese hands. The Chinese bought and married their way under this wing, giving large shares of their companies to the Thai nobility. A good example of military and political patronage can be seen in the family of the late Chin Sophonpanich, the founder and former chairman of Bangkok Bank, Southeast Asia's largest regional bank. Its board of directors has included deputy prime ministers and speakers of the Thai Parliament; and the chairman of the bank for sixteen years was Field Marshal Prapass Charusathiara, who was for a time also deputy prime minister. Chin, who was largely responsible for amassing the family fortune (now estimated at US$2 billion), began his working life as a cook. He then became a clerk in a construction company and went on from there to become one of the most significant and influential men of his generation in Southeast Asia.

The Sophonpanich empire is also a classic example of the Overseas Chinese network. It has been said that every successful Overseas Chinese has had links with Bangkok Bank at one time or another. Chin lent money to Overseas Chinese when foreign banks would not do so; among them was Liem Sioe Liong. The bank's network today spans Hong Kong, Tokyo, Osaka, Singapore, Kuala Lumpur, and all the other principal capitals of Asia, as well as London, Hamburg, New York, and Los Angeles. Today, Chin's son Chatri has overall control of the Bangkok Bank empire. His eldest son, Robin, has lived all his life in Hong Kong, where he is known as Robin Chan and runs a bank specialising in trade finance for Teochiu customers.

Yet even Thailand tried at one time to restrict the Chinese capitalists. It was the first of the Southeast Asian countries to prevent the Chinese from taking too much control of the economy. From the late 1930s to the mid-1950s, the government took over many Chinese private businesses. One such company was the Thai Rice Company. If the government had not done so, the country's largest industry, its chief export, and the staple diet of the people, would have been controlled by the Overseas Chinese.

Apart from Taiwan, Singapore is the only place in the diaspora where the Overseas Chinese are politically, as well as economically, dominant. Historically, they have had an easier time making money there than anywhere else in Southeast Asia. Ironically, though, the country has thrown up fewer and blander entrepreneurs. Ethnic Chinese make up three-quarters of the population. And, since independence, Singapore has been ruled by Chinese prime ministers — Lee Kuan Yew for thirty-two years, until he ceded his position to Goh Chok Tong in 1991. The Chinese in Singapore have come a long way since the first junk from the port of Amoy (now called Xiamen) in the southern province of Fukien (Fujian) landed on its shores in 1821. The country today is a success story, the

Switzerland of Asia, which many have claimed would not have been possible without the Chinese. The country is clean, well-ordered, and essentially free of corruption. Singaporeans are well-educated. The country works.

Though Singapore considers itself a multi-racial society, the Singapore government has been promoting strongly the use of Mandarin since 1979, and Confucian values are much touted. But despite this flowering of Chinese culture, the Singaporeans probably have the least spiritual and emotional affinity with the People's Republic of China of all the Overseas Chinese communities.

Why have the Chinese in these countries been so successful? Perhaps there is something in what is commonly said, that the capitalistic streak is inherent in their nature. Couple this with an immigrant mentality, a sense of opportunism, and an ability to adopt a single-minded focus on work, and one has a people driven by the need to make a fresh start in life in somebody else's country. If the need to survive provided the energy, then the dynamo was the desire to make money quickly so that they could return, or at least retire, to China. For many this remained a dream; they never saved enough to return. But in times of adversity, Overseas Chinese have returned to China in droves.

The Chinese way of business is particularly successful in countries where information is at a premium. In Europe and the United States, who is doing what, and the cost and availability of capital, can be determined from many sources. But in Asia Pacific, especially in China and Southeast Asia, such information is not usually in the public domain. Businessmen have to get it by means of their network of contacts, and at this the Chinese excel. Chinese information networks extend throughout the Southeast Asian finance and distribution industries, cemented by family, friendship, provincial and cultural ties, and sometimes by shrewd cultivation of the right politicians. When Suharto was fighting in the jungle, Chinese money paid for his weapons and troops. When the jungle guerrilla became president of Indonesia, he rewarded his backers.

During the 1950s, Mao Zedong referred to the Chinese abroad as Chinese nationals. He urged the Overseas Chinese to return to their homeland to help build the new China. But during the 1960s and 1970s, the Chinese leadership changed its mind. Instead, it advised these overseas kith and kin to assimilate into the country in which they lived so that they could create beachheads of influence and at the same time continue to remit foreign exchange to their families at home. When Deng Xiaoping resurfaced as a power in China, he also wooed the Overseas Chinese.

While the Overseas Chinese are far from being a homogeneous group, it is almost impossible to cure them of their cultural and family links with China, especially with their ancestral village and province. Wealthy businessmen, even those who are the second or third generation living abroad, remain sympathetic to, and concerned about, mainland China. These Chinese provide a continuing source of philanthropic aid, building universities, hospitals, and social institutions in China, once again usually directed towards their ancestral villages and provinces. They have also been among the successful small investors who helped to fuel the mainland's engine of growth in the 1980s. The Overseas Chinese in Hong Kong alone are the source of some 55–60 per cent of China's foreign investment, and the other Overseas Chinese supply perhaps another 20–25 per cent.

This Overseas Chinese community forms a strong and vital network between the countries of Asia Pacific. There are those who would argue that the 'clubbiness' of the Overseas Chinese would mitigate against such a development. I would argue that, while in the past this may have been true, it is less so today and will be increasingly less so in the future. As the global business world's practices transcend the region's cultural and national barriers and lead to the regional business practices in turn becoming more sophisticated and transparent, the Overseas Chinese will need all the resources they can get, including assistance from the people of other races, particularly from those in their own region, in order to retain what they have, let alone grow.

Thus this community has the potential to be a powerful force in tying the region together, through family, economic, and political linkages. It is also in the best interests of the Overseas Chinese to support such an effort. By being part of a developing Asia Pacific community, the countries of the region will no doubt have the incentive to condemn any single Asia Pacific country government that demonstrates too overt a racial prejudice towards its own domestic Overseas Chinese community. Such actions would only add to regional tensions and would risk such community's polarisation towards mother China. This could then give rise to a real Greater China, which might take a more dominant position in the region. Such a scenario should be avoided at all costs, as the resulting hostile chain reaction throughout Asia would lead to confrontation and, ultimately, to possible military confrontation.

INDIA
Counterbalancing the Greater China Threat

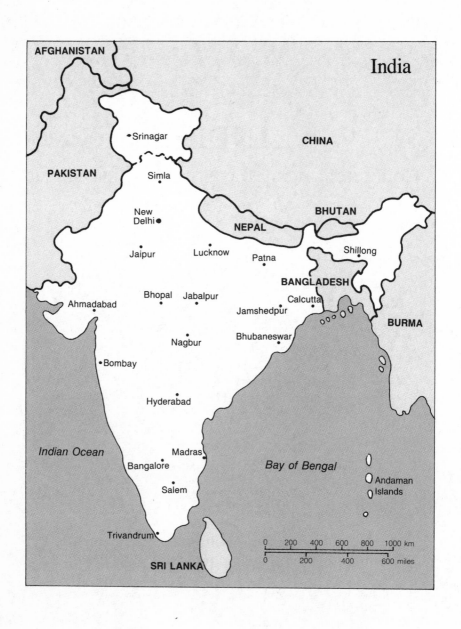

INDIA

Counterbalancing the Greater China Threat

First impressions of India tend to be superficial and focus on its poverty, backwardness, and the suffering caused by natural disasters such as floods and famine and the country's frequent civil disturbances. The overriding impression is one of chaos, albeit fascinating chaos. But impressions such as these belie the underlying truth, making India one of the most misunderstood countries in the world.

According to the world's purple press, India is always on the verge of political disintegration, starvation, or worse. However, it is essential always to put things in perspective. Sikh terrorism in the Punjab and Tamil separatism in South India have made international headlines. But few realise that the Sikhs comprise only 2 per cent of the population (842 million in 1991) and, more importantly, that these divisions have existed for more than three centuries. The statistics of daily violence in India would probably compare favourably with those of the United States, which has one-third of India's population. Flood, droughts, and famine have similarly attracted the attention of the media. The Indian government has made enormous advances in ensuring programmes to provide medical assistance, stockpiles of food, and other such measures, and these calamities in fact affect relatively few people in percentage terms. While many assume that India will be torn apart by its internal divisiveness, in fact, apart from intermittent periods of upheaval, it is a remarkably integrated country with a wonderfully rich culture dating back to the third millennium BC. It also has a strong tradition of democracy. One-party government gave way to multi-party democracy ahead of virtually all its Asian neighbours.

The second, and more realistic, reaction by visitors to India stems from its voluptuous, opulent, and even violent excess. There is no country in the world that assaults one physically, intellectually, and spiritually, in the way that India does. India is a land of enormous contrasts and wide disparities. But despite this, there is unity in its diversity.

Physically, the country is vast, embracing savannahs, soaring mountains, deserts, rain forests, and the vast rivers which give physical and spiritual life to the people. The awesomely powerful tigers, the iridescent peacocks, the flatulent warthogs, the grey elephant juggernauts solemnly pacing the jungles and roads of India, and the rest of India's teeming wildlife create a wonderful kaleidoscope of movement. The vivid, extraordinary colours and the other elements of India's visual cornucopia; the olfactory assault of the incredible smells of exotic spices and overflowing effluvia; the astonishing tastes: spicy, fiery, subtle; the sounds: the cawing of vultures at the *ghats*, the babble of dozens of dialects, the endless strident hooting of vehicles; the touch and textures of smooth silks and cool marble — all this enveloped in heat and dust, except for the almost Swiss-like meadows of the Himalayas, leaves the foreign visitor gaping in amazement, and often prostrated by the overall experience.

Intellectually, India's ancient civilisation and multi-faceted culture can leave one virtually stunned. Discussion on any subject usually leads to an onslaught from the articulate, intelligent, and demanding Indian interlocutors, with the result that the bemused visitor is often left reeling against the ropes, wondering what hit him. One could spend the rest of one's life in India and never be bored; alternatively, one could be driven completely insane.

Spiritually, the juxtaposition of poverty and the capitalist Rolls-Royces sets the tone. The poor stall owner watching his meagre offerings being eaten by a holy cow contrasts sharply, but is in harmony, with the Harvard or Oxford University-educated executive, with the virtually naked fakir meditating in the midst of sufficient chaos and disorder to make one wonder if World War III was not about to start, and with the poor farmer trekking a hundred miles to burn his dead on the banks of the Ganges, having spent most of his savings on the wood for the funeral pyre — they all seem to have their place and a purpose. And they all have much in common.

Indians, be they rich or poor, literate or illiterate, are generally spiritually minded. Religion (as a spiritual philosophy) is central to their lives, and everything revolves around their spiritual beliefs. It is the very genuine and daily practice of its various spiritual beliefs that gives India an extra dimension, in the form of greater resilience and strength to withstand the vicissitudes of life, and makes India both fascinating and terrifying. Few, if any, other countries have this constant and palpable presence of God in all His various forms.

After its independence and during the Cold War period, India made a policy of being loquaciously non-aligned. As a consequence, it became very introverted and left the rest of the world to its squabbles. At the same time, pleading poverty, it made sure it got more than its fair share of the available aid from all sides. One of India's great strengths — and weaknesses — is its bureaucracy, which it inherited from the British Raj. The bureaucracy's strength is that it ties this fractious country together and provides a vehicle for the creation and implementation of a truly national policy. It adds stability to the political process of governing the country — one may see governments come and go, but the administrative machinery continues. Its weakness is that, until the 1991–1992 reforms, it strangled initiative in the private sector and discouraged foreign investment. Additionally, it has been the source and focus of considerable corruption. However, to be fair, India's democratic political Tower of Babel makes it a difficult and risky business for the much-maligned bureaucrat to take any decisions that are in the least bit controversial.

Directed (some would say, misled) by the world's headline-seeking media and assisted by the Indians themselves, the world is often led to assume that India is virtually destitute and in constant need of aid. On the contrary, it has great economic strength, thanks to its successive governments and their bureaucrats. It is slightly more than self-sufficient in food (unlike most countries) and is even beginning to enter the field of agro-product exports. It has considerable self-sufficiency in energy (some 40 per cent) and adequate natural resources, such as coal and iron ore. It has developed all the basic heavy industries, including shipbuilding, and iron and steel. The subcontinent's industry, while untested internationally, produces everything necessary for a strong exporting economy. Added to these factors is probably the most unrecognised of India's economic strengths, namely its new and enormous middle class of at least 100 million people (some say as many as 350 million). They are well-educated, articulate, entrepreneurial, and have considerable disposable income. They thus represent one of India's major resources, provided they don't continue to be strangled by the bureaucracy and the constantly grand-standing and bickering politicians. If the Indian government and its bureaucracy can take advantage of this strong collective position, the building-blocks for a change in India's Third World underdeveloped country status are more or less in place.

India, long protectionist and economically introverted, is now pursu-ing an outward-looking economic policy. As it does so, it will be forced to look towards Asia Pacific rather than to the West. The Soviet Union has no more aid — indeed, it no longer exists. Britain is too involved with the EC. The Middle East is in a state of turmoil. And America has other fish to fry.

Moreover, Asia Pacific, particularly Japan, needs India as one of the counterbalances to China. The basis for an India–Asia Pacific relationship is already in place. India is a member of the Asian Development Bank and other such Asian organisations. While networks of Indian businessmen have spread extensively throughout Britain, the United States, and Africa, a number have also spread throughout Asia Pacific, creating ties between India and many of the region's nations. These ties provide the foundation for a strong relationship with the region. With the extraordinary changes that have recently taken place in the world, most nations are being obliged to rethink their priorities. For India to think that it is exempt from this soul-searching process would be irresponsible. Indeed, it has finally begun to grow out of its traditional response of endless, articulate debate leading nowhere — certainly, the rest of the world has had enough of that — and it now appears to be moving into an era of real reform.

Perhaps the best way to begin to understand the country's richness and diversity is to think of India's cuisine. Indian cuisine is incomparable in the variety of its curries, the range of its spices, and its other equally challenging dishes, from *vindaloos* to fiery mild *kormas*, from the subtleties of the *tandoor* oven to the sweetness of desserts like *gulab jamon*. Even the simplest dish contains a multiplicity of spices, and the range of tastes is endless.

Indian society and culture is a similarly rich blend of hundreds of influences from the entire Eurasian land mass and beyond, a crossroads and meeting-point for East Asians travelling west and for Europeans, Muslims, and Central Asians travelling east. India is a unique absorber, soaking up the customs and beliefs of the peoples who invaded it or simply settled there, whether it be democracy or Islam, blending them all together in one gigantic pot. Today there are seventeen official languages in India, and hundreds of minor languages and dialects.

But India was not only a magnificent importer of culture, it was also a great exporter. Its early language, Sanskrit, is the source for Indo-European languages such as Greek and Latin. And Buddhism was born in India, in the guise of Siddhartha, the son of a Nepalese tribal chief. He later travelled south to what is now the Indian state of Bihar, where he found enlightenment. India is also home to another of the world's great religions, Hinduism, which preceded Buddhism. The Buddhist religion has spread throughout Asia and the world, but has virtually disappeared from its land of origin. By contrast, Hinduism moved eastwards to Southeast Asia, where it was later supplanted by Islam; only a few pockets, such as on the Indonesian island of Bali, remain.

It is not difficult to see why Hinduism flourished in India; it is a perfect example of a religion influencing society and vice versa. The profusion of deities gave an enormously wide choice of gods to worship and helped to establish a caste system which has survived for more than 3,000 years. One interesting point is that the *Vedas*, a huge body of religious literature written in about 1000 BC which forms the basis of Hinduism, is not readily accessible to the vast majority of Indians. Indeed, very few among even the educated classes have read any part of the vast literature. But the epics themselves have become part of the folklore, not only of India, but of the whole of Southeast Asia.

The word 'Hindu' is not of Indian origin, but is the ancient Iranian word for the river Indus which came to be applied to the people living in the land of India — although today the river is in Pakistan. The religious lore contained in the *Ramayana* and the *Mahabharata* epics remains part of a living tradition. Many of the ancient shrines are still centres of pilgrimage and active worship, while the erotic carvings to be seen in places such as the Lingaraja temple at Bhubaneswar show that ancient Indian culture and religion had a strong worldly orientation, a vigorous enjoyment of physical life.

Until the Turko-Afghan conquest of India in the twelfth century, the elements which came from outside India were absorbed into the civilisation of the area. The Greeks, Kushans, Huns, and central Asians who successively entered the region have left few distinct traces. This is largely true, too, of the Turks, Afghans, Persians, and others who ruled India, or parts of it, from the late twelfth century until the Europeans came on the scene some three hundred years later. However, their presence can be detected in the large number of Perso-Arabic and Turkish words absorbed into Indian languages, as well as in the one cultural element they brought which was not absorbed by Hinduism, namely Islam. Although the religions remained separate and distinct, the civilisation that came to India with Islam proceeded to influence almost every facet of life, creating what can best be described as an Indo-Islamic culture, particularly in northern India and the Deccan.

Two debates have arisen regarding the relationship between India and Islam. The first is historical. Western historians describe the Turko-Afghan dynasties and their successors, the Mughals, as the period of Muslim rule in India. Many historians argue that this is not true. The Muslim community did not rule, they say, for it enjoyed no special privileges and after the initial conquest its leaders shared power with indigenous potentates.

The second debate concerns the theory that there were two 'nations' in India, following the arrival of Islam. This view is the rationale on which the modern state of Pakistan is based. But many would regard this idea as ahistorical. After all, the concept of nationhood did not emerge in India until the mid-nineteenth century. There was a Muslim élite at the time, to be sure, but the country was ruled by the British.

These debates may seem obscure, but they go to the heart of the Indian identity. For if it is true that India is a truly syncretic civilisation (as well as a modern nation-state *de jure* and *de facto* following Partition in 1947), this gives hope for the rest of Asia Pacific. India can show the rest of the region how to absorb external influences without losing its sense of identity. Indeed, it is more accurate to say that India is not one nation, but many; a world unto itself, but highly receptive to the world outside, given half a chance.

Compare the way that India and China absorbed Western influences from the beginning of the eighteenth century. For China, these forces took hold at a time when its civilisation and system of government were waning. The pressure from the Western imperial powers was probably even more traumatic for China than for India. In the former's case, it led eventually to nationalism and totalitarianism, combined under Mao Zedong. India, on the other hand, developed into a vigorous, albeit highly self-protective, democracy.

China has made greater economic progress than India in the early 1990s, but the Chinese still have another trauma to come: the ultimate battle between a 'communist' party monopoly on government and, in effect, a capitalist market economy. India could become a serious economic competitor for China. And it could do so without facing the tremendous political upheavals potentially awaiting China, because the Indian political system is more seasoned and pluralistic — that is, if it can overcome the ominous Hindu self-determination movement (with overtones of ethnic cleansing) that emerged with a vengeance in late 1992 and early 1993.

The standard cry is that India is an economic miracle waiting to happen — unfortunately, many have grown tired of waiting. For Indians, global entrepreneurship is as long established as bathing in the river Ganges. The currents of people and goods that have crossed its land have taught Indians the value of trade, and in all countries, commerce is the foundation of entrepreneurship. Who are the merchants to be found buying groundnuts from Ghana and selling them to Hong Kong in return for plastic flowers exported to Dubai? Not the Overseas Chinese, but the Indian diaspora. They take huge risks for the thinnest of profit margins. They go where other Asian businessmen fear to tread. But the entrepreneurial drive of domestic Indians has been stifled in a straitjacket of bureaucratic controls that, until recently, emasculated every facet of economic life, all in the name of self-sufficiency and non-alignment.

India's other major advantage over China is its well-established, educated middle class. The vigour of the country's industry has created this enormous middle class, which essentially announced its arrival in the 1980s. Its members had money to spend and splurged it on company shares, cars, bathroom tiles, chocolates, and designer clothes. Most economists' estimates define the top 12–40 per cent (by level of income) of the Indian population as constituting the middle (and upper) classes. This translates to a figure of some 100–350 million, which, even at the lowest estimate, is more than half the population of the United States, and only slightly less than the entire Japanese population.

This middle class constitutes the key source of national savings, which pumps money back into the economy. For a developing country, with an overall 1990 GNP per capita of US$350, India has a relatively high gross domestic savings rate — 20 per cent of its GNP in 1990; in the United States and Britain, the rate is less than 10 per cent. Yet the government has a domestic deficit, and although the private corporate sector has a positive savings rate, it ranges between only 2 and 4 per cent. When one considers that in 1992 around 25 per cent of the population was living below the poverty line and another 15–20 per cent was living barely above it, the importance of the middle class as a source of capital for investment is clear.

Given its numbers, the middle class obviously provides a substantial and growing market for consumer goods, and much of the industrial growth of recent years has been a direct result of this surge in demand for goods that were previously considered luxuries. From the viewpoint of foreign investors, at current levels, a fully qualified engineer with two to three years' experience can be hired for as little as US$250–300 per month. Similar rates apply for accountants and junior business executives. It is not surprising, therefore, that, given the recent reforms of Prime Minister Narasimha Rao's government, many international companies in selected industries — for example, software engineering — have chosen to locate large operations in India.

Although extremely conservative in many ways, the middle class is still likely to be the harbinger of social change in India. This is due partly to rising education levels but also to increased exposure to international society through overseas travel. The fact that younger people in India today are marrying outside their immediate castes and societies is due largely to changing opinions within the middle class. Resistance to the practice of giving a dowry has also come from this class.

Finally, the middle class could act as both a stabilising factor and a factor of change in Indian politics. The stability it could impart is founded on the stability of the political system itself. Successive elections have shown how steadfastly India has adhered to democracy. Any attempt to change this — as in 1975–1977 when Emergency Rule was imposed by Prime Minister Indira Gandhi — has met with strong resistance from the middle class. And yet, because of its ability to influence political opinion, it is also in a position to bring about change within the system. Thus, the middle class waited for the return of democracy during Emergency Rule, and when elections were finally announced in 1977, showed its disapproval by electing, for the first time since independence, a non-Congress government. Much the same thing happened again in 1979, when the electorate felt that the Janata government simply could not deliver the goods. More recently, in 1989, the same electorate that swept Rajiv Gandhi into office on a tidal wave of emotion in 1984 did not hesitate to pull the rug from under his feet when his 'Mr Clean' image was tainted by allegations of corruption. Such political maturity is a significant step in the further strengthening of democracy in India. It is this class which provided the foundations for the 1992 elections and for the reforms of the then newly elected Prime Minister Rao's government, which were draconian by previous Indian standards. It is this same class which will be needed to see the reforms through the thickets of political and bureaucratic self-interest and self-doubt, as well as to neutralise all the government and private-sector political skullduggery which will take place during the process. It will thus provide a critical contribution to India's future economic growth.

These people are capable, if given more freedom, of invigorating India, its politics, its economy, and its linkages to the rest of the world. However, until 1991, the politicians and bureaucrats had presumed that they knew best. In their tortuous way, they required the middle class to waste millions of man hours in obtaining the licences, authorisations, and permits, and meeting all the other dreaded conditions of Indian bureaucracy needed to start a business. This had to end if India wished to be able to exploit its current natural advantages. The middle class not only provides a substantial market for consumer goods, but also provides a platform — following the model of Japan's early, post-World War II economic history — for the guaranteed consumption of domestic products, initially whatever their quality. As consumers become more sophisticated, they will demand goods of a higher quality, which will bring India into the international marketplace with a specific cost advantage. These conditions will also provide incentives for foreign investors to participate in building India's next generation of industries. If it does all this, the Indian government will have achieved one of its constantly-stated aims: namely, uplifting the living standards of its large, disadvantaged population. Compared to the late 1970s, however, when some 45 per cent of the population lived below the poverty line, the 1992 level of less than 25 per cent is a considerable achievement.

The daunting system, as it existed before May 1991, was assessed by *The Economist* more or less as follows. India's trade regime was straightforward for consumer goods. Imports of these were forbidden. Only a few essentials such as medicines were exempted. The system for capital goods was more flexible. These were divided into 'restricted' and 'open' general licences (OGLs). Goods on the restricted list required an official licence. The relevant ministry would have to certify that the import was 'essential' and award it an 'indigenous angle clearance', meaning that a similar product could not be supplied in reasonable time by an Indian firm. No special licence was needed for OGL capital goods. Things were more complicated for intermediate goods, which were divided into banned, restricted, limited-permissible, and OGL. Different sets of criteria and permissions applied; licences were required for both the restricted and limited-permissible categories. There was more: imports could be bought only by an 'actual user', so intermediaries were banned. As part of the domestic capacity-licensing scheme, firms were obliged to sign up for a 'phased manufacturing programme'; they were allowed to expand capacity, but only if they promised to reduce the import content of the goods they produced. An entirely separate set of procedures was used to monitor imports slated for reduction under the programmes. Then there were sixteen government monopolies that were granted licences for imports such as oil, steel, and newsprint. Finally, to be on the safe side, there were tariffs, which were the highest in the world.

All this began to change soon after *The Economist*'s report appeared. Prime Minister Rao, a former foreign minister who was heading into retirement after a heart operation, arrived at a unique point in time for India. He had the vision and determination to seize the day. But to understand the dimension and achievements of his government's reforms, it is necessary to see why India had gone down this economic *cul de sac*. The answer, in a word, is history. India's colonial past under the British demonstrated to the subjugated people that trade meant exploitation by foreigners. Jawaharlal Nehru, India's first leader after independence in 1947, looked towards the Soviet Union as a model of what could be achieved in transforming a backward society into an industrial behemoth. Central planning was the key. The commanding heights of the Indian economy were duly nationalised. This policy nurtured three great interest groups determined to ensure that India stayed that way: a twenty million-strong bureaucracy; a political party, now called Congress (I); and a group of constantly complaining business-men who grew fat behind the shelter of the world's highest trade barriers.

For the next thirty years, India pursued a policy of 'self-reliance', so that Indian industry came to produce just about everything — basic metals such as iron and steel, machine tools and industrial machinery, transport equipment, including passenger cars and railway engines, electrical and electronic consumer durables, products for industrial use, textiles, foot-wear, paper, pharmaceuticals, computers, even nuclear plants and com-munications satellites. This diversity seemed impressive, but in reality the industries concerned were often inefficient. Furthermore, they were crippled by bureaucratic legislation. For example, to install a new piece of machinery, a factory-owner needed to obtain a government permit. To obtain a permit, he would have to show he had prior permission to expand. Such a regulatory environment, of course, was a breeding-ground for corruption.

It became evident in the mid- to late 1970s that changes were needed. As most of India's goods could not compete internationally, exports had never really taken off and yet imports were rising, leading to a balance of payments crunch. At the same time, it became increasingly apparent that the burden placed on the public sector had become too much for it to bear and that its losses had become a major drain on national resources.

Industrial growth itself slowed sharply towards the end of the 1970s, the more so as it was struck by external factors, such as the steep rise in oil prices. Policy-makers gradually began to change tack. Economic liberalisation — which, in effect, meant loosening some of the controls and the regulatory framework of the economy — began in the early 1980s. It was only when Rajiv Gandhi came to power, however, that the process received a big boost. His government concentrated on removing controls on industry and supporting economic growth with tariffs and reduced taxes. The new policies had immediate positive results. Average annual industrial growth during the 1980s jumped to almost 8 per cent. The previous shortages of key industrial products like cement and fertilisers soon turned into gluts as production increased sharply. The demand for consumer goods soared. The output of passenger cars, two-wheelers, colour televisions, sound systems, kitchen appliances, and household furnishings multiplied several-fold in a matter of a few years. Sunrise industries such as electronics and computers also received a boost. And exports revived strongly; between 1988 and 1991, the growth rate in exports ran at close to 20 per cent annually, though exports of manufac-tured goods remained pathetically low, at 5 per cent of GDP. Exports fell back sharply in the second half of 1991.

For a while it seemed that Indian industry had taken off once again and that there could be no turning back. But as the political constraints on the government mounted in the run-up to the 1989 elections, the pace of liberalisation slowed. These political constraints were to be expected. Politicians and bureaucrats did not relish the idea of their no longer being able to control the fate of large industrial projects. They also became worried that a traditional source of illegal, corruption money would no longer be at their command. The domestic businessman himself had suddenly realised the virtues of a protected environment, free of compe-tition. The bottom line was that economic liberalisation meant the strong nexus between bureaucrat–politician–businessman, which had developed over the last thirty years, was suddenly under threat. Hence, resistance to reforms was considerable; the cosy (or some say unholy) triangle, for those within it, worked too well.

Rajiv Gandhi's Congress (I) party lost the elections to a coalition of parties, whose ideologies ranged from the extreme left to the extreme right. V. P. Singh took over as prime minister in late 1989, but his minority government was unable to make significant progress.

Nothing much happened until Narasimha Rao came to power after the collapse of the minority Chandra Shekhar government, which led to a general election being held in May 1991. During the election, the Congress (I) party leader and former prime minister, Rajiv Gandhi, was assassinated. Voters swung to his party and Rao was selected as a consensus, stop-gap leader of the new government. By deftly handling his party's factions, he was able to put a number of reformists into the top economic portfolios, such as his new finance minister, Dr Manmohan Singh, and the former Indian Reserve Bank governor, S. Venkitaramanan, both extremely experienced and capable bureaucrats. These and other reformists then collectively introduced the boldest economic reforms seen in India since 1947.

Rao would have faced fiercer opposition if the economy had been less weak and if there had been much of a choice in what economic measures to adopt. As it was, growing external and fiscal deficits brought India to the brink of default on its foreign borrowings, totalling more than US$70 billion, the largest in Asia. This was a traumatic situation for a country that prided itself on paying its debts on time. India's public finances were in a parlous state, because of growing subsidies for agriculture and industry, the relic of governments which could see no way out except to pile on the cash for ever-diminishing returns. By early 1991, the Indian economy was on the ropes.

The International Monetary Fund attached stringent conditions to emergency loans sought by Finance Minister Singh of both some US$2.8 billion to mid-1994 and some US$7–9 billion to around 1998/99. Rao's government devalued the rupee by nearly 20 per cent in July 1991. A sweeping simplification of the foreign-trade regime was announced in the same month, under which all but a few essential imports were tied to earnings from exports. The instrument for this was a second currency, 'Exim scrip', which would be earned at the rate of 30 per cent of export receipts and which would be freely tradable. All import items would be shifted progressively to the OGL, and export subsidies were withdrawn immediately. Full convertibility of the rupee for trade payments was promised to follow, and this subsequently took place in 1993.

From there, the government went on to introduce a tough budget intended to cut the central government deficit by 13 per cent. In addition, industrial policy was scrapped for all except seventeen sectors. The Monopolies and Restrictive Trade Practices Act was stripped of provisions which had previously required all companies above a certain size to seek government clearance for any expansion or diversification. Foreign joint ventures were promised virtually automatic approval for foreign equity up to 51 per cent in a wide range of designated priority areas, as long as foreign equity covered the foreign-exchange requirements of the start-up capital. This has resulted in major multinational corporations such as IBM, Texas Instruments, General Electric, Motorola, and Coca-Cola tying up with Indian companies or setting up export-oriented projects. Other multinationals are consolidating their existing presence in India by increasing their equity in order to obtain a majority ownership position under the legislation. The results have been impressive: in 1990, the government approved only US$90 million of foreign investment. However, in the twelve months after the new regulations came into force, foreign investments approvals leapt to US$1.23 billion. Unlike China, which has attracted much larger amounts but essentially for the private-sector manufacturing sector, much of this investment is going into infrastructural projects such as two power-generation projects producing 1,000 megawatts where the US company foreign partners hold 51 per cent of the equity.

It is also worth noting that India is as advanced technologically, if not more so, than many of its Asian neighbours. India has developed a surprising range of self-sufficiency in this arena: it has parked in geostationary orbit an Indian-designed and manufactured satellite for weather forecasting, telecommunications, and television broadcasting, using its own launching rockets. Indian technology will provide some 50 per cent of the 11 million telephone lines to be installed by 1997. It has made considerable strides in the development of computer software. In the arms sector, it has developed and test flown an advanced light attack helicopter, and it has ambitious programmes for battle tanks, missiles, nuclear submarines, and combat aircraft. While India has and will, of course, continue to depend on foreign technological assistance, all these projects demonstrate the depth of scientific and technical human resources available, all of which will no doubt contribute more and more as India's economy opens up.

Various measures have also been taken to lure back capital held overseas by non-resident Indians (NRIs), offering attractive deposit rates on foreign-currency accounts in India with no questions asked. NRIs may have as much as US$70 billion in capital stashed away abroad, and it has been a long-held ambition of the government to tap into this source of sympathetic capital.

Rao's new reform policies met with approval from most domestic industry associations, although there was general unease among workers at the hundreds of loss-making state enterprises. They need not have worried, at least for the moment. The government promised only that a new body similar to the Board of Industrial and Financial Reconstruction would be charged with rehabilitation schemes for public enterprises. However, profitable state-owned companies, such as those in the hotel industry, were put on the selling block.

But India is not out of the woods yet. By 1992, although inflation had fallen to 6.9 per cent (the lowest in twenty-five years) from nearly 17 per cent in 1991, economic growth had fallen to about 3 per cent a year, from more than 5 per cent in 1990, and resistance to further economic reforms from vested interests remained intense. Furthermore, although this could stand it in good stead in a regional trade war, India's dependence in 1992 on international trade (that is, the value of its exports or a share of its GNP) is only 7 per cent. This compares with Indonesia's 25 per cent and Thailand's 30 per cent for the same period. Ironically, it is this high degree of self-sufficiency that has no doubt diluted its interest in integrating into the international economy. Despite all this, it seems clear that India has made a giant leap forward. It is rejoining the world economy. There may be reverses in the future, but India's economic progress seems more assured than perhaps at any time since independence.

India has no option but to integrate into the global economy, largely because of its foreign debt of US$70 billion. In order to repay this debt, it will have to generate surplus foreign exchange through increased exports. But exporting is not easy. The implications are that Indian manufacturers will have to be induced through increased competition to reduce costs and improve quality. The process appears to have begun.

Indian corporations are now, for the first time, making serious efforts to improve quality. For example, at least thirty companies have acquired the international ISO 9000 accreditation. Also, many corporations are at different phases of implementing total quality management (TQM) within their organisations. Indian industry is slowly realising that the customer is king, and it is making an effort not only to catch up generally with the rest of the world but also to excel in certain niche markets.

In the early 1990s, a resurgence of the endemic Hindu versus Muslim problem almost brought the country to a standstill. The same middle and business classes must put real pressure on the Rao government to regain control over the Hindu versus Muslim conflict, occasioned anew by the late 1992 razing of the four hundred-year-old disused Muslim Babri Mosque at Ayodhya, some 500 kilometres east of Delhi, by 150,000 or so Hindu believers. India's population is made up of around 83 per cent Hindus and 11 per cent Muslims; the remainder are mainly Sikhs and Christians. This event was a delayed follow-up to the clashes in 1990 over the same issue, which left hundreds of people dead. This sectarian conflict, and each government's seeming inability to manage such conflicts more effectively, is of course India's other Achilles' heel. Few things are more off-putting to the foreign investor and businessman than the thought of sectarian riots raging across the country, causing widespread death and property damage, while the government stands by, seemingly paralysed. In the related late 1992/early 1993 Babri Mosque riots, despite police and army intervention, considerable loss of life and property damage occurred in New Delhi, Bombay, and elsewhere. The government must take more initiative to resolve these problems. Rao's government appears unable/unlikely to do so because of the fanaticism of the protagonists and the democratic forums they abuse in the furtherance of their own personal goals.

The politicians themselves will no doubt continue to take sides and again debate endlessly, so it is up to the business community and the middle classes to take a stand; they also have a strong business and lifestyle incentive to do so. Sadly, all this is also largely a problem of India's old caste system, where the upper-caste Hindus, the Brahmins, have dominated the Hindu world for thousands of years and still largely do so. There are many who claim that the lower-caste Hindus are still socially and economically exploited by the upper-caste ones — historically, they have been, and certainly today the people in rural India seem to believe so. The sectarian conflicts are also thought by some to be supported by the upper-caste Hindus in order to disadvantage and, in turn, economically exploit the Muslims.

Thousands of years ago, Aryans migrated from central Asia to the Indian subcontinent. The Aryan holy books, the *Vedas*, were a general potpourri of stories about their numerous gods, prayers, and general philosophy. As the Aryans mixed with the local tribes, the latter's gods and beliefs joined the Aryan ones. As all these people lived around the Indus River, their collective agglomeration of beliefs and gods eventually became called 'Hinduism'. Like Buddhism, Hinduism is more like a society with endless alternatives as to, and dizzingly varied rules governing, the way one may choose to live, rather than a religion with a specific god and creed or a church organisation. Buddhism, Jainism, and Sikhism are essentially branches of the main Hindu 'religion', with each branch being developed by its relevant *guru*, or spiritual leader. The nature of 'caste', as originally defined in the Hindu scriptures, is set out as the different professions a man may choose. In early times, everyone was quite free to make any choice. A man could be a ruler, warrior, teacher, priest, tradesman, server, and so on, depending on his chosen profession. However, because of the corruption of the system brought about by vested interests over the centuries, this definition of a man's profession/caste being a voluntary one changed into a man's caste being defined by his birth into it. Many Indians consider that the differences between the various castes became much more pronounced after India's independence from Britain. Another way of putting it would be to say that the then, and subsequent, urgent desire of democratic political parties to create 'captive' voting groups focused in on, reinforced, and even probably exaggerated, the caste factor.

The late 1992/early 1993 sectarian riots, which signalled the emergence of extremist Hindu groups, added an even more ugly dimension to this question of 'voter banks'. It appears likely that future political party platforms will be aimed at encouraging this ethnic separation and then counting on receiving the support of such clearly polarised groups or voter banks. Obviously, with such a massive majority in population terms, the extreme Hindu politicians and their less-salubrious allies will secure a distinct advantage, not only over the Muslims, but also over their more reasonable and non-secular political rivals.

This phenomenon has considerably distorted the evolution of India's post-independence culture and society. Hinduism, like Buddhism, was, and should theoretically still be, extremely liberal in its outlook — for example, it never encouraged proselytisation. Certainly, a review of the past history of India would give considerable evidence of this. It was able to absorb, and make use of, the many external influences visited upon it over the centuries. It is thus particularly tragic that the sectarian riots of 1990, and of late 1992/early 1993, of which the latter left over a thousand people dead, have occurred. What is even more disturbing is that this is the first time in India's history that the concept of a 'Hindu state' has been actively advocated. Further, these riots have split the Hindu people into secular versus non-secular opposing sides.

With the advent of this surprising and frighteningly extreme sectarian polarisation, India is facing its greatest challenge since its independence in 1947, which left between 500,000 and a million dead in the Hindu–Muslim clashes in the four months following the partition of British India into India and Pakistan. As noted in the *India Times* on 21 December 1992, extremists on both sides have been squabbling, if not fighting, over the Babri Mosque since the mid-nineteenth century. In recent times, a Hindu organisation, the National Volunteer Corps (or Rashtriya Swayamsevak Sangh, its Hindu name, and referred to by its initials, RSS) and its affiliates, including the Shiv Sena (Lord Shiva's army), have gained considerable public support for their dedication to the revival of Hinduism and its ancient warrior virtues. This development originated when the BJP, already in touch with these militant groups, supported in 1989, the cause of building a Hindu temple next to the Babri Mosque with the consent of Rajiv Gandhi. The BJP, in the event, correctly assumed that this action would provide substantial political support for the Party. BJP leaders then escalated the stakes by causing the Babri Mosque sectarian riots in 1990, which effectively resulted in BJP winning four state government elections and 119 seats in the 1991 general elections, which brought Rao into power.

The next stage was when Rao got involved in July 1992 in trying to mediate between the BJP and various Muslim groups over their respective desires concerning the Babri Mosque. When the October 1992 deadline for a resolution expired, the Hindu extremist groups called for another rally on 6 December 1992 at the mosque. The extreme militants were now in the ascendant; graffiti appeared with slogans such as 'Hindusim is for Hindus, death is for Muslims'. Many Hindu followers were prepared to die for the Hindu god Rama and the cause. Events rapidly escalated out of control. The state government of Uttar Pradesh (BJP party) took no steps to stop the demolition of the Babri Mosque, despite having control of the police who did nothing and the authority to use 14,000 federal troops stationed near Ayodhya for the express purpose of controlling any possible riot. Rao then dismissed the state government, and the two key BJP leaders were arrested. Matters worsened, the violence spread, and although the BJP leaders initially deplored the violence and loss of life and property, they soon changed their tune. They then declared they could not withdraw and that they would have no choice but to 'continue riding the tiger'. BJP president Joshi went further by saying just before being taken into custody, 'The Government has declared war on us. The war is on.'

Unfortunately, subsequent events seem to have proved him right. The sectarian violence worsened and spread to many cities in India, in particular to cosmopolitan Bombay, which has always prided itself on its sophisticated, multi-ethnic, commercially-oriented society — yet it ended up with more than five hundred dead and a thousand injured, as well as extensive damage to property. This general violence was further exacerbated by the formation of alleged unholy alliances between the extremist factions and criminal gangs, both sides using each other to further their respective goals. The issue became even more complicated by the clear unwillingness of the police to step in, and by the frictions that existed between the state government and the Defence Ministry. These frictions and resulting inaction by the state caused Rao's government to appear paralysed. Finally, the army moved in and put an end to the violence.

More importantly, the country's self-esteem was severely damaged.

Bombay's credibility, as India's premier commercial centre, was also severely damaged. It now has to live with an ethnic group distrust that could take years to eliminate. The only positive note is that this divide between ethnic communities was primarily apparent in urban cities, rather than in village communities, where the closer interrelationships of village life acted as a buffer to extremist tendencies. However, with a continuation of this urban polarisation, egged on by the various political interests, this could change for the worse.

When the BJP leaders were released on 10 January 1993, they returned to New Delhi as heroes. The BJP rapidly took the position that Rao's government was ineffective and that it should resign. The position of the BJP and its affiliated Hindu organisations is now very different from that of the Congress (I) Party. Rather terrifyingly, the BJP would appear to want to build nuclear weapons as soon as possible, reverse Rao's economic reforms, ban foreign investment, and accentuate, with as much vigour as possible, the nature of Hinduism in India's culture, education, and achievements. Bal Thackeray, the head of the Shiv Sena, stated in an interview in January 1993 that, among other things, India was a Hindu *rashtra* (nation), that he didn't care two hoots for India's international image, that he hoped the Muslims had understood their lesson well, and that the Hindu god Shiva (who opens his third eye to destroy) had now opened his third eye. While one can take a view on the importance or relevance of such statements, the level of concern escalated dramatically when BJP's principal spokesman, Kavel Malkani, stated in January 1993, 'The aim is to make India a great country. We should go nuclear and sign the Nuclear Non-Proliferation Treaty as a nuclear weapons state. The whole world will recognise us by our power.' By February 1993, it was obvious that the BJP was out to topple Rao's government. Hopefully, India will come to its collective senses and realise that such political exploitation by relatively few extremists puts at risk the future of the entire country. Rao and his political colleagues, the middle classes, and indeed anyone in India with any sense of objective reality, must come together to ensure that such political opportunism, racism, and religious extremism do not spread out of control, as it did in a similar way in Nazi Germany and Iran.

T he reason for this lengthy account of the Babri Mosque-related events is to make clear the point that, in the context of India's post-independence history, India had suddenly, and to its horror, arrived at a crucial watershed. The problems of its excessively democratic processes, its vast bureaucracy, its past fixation with non-alignment, its slow reforms, and so on, pale into insignificance when compared to this crisis. If the Rao government does not take urgent and highly specific action to put down this new ethnic and 'religious' nationalism, all of which fly in the face of Mahatma (M.K.) Gandhi's and Jawaharlal Nehru's great liberal and pacifist tradition, India could be facing a very bleak future. However, unlike fundamentalist Islam, which in its extreme forms can threaten the rest of the world, fortunately extremist Hinduism is effectively confined to the subcontinent.

Why has all this happened? After being the butt of derision or condescension, why did militant Hinduism suddenly leap into such prominence in 1992? One reason is certainly that, although the National Congress Party, which has held power virtually continuously since India's independence in 1947, and which strongly espoused secularism and democracy, has in recent years lost its way and become less efficient and more corrupt. In the process, India as a whole also appears to be losing its way, its goals, and its sense of national unity. Instead, India has begun to degenerate into a multiplicity of different factions, of different parochial goals, all as diverse and complex as its culture. And, in an unfortunate reversion to its historical traditions, many of the different factions appear quite happy to resort to violence — with the passive acquiescence of society, which tends to see these violent law-breakers as heroic upholders of the new factional goals. This underlying problem has also, no doubt, been exacerbated by the fact that more than 200,000 Hindus have fled Kashmir after many were killed and their temples damaged by Muslims, and that thousands of Hindus have either been forced to flee, or been killed, by Sikh secessionists in the Punjab. This has no doubt led to a feeling of Hindu insecurity and an inchoate desire to do something about this perceived persecution of their fellow Hindus.

The BJP, to some extent unwittingly, became the catalyst for giving a sense of focus to address all these malaises. On a narrower front, the Hindu militant arm — the RSS — has done much to facilitate this sudden focus.

It was founded in the 1920s to revive the primacy of the Hindus in India, who the RSS leadership felt were evincing all the characteristics of a conquered race and who were riven by divisions of region and, most importantly, caste. They saw Gandhi's concept of non-violence as being an alien Christian one which weakened the old Hindu warrior tradition of killing one's enemies. Thus, the BJP once again unwittingly found itself with an instant force ready to do its bidding in the furtherance of Hindu supremacy — what the BJP did not realise was the extent to which the RSS and other similar groupings would resort to violence in order to achieve this end.

Ultimately, the problem facing India is how to deal with the internal Hindu problem of how the secular and opposing communal Hindu groups will deal with the minority Muslims. It is not the problem of the Hindus versus the Muslims. What the BJP claims is that it is secular, that it has Muslims (token?) in certain party posts, that Hinduism is the best way of creating a new communality of spirit and purpose to enable India to deal with the challenges of the twenty-first century, and that a Hindu theocracy (as in Iran's Muslim theocracy) has no place in its strategy. Rather, it intends to exploit the Hindu holy men to achieve its aforestated goals and not end up sharing power with them.

There are, however, ominous over- and undertones to the events of 1992–1993. The police have become visibly involved in politics by harrassing the opposition and protecting even the most outrageously criminally involved, or criminally connected, ruling party members. The BJP uses the same double standards as all its predecessors in the game of victory-at-all-costs — its central leadership cloaks the brutal activities of its local leadership. What all fear is that the BJP hardliners, having gotten away with 'bloody murder', now have the heady scent of success filling their nostrils and inflaming their brains. Too often in the past, those who have thought to ride the tiger have ended up being eaten by it. Try and argue the rule of law, democracy, and the good of the whole with the Hindu holy man, the sadhus, or their equally fanatical followers, and they will give not a jot for such alien babbling.

All in all, this is a complex stew, but one that must be dealt with. The politicians don't seem able to, so it is up to the middle classes to do so.

Unlike the mobs of fanatical believers, who generally have nothing, and therefore nothing to lose, and who are whipped into a frenzy by their leaders, the business and middle classes now have a great deal to lose. It is therefore doubly curious that in early 1993, according to many sources in India, the country was split approximately 50:50 in terms of support for the extreme, anti-Muslim position taken by the Hindu-nationalist BJP — including solid support from the middle classes. This, on the face of it, is completely illogical. If this development is not nipped in the bud by a determined government and with strong national, and rational, middle-class support, those events could presage a dangerous reversal. And many of India's hard-won recent reforms will be for naught. This is yet another example of the endlessly fascinating, yet infuriating, aspects of India. The Indians really do seem to be their own worst enemies.

Despite the BJP's criticisms of lack of government leadership, Rao and his team implemented two important reform initiatives in early January 1993. The first was to reduce the excessive subsidies provided by the government on the price of various grains, which had resulted in artificially depressed prices being paid to the farmers. With such a move, the government has clearly signalled to the rural community, which consti-tutes around 75 per cent of India's population, that it is serious about increasing the rural community's prosperity. The second is that the government officially promulgated an ordinance substantially amending the Foreign Exchange Regulation Act 1973 (FERA), bringing the Act into line with recent industrial, trade, and exchange rate liberalising reforms. Then, in Finance Minister Singh's 1993 budget, which he announced on 27 February, further important reforms were initiated. They included the rupee's free flotation and full convertibility on the trade account, a reduction on the ceiling for import duties from 110 per cent to 85 per cent, an increase in the government's outlay on agriculture, education, and infrastructure, and a concessional 30 per cent tax (from 50 per cent) on short-term capital gains by foreign institutional investors. This will hopefully demonstrate, not only to the world at large, but also to India's middle class, that Rao's government means business, and that it will not be distracted from its vital reforms by the rabid, xenophobic babblings of the BJP and other Hindu extremists.

India should be welcomed into the Asia Pacific community. Why should Asia Pacific accept India? There are several reasons. As the world's largest democracy, India can provide a contrasting role model in bringing democracy to the region — although it is not certain that the other countries of Asia wish to replicate entirely India's democratic Tower of Babel! More importantly, no one country should be allowed to dominate Asia Pacific. Another Greater East Asia Co-Prosperity Sphere led by any country would be a disaster. Although Japan is economically very powerful, it is Greater China, if not China itself, which could threaten domination. India has the potential to assist in obviating such a threat. India, combined with the other countries of the subcontinent, has a population somewhat larger than China's. Both India and China command huge potential markets, while in both, labour costs remain low. Each country has a history and tradition that dates back thousands of years, and both have been accepted as ancient civilisations. In recent times, they have embarked on economic reforms to help them move away from socialism and into the age of capitalism — admittedly with varying degrees of success. Chinese and Indians alike have spread throughout the rest of Asia Pacific, as well as to many other parts of the world. And in the centuries of migration they have helped to create important overseas networks. The 'Overseas Indians' — or NRIs, as they are referred to by the Indians themselves — are potentially, together with the Japanese, the major competitors of the Overseas Chinese in Southeast Asia.

Historically, India and China have had similar aspirations to be a regional superpower. And India has traditionally seen China as a threat and a rival, owing to the intermittent border skirmishes which have disrupted the Indian-Chinese border for decades. It may be that this rivalry alone is reason enough for India to try and ensure that China does not come to dominate the region. India is therefore one of the key elements in providing the necessary balance to China in the new Asia Pacific.

The challenge for India is not only to open up its economy as described above, but to make a decision as to where its future lies. Traditionally, India has had close ties with Britain and, to a much lesser extent, the rest of Europe. It relied heavily on its ties with, and economic support from, the Soviet Union. It has also enjoyed close trading ties with the Middle East. At the same time, it has exasperated the world with its 'non-aligned' position and related partnerships. Britain, with its involvement in the EC and its own economic problems, is likely to provide little support in the future. The Soviet Union no longer exists. The Middle East will no doubt continue to be a trading partner, but in the global regional realignment of trading communities it has no significant economic partnership role to offer India. And to develop closer ties with the Islamic world of the Middle East could lead to further sectarian tensions within India. Finally, there is now little meaning in being 'non-aligned'.

India is now effectively in a vacuum. Asia Pacific needs India's resources and needs it to counterbalance the future Greater China. Asia Pacific (and, for that matter, the rest of the world) also needs to ensure that India doesn't embark on a too self-serving course of nuclear armament. India's alleged secret attempts in 1992, albeit unsuccessful, to find sources of enriched uranium in Central Asia bode ill, despite India's possibly justifying that it needs such weapons as a defence against ex-Soviet bloc nuclear weapons falling into the hands of volatile Islamic states to the west of India. The United States, Japan, France, Germany, Britain, and Russia have put pressure on India to sign the Nuclear Non-Proliferation Treaty (NPT) and to agree to the International Atomic Energy Agency (IAEA — based in Vienna) monitoring all its nuclear plants. The Asia Pacific countries should lend their support to this objective. Indeed, the rest of the world should also exert more pressure through the United Nations and, if necessary, threaten sanctions. It goes without saying that other would-be regional nuclear players should be treated in a similar fashion.

Conversely, while undergoing the trauma of restructuring both its economy and, as a result, to some extent its society, India must make a decision as to which alliance in this new world order will best serve it, at least over the medium term. As it opens its economy, India will not only automatically enter the gravitational pull of the vibrant economies of East Asia but will also need them and not the stagnant economies of the Middle East and Europe. In partnership with the countries of Asia Pacific, India has an important role to play. However, it should not be side-tracked by chasing memberships in organisational chimeras, such as APEC, which will provide little in the way of concrete benefits and thus waste valuable time, and political and human resources — unless membership is taken for the simple, cynical reason of being able, in the short term, to gather more information and have more influence. Instead, it should focus on what its realistic medium- to long-term goals should be and then pursue them in a disciplined manner, such as membership in ASEAN.

On a more practical note, India should realise that it can also learn some useful lessons from Greater China. Specifically, China's current growth is being fuelled primarily by the Overseas Chinese of Hong Kong, Taiwan, and elsewhere. India has its own pool of non-resident Indian capital and expertise to tap — this should be its primary source of direct foreign investment. Instead of only offering its Overseas Indians special domestic deposits at attractive interest rates, with no questions asked, the government should focus more on persuading its Overseas Indians to invest in businesses in India. This, in theory, should attract a much greater influx of funds than the special deposit mechanism, which is effectively only an income-earning, charitable donation mechanism. This would also enable India to tap into the substantial business and other technical expertise of its NRIs, as well as into their worldwide business contacts, thus emulating the Overseas Chinese model. Possibly the only way to break this seeming log-jam of NRI disinterest is for India to remove its foreign exchange controls.

To do something concrete in this arena is vital, as India must also realise that China is its greatest competitor, not only in the region but worldwide. In this context, it is worth pointing out that, although India has made major reforms since May 1991, the world has grown weary of waiting over the last forty years or so for India to finally grow up and join the real world. As a result, the world has become generally cynical about India, which has led, and could continue to lead, to the rest of the world reasonably assuming that, the more everything changes, the more everything remains the same. India, its government, and its businessmen must therefore ensure the broadest possible dissemination worldwide of the facts about these new reforms. More importantly, they should not now sit back in an orgy of self-congratulation and enter into another highly politicised and articulate debate, lasting forever, about what to do next. Instead, they must realise that these reforms are only a beginning and that, if they are to survive, they must continue with renewed vigour to press for further and even more fundamental reforms and changes.

To remove all foreign exchange controls, while a nightmarish thought no doubt to many politicians and bureaucrats, could possibly trigger off an enormous upsurge in foreign direct investment, tie India's economy into the world market, and bring about dramatic survival-driven efficiencies — all the while maximising India's many real strengths. Obviously, there is a very real risk involved in doing this. In this connection, it is interesting to note that when President Ramos came to power in the Philippines in May 1992, one of his first acts aimed at revitalising the flagging Philippine economy was to remove all foreign exchange controls. His decision occasioned considerable alarm, both domestically and abroad, with most predicting a substantial devaluation of around 20–30 per cent and a huge outflow of capital. The reverse happened. The peso revalued by around 15 per cent and there was an inflow of capital. This is not to say that the same would automatically happen in India's case, but it is an interesting indicator.

In today's trade-driven world, not to take risks in order to grow is to invite both stagnation (if not a decline) and the disinterest of the rest of the world. If India takes further major reform steps, it will generate real interest, particularly from India's potential main trading partners, Japan and Korea. Interest could also possibly be generated from the more entrepreneurial and adventurous Overseas Chinese, as well as from other foreign investors who are investing in China. At least some of these investors must be worried about the inherent instability of China as it moves towards creating a more capitalist economy, while trying to retain control of its rapidly evolving society. It should not be forgotten that India has much to offer international investors. It has English as its business language; a proper legal and accounting system; well-established stock exchanges and a domestic capital market; an educated labour force; in addition to space and a reasonable nationwide infrastructure. In contrast to the tired discussion about whether or not India will ever make it, China, after suffering for years from the lack of interest of most Overseas Chinese and foreign investors, is now, with its dramatic reforms, deemed by many to be the hottest game in Asia. To overcome international investors' negative preconceptions and redirect some of their interest towards the subcontinent will be India's main challenge over the next few years.

If this challenge isn't already difficult enough, India must also deal with its overly democratic system, which tends to bog issues down in political debate that leads nowhere. Its much-vaunted and admired democratic processes are, in effect, its Achilles' heel. In order to assist in the process of developing a functional democratic system, India's businessmen and middle classes must take a more proactive role and insist on a pragmatic approach to ensure not only India's survival, but its growth in the coming cold trade war period.

What India must also realise is that, sadly, there is considerable Asian distrust of India's aggressive business practices, its seemingly endless turmoil and confusion, and its propensity to indulge in endless debate — with little resulting action. Further, its overly democratic and bureaucratic processes, which seem to slow any foreign initiative in India down to an arthritic snail's pace, do not exactly encourage the Asia Pacific investor or businessman to make much of an effort. After all, there are so many other interesting investment alternatives in the region. This is borne out by the geographical origin of the post-1991 reform mini-surge of investment in India — little is from Asia; most of it is from Europe and the United States, and it wasn't much at that!

Conversely, for all the reasons explained above, Asia Pacific should welcome a reforming, revitalised India which is clearly focused on the East. This development would create a more balanced regional community. However, despite its brave new steps, without a stronger internal commitment to an internationally intelligible course of action, and without Asia Pacific as a regional partner, India can only flail around in an increasingly disinterested world. To remain irrationally independent can only lead it nowhere in a trade-driven, regionalising world. It can only result in India continuing to be exploited by the three regional trading communities and return the country to its original paranoid position of closing itself off in order not to be exploited by the rest of the world — in such case, there will be little foreign investor incentive to try and make any sense of the Indian equation! If it fails to become a member, if not one of the pivotal members, of the Asia Pacific community, India risks becoming an anthropological and cultural sideshow. In the worst case, in its desperation to flex its cultural and national identity muscle, it could become a nuclear wild card. This could have very serious consequences *vis-à-vis* both some of its unstable Muslim neighbours and the rest of Asia.

AUSTRALASIA
A Rudderless Ship Drifting towards Asia

AUSTRALIA
NEW ZEALAND
PAPUA NEW GUINEA

AUSTRALASIA
A Rudderless Ship Drifting towards Asia

The two main countries of Australasia — Australia and New Zealand — have spent most of their modern history trying to work out their identity. History and culture tie them to the West. And yet, if one considers their respective economies and glances at a map, it is clear that Australasia's primary link with the rest of the world should be with Asia.

Australasia is young, and has all the untapped potential and youthful enthusiasm that this implies. Perhaps because their identity is so un-formed, Australians assert their 'Australianness' and New Zealanders their 'New Zealandness', even if they are not sure what this means. Papua New Guinea, the third country within Australasia, is only just emerging from its Stone-Age culture and has yet to evolve a national identity. All three countries find it hard to fit into the world community.

Two centuries ago, Australia was a vast *tabula rasa*. For millenniums, the country was sprinkled with aboriginal peoples who hunted a little and foraged for plant roots and grubs. Once in a while, a Malay fisherman or an Indian trader might be blown off course and make a landing on the uninviting terrain of northern Australia, but such visitors never stayed long.

Practically no one stumbled over New Zealand, and those who did were repelled by the warlike natives, the Maoris. Paddling simple canoes, the Maoris migrated to New Zealand from Polynesia in about AD 1100. These people have changed little over the centuries.

Papua New Guinea, populated some 50,000 years ago by the Melanesians, is the least known of any country in the world. Many of its Stone-Age tribes survive today, co-existing somehow with their more modern brethren in a country that has only recently seen the arrival of the twentieth century in all its bewildering forms.

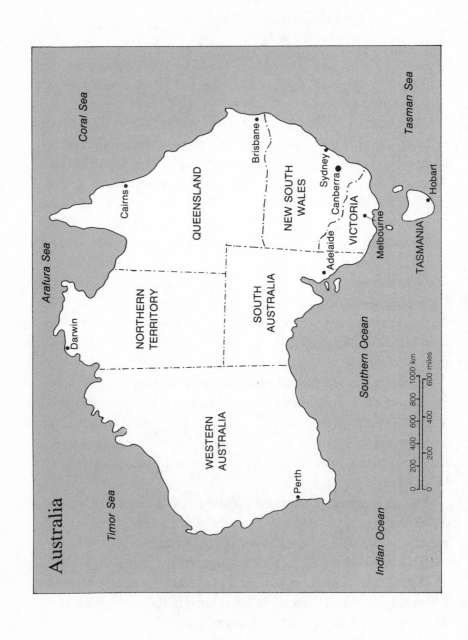

Australia

AUSTRALIA
Its Main Option is to Join Forces with Asia — Is it up to it?

Like their Asian predecessors, the great European explorers were not overly curious about the 'South Land'. The great kingdoms of India, China, and Southeast Asia offered more than enough gold and spices to keep European adventurers busy. On their maps, pilots drew an imaginary coastline and called it *Terra Australis Incognita*, or 'Unknown South Land'. Once in a while, there would be a rumour about it. The Spaniards speculated that King Solomon's gold mines might be located there. It was only after more than a century of European sea trade in Asia that the Dutch got around to exploring Australia's northern and western shores.

Discovery came in fits and starts when ships were blown off course. And when the Aborigines turned out to have nothing to trade but curved sticks and dingoes, the businesslike Dutch quickly forgot about colonising 'New Holland'. Another century passed before Captain James Cook went further south and was rewarded for his curiosity. Cook charted the continent's fertile east coast in 1770 and claimed New South Wales for the British Crown.

It was at about this time that Britain, having begun to industrialise, was running into all sorts of problems. As the cities swelled with countrified factory workers, pickpockets and petty thieves followed. The prisons and workhouses were filled to the point of inhumanity, even by eighteenth-century standards. The courts were reduced to housing convicts on old sailing ships moored in the Thames. The Crown needed to solve this prison problem; it also needed settlers to back up its claim to New South Wales. Few, besides adventurous, fortune-seeking second and third sons, would voluntarily ship out to a place so far away. To the eighteenth-century mind, Australia might as well have been the moon. But convicts might choose the gruelling three-month sea journey if a new chance was possible following the years of hard labour. It seemed the perfect solution. Thus was born Britain's convict colony in Australia.

In 1788, Captain Arthur Phillip landed a company of more than a thousand, including 717 convicts, 118 of them women, who set about building the village that would become Sydney. During the first years of the settlement, the spectre of starvation was never far away. Recalcitrant convicts were flogged almost to death. The officers, who were in the minority, could not afford to lose their grip on power. If there was a convict rebellion, a year might pass before any help came from home. Ironically, the officers mounted a rebellion of their own when the governor threatened their monopoly on the rum market. These were times of rum and ribaldry, escapes and executions. There were officer uprisings, convict revolts, even cases of cannibalism. Some historians claim that the convicts were more sinned against than sinning. Others point to the known depravity of the convicts and the widespread degradation which necessitated such a severe system to keep order. The truth probably lies somewhere in-between. But no historian can deny that early Australia was a brutal, tough place.

The British slowly enlarged their sphere of influence in Australia. Settlers started new towns along the temperate-zone coastline. The governor moved a maximum security convict settlement to the island of Tasmania, off Australia's southern coast. Then, in 1813, explorers crossed the Blue Mountains, west of Sydney, and discovered the vast pasture lands beyond. More and more settlers landed in Australia, using convict labour to establish sheep stations beyond the mountains.

Britain's industrialisation dovetailed further with Australia's development, as the woollen mills of Manchester and Birmingham drew increasing supplies from Australia's flocks. By 1821, 300,000 sheep grazed there; twelve years earlier, there had been only 26,000. Times were wild. The sheep runs had no fences and the sheep owners no title to the land where they grazed their stock and, at first, paid no rent. Squatters poached and raided. But the flocks continued to grow. Raw wool made fortunes for the second-generation shepherds, known as 'the squattocracy'. Society was sharply divided between the haves and have-nots. Smaller settlers and farmers began to oppose the use of convict labour, less for humanitarian than for economic reasons. Between 1840 and 1868, the export of Britain's convicts to Australia gradually came to an end.

In 1851, the cry of 'Gold!' blurred the class divisions. For ten years, prospectors flocked to the eastern diggings, doubling the population to more than 1.1 million by 1860. A new rush began in the 1890s when gold was discovered in the west. Many prospectors came in search of gold because they were disaffected in their home countries. When the gold ran out they entered business, mounting a successful challenge to Australia's privileged classes. Their labour made it possible to create manufacturing plants, and industry developed rapidly.

Like the United States a hundred years earlier, the various colonies in Australia began to have troubles with intra-colonial trade in the 1890s. The vast expanse of ocean isolating Australia was its first trade barrier. Goods took forever to arrive from Britain and cost a fortune to transport. As a result, a number of import-substitution industries had grown up since the 1850s in Sydney, Melbourne, and Hobart: coach-builders, candle-makers, foundries, breweries, textile mills, and the like. Towards the end of the nineteenth century an economic depression settled over the world. The activities of other nations in the Pacific began to alarm Australians. The need to stop the colonial bickering over trade, and to co-ordinate defence policy and external relations, transformed vague ideas about political federation into positive action. Although there were bouts of opposition, Australia adopted a federal constitution in 1901, and became a consolidated nation acknowledging allegiance to Britain. From this time, protectionist policies, in manufacturing, banking, transport, and a host of other areas, were enforced by statute.

New Zealand spurned the invitation of the Australian colonies to join them in establishing the Commonwealth of Australia. Diplomatic ties across the Tasman Sea developed slowly. Economic links that had bound the colonies together in the nineteenth century were severed as both Australia and New Zealand sought to protect their domestic producers from foreign competition. But the tie with Britain was not so easily severed, nor did Australasians want to break with the British completely. Britain continued to be the major trading partner and role model for both countries.

If ever there was a country chock full of the stuff that factories and trade surpluses are made of, Australia is it. But a good start from Mother Nature is not always enough to foster prosperity. Sound management has as much to do with success as anything else, and Australia's management of its economy has resulted in a deep malaise rather than booming industries.

The land Down Under is a geologist's dream. Australia has about one-quarter of the world's reserves of lead, zinc, silver, and cadmium. The Broken Hill lode has yielded approximately 168 million tonnes of lead, zinc, and silver ore, and it is estimated to contain some 30 million tonnes more. There's gold in the hills. More than 241.3 tonnes of gold had been recovered by 1990. There is iron ore to make into steel, copper for pipes, aluminium for machinery and airplanes, as well as nickel and zinc — enough to make the country self-sufficient in all these minerals and have plenty left to export. The list of other mineral deposits is seemingly endless: manganese for steel-making, tungsten for light bulbs, bismuth for medicinal drugs, and tantalum for incandescent filaments. Rich coal fields provide more than enough energy to power all these factories, and lie conveniently near the major cities and the coast.

In addition to its mineral treasures, Australia is rich in food. Although the Australian continent is the driest in the world, irrigation has made it possible to develop the land away from the coastal areas where there is relatively high rainfall. Periodic droughts still hamper agriculture, but despite this, Australia has become a world leader in producing dairy products, meat, and wool. The development of refrigeration made meat export practical and opened the way to markets for surplus sheep and cattle.

During World War I, shortages of imported goods from Britain and elsewhere spurred industrial expansion, which continued in the 1920s as Australia became self-sufficient in steel production and moved into other areas. But the real rush came after World War II, when major enterprises were launched. By the 1960s, it was producing home appliances, automobiles, farm implements, locomotives, and ships.

The government's vision was that Australia was simply a small country waiting to grow up. With some government prodding, the small economy would develop into a big economy. For a while, Australia could import the building-blocks of grown-up industries — parts for cars, steel plants, and airplanes — but as the economy grew, Australia would become self-sufficient, no longer needing to import manufactured goods. So the government protected what were considered promising infants, keeping mature foreign competitors out.

Despite the government's vision, Australia remained a relatively small country in economic terms. Its GDP in 1990 was US$296 billion, smaller than that of China and Japan, but bigger than India's. And yet, because the government had decided it was going to be a big country, Australia did few of the things that small economies do to survive. In order to compete in industries where the size of markets is important — such as steel and heavy machinery — small economies have to export. And without the resources to compete in all areas of industry, most small economies specialise. They might export a particular variety of machine tool and import another. Australia, however, did not trade much within industries. It eschewed specialisation, implying that it produced everything necessary for a particular industry. Yet at the beginning of the 1970s, while Australia was producing a mix of goods not very different from that of other small economies, exported goods accounted for only 15 per cent of the products made. High protective barriers covered the costs of this policy. Cars, for example, were protected by a tariff of 100 per cent on foreign imports; clothing and textiles by tariffs of 40 per cent. This guaranteed easy profits for the protected industries, which were redistributed to the workers in the form of high wages. In reality, these workers were being subsidised by the export income guaranteed by Australia's food and mineral exports.

With the important exception of steel, high wages kept Australian prices uncompetitive in the world market. Neither market conditions nor government policies encouraged Australian industry to be very competitive. Australia contented itself with manufacturing goods to sell at home. And, although the country is a world leader in mineral, meat, and agricultural research, Australian industry became notorious for investing relatively little in the research and development which might lead to new industries and new markets. As early as the mid-1960s, it became clear that import substitution alone would not prod the economy into adulthood. A decade later, the government abandoned 'made-to-measure' tariffs which kept targeted foreign goods out of the running in Australian markets. The tariff on foreign cars was reduced to 35 per cent (further reductions are planned in the future), while tariffs on clothing and textiles were planned to be reduced to 25 per cent. But by the 1980s, these highly protected industries accounted for a relatively small share of the Australian GDP. As a 1992 *Economist* survey puts it, the fundamental problem with the Australian manufacturing base is that it is too broad and too shallow; it needs to become narrower and deeper to compete in international markets.

Australians often take it for granted that they have not just a comparative, but an absolute, advantage in rural production. The data do not bear this out. Farm productivity has been growing less rapidly in Australia than elsewhere, and in the long term, as agricultural technology makes it cheaper to produce a kilo of flour elsewhere in the world, it will be difficult for Australian farmers to keep up. Agricultural protectionism in Japan, South Korea, and Taiwan, as well as in the United States and Europe, has made things even more difficult for the Aussie farmer.

Australia also failed to make effective use of that most important of natural resources, its people. Australians liked to think of themselves as a relatively well-educated nation, who therefore must have an edge in sophisticated activities. However, while Australia spent a relatively high share of its GDP on education, in the 1960s and 1970s, only approximately 50 per cent of students finished high school. Many left school with no certified skills and little hope of acquiring any. The fragmented system did not permit a lifetime approach to training and career development. Narrow, craft-oriented apprenticeships did not encourage the development of several skills, which would be more appropriate to today's sophisticated industries. As a result, Australia's service industries have lagged behind those of other countries. But the government has taken steps to combat this 'education gap' and these problems are being rectified. By giving grants to families whose children continue their schooling beyond the minimum school-leaving age, and by raising the age at which young people qualify for the dole, the proportion of children completing twelve years of schooling has doubled since 1981.

Until recently, each time the intrinsic problems in the economy grew large enough to force the government into action, a boom in the international minerals markets would bail it out and postpone reform. For most of the two centuries of European settlement, Australia has luxuriated in high returns from its mineral and agricultural resources. In the 1970s and early 1980s, Australians began to worry about what some called the 'Dutch disease' — when resource exports bring in so much money that industry, suddenly superfluous, starts to dismantle — but the problem turned out to be imaginary. However, both mining and rural 'terms of trade' (the prices of rurally-produced goods compared with the price of urban-produced goods) started to deteriorate as the 1980s drew to a close. In fact, new technologies were making the use of minerals more efficient and processing less costly. Mineral production itself has become more efficient. Australian companies have tried to respond by exporting commodities which have been at least partially processed. For instance, while exports of bauxite have remained more or less static, exports of alumina and refined aluminium ingots have grown rapidly. However, overmanning, low-productivity work rules, and slack management hamstring the mineral industry. Minerals can no longer dig the country out each time the going gets rough.

Australians have traditionally distrusted authority in the form of big business and big government, and have banded together in powerful unions since the country first started to industrialise. In 1911, 25 per cent of all employees were union members. Today, the figure is 60 per cent. Throughout the 1980s, these unions have been a thorn in the country's side. Strikes have hobbled the economy and continue to do so.

In 1989, a protracted pilots' strike brought the domestic airlines to a halt. The pilots, who earned an average of A$80,000 a year, demanded a 30 per cent pay increase. The government had to call out the air force, and enlist the help of foreign airlines, to break the strike. Part of the reason Canberra set such extraordinary precedents was that the strike threatened a six-year-old wages accord. The accord gave workers modest but evenly spread wage adjustments. Negotiators hoped this compromise would enhance the economy's competitiveness as well as get the large army of unemployed — 8–11 per cent of the workforce at any given time — off the dole. The accord did keep the industrial peace for several years, but the years of restraint have made workers, not just the pilots, restless for big wage hikes. The government has also had serious problems with the maritime unions. While the manning levels of ships have been reduced and are now close to international standards, other restrictive practices imposed on ships docking in Australian ports have made intra-coastal shipping prohibitively expensive. According to *The Economist*, in 1991 it cost five times as much to ship salt from northwestern Australia to Fremantle in Western Australia as it did to ship it to Japan.

Both mining and agriculture would benefit from a governmental attack on labour practices. If these problems continue, or if strikes again hit crucial industries such as the airline transportation system, Australia's image with overseas investors will remain tarnished.

It is not just the workers who give Australia a bad name with international investors; those at the top have also done their fair share. In 1985, takeover barons ran riot through Australia's stockmarket, and a generation of wheeler-dealers arose. By the end of the 1980s, many of these overnight successes were staggering under the burden of huge debts. Alan Bond, the most famous of these faltering barons, built an empire in just a few years of takeover deals. But between 1989 and 1991, his Bond Corporation struggled to sell off assets in order to meet interest payments. Finally, like many of his ilk, he was forced into bankruptcy. He was later charged over his role in the failed rescue bid for the Rothwell's banking group and subsequently spent time in gaol. Foreign investors and banks got severely burned by Bond, and by other enterprises like his.

From being the wealthiest country in the world at the turn of the last century, and the third wealthiest at the end of World War II, Australia had slipped to eighteenth at the start of the 1990s. Its share of world trade has halved since 1953, from 2.6 per cent to around 1.3 per cent. In 1986, Paul Keating, the then treasurer, warned the public that Australia's terms of trade had become so bad that the country risked becoming a banana republic. At a time when the economies of Japan, Korea, and Southeast Asia were taking off, Singapore's Lee Kuan Yew pointed out that Australians were fast becoming 'the poor white trash of Asia'.

The government took drastic steps. It reduced tariffs and let in a flood of foreign goods to shock domestic industry into action. It opened its financial sector and removed foreign exchange controls in order to attract foreign investment. The Australian dollar was allowed to float, which in turn caused it to devalue, thus making heavy industry more competitive.

The new policies concentrated on developing a competitive industrial structure, and took international markets into account when setting wages. It was widely agreed that manufacturing could not continue to grow unless Australia turned to foreign markets. As a large country, Australia had difficulty in accepting the reality of being a small economy, but in many respects it is closer to doing so than at any time in the past.

By 1987, Australia had emerged leaner, more efficient, and more competitive. Unfortunately, the success of the reforms has proved short-lived. Australian manufacturing has not had the spare capacity or the market orientation to replace imports or produce more exports. And although the economists planned to liberalise protected industries slowly, helping them out of their slump promises to be even more costly than protectionism. Except in the vigorous tourism sector, the much-needed investment upsurge has failed to materialise. In the late 1980s, Australian firms were hesitant to build new plants, and their potential customers at home were as hungry as ever for imported television sets and the like. Instead of balancing capital imports against capital exports, Australia piled up loans owed to foreign creditors.

Few economists still think that Australia's post-war dream of shifting its reliance from agriculture and resources will happen soon. Raw ore, wool, wheat, and other commodities still account for 80 per cent of the country's exports. Across the board, Australia in the 1990s remains one of the world's most protectionist industrial economies. Tariffs average 20 per cent, although the Labor government is committed to reducing these to 5 per cent by the year 2000. Industry is still relatively heavily regulated to little purpose, this involving costly armies of administrators under pressure to perform, which means regulating to the point of markedly reducing productivity. Clumsy government attempts to intervene in the market to support domestic industry have failed. Between 1988 and 1991, the Australian Wool Corporation, for example, bought up much of the wool clip in an attempt to maintain the price, only to be left with a largely illiquid or unsaleable stockpile. Australia's industrial relations record is among the worst of the industrialised countries. Its workforce is poorly trained. Much of the publicly-owned 'public goods' sector is inefficient. Some of the leading protected domestic suppliers plagued their captive customer base with poor-quality goods and lagging delivery times. Others are so tied to outdated technology that their costs are inordinately high. Both groups accuse Asian competitors of 'dumping' their goods in Australia. In doing so, Australian industry is biting the hand that could feed it.

Australasia has the most rapidly growing markets in the world on its doorstep. It is only now beginning to use them. In fact, Australia's exports to ASEAN countries grew in nominal terms by 400 per cent between 1980 and 1991. By 1992, in export market terms, the ASEAN market was larger than those of either the EC or the United States. Further, between 1987 and 1991, Australia's exports of high value-added manufactures to ASEAN countries grew faster than any such exports to any other major market. ASEAN is also an important export market for Australia's high value-added service exports, with educational services being a prime example.

Isolation and cultural bonds to Europe and North America have made Australians suspicious of the crowded, booming countries of Asia. At the same time, Asia has reason to be sceptical of Australia's commitment to the Asia Pacific region. Australia's ties to the West run deep. Although from the beginning it has been a nation of immigrants, Caucasians overwhelm the other races. When the gold rushes brought thousands of Chinese to the continent, alarmed Australians introduced the White Australia Policy, which banned settlers from Asia. Even at the end of the nineteenth century, native Australians still referred to Britain as 'home'. The 'bush' poet Henry Lawson, for example, wrote about 'going home' before he visited London in 1900. A prominent politician, visiting Britain for the first time, noted in his diary, 'At last we are in England. The journey to Mecca has ended.' Australian trade unions, universities, and corporations have modelled themselves on their British counterparts. Australian foreign policy has been contained within the imperial structure. In turn, Australia confronted and fought the German, Italian, and Japanese threats to British imperialism. When World War I began in far-off Europe, Australians reacted instinctively and contributed 329,000 volunteer servicemen from a total population of less than 5 million. The country sent a million of its 7.1 million people off to battle in World War II.

Soon after World War II, the Australian government decided to encourage immigration at the annual rate of 1 per cent of the population. Canberra, which had long helped British immigrants with the cost of moving, began to assist non-British settlers on a large scale. When Australia also started to accept refugees, the flow of immigrants became a flood. From 1946 to 1965, Australia took in more than 2.3 million permanent new arrivals, a greater rate of increase than ever before. More than thirty nationalities joined in the rush — Italians, Greeks, the Dutch. But no Asians. Australia's immigration policies virtually banned the entry of any Asian person for permanent settlement.

World War II, while reaffirming Australia's blood ties to Europe and North America, had also underscored how distant the West was, and how close the East. During the Pacific campaigns, the British Royal Navy could not defend Australia's shores alone, and the Japanese bombed Darwin, Wyndham, Broome, and other northern outposts. The fall of Singapore, and Japanese submarine threats to Sydney's harbour, shocked the nation into its first recognition of Asia's proximity. Many Australian servicemen were captured and kept in poor conditions by the Japanese, and the experience left them with bitter feelings. Yet, pragmatically, immediately after the war ended, one of the country's first two ambassadors was sent to Tokyo.

The second ambassador went to Washington. As Australians became painfully aware of their isolation from kindred European communities, Canberra gravitated to the United States, then the new Pacific power. Their concern grew more intense in the 1950s, when communist power was consolidated in China and communist influence expanded in some of the newly-independent countries of Southeast Asia. Australia followed Washington, not London, on policy towards mainland China, at first refusing recognition of any kind. It joined the ANZUS defence alliance with the United States and New Zealand, as well as SEATO, a now-defunct defence treaty between Australia, America, Britain, France, the Philippines, Thailand, and Pakistan. Australia and New Zealand joined in the Cold War chorus of anti-communist 'containment' rhetoric.

At the same time, perhaps to keep Asians in Asia, Australian government spokesmen emphasised the need to overcome the prevailing poverty, disease, and hunger in underdeveloped lands with rising populations.

Both Australia and New Zealand supported the Colombo Plan, designed to raise the standard of living in South and Southeast Asia.

In the 1960s, Australia began to look more seriously towards the north for potential trading partners. This process had already begun two decades earlier. Trade was the first step to developing a relationship with Asia. Direct investment follows trade and is followed in turn by immigration.

In 1966, the Australian government finally decided to relax its immigration laws. Asians now found it easier to obtain residence permits. And if they wanted to become Australian citizens, they no longer had to wait fifteen years but could do so in five years, like everyone else. Still, these new laws were aimed mostly at Asians with special skills. Policy-makers did not expect the new standards to increase non-European immigration much beyond the seven hundred non-Europeans permitted to enter annually in the mid-1960s. Big differences remained between the criteria for admitting non-Europeans, part-Europeans, and Europeans. Only in January 1973 did the government come up with a wholly non-discriminatory immigration policy.

By the late 1980s, this policy had radically changed the Australian immigration picture. In Asia today, the advice of the old and wise to the young and adventurous might well be, 'Go south'. In Hong Kong, Jakarta, and Manila, people live elbow to elbow in cramped apartments. They commute along crowded streets choked with traffic and exhaust fumes, to work at grinding jobs. Without connections, it is difficult for the talented but poor to advance. If they cannot rely on friends or family, the paths to success are often blocked. Down Under, it's different. Australia has space — dump India, Mexico, and France into it and you would still have lots of room left over for kangaroos. Yet only 17 million people — fewer than in Taiwan and about the same as in Sri Lanka — live in Australia.

Since 1980, between one-third and a half of Australia's immigrants have been from Asia Pacific. Asians alone could easily take up all the 140,000 or so places offered each year. In 1989, for example, more than 1,800 Philippine women married Australians. Their relations may follow them in the years to come. Only four Australian immigration officers were based in Hong Kong in the mid-1980s. By 1990, there were eleven. By the end of 1992, Southeast Asia provided almost 40 per cent of total emigration to Australia, and the immigrants are certainly assisting in the trade flows with the north.

These changes kicked up a storm of debate. In sharp contrast to twenty years earlier, however, the main argument was not over where immigrants should come from, but over what economic contribution they should make to their new home. The big question became not who to keep out, but how the numbers to be admitted could be increased. Australia argued over whether it should aim to assimilate the new arrivals in American melting-pot style, or whether the country should preserve the immigrants' diverse cultural heritages. Should it promote business migration or humanitarian immigration of refugees or family members? Faced with potentially explosive arguments on every side, the Labor government took refuge in a common political solution. It set up a committee to study the issues.

The Fitzgerald Report, released in June 1988, was brutally frank about the costs and benefits of immigration, and based its main proposals on the economic gains which immigrants could bring. The committee recommended that 150,000 migrants should be admitted in 1989/90. They should be chosen on the basis of their skills. Beyond those obvious benefits, the report claimed that a larger population would make transport and communications cheaper per head. Immigration would also delay, slightly and temporarily, the ageing of Australia's population. Environmental problems, the report said, would be easier to clean up if there were more people to pay for them.

The Fitzgerald Report lent weight to an existing trend towards trying to make Australia attractive to migrants who could pump up the economy. Business migrants must show they have attained a certain level of business acumen according to specific criteria, one of which is to demonstrate that they hold assets of not less than A$350,000 in one or more businesses. A 1985 survey of ninety migrants under the programme showed that eighty-six of them had set up businesses in Australia, or were in the process of doing so. According to the Immigration Department, migrants in the sample had spent US$67 million and generated 1,092 jobs. Asians have been particularly drawn to Western Australia, where the Asian-origin population accounts for 7 per cent of the total, twice the national average.

Australia's migration programme holds out a promise of business contacts, skills, and language acquisition that could overcome some short-term bottlenecks in doing business with Asia. Yet it has been impossible to debate the subject in broad national terms without running into the narrow self-interest of various ethnic communities representing past immigrations. The Fitzgerald Report incurred the wrath of the ethnic Italian and Greek communities, who thought it insultingly implied that their immigration hadn't helped the country. Parts of Anglo-Saxon Australia became gripped by the fear of a 'yellow peril'. In Western Australia, a small group of right-wingers put up posters opposing Asian immigration. In late 1989, commentators began questioning whether the country could sustain high immigration levels. Controversial Sydney radio commentator Ron Casey was sacked, but got remarkable support, for his claim that Australia risks being swamped by an 'alien culture'. In 1988, former Liberal Party leader John Howard suggested that Australia revert to partially racial criteria for the selection of migrants. Opinion polls at that time showed a disturbing degree of support.

The cost of these outbursts is high. Every time racial bigotry surfaces in debate, it makes headlines in Asia, reinforcing the widely-held view that the White Australia Policy is far from dead. Many Asian immigrants, faced with hostile attitudes, come to the conclusion that Australia is not the home they want. Often Asian newcomers never get beyond the racism to develop friendships with white Australians.

Cultural, intellectual, and youth exchanges between Asia and Australia can help stop the backlash. But in all the debate over Australian racism, it is often forgotten that the Australian people have already adjusted to a nearly tenfold increase in Asian population since World War II. More than 600,000 Asians now live in Australia, 3.5 per cent of the population. There are already scores of thousands of young Australian-born 'Asians'. Nearly all of them think like Australians, speak with broad Australian accents, play cricket or Australian Rules football, and are in many respects as assimilated into the Australian way of life as their counterparts from Greece, Italy, Poland, or Britain. By the year 2010, ethnic Asians are expected to make up 7 per cent of the Australian population. But by that time, the very terms 'Asian' and 'Australian' may have become far more blurred than anyone is yet prepared to recognise.

Located on the southern periphery of the Asian land mass, balancing Japan, Australia is ideally positioned for a thriving relationship with Asia. It would be easy to send not only mineral and agricultural products, but also services and processed raw materials, to the thriving cities to the north. In return, Australia could import most of its consumer goods and a substantial share of standard industrial needs from manufacturing centres in Hong Kong, Seoul, Tokyo, Bangkok, and other cities. Being so naturally dictated by geography and resources, the trade would be vigorous. It could supply the markets and the money necessary for Australian industry to specialise and enjoy economies of scale. Linked to the fastest-growing region in the world, Australians could earn one of the world's highest per capita incomes. Squeezed from east and west by the larger powers of Europe and North America, Asia and Australia could co-operate diplomatically and work steadily towards stability in the region.

Before World War II, Britain was Australia's single largest purchaser and supplier, providing 52 per cent of foreign investment; only 10 per cent of Australia's exports went to Asia. Since the war, Australia has rapidly expanded its food and raw material exports to Japan. By the 1960s, exports to Asia had trebled as Australia sent boatload after boatload of meat, minerals, and wool to Japan. Asia is now Australia's largest market by far. Japan alone buys more Australian goods than the EC and the United States combined, and Asia's demand for Australian crops, meat, and metals continues to grow. Much of Asia lacks enough agricultural land to feed its people, and rapid urbanisation and population growth are reducing the supply of farmland further. Asian diets are also changing — Asian people are eating more dairy products, meat, and wheat — which benefits Australian farmers.

In return, Japan has become a leading supplier of manufactured goods to Australia. The expansion of trade was managed by the Japanese and was backed by Japanese investment in Australia. As other East Asian countries began to increase their purchases of agricultural and mineral products from Australia, the trading pattern was repeated. In the short term, most economists believe the strength of the Australian economy depends directly on the dramatic increase in Japanese demand, which is firing up the rest of Asia.

The surplus economies of Asia, particularly Japan, and the newly-industrialising countries — Taiwan, South Korea, Hong Kong, and Singapore — provide much of Australia's foreign capital. Eight Japanese power and gas utilities have contracts to buy liquified natural gas from Australia. Up to May 1989, Japanese investors had bought more than US$6.1 billion in Australian real estate. But so far investment from Asia has been largely in tourism, a healthy sector of the economy. As incomes rise in the boom countries of Asia, the number of Asians who visit Australia increases. The Australian Tourist Commission has predicted that the total number of tourists will rise from under 2.5 million in 1991 to 6.5 million in 2000, and that by then, half of these tourists will be Asian. Major Japanese investors now own four of Perth's six major hotels, and a fifth is owned by Malaysian interests. Singaporeans and Malaysians have bought several hotels in the three-star range, as well as open land and housing. As Australia integrates into the competitive community of Asia Pacific, its economic advantages will lie not in manufacturing, but in its natural resources and its attraction as a tourist, and possibly a retirement, destination.

The United States and Europe continue to be valuable trading partners, but the American economy faces hard times. Australia has repeatedly run into American import barriers, as well as American dumping of agricultural products where Australia sells or aspires to sell. In early 1992, it was clear that President Bush's administration was determined to continue protecting America's internationally uncompetitive farmers. Exports to the United States of Australian beef, sugar, and dairy products are limited by quotas. The effects of EC protectionism on Australia are even more serious. Australian butter no longer makes it on to British supermarket shelves, and exports of Australian beef have declined from 120,000 tonnes a year to Britain to 5,000 tonnes a year to all the countries of the EC combined. So, in trade terms, Australia's problems are the same as in the rest of Asia Pacific.

Japanese academics were the first to suggest the idea of a Pacific free trade area in the 1960s. Australian prime minister Bob Hawke revived the idea on a visit to Seoul in 1989. Hawke suggested forming the Asian Pacific Economic Co-operation grouping (APEC), which would be a common platform from which the region could talk to the rest of the world. The group would help to ease trade in services, tourism, and direct foreign investment. It would protect regional interests in wider economic forums, but would stop short of being a trade bloc. Australian officials were quick to point out that a Pacific initiative would not diminish the importance of Australia's links to the West. Unfortunately, this initiative lost its purpose and the chance of developing any real credibility as the Hawke government bowed to almost immediate pressure from the United States for its inclusion. Canada closely followed suit. APEC became effectively a meaningless soapbox, as it encompassed countries on both sides of the Pacific which had fundamental conflicts of interest in terms of their future economic and political goals.

Both Asia and Australia would benefit from sharing in a loose grouping. While Australia would profit from contact with the vibrant economies of Asia, it is also true that in negotiating trade issues with the United States and Europe, Australia can exploit intangible advantages which no other country in Asia Pacific has. Because they have a shared language, culture, and past, Australians simply have less trouble developing rapport with American or European negotiators, sitting down over a drink and talking things out. Asia could profit by using Australia as one of its standard bearers.

This is as true in diplomacy as in trade. As its bond with the United States has weakened, Australia has tempered its attitudes towards communism and recognised the governments of the People's Republic of China, Vietnam, and North Korea. In the past, Asia has not exactly welcomed Australia's attempts to be a political player in the region. In 1984, ASEAN foreign ministers firmly rejected Australia's offer of Canberra as a venue for a meeting on the Cambodian problem. However, in the same year, Australia and China established direct air links, and a steady stream of visits by high-level leaders began.

The economies of Japan and Australia are both dependent on safe shipping lanes and free trade. Thus their defence interests coincide in many areas. Both must develop new policies as external superpower influence in the region wanes. From the beginning of the 1980s, limited military contacts have been instituted between Japanese and Australian forces. Australian-Japanese co-operation, within an enlarged framework led by the United States, could complement whatever level of American defence presence remains in Asia Pacific for the remainder of this century.

Many things still stand in the way of Australia's evolution as an East–West ombudsman. An evolving defence role could be distorted by the problems New Zealand has created within the ANZUS alliance. As a result of that government's strong anti-nuclear stance, the United States withdrew its military assurance to New Zealand in 1986. ANZUS has not died, but the Australia–United States tie was tested even before the ANZUS dispute. In April 1984, Australia's foreign minister pointed out quite bluntly that the Americans had never given Australia a guarantee that the United States would come to its aid in an emergency. And in 1985, Australia backed out of participation in the United States' MX missile-testing projects. Despite the Labor government's victory in the March 1993 general elections giving it a remarkable and record fifth term in office, it is under continuing pressure to ensure that its measures lead to an economic revival in the reasonably near term. Without such improvement, Australia will continue to be rent with internal debate and indecision as to where its future should lie.

Perhaps Australia has not always fared well in international economics and politics because it is essentially insular. While all governments can be sidetracked by domestic issues, this is doubly true in Australia. The rest of the world is so far away that domestic problems must always seem more urgent. When Australia's Aborigines clamour for land rights, when labour unions press for higher wages, when housewives demonstrate for disarmament, their calls must seem much louder than the complaints of Washington congressmen or London parliamentarians half a world away.

T he opportunities for Australia's future will come from beyond the vast tracts of ocean that isolate it; more and more they will come from the north. Already some have had grandiose visions of what such a relationship could bring. A supercity project, called the 'Multi Function Polis', first proposed by the Japanese in 1987, envisioned a metropolis of the future with a population of about 250,000 skilled workers drawn mainly from North America, Europe, Asia, Australia, and New Zealand. Consultants have estimated it would cost up to A$9.75 billion to build the international city near Adelaide, incorporating industries, research, education, training, and leisure for the twenty-first century. It was suggested that the project could open a new, creative era of Australian-Asian co-operation. When the plan was first proposed, it became a political football, exposing the dark side of Australia's relationship with Asia and becoming a touchstone for anti-Japanese sentiment. Opponents have claimed that Australia should debate more serious issues than a Buck Rogers future city. And near the end of the 1990 election campaign, opposition Liberal Party leader Andrew Peacock said he would drop the plan because it would create an exclusive enclave. Such a city, he said, would be socially divisive and could cause a backlash against foreign investment and immigration, much of which is from Asia. The project is still on, but no doubt it will drag on for a long time to come.

The Multi Function Polis will not make or break Australia's future. But similar proposals will. Australia can open itself up to joint ventures with Asia, or it can choose not to do so. It can open its markets and invigorate its industry in order to compete with Asia, or not. It can choose a clear course in international affairs, or not. It can benefit from both Asia and the West, or not. Perhaps Australia can continue to look inward for a few more years without serious consequences. Perhaps Australians will be content to drift alone, neither part of Asia Pacific nor of the West. But the best bet is that harsh reality will prevail. An Australia which is truly part of the vibrant community of Asia Pacific will be better equipped to compete in world markets.

And at last, it seems that at least part of Australia has come to its senses. The country is currently under political leadership which is determined that Australia be seen as a part of Asia Pacific. Prime Minister Paul Keating, who won, with a majority of more than ten seats, the March 1993 elections, has clearly committed his government to shaking off Australia's image as a Eurocentric economic backwater that is out of tune with the dynamic Asia Pacific region.

Instead, as Keating puts it, Australia is going to be Asia's 'odd man in'. Both Australia and the rest of Asia agree that Australia will never be fully Asian. It is culturally Western, and racially still mostly European in spite of increased Asian immigration. It will take more than one government to change the colour of Australia's skin. But what Australia should aspire to is to be a truly competitive country that is fully integrated into the economic and geopolitical life of the region in order to be a part of the economic success story that is synonymous with Asia Pacific.

What has forced Australia to focus northward? In no small part, it is the severe recession, almost a depression, that has gripped the country since the late 1980s — the worst since the 1930s and one which threatened in the March general elections to oust the Labor government from power after a decade in office. Keating himself has blamed the country's economic ills on years wasted in Anglophilia, torpor, and continuing psychological ties to Britain, all of which were debilitating to Australia's national culture, its economic future, and its logical destiny as a member of Asia Pacific. So, for example, when Australia issued, in 1992, a new A\$5 note bearing the visage of Queen Elizabeth II, Keating was quick to denounce it as a national embarrassment. It was time Australia made the break with Britain. Keating went as far as to suggest that the Union Jack be removed from the upper corner of the Australian flag.

In his first year of office, Prime Minister Keating made two visits to Asia. In Tokyo, he went to the extreme of taking Japan's side in its trade frictions with the United States. He further stated publicly that he shared Japan's suspicions regarding the new NAFTA agreement between the United States, Canada, and Mexico. Despite often vociferous outcries, Keating has been unashamedly pro-Japan. It has paid dividends. Keating used his visit to Tokyo to raise APEC's profile and, consequently, also that of Australia. The Japanese prime minister, Kichi Miyazawa, gave Keating 'full backing' for his plan to hold regular summit conferences among the fifteen member states of APEC on both sides of the Pacific. On the issue of defence, the Australians on the Tokyo visit even suggested that Australian and Japanese forces carry out joint exercises.

Unfortunately, however, APEC is a red herring — and the sooner the Australian government realises this the better. Keating and Australia would be much better off in pursuing a closer relationship with the ASEAN leaders, particularly those of Indonesia, Malaysia, Thailand, and Singapore, as well as China and India, in order to complement their relationship with Japan. Indeed, it is quite conceivable that, in the not-too-distant future, Australia could, and in my opinion should, apply for membership in ASEAN. This would give substance to the existing trade realities, as well as clearly nail Australia's future's flag to the Asia Pacific regional mast.

Keating's statements may have been somewhat exaggerated. But his government's earnestness in its quest to become more closely tied to Asia has not gone unnoticed by Australia's northern neighbours. Australia's position in Asia Pacific is becoming more obvious. The attitudes of the Asian countries have become decidedly warmer and friendlier. There have been more top-level visits by Australians to Asia than ever before. There is more common membership in regional organisations, which are most often vehicles for promoting trade liberalisation — a buzzword in Asia Pacific. The shift in Australia's trade over the past decade has been so marked that 61.5 per cent of its exports in 1991 were with Asia compared with 11.8 per cent with North America (down 5.4 per cent since 1990) and 14.1 per cent with the EC (down 8 per cent since 1990).

One of the remaining problems regarding Australia's national identity is its relationship with Great Britain and with Queen Elizabeth II as its 'head of state'. The issue has led to considerable domestic schizophrenia, as well as to confusion amongst its Asian neighbours as to what, exactly, Australia is. With the formation of the Republican Movement in Australia, there has been increasing public support for Australia to become a republic. The January 1993 Quadrant poll figures indicated that 65 per cent of the Australian population was in favour of an Australian republic, with an Australian president who would fulfil the functions of the current governor-general appointed by Great Britain. He would not have any of the executive functions held by the US and French -presidents. The Movement's target date for Australia to become a republic is the year 2001. If achieved, this restructuring of Australia's identity should give it a greater sense of self-confidence. And it should facilitate considerably the improvement of its relations with its Asian neighbours. It could also possibly make it easier for Asia to consider Australia as a free and independent member of the Asia Pacific region.

As Richard Braddock, head of economics at Sydney's Macquarie University, put it, 'We are Asianising. We are, in trade and investment, an Asian country, but only recently has this been accompanied by a gradual cultural realisation.' Admittedly, the Australian public is much less enthusiastic than its political leaders about even partially abandoning its white cultural roots, and adopting in their place more Asian ones. But times are changing. And where better to nurture new ideas than in the schools. The teaching of Asian languages, notably Japanese, but recently Mandarin as well, is spreading throughout the Australian education system. The state of Queensland even went so far as to formulate a policy stipulating that all schools offer an Asian language as an option. What is more important and encouraging is that this is being welcomed by students. In recent years, there has been a dramatic increase in student exchanges in both directions. This bodes well for the future, as it is these new generations which will create the people linkages that are so important in tying the region together. They will be able to do so, unburdened by the baggage of World War II memories and Cold War period attitudes. They will also be driven by new realities and new freedoms. Encouraging even more immigration from Asia, in the form of people wishing to flee its overcrowded and polluted cities, or to invest in Australia, should become a priority, particularly in the case of the young, professional middle classes. This will greatly assist in tying Australia firmly into Asia and the region's future.

All of these indications augur well for Australia's future. The Liberals under Hewson, leader of the main opposition party, want to make Australia Asia's 'odd man in' as an open, competitive economy. Yet Hewson is also keen to see Australia apply for NAFTA membership — at worst, this proposed initiative is nothing more than political opportunism of the crassest kind on the part of the opposition party, or of wanting to have its cake and eat it too. At best, such a move would be shortsighted in the extreme, carry unfortunate racial undertones, and leave Australia with little hope of being any more than a distant and irrelevant appendage to North America. Distractions of this kind can only dilute Keating's drive to focus the country on the issues essential for pursuing a firm budgetary course, for its evolution into a productive economy, and for giving its people a clear sense of Australia's role in the new world order. Keating has shown considerable vision and tenacity. With his new electoral mandate, he now needs a unified country behind him, so that he and the country can successfully capitalise on the pain and sacrifices of the last four years.

The argument that Australia should have some insurance in the event that Asia rejects it, has some substance. However, as Asia might see it, a largely white Australia might wish to remain allied to the West (with the United States replacing, or being additional to, Britain); if rejected, Asia would be its second option. The realities, including the trade flow figures, would argue that an association with Asia should be Australia's first choice. Just as the Japanese, who are nervously looking from one side to the other, have to make a choice and live with the consequences, so should Australia.

Australia would be much better off proposing membership in ASEAN's Asian Free Trade Association (AFTA). Conversely, by unreservedly joining Asia, Australia can take its place as a full partner providing needed natural resources, agricultural commodities, land, and a bridge to the West. Asia, in turn, can provide Australia with its discipline, dynamism, markets, and capital. As importantly, Asia can give Australia a sense of real focus and purpose, something it has lacked for many years.

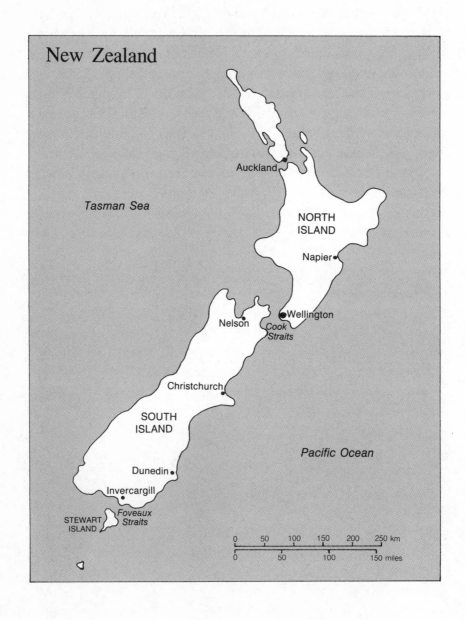

New Zealand

Tasman Sea

Auckland

NORTH
ISLAND

Napier

Wellington

Nelson

Cook
Straits

Christchurch

SOUTH
ISLAND

Pacific Ocean

Dunedin

Invercargill

STEWART
ISLAND

Foveaux
Straits

| 0 | 50 | 100 | 150 | 200 | 250 km |

| 0 | 50 | 100 | 150 miles |

NEW ZEALAND
Can it Afford the Luxury of Remaining European?

Some 2,000 kilometres southeast across the Tasman Sea from Australia lies one of the world's most beautiful countries. New Zealand is a land of lush, semitropical rain forest, cascading waterfalls, glaciers, and snow-capped peaks — the stuff of picture postcards. The country is made up of thousands of tiny islands and two main long, narrow islands divided by a thin strait — all being so far from the nearest large land mass that they have their own distinctive flora and fauna. It is a mountainous country, with only a quarter of the land lower than 200 metres above sea level.

No one knows when New Zealand was first populated. Radiocarbon dates for the earliest-known human occupation suggest that man only arrived in New Zealand in around the eleventh century, though it is thought that initial settlement probably occurred somewhat before then. In any case, no other relatively large geographical territory anywhere in the world remained undisturbed for millions of years, unnoticed and unappreciated by man.

Then great sailing canoes arrived from the islands of East Polynesia. The East Polynesians were island dwellers, canoe builders, navigators, fishermen, and crop growers. They were thought to have been driven out to seek new land because of too high a population, and the consequent tribal wars, at home. Additionally, these were people of what is termed the 'Lapita culture', a people who had it in their blood to move on and explore new, unpopulated oceanic areas in the tropical-temperate Pacific waters. The Lapita people were skilled long-distance nagivators and always lived close to launching points for ocean-going craft. The earliest canoes probably came from the Tahiti area, the Cook Islands, and the Marquesas. These East Polynesians were the first settlers in these new unpeopled islands, where they became the initial Maori population of New Zealand

The Maoris' own accounts of their arrival from the island they called 'Hawaiki', the last departure point of their ancestors, suggest that the first canoes landed in the East Cape–Bay of Plenty area of New Zealand's North Island. They were astounded by the coastline that seemed to go on forever and by the immensity of their new home after the small isles they had left behind. They named their discovery *Aotearoa,* or 'Long White Cloud', and *Tiritiri o te Moana,* 'Gift of the Sea'. Onshore, they found plenty of timber with which to repair and replace their canoes. It did not take the original Maoris long to circumnavigate and explore the entire coastline of New Zealand. They shared out the islands between the tribes, and began moving inland by the fifteenth century.

For a long time, the Maoris had the gift of the seas around New Zealand to themselves. They fished, grew crops inland, and developed a unique culture considered to be one of the most advanced in all Polynesia.

The arrival of the early Europeans in New Zealand was haphazard and brutal. A Dutch navigator first happened upon the islands in 1642. It was another 150 years, however, before a handful of British seamen and traders settled there. Their small, white communities were swelled with seamen who had deserted their ships, and with convicts who had escaped the penal colonies of Australia.

The sealers began arriving in 1792 and virtually denuded the South Island waters of what had been flourishing colonies of seals through their ruthless hunting. Whalers, too, added to the destruction. Between them, they also brought a multitude of land-based evils which caused Charles Darwin to describe them as 'the very refuse of society' after his 1835 visit. What with Australian convict escapees, runaway sailors, and a flourishing brothel industry, New Zealand became known as 'the hell-hole of the Pacific'.

Missionaries arrived in 1814 to save the people from their degeneracy and lawlessness. Generally, the native Maoris saw the solution as getting all the newcomers to go away, although there were many who wanted them to stay so as to provide a source of trade. They knew nothing of the settlers' pottery or metalworking, and most had no desire to know. The men of the Lord had barely the time to build their chapels before the Maoris, having obtained gunpowder and muskets, started fighting each other and the settlers. The islands were thrown into such turmoil that even the missionaries, who had opposed British annexation, pleaded with the Empire to restore order. The Union Jack was raised over the islands in 1840.

Waves of migration since then have transformed the country into the land of milk and honey. The earth is fertile. New Zealand is well-suited to agriculture, with 65 per cent of its land devoted to farming and dairy and sheep herding. There are no irrigation problems. The standing joke about the country is that there are more sheep than people: some 70 million sheep and 10 million cattle to its 3.45 million population. New Zealand is a world leader in the production of dairy products, meat (primarily lamb), and wool. One in every forty New Zealanders is a farmer. Tens of thousands more depend on agriculture for their livelihood.

But things turned sour with the post-war decline in prices for agricultural commodities, which make up 62 per cent of the country's exports — such decline being an almost direct result of the formation of the EEC. The country's cradle-to-grave welfarism also took its toll. The country went from having the world's third-highest standard of living forty years ago to being number 23 in 1991, overtaken by such countries as Hong Kong and Singapore.

Like its larger neighbour, Australia, to the northwest, New Zealand had also gone the protectionist route. It relied on a narrow export base of agricultural primary products to support an extensive welfare state. Industry remained small-scale, making goods to sell at home. The government managed industry. When its terms of trade (the ratio of export prices to import prices) fell by 30 per cent from the mid-1960s to the mid-1980s, the response was to subsidise the principal export industries. This only made matters worse.

When the Labour government of David Lange came to power in 1984, it took similar steps to those adopted in Australia, only more radical still. It desubsidised and deregulated. Public expenditure was severely cut back, largely by removing public purse support for the productive sector. The aim was to free the economy by reducing protection against imports and increasing competition and efficiency. It was a Labour government, rather than its predecessor conservative government, the National Party under Prime Minister Robert Muldoon, which introduced the radical reforms necessary to get the country back on its feet. It deregulated the financial markets, floated the currency, removed import licences, reduced tariffs and export incentives, commercialised many government trading departments, introduced a comprehensive value-added tax, and slashed personal and corporate tax rates. Initially, New Zealand business was jarred by contact with the rough world outside the heavily regulated and protected economy it had hitherto known. Manufacturing output contracted and farm income dropped sharply. When the right-wing National Party took over after a general election in October 1990, it pursued even tougher reform policies than its predecessors, dismantling parts of the welfare state and introducing sweeping labour reforms.

After a seemingly endless recession, New Zealand finally appears to be on the road to a full recovery, while at the same time providing an example to Australia and other protectionist parts of the world. After seven years of punishing free-market reform, inflation in 1992 stood at 0.8 per cent, the lowest in three decades and one of the lowest in the world. Yet only as recently as 1989 it was running at 12 per cent. New Zealand business by the end of 1991 had labour cost advantages over Australia of up to 50 per cent in some sectors. This encouraged New Zealand exports to Australia and further afield. It has also encouraged foreign companies to consider New Zealand as a business base for the southwest Pacific and, to some extent, as an English-speaking base for exports to Southeast Asia.

Unlike its Australian neighbour, which in 1992 began to project itself as Asia's 'odd man in', many New Zealanders cling fondly to their British ties. The fashion of late among New Zealanders of European descent is to rediscover their roots.

New Zealand has been ethnically and culturally connected to Polynesia for around a thousand years. Less than two hundred years ago, its population and cultural heritage were completely Polynesian. But now cultural traditions that are mainly European, and particularly British European, have taken over. Four-fifths of New Zealanders are now of European stock. The white Kiwi, or *pakeha* as he is known to the Maoris, originated mostly from Britain, with a smaller number coming from the Netherlands, Yugoslavia, and Germany.

The indigenous Maori, who account for only 12.4 per cent of the population, are the next largest group. After 150 years of British colonisation, they are the worst-off group in the country. Proportionately more of them are poorly educated, unemployed, and in gaol. For the period from the 1840 Treaty of Waitangi until 1912, the Maoris lost as much as 95 per cent of their land through systematic violation of their rights (as stated in the *Far Eastern Economic Review* of 28 October 1992). The ruling National Party in 1975 established a Waitangi Tribunal, which was reinforced in 1985. The tribunal has been charged with the painstaking task of working through thousands of land claims, as it is determined once and for all to resolve all the land grievances of the Maori tribes by the end of the century. A lasting racial accommodation is critical to the country's social stability. Immigrant Polynesians from the South Pacific islands make up another 3.5 per cent, the third-largest group of the population. Asians account for only 1 per cent of the population.

New Zealand is like a slice of Europe cast adrift in the southwestern reaches of the Pacific Ocean — closer geographically to Asia than Europe, but spiritually Westernised. Its trade unions, universities, and corporations are modelled on those of Britain. New Zealanders, like their Australian cousins, made a major contribution proportionately to the British war effort during World War II, suffering over 39,000 casualties in the process.

The country's native animals and vegetation are symbolic of its isolation. A vast proportion of the native fauna and flora are to be found only in New Zealand. The country has had to bring in other species of plants and animals. These animal immigrants have thrived at the expense of the native species, which are fast becoming few and far between. However, through rigorous quarantine and import restrictions, New Zealand has kept out many specimens of wildlife which plague the rest of the world — there are, for example, no snakes to be seen anywhere, not even in the zoos.

In terms of people, Britain has been the source of most of New Zealand's migrants. From 1947 to 1974, thousands made their way to New Zealand under the assisted/free passage scheme to attract industrial and agricultural workers. And the country wants to keep it that way. Britons are targeted again in a new migration policy introduced in early 1992 which aims to generate a net immigration of around 20,000 a year. This is to compensate for a yearly net emigration of around 16,000, as people fled the recession of the 1980s. Other Europeans are also encouraged, including those from poor former Eastern bloc countries.

However, Asians from Hong Kong, Malaysia, and particularly from Taiwan, have found a way into the country through the government's various immigration schemes for entrepreneurs, which schemes they dominate. In came those with business experience but, more importantly, with at least NZ$250,000 to invest in job-creating businesses. Some 14,570 migrants — including 5,586 from Taiwan, 4,699 from Hong Kong, and 1,688 from Malaysia — had obtained New Zealand citizenship under that scheme by the end of 1990. Unfortunately, many Asians abused the scheme. Little track was kept of whether they did, in fact, invest in the country. Many put in the minimum of time and money necessary to obtain an official residence permit and then returned home. Stricter guidelines are being imposed on future 'entrepreneur scheme' migrants. In order to obtain an entry visa, they will need at least NZ$500,000 to invest and enough to buy a house. Furthermore, they will not be granted residency until that money is invested in acceptable projects such as joint ventures, industry, exports, or tourism.

The reorientation towards European immigration was in part a result of rising Asian immigration, which tripled as a percentage of the total during the 1980s to near-European levels. New Zealand is afraid of Asian enclaves taking shape. These fears seem absurdly exaggerated. There has been only a tiny Asian community since the first Chinese established themselves during the gold rushes of the 1860s. Together with the more recent Chinese and Indian migration, Asians make up just 1 per cent of the population. Prime Minister Jim Bolger has said, though, that encouraging Europeans to migrate to New Zealand did not reflect a desire for a 'white New Zealand', and that the general immigration policy would be even-handed between Asian and other sources.

Old friendships with the West are slowly crumbling. New Zealand's ban on nuclear-armed or powered ships caused a rift with the United States, which neither denies nor confirms whether its naval ships carry nuclear weapons. Effectively, all US naval ships are barred from entering New Zealand waters.

This stipulation led in 1986 to the United States removing New Zealand from the forty-year-old ANZUS (Australia, New Zealand, and

United States) defence pact and put an end to intelligence exchanges and military exercises with the United States. The New Zealand government is now in the sticky situation of trying to ingratiate itself back into the ANZUS alliance, while at the same time remaining true to its non-nuclear stance, which is much favoured by the public. The 1991 American decision to remove tactical nuclear weapons from its naval ships has alleviated the stalemate between the two countries, but the problem has yet to be fully resolved.

It is also dawning on New Zealand that its links with the United Kingdom are fast fading. The death-knell was first rung when Britain, then New Zealand's biggest market, entered the EEC in 1972. Though Britain negotiated special quotas for New Zealand butter and lamb, New Zealand's access to the EC is now restricted. Britain's status as New Zealand's largest importer has fallen rapidly since 1980. That year, Britain was New Zealand's number one market, buying 14 per cent of its exports. This share dwindled steadily over the years to become a mere 6 per cent in 1991.

Potential for trade expansion in the United States is also limited, since the United States imposes a number of restraints on New Zealand's agricultural exports. Legislation sets an annual limit on beef and veal imports, allowing more to be imported when US domestic production is low and vice versa. For other agricultural products, after two years of unrestricted access, voluntary restraints were imposed from the last few months of 1991. The quota controls were applied to dairy products, especially butter, cheese, and milk powder.

Why should the United States and the EC, who themselves are already saturated with dairy and meat products, want yet more of the same from New Zealand? The fact that it would be probably much cheaper is irrelevant — their respective powerful farm lobbies would ignore such practicalities. New Zealand's leaders are currently engaged in GATT negotiations to remove or minimise subsidies and other forms of restrictions on international agricultural trade. Much of the EC production is sold on world markets at only half, or even one-third, of its production costs. New Zealand farmers with no subsidies or government assistance receive only a quarter of the price paid to EC farmers for their milk, for example. New Zealand's dairy industry has said that the EC's politically managed agricultural system is worse than the rigidly controlled agricultural systems of the former Soviet Union and eastern Europe. If the November 1992 GATT preliminary agreement fails to hold up, New Zealand's government has stated publicly that it will consider applying for membership in NAFTA, as it seems, erroneously, to believe this will guarantee a market share there for New Zealand's agricultural exports. In fact, New Zealand would be competing head to head with probably the United States' strongest lobby, its farm lobby, which faces little competition for New Zealand-type products from either Canada or Mexico and which would put up strong resistance to such new competition from New Zealand.

If it was more realistic, it should see that trying to sell meat and milk to the United States and the EC is like selling tea to Sri Lanka. New Zealand should instead regard itself as the South Pacific farm of Asia. Like Australia, New Zealand is well placed to participate in the economic dynamism of Asia Pacific. Already, just by looking a little to the north, New Zealand has found new markets. China is fast emerging as a major customer for New Zealand wool. It was the single largest buyer of New Zealand wool, importing NZ$422 million worth, during the period 1988–1989. New Zealand has taken part in livestock and pasture development projects in China, and several joint ventures have taken place in light industry. Chinese and Taiwanese corporations have also invested in forestry and property in New Zealand.

Although meat and dairy products do not form the traditional fare of Asians, the more affluent, younger generation have developed more Westernised palates. The opening of the Japanese beef market, currently under way, is expected to expand the world's red meat trade by 500,000 tonnes. At the same time, demand from South Korea and the rest of Asia is also picking up.

New Zealand's trade with Asia is steadily expanding. For the year ending June 1992, Asia, including China, Taiwan, and Japan, accounted for 34.8 per cent of New Zealand's total exports, as against 16.6 per cent for the EC and 12.8 per cent for the United States. Japan alone bought 15.3 per cent of New Zealand's exports, and is poised to overtake the EC as New Zealand's second-largest export market after Australia. South Korea will likely soon surpass Britain as the country's fourth-largest single-country trading partner. While the Americans and the Europeans are buying less from New Zealand, trade with Asia is booming. Dairy products account for over half of total exports to the ASEAN countries of Indonesia, Malaysia, the Philippines, Singapore, Thailand, and Brunei. Malaysia is New Zealand's largest export market for milk products. In the year ending June 1991, sales to Taiwan, New Zealand's sixth-largest export market, were up by 46 per cent, South Korea by 40 per cent, China by 85 per cent, Hong Kong by 42 per cent, and India by 41 per cent. Sri Lanka is also an important market for its milk products. These economic realities should be recognised politically!

New Zealand's foreign policy makers acknowledge that the relationship with Japan is the country's most important. Their economies are complementary, and each has in abundance products that the other needs. New Zealand provides a good share of Japan's imports of beef and dairy products. And Japan is a major supplier of cars, machinery, communications, and electrical equipment to New Zealand. The two countries are working towards a closer trade and economic relationship. Regular consultations are held between the two governments at ministerial and other levels. Close contacts are also maintained between the business communities of both countries.

Ties with Australia are better than they have been since 1900, when New Zealand spurned the invitation of the Australian colonies to join the Federation of States, when the Commonwealth of Australia was established. Diplomatic ties across the Tasman Sea developed slowly. And economic links which brought the colonies together in the nineteenth century were severed as both Australia and New Zealand sought to protect their domestic producers from foreign competitors.

Today, the two countries have a special relationship. There is no better indication of this than the 1982 Closer Economic Relationship (CER) agreement. There are no barriers or border restrictions on trade or goods between the two countries. Under the CER agreement, trade has blossomed between Australia and New Zealand, with New Zealand turning out to be the principal gainer. Under the agreement, goods move as freely as the people of each country can move to the other. The next stage of the CER agreement is to make other things compatible, such as taxation, commercial law, and the investment environment — similar to the EC but without the bureaucracy. The New Zealand National Party government sees the CER as a model for agreements with other Asian countries.

Since 1983, total trans-Tasman trade has grown from NZ$2.5 billion to NZ$6 billion. Australia is New Zealand's largest export market, taking 20 per cent of its exports, while New Zealand is Australia's fourth-largest trading partner. New Zealand buys 20 per cent of its imports from Australia. Two-way investment has also increased dramatically, particularly in Australian investment in New Zealand because of its deregulated financial market.

However, although Prime Minister Bolger has said, 'The biggest trading interest, and therefore foreign policy interest, we have is Asia', the country finds it hard to open itself up to Asia. When it comes to investment, for example, there is strong opposition, both from within the government and from the public, to the small but growing levels of Japanese and Taiwanese investment, particularly in housing and tourism. Tales of Japanese investors setting up Japanese-supplied and Japanese-staffed enclaves in Australia have alarmed many New Zealanders. Concerning New Zealand's farmland, Bolger said in November 1990, 'I do not believe New Zealanders want to sell, and I do not want to sell, farmland in great chunks to overseas owners of any description.' He added that any such sales would have to be productive for New Zealanders, as well as for the foreign owners.

New Zealand's days as the land of milk and honey could return. But its desire to remain predominantly white can only complicate matters in a country that is only just coming out of a major recession. New Zealand is as uncomfortable with its Asian migrants as it is with its location on the fringe of economically affluent Asia. At the same time, it is going through an identity crisis of sorts. It appears to hanker after closer ties with the United States and Britain, but this is becoming increasingly difficult to sustain, and Australia, as a substitute, provides cold comfort. On the other hand, the more realistic New Zealanders are anxious to be a part of any sort of Asian grouping.

In the harsh reality of the 1990s' new geopolitical and primarily trade-driven equation, New Zealand has little choice. Its distant geographical location and tiny population make it largely irrelevant — particularly if it is too demanding in its requirements. North America and Europe have no need for its products, and their exports to New Zealand are expensive, partly because of the distance. On the other hand, New Zealand has excellent political and economic relationships with Australia, and it is already beginning to find substitute markets in Asia for its export products. Likewise, Asia should be able to provide it with manufactured goods at a competitive price. New Zealand — and, for that matter, Australia — should also take note of the fact that a number of commentators have proclaimed that, by the middle to the end of the twenty-first century, the distinction between white and yellow races in Australia, and possibly New Zealand, will be largely academic, because of increasing racial miscegenation. Increasing global tribalism makes this prediction questionable — however, the youth of the future could easily prove these commentators right. What must also not be forgotten is that the youth of today do not bear the prejudices of the pre-World War II generation; they are much more tolerant, and are looking for an opportunity, any opportunity, to survive in this increasingly complex world. Therefore, the question of whether one works in Tokyo or Singapore, or is married to a Thai or Chinese, could become of increasingly less consequence to the young New Zealander and Australian.

Why delay the inevitable; why create racial tensions instead of a partnership? Despite its remarkable economic reforms and the extraordinary competitiveness of its agro-products, New Zealand risks becoming an economic and political dead-end, unless it makes a major adjustment and creates a *raison d'être* for one of the evolving trade regions of the world to invite its participation. After all, it astonished the world with its recent reforms and its new competitiveness on the world's trading stage — why not do so again by actively developing a role for itself in its home territory, the Asia Pacific region, and stop wasting time chasing NAFTA chimeras. Asia Pacific, too, should recognise the benefits of New Zealand's involvement in the region and actively encourage and support it.

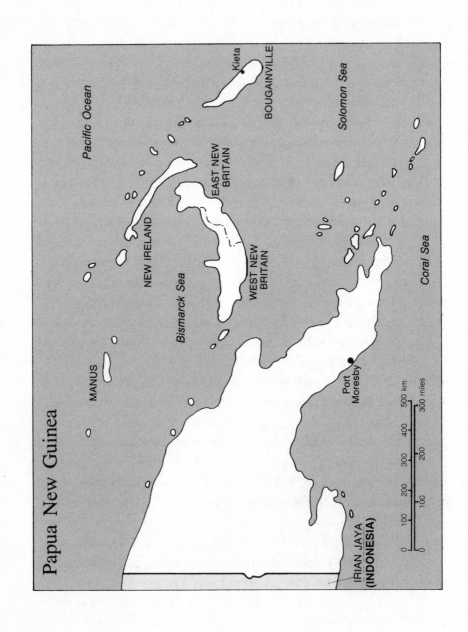

Papua New Guinea

PAPUA NEW GUINEA
A Leap from the Stone Age into the Twentieth Century

Between Southeast Asia and Australia lies the little-known country of Papua New Guinea (often called PNG). Until the 1930s, most of its people were still living in the Stone Age. Cults and sorcery flourish even today, and tribal warfare with bows and arrows remains common. However, the country is rich in minerals, with some of the world's biggest copper and gold mines, as well as having extensive oil resources.

PNG is one of the world's most sparsely populated countries, with the highest density of languages. Its land area exceeds that of Japan, yet its population of just 3.9 million is around 3 per cent of Japan's. The tribes of PNG speak over 700 distinct languages, almost half the world's known languages.

It is a mountainous country, with peaks reaching 4,000 metres. About 80 per cent of the island is covered in dense, tropical rain forest, one of the largest areas of primary jungle left in the world. This is one of the last of the world's largely unknown countries, though it lies barely 160 kilometres north of Australia. It consists mainly of the eastern half of the big island of New Guinea, and a few smaller islands to the northeast. The western half is the Indonesian province of Irian Jaya.

Nearly all the people are Melanesians who settled in the New Guinea islands some 50,000 years ago. They lived in small warring tribes and clans in the valleys, in the mountains, on the coastal plains, and on the scattered offshore islands. They knew nothing of metal tools or the wheel. The Europeans discovered the islands in the 1800s and explored them with great difficulty, as much of the coastline was, and still is, barely accessible. The Dutch claimed the western half of the island — now Irian Jaya — as part of Indonesia. The eastern half was shared by the British, in the south, and the Germans, in the north. The island's high mountain ranges, all covered with dense forests, made it virtually impossible for the early European colonists to penetrate the interior, and both the British and the Germans viewed their stakes in New Guinea largely as strategic ones. The tribes of the island were thus left largely untouched by the European settlers. Late in 1906, British New Guinea was renamed Papua New Guinea and handed over to Australia to administer. In 1920, the League of Nations handed German New Guinea to Australia as a mandated territory and it was added to the old British New Guinea. With air transport becoming available, along with Australia's experience and interest in prospecting the country for mineral resources, the exploration of PNG became somewhat less formidable. The discovery of minerals fuelled further exploration, with the result that some of the largest gold and copper mines in the world have been developed. As recently as thirty years ago, an expedition team was prospecting in an area near Mount Fubilan about 20 kilometres from the border with Irian Jaya, which area was still marked 'unexplored' on their maps. The mountains and dense jungle make clearing the area a nightmare, even with modern bulldozers and light planes.

Since its independence on 16 September 1975, the island has established a Westminster-style parliament, but with a distinctive PNG flavour. Political parties are based on personality and tribal ties, not ideology; and prime ministers can be challenged at any time after their first six months in office. These factors have led to six changes of PNG's leadership since 1975. The personalities that dominate the political merry-go-round are PNG's founding father, Michael Somare, now Sir Michael, and Rabbie Namaliu, both of the Pangu Party, and Paias Wingti of the People's Democratic Movement Party, which party currently leads the ruling coalition government, having taken over from Namaliu at the general election in June 1992. Throughout PNG's independent political history, all three men have at various times led the country or held other office.

PNG is an unusual island — rich in some ways, but primitive in others. The capital, Port Moresby, is not linked by road to any of the country's other major towns. Most of the country can only be reached by plane or boat. About 80 per cent of the people live in villages, with nearly half of these located in the mist-shrouded central highlands and mountains. The people speak a pidgin English called Tokpisin and are poorly educated, with only 30 per cent of adults being literate. There is also a shortage of skilled labour, yet wages are high because of the legacy of the country's Australian mentors' centralised wage-fixing system.

Papua New Guinea has been described in *The Economist* as a 'colonial cocktail', with an Italian political system, an African infrastructure, a German monetary policy, and an Australian labour market. The local currency, the kina, has been steady following a 10 per cent devaluation in January 1990. The budget deficit has been cut from 6 per cent of GDP in 1980 to 1 per cent in 1988.

The island is blessed with natural resources. The surrounding seas teem with fish; its soil is fertile and rich in minerals. Its major agricultural products are coffee, cocoa, copra, copra oil, palm oil, rubber, and timber. Gold and copper are the country's main exports, accounting for more than two-thirds of the total. Its two copper mines are among the world's biggest. The new Porgera gold mine exceeded expectations to produce 1.2 million ounces in 1991, its first full calendar year of operation, making it the largest gold mine outside South Africa and one of the top three in the world. Another mine in the pipeline, when fully operational, will be the world's largest gold mine. There was a record production of 1.95 million ounces, or 60.78 tonnes, of gold in 1991, making PNG the world's sixth leading gold producer. Gold output reached approximately 100 tonnes in 1992. More recently, oil has been discovered. In 1992, the US$1 billion Kutubu oilfield's output contributed US$2 billion to total exports, and is expected to contribute, at worst, some US$2.4 billion in 1993. Together, mining and petroleum account for 80 per cent of PNG's total exports.

But unrest has been brewing on the small island of Bougainville since PNG was made independent. Bougainville, which is culturally and racially different from the rest of PNG, asked for, but failed to get, its independence. The self-styled Bougainville Revolutionary Army was formed in 1976. Aggressions escalated in the 1980s, and in 1989 the Bougainville copper mine, the world's largest, had to be shut down — the amazed engineers had the startling experience of being shot at by Stone-Age tribesmen armed with bows and arrows, as well as shotguns! The mine's closure deprived PNG of 45 per cent of its export earnings and 17 per cent of its government revenues that year. The PNG government has since then maintained a blockade of the island, which is now under the internal control of the Bougainville Revolutionary Army.

Since its independence, the island's leaders have sought membership in ASEAN, but their request has been turned down. PNG's Melanesian people see themselves as part of the Pacific, rather than of Asia, and Asians feel little affinity with them. However, the country has been invited to sit on three ASEAN committees — on food and agriculture, human resources development, and science and technology.

The island was also excluded from the Australian-initiated APEC, due in part to Australian oversight. But fences may be mended soon, as PNG is expected to join APEC in 1993. Australia is, after all, PNG's oldest friend and its biggest aid donor. Under the Papua New Guinea–Australia Trade and Commercial Relations Agreement, first introduced in 1977 and renewed regularly, PNG has duty-free and concessional access to the Australian market and is offered assistance in quality control, market research, and small business development.

It is with its geographically closest neighbour, Indonesia, that relations have been difficult. The problem is that PNG is on the receiving end of a pressure cooker. Overpopulated Java has pushed its people to settle in Irian Jaya, and the local inhabitants do not like the new Javanese settlers — the Irianese are Melanesians like the people of PNG. Indonesia has great difficulty policing the 800-kilometre border between Irian Jaya and PNG. Skirmishes are frequent between Indonesian soldiers and a small guerrilla group fighting for an independent Irian Jaya. This has led to frequent Indonesian military incursions across the border into PNG. Rebels have also fled into PNG seeking refuge. While PNG had previously viewed Indonesia as a dangerous neighbour with territorial ambitions towards PNG, in the mid-1980s both sides realised the need for better bilateral ties, and in 1986 they signed a friendship treaty. Then, in early 1992, former prime minister Namaliu signed the Status of Forces Agreement (SOFA) on his visit to Indonesia. The Agreement provides for expanded co-operation in defence activities, including joint military training, exchanges of personnel, and civic missions.

PNG has also won over China as an investor. The South Pacific Games, which PNG hosted in 1991, was almost entirely China's project. China signed an investment promotion and protection agreement, and provided a US$15 million interest-free loan, plus the design and much of the labour to erect the purpose-built stadium in Port Moresby.

Improving ties within the region can only be of benefit to PNG. A country which has gone from the Stone Age to the twentieth century in only two generations and which has such a wealth of resources has the potential to become a useful participant of the Asia Pacific region. However, given its constantly changing, and very tribal, system of government, and given the other requirements of the advanced countries of the Asia Pacific region in creating a regional forum, it is unlikely that PNG will participate in the first few stages of development of such a regional forum.

KOREA

The North–South Equation — with a Possible
Nuclear Twist

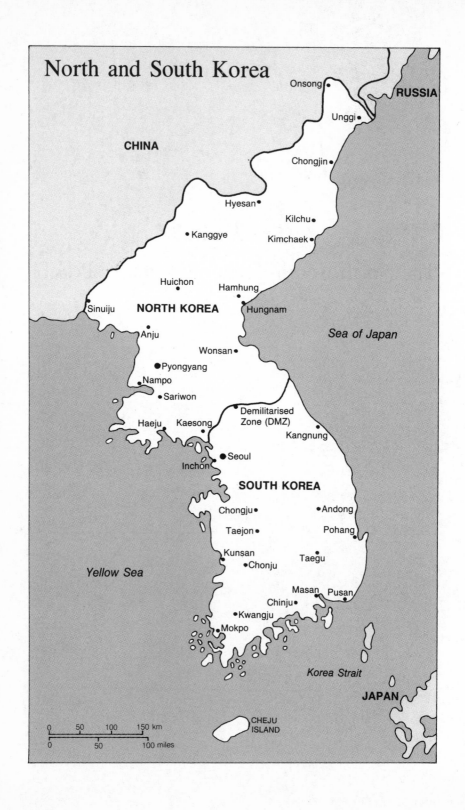

North and South Korea

RUSSIA

CHINA

- Onsong
- Unggi
- Chongjin
- Hyesan
- Kilchu
- Kimchaek
- Kanggye
- Huichon
- Hamhung
- Hungnam

Sinuiju

NORTH KOREA

- Anju
- Wonsan
- Pyongyang
- Nampo
- Sariwon

Sea of Japan

Haeju Kaesong

Demilitarised
Zone (DMZ)

- Kangnung

Inchon ● Seoul

SOUTH KOREA

- Chongju
- Andong
- Taejon
- Pohang
- Kunsan
- Taegu
- Chonju
- Masan Pusan
- Chinju
- Kwangju
- Mokpo

Yellow Sea

Korea Strait

JAPAN

| 0 | 50 | 100 | 150 km |
| 0 | | 50 | 100 miles |

CHEJU
ISLAND

KOREA

The North–South Equation — with a Possible Nuclear Twist

Dawn had barely broken in Manila, and in the Westin Plaza's coffee shop the waitresses had just begun serving the first customers of the morning. One customer, at least, was not pleased. Not at all. He was a senior South Korean bank executive who, despite his rank, had come to check on the breakfast arrangements his chairman was to have with a European banker. When he saw the coffee shop, he shouted at the European. The coffee shop, he yelled, was not appropriate. Not at all. He and his chairman were important people with important business to discuss. Only with great difficulty did the European convince the Koreans to continue with breakfast. He would be forced to pay for his gaffe in coming weeks as his Korean opposite number made negotiations difficult. However, in the end, they became close friends. In future, the European would always be careful about showing proper respect to any Koreans he dealt with. That European was myself.

Of course, although his reaction was not necessarily typical of all Koreans, the important banker from Seoul had good reason to expect better treatment. He and his country, focused for so many years on survival through personal sacrifice of all kinds, have finally found success. They also need respect because, historically, they have never had it. Their reactions are intense because they have suffered centuries of abuse.

The breakfast disaster was also a good measure of the Korean temperament. When negotiating with Koreans, it is best to forget the popular images of the polite businessman, the demure courtesan. Forget the bowing and the polite smiles. Forget most of the Asian stereotypes. The bitter past has made Koreans into different stuff. Of course, Koreans can be as polite as anyone. Refined, delicate courtesans do exist in Seoul's *kisaeng* houses, the Korean equivalent of the Japanese *geisha* houses. But they, too, can be very direct. If Koreans don't like something, they may become angry. A business meeting may be punctuated by bowing and smiling, but if your potential partner disagrees with you, don't expect him to keep quiet about it. If a customer thinks the price is too high, pounding of fists on tables may follow. While their neighbours the Japanese seldom, if ever, raise their voices in anger, Koreans don't hesitate to yell, board-room or no.

Behind the anger lies melancholy. There is an abiding sadness in Korea and an individual internal acknowledgement of their *han*. This is a uniquely Korean concept, and a crude translation would be that their *han* must be to grit their teeth and finally overcome the disadvantages of their race's history of constant subjugation and deprivation in order to succeed in the future. *Han* is a result of the Koreans' accumulated yet involuntary patience and obedience to a stronger power or authority, as embodied by a weak nation *vis-à-vis* a stronger one during Korea's long history. *Han* is more or less related to perseverance and defensiveness. You can hear their *han* in their music and find it in their literature of separation, deprivation, and loss. The Korean language does not allow Korean birds to sing; they cry. The most popular beauty spots in Korea are those associated with tragedy, such as the Rock of Falling Flowers where court beauties threw themselves to their deaths rather than be dishonoured by invading Chinese. What draws Koreans to such music, such stories, such places? Perhaps it is their *han*: their regret, or even their anger, defensive-ness, or frustration at never being complete — perhaps all of these. Or it may simply be centuries of bad luck.

There is another unique and rather paradoxical characteristic of Koreans: they wish to avoid conflicts and to have harmonious relation-ships. They seem to want to forgive and be forgiven — the term they use is '*kibun*'. It is no doubt due to this attitude that they feel so strongly about receiving an unequivocal apology from Japan regarding Japan's historical behaviour towards Korea, before they can really begin the process of building a long-term relationship with Japan. It is possibly due in part to this attitude that a surprisingly high percentage of South Koreans, around 40 per cent and rising, are Christians. They appear to need to go to church each week in order both to be forgiven for their sins and to live in a harmonious relationship with God. Many other factors have also influ-enced the propagation of Christianity in Korea: traditional worship-oriented Shamanism; the process of Korea's modernisation after the Korean War being linked to the advent of Christianity in Korea; the initial, almost faddish interest in Christianity which made its believers feel superior to the followers of Buddhism and Shamanism; and the atavistic need to believe in some greater being in order to cope with the tragedy of the Korean War.

It has been a long, hard journey to South Korea's present prosperity. Tribes from Central Asia first wandered on to the peninsula about ten thousand years ago. Some of these tribes also made it to the West and, as a consequence, the Korean language has roots in common with Turkish, Finnish, and Hungarian, as well as with Chinese and Japanese. Korean legend states that, in the year of Wu-Chen of the Chinese Tan Yao period in 2333 BC, the first ruler of Korea, Tankoon, was the son of the Creator. Tankoon chose Pyongyang, the current capital city of North Korea, as the capital of his new country, to which he gave the name 'Chosun', meaning 'the Land of Morning Freshness' or 'of Morning Calm'. The Korean people have great pride in their more than 4,300-year history. Much later, around 194 BC, the Chinese took vague control over the northern two-thirds of the peninsula for four centuries, playing a role similar to that of the Roman colonists in Britain. Then, in the third and fourth centuries AD, invaders overran North China, and China's nominal Korean colonies sank into oblivion.

Three small, native Korean kingdoms grew into the power vacuum: Koguryo in the north, Paekche in the southwest, and Silla in the southeast. For a century or so these kingdoms fought each other, and although Koguryo was the dominant power, it never managed to conquer its two rivals. In the seventh century AD, Silla emerged from the bickering, made a practical alliance with China's new T'ang dynasty, destroyed Koguryo, and by AD 668 it had unified the peninsula. A hundred years later, rebellion and warfare engulfed Silla. One force eventually prevailed, and in 918 their leader, Wang Kon, renamed the newly reunified state 'Koryo', from which Westerners derived the name 'Korea'.

The battles and wars continued. Small states in Manchuria harried Korea from the north, and Japanese pirates made raids on the coast. In the early thirteenth century, Korea suffered a devastating Mongol assault. For the next hundred years, the Mongols propped up the figurehead Koryo rulers, marrying Mongol princesses into the Korean aristocracy and practically making it a branch of the Mongol ruling house. The Korean élite hated the Mongols for the political and spiritual oppression they imposed; the peasants hated them for the heavy taxes they levied to support their military adventures. But when the Mongol empire collapsed, Koryo toppled soon after. A Korean general, Yi Sung-Kae, seized control of the government, and in 1392, he established the Yi dynasty with himself as Korea's new emperor.

The Yi dynasty could not maintain itself without the support of the equally new Ming dynasty in China. So they quickly established tributary relations with Peking, and, as a vassal to China, ruled the peninsula until the nineteenth century. However, bitter factional disputes plagued the dynasty to the end and the invasions did not abate. In 1592, Japan's rulers succumbed to an Alexandrian desire for more worlds to conquer and launched an all-out attack on Korea, quickly capturing Seoul before they were subsequently thrown out of the country. On their second attempt, the Japanese were defeated again by the Korean general Yi Sun-Shin in a series of brilliant naval victories. More destruction followed in 1636, when the Manchus marched down the peninsula in two successive waves. The fields were trampled by battle, and agriculture declined. In the chaos caused by invasion, control slipped from the government. Although the Yi dynasty survived in form, in substance, it never really recovered.

Koreans spent the eighteenth and nineteenth centuries looking inward, their old feudal culture stagnating on the backs of overburdened peasants. These were the years of the Hermit Kingdom. Sheltered by their Chinese masters, the Koreans were largely invisible to the rest of the world, and wanted it that way. These recluses from the rest of the world spurned Western goods, martyred missionaries, and passed on all requests for diplomatic relations to Peking. Korea's rulers thought even the Japanese were too Westernised.

In the late nineteenth century, Korea disintegrated into blocs of rival cliques. Infighting became more important than governing. Without strong central control, the government caved in to mounting pressure from abroad. Korean misgivings about allowing foreigners entry proved well-founded. In 1876, Korea signed a treaty with the Sun Emperor allowing the Japanese trading rights and concessions. Once the Japanese marched in, Korea became a helpless pawn, a prize to be fought over by two powerful rivals. First the Chinese manipulated the Koreans, until they lost the first Sino-Japanese War of 1894–1895 and had to give up their claims to Korea. The Koreans then relied on Russian backing to keep the Japanese at bay. But when Russia lost the Russo-Japanese War in 1905, the Czar sacrificed Korea as part of the price of peace.

The Japanese disbanded the Korean army in 1907 and forced the last Yi dynasty emperor to abdicate. Then, in 1910, they formally annexed Korea, which remained a colony until the Japanese surrendered to the Allies at the end of World War II. After the war, Korea again became a pawn in the game between larger powers. The fragile alliance between the United States and the Soviet Union had already begun to fray in the closing days of the war, and Korea, not unlike Germany in the same period, was caught in the middle. When the tie between the large powers snapped, the small countries were the losers. Pronouncing the importance of an independent Korea at some vague future date, the great powers agreed to an international trusteeship, similar to the solution in Germany. The Soviets, coming in from the north, and the Americans, advancing from the south, agreed on the 38th parallel as the dividing line between their spheres of influence. This left all the natural resources — hydroelectric dams, and coal and other minerals — in the northern part of the country.

Realising that the Soviets considered the 38th parallel a permanent boundary, the United States tried to involve the UN in Korean unification. In the immediate post-war period, the Russians agreed that unification was a worthy goal, but only if achieved on their terms. Rivalry escalated into war in 1950. In a surprise attack, North Korean troops poured over the 38th parallel on the pretext of repelling a non-existent invasion from the south. In response, President Truman committed American forces to defend South Korea and at once secured the support of the UN in the name of collective security. Forces were sent from sixteen other countries.

All-out fighting lasted only about a year. During those twelve months, armies staggered back and forth across the peninsula, blowing up each other and the countryside, baking in the summer, and freezing in the winter. Seoul changed hands four times and was stomped into muddy chaos. The roads and factories the Japanese had built were destroyed. Farm fields lay ruined, leaving the farmers homeless. The North Koreans came close to pushing the Allied forces south into the sea. Only a daring landing behind the lines at Inchon, the port for Seoul, staved off disaster. Then UN forces pushed the North Koreans towards the Yalu, on the border with China. Terrified of an American invasion, China rushed to the aid of her fellow Communists.

Finally, the UN troops reached a stalemate with the North Korean troops and their Chinese allies. In 1951, armistice talks began at a small village called Panmunjom. As these talks limped along during the next two years, the killing continued. When a truce, never a peace, was finally declared, around 2 million lay dead, including 140,000 UN soldiers (mostly American), 300,000 South Koreans, and an estimated 1.4 million North Koreans and Chinese. Korea's male population and its intelligentsia had been decimated.

Since then, both Koreas have exchanged the chaos of actual war for a constant state of mutual military preparedness. The legacy of war has given a twist to Korean social attitudes, despite their classic Confucian origins. More specifically, while hierarchy pervades Korean life, many Korean subordinates will openly disagree with a colleague or a foreigner. Such behaviour would be an unthinkable breach of propriety in Japan. Koreans maintain loyalty to another individual or the system, but only if that other individual or system is backed by power. When a Chinese defector flew a MiG fighter jet to Seoul in 1986, some maids in the houses of the South's wealthy put down their tools. A MiG jet could signal an invasion. The servants stopped working and waited to see who their new masters would be. There is an old joke amongst Koreans: if the governor of a province died, no one would show up at his funeral, but if his dog died everyone would show up! A people who have had to adjust to one overlord after another cannot afford to be too loyal to anyone.

However, Westerners often find the Koreans the most approachable of all Asians. Their practical independence strikes a chord of recognition. The Koreans have little of the Chinese arrogance or the Japanese reticence which Westerners often find so frustrating. They have not enjoyed dominance, as have the Chinese, nor sustained insulation, like the

Japanese. They haven't had the luxury of being able to sacrifice effective-ness for subtlety. They are a hard people, forged in the fire of centuries of hardship, pain, brutal masters, and concern about their future. Koreans insist on dignity and respect from foreigners, but because Korea's worst colonial experiences have been at the hands of other Asians, not Western-ers, they have none of the confused feelings towards the West which affect many other Asian nations' relationships with Western powers.

The surest way to see Korean temper burst forth in full flower is to tell a Seoul businessman that he and his colleagues are like the Japanese were twenty years ago. It is equally risky to make the same comparison to the Japanese. Historically, the Japanese have always worried the Koreans, and the reverse is also true. During the thirteenth century, Genghis Khan launched two assaults on Japan from the Korean peninsula. The fact that the Mongol emperor and his Korean troops were unsuccessful does not dull the memory in the Japanese mind. However, the memory that looms largest in the Korean-Japanese relationship is Japan's reign as Korea's colonial overlord from 1905 to 1945, although Japan only officially annexed Korea in 1910.

The Japanese imposed a harsh rule on the peninsula. Japanese military police brutally crushed any signs of resistance; thousands were killed. The Japanese forbade use of the Korean language and forced Koreans to take Japanese names. Japan developed the country economically, building new roads, mines, power plants, and factories. But Koreans benefited little. Few were allowed advanced education, as the Japanese considered them little better than their own *Eta*, or 'untouchables'. The colonial govern-ment forced hundreds of thousands of Korean men to emigrate to Japan to fill the jobs vacated by soldiers. Thousands of Korean women were forced to act as 'Comfort Women' for the Japanese soldiers. As Japan's fortunes declined during World War II, crops grown by Korean peasants were taken to feed Japanese troops. The Koreans were reduced to eating tree bark, boiling the skin underneath into a rough cake.

Both sides have their grievances. The Japanese call the Koreans crude and vulgar; the Koreans call the Japanese devious. Both protest too much. The vigour of their deep-seated competition is born of a recognition of historical and economic similarities. Most of all, the two are similar in their absolute need to win. Since the war, the intensity with which the South

Koreans have laboured has been cause for more and more worry for the Japanese. The Japanese, often accused of being workaholics themselves, are now accusing the South Koreans of working too hard. In the medium-term future, it is unlikely that South Korea will overtake Japan economically. But the sound from behind of Korean footsteps is sure to keep the Japanese on their toes.

After the Korean War ended, South Korea was little better off than any Third World country. All the country's resources lay in the north, behind barbed wire, machine guns, tanks, and many divisions of North Korean soldiers. The supply of electric power from North to South Korea was cut. The fields were in need of fertiliser, terracing, and rebuilt irrigation systems. Denied advanced education by the Japanese and by the chaos of successive wars, the populace, though literate, was unsophisticated. Refugees from North Korea and repatriated Koreans from Japan swelled their numbers at a time when the country was least able to cope.

During the 1950s, South Korea's economy became locked in a vicious circle of poverty, hyperinflation, and high dependency on foreign aid. Until 1959, the most conspicuous feature of finance in the Republic of Korea was that between a half and one-third of the general budget was provided by American economic aid. The economy focused inward, on making enough basic goods so that things like shoes and toasters would not have to be imported. Survival seemed the highest goal. At the end of the 1950s, South Korea was still poorer than Sudan.

In 1960, demonstrations toppled Synghman Rhee, the country's first president. Although Rhee had been installed via free elections soon after World War II, his presidency was soon followed by Korea's tradition of authoritarian rule. With his demise, the country flirted briefly with democracy, but the new democratic party could neither fulfil the high expectations of the demonstrators nor hold the contentious nation together. After nine months, a military coup brought General Park Chung-Hee to power. Only then did South Korea begin to modernise. As a result of a shift in its Far East policies, the United States began trimming its aid to South Korea in the 1960s. If it had been left unremedied, Korea's attempts to establish a strong economic base could have faltered, if not failed. Fortunately, Japan stepped into the breach and, in 1965, it extended some US$500 million in unconditional and conditional aid.

This aid made a material contribution to Korea's modernisation.

As an officer in the Japanese colonial army during its occupation of Korea and northern China, Park had seen with his own eyes the industrial and infrastructural development wrought by the Japanese during their brief tenure. He drew his inspiration from late-industrialising countries like Prussia, Egypt, Turkey, and especially from the Meiji reformers who had consciously yanked Japan into the modern era. Park and other Koreans may have heartily disliked the Japanese, but they respected Japan's success and power. And like the economic *daimyo* and *samurai* of the Meiji period which reformed Japan's traditional economy and brought it into the modern, industrial age, Park believed in a strong and interventionist state. Political and economic revolution would be carried out from above. Park even borrowed a Japanese name for the reform programme he introduced in 1972. He called his measures *Yushin*, from the Japanese *ishin* or 'renovation'.

In the name of national stability and security, Park reduced and diluted the powers of the National Assembly, debilitated his own political party, muzzled the press, and emasculated the labour movement. Like Japan in the 1930s, South Korea in the 1960s and 1970s aimed to create and sustain what the first Japanese reformers referred to as *fukoku kyohei* — literally, a rich country and a powerful military. Rival politicians were imprisoned and, with nearly all political power vested in the office of the president, Park had the authority to issue emergency decrees at any time. He declared martial law in 1965, 1972, and 1975. Human rights and democracy took a back seat.

Park's regime crushed dissent in churches and universities. As in Japan, successive South Korean regimes actively pushed mass education as the key to economic modernisation, so that today an impressive 98 per cent of the population is literate. But among the lessons graduates were taught was the maxim never to question the military.

Free from inconvenient objections by the masses, Park proceeded to take the economy in new directions. Throughout the most repressive days of the government, the economy was run almost as a separate country. In a series of five-year plans, the basic idea of Park's economists was to use the country's only resource — people — and train them to make increasingly complicated, and thus more expensive and profitable, products for less than the competition. As in Japan, South Korea gradually moved from producing just what it needed to producing extra goods for export. Big became beautiful. Industries expanded and diversified. Advanced technology was imported and paid for with foreign loans in an effort to spur development. South Korea wanted to get things done, and quickly. It wanted to stop making toys and start smelting steel.

Park got results. Soon South Korea was producing above-average quantities of food, textiles, clothing, paper products, chemicals, and metal products. Industry led the boom. Manufacturing more than doubled in the fifteen years after 1960. Dependence on agriculture and forestry almost halved during the same period.

These changes were not wrought by legions of small firms, as in Hong Kong or Taiwan. The South Koreans built sprawling conglomerates, just as the Japanese had in the decades before World War II. Called *Chaebol*, in Korea these conglomerates have been compared to octopuses. They have arms all over the place and insatiable appetites for expansion and diversification. Like Japan's pre-World War II *Zaibatsu*, the *Chaebol* were dominated by a few families who rose to great wealth and prominence. They were the titans of the domestic business sector and provided the shock troops of the export drive.

As the Japanese Ministry of International Trade and Industry acted more as a promoter and protector of industry than as a regulator, so the South Korean government unabashedly favoured the *Chaebol*.

The big Korean conglomerates got all the breaks. Exporters could get bank loans at heavily subsidised rates. The tariffs on their imported raw materials were suspended, along with their income tax. These policies could cut a company's costs by as much as 40 per cent. By 1981, the top thirty conglomerates accounted for 60 per cent of the nation's GNP, and the top ten conglomerates controlled 29.3 per cent of South Korean exports in 1983. As the *Chaebols* grew, so did Korea's economy.

Many famous *Chaebols* arose from the ashes of the Korean War. Notable among them were the Samsung Group founded by Lee Byung-Chul, whose son Lee Keun-Hee now runs the group; the Lucky-Goldstar Group founded by the Koo and Huh families; the Hanjin Group (Korea Air) founded by Cho Choog-Hoon; the Lotte Group founded by the prominent Korean-Japanese industrialist Shin Kyuk-ho; the Kum Ho

Group founded by Park In-Chon and now run by his son Park Seong-Yawng who has a PhD from Yale; the Hyundai Group founded by Chung Ju-Young and now run by his younger brother Chung Se-Young; and the Hyosung Group founded by Cho Hong-Jae. One of the most famous *Chaebols*, the Daewoo Group, was founded by Kim Woo-Choong in 1967. Kim claims not to have taken a day's holiday since beginning work as a pre-teen paperboy. With a wealthy partner, he started Daewoo as a small-scale textile operation. They began by copying American-made shirts 'down to the last stitch' and selling them to the Japanese who in turn sold them to the United States. Kim soon discovered he could go around the Japanese and sell directly to such retailers as Sears, JC Penney and K-mart. To export was to be a national hero, and Daewoo had found one of the best ways of doing so. The praise and regulatory favours followed. When the United States put import quotas on Korean goods, Daewoo was strong enough to take over floundering firms that did not have the *Chaebol*'s access to capital. Daewoo grew even bigger.

South Korea grew steadily richer. But in the early 1970s, the results were not evident in the countryside where most people still slept in thatched houses and walked wherever they needed to go. So, in tandem with the industrial efforts of *Chaebol* like Daewoo, Hyundai, Samsung, Lucky Goldstar, and others, President Park introduced the *Saemaul*, or 'New Community' movement. Park appealed to the Confucian sense of shame and the Korean sense of competition. The government made building materials and funds available to villages. Those who built the best school or the best bridge, got more building materials and funds. *Saemaul* energised the population. It modernised the countryside while creating a demand for products from the growing *Chaebol*.

By the mid-1970s, Park's economic planners had had enough success with light industry to begin encouraging ventures into heavier territory. South Korea started developing iron and steel, electronics, and petro-chemicals. In 1976, President Park asked Kim Woo-Choong to take over a money-losing, state-owned machinery plant. Daewoo Heavy Industries was born. Kim himself moved into the plant for nine months and worked like a slave, making the company profitable and the cornerstone of a huge expansion by Daewoo. Park continued to give the *Chaebol* industrial presents. He gave Daewoo a car company and then a shipbuilding yard.

Daewoo didn't even want to go into shipbuilding. But while the Daewoo chairman was away, Park simply announced that the *Chaebol* would be taking over the yard. The move typified the government's heavy-handed style. The flip-side to enjoying the government's largess was that Kim couldn't refuse. During the 1980s, the yard at Okpo swallowed US$500 million of Daewoo's capital, but it is now considered one of the best in the world.

Everything seemed to be going wonderfully, at least on the economic front. Then, in August 1979, Park ordered riot police to raid a workers' sit-in. The police brutally beat the workers and killed one labour leader. Soon after, Park ousted opposition leader Kim Young Sam from the National Assembly. Outrage at these incidents fuelled large demonstrations. The director of the feared Korean Central Intelligence Agency, afraid that Park's hard line against dissent would provoke violent revolution, assassinated him in October. At his death, President Park's economic policies were thrown into doubt. A subsequent oil price shock rocked the Korean economy. The government involvement, which had first spurred the economy, had become invasive. Too much bureaucratic interference had led to inefficiency. The country had begun to struggle. Growth slowed, replaced by contraction. South Korea's debt climbed to US$46 billion.

Park's successor, Choi Kyu-Hah, began to loosen the government's grip, releasing political detainees and promising reform. People started to talk about the possibility of a return to Korea's old civilian constitution. But not for long. General Chun Doo-Hwan, commander of the Army Security Command and the man appointed to investigate Park's assassination, marched down to Seoul in mid-December 1979. After a spectacular shootout, Chun arrested thirty generals as well as the army chief of staff, charging them all with complicity in Park's murder. From then on, Chun ran the government. The president was president in name alone, until 1980 when Chun also took that position for himself.

After Chun's coup, student and labour unrest erupted around the country. Students set 17 May 1980 as the deadline for the government to announce publicly its schedule for a return to civilian rule. But when 17 May arrived, the government declared martial law instead. Police and militia fanned out over the country rooting out all sources of discontent.

In Kwangju, a southwestern city traditionally at odds with central government, the students reacted to the crackdown. A brutal battle ensued. Demonstrators threw stones, Molotov cocktails, and sticks. Police responded with tear gas and pepper gas, and then Special Forces troops were brought in. For reasons still unexplained, the troops let loose, beating, stabbing, and mutilating unarmed civilians. Though reports conflict, stories of random and senseless violence abound. When a mother protested about rough treatment of her daughter, they were both shot on the spot. Ten high school students were killed in front of a police station. Public buses were randomly searched for people under thirty, whose hands were then bound with barbed wire before they were marched off, never to be seen again.

Enraged citizens, who would never normally consider taking to the streets, rose up with guns seized from nearby armouries and drove the troops from the city. Kwangju became a law unto itself. Daily demonstrations called for democracy, unification, and an end to military rule. Organisers formed a committee to negotiate with the military, and requests were made for American assistance in the talks. The assistance never came. Instead, the United States backed Chun's claim that the 'Kwangju Incident' was a threat to national unity. The government moved two regiments of Special Forces troops from the front lines on the Demilitarized Zone to engage in the fighting. The troops retook Kwangju.

While Chun was in power, thousands of people suspected of subversive thought or activity found themselves in prison or without a job, and a new press law put the media under strict government control. But in 1986, after seven years, the harshness of Chun's regime drove tens of thousands into the streets. Chun couldn't intimidate everyone. In 1987, he was forced to step aside for military classmate Roh Tae Woo.

F avourable economic circumstances, coupled with a series of reforms, saved South Korea. In 1986, the Japanese yen climbed to an all-time high against the American dollar, making Japanese goods suddenly very expensive. As the Korean won was pegged more or less to the American dollar, between 1986 and 1988 the won fell as the dollar fell. Korean goods became the best substitute for Japanese low-to-middle end products. And Korean industries developed apace with Japanese industry, albeit many years behind. Koreans bought low-level technology from the Japanese and then produced it more cheaply than was possible in Japan. As Japan car companies went up-market with luxury sedans, Korea introduced the Hyundai econobox car. Japanese firms invested in high-definition television, while Korean companies started producing black and white televisions. Then the bottom fell out of the oil market and slashed the power bills of Korean factories in half. Growth between 1986 and 1988 averaged 12 per cent a year. In 1988, the country displayed its wealth to the world, successfully hosting the Olympic Games.

Soon, however, problems began to surface. Like Japan, Korea's success incurred the ire of the United States, its largest export market. Korean exports to the United States had grown at an average annual rate of 20 per cent between 1982 and 1986. From 1988 to 1989, Korea's trade surplus with the United States halved. But acrimonious debate continued, despite a trade agreement that declared an uneasy truce. The Americans threatened retaliation if Koreans didn't allow imports of certain American products. Following the strategy of the American multinationals during the 1950s and 1960s, the Japanese muted the effects of protectionism by building plants around the world. However, the Koreans did not have the money to pursue this strategy.

South Korea also struggled with labour problems. When controls were relaxed in 1987, unions launched more than three thousand labour disputes. These were hard, confrontational, and often very violent affairs, not the polite, lunchtime strikes of the Japanese. Management, used to a docile workforce, became confused. Partly in reaction, Kim Woo-Choong published *It's a Big World and There's a Lot to be Done*, exhorting workers to put aside self-interest in favour of national greatness. The book became a bestseller in South Korea. A poet-dissident, Park Noh-Hae, slammed back with *Our Love and Our Wrath*, which exhorts Korea's leaders to ensure the country's greatness through a fair division of its wealth.

South Koreans still work hard. They put in an average of ten more hours per week than the Japanese, fifteen more than Americans. But there has been a change in attitude. Even with pay increases, productivity is on the decline. The people, quite reasonably, want more.

Social differences in South Korea remain stark. There is still an acute shortage of housing. People live in plastic-wrapped lean-to's next to apartments costing US$250,000. Bicycles carrying wooden crates vie for space on Seoul's clogged arteries as US$25,000 cars whizz by. Around 20 per cent of Koreans control 42 per cent of the wealth. Hard work and low wages have created Korea's boom, as they did in Japan twenty years ago. But Koreans are not willing to take voluntary pay cuts, as Japanese workers have done when their economy was hard pressed. Korean workers want their share.

The anger in the workforce might not be so violent if Korea did not have such a tradition of heavy-handed labour policy. Until a few years ago, the Labour Minister often used plainclothes police — euphemistically called the 'Love the Company Corps' — to storm factories where strikes or sit-ins were under way. High wages, strikes, collective bargaining procedures, and the like were 'inefficiencies' which jeopardised export competitiveness.

A series of labour laws in the early 1980s stripped the unions of any real power. Unions depend on the state for legal recognition and the right to formally represent worker interests. The government can remove union leaders or disband unions, which are forbidden to co-operate with, or contribute any money to, political parties. A Labour Party is technically impossible. Industry-wide unions are discouraged in favour of less efficient local unions. When martial law was imposed in 1980, thousands of union members, both officers and rank and file, were purged from their organisations. They all went to rectification camps to have their thinking purified by hard work and callisthenics. At the time, the ex-president of a Seoul chemical workers local union told the *Korea Times*, 'The government always says that we are communists just because we try to get our rights. We're not communists. We don't have any sympathy for North Korea. All we want is justice and the chance to live a decent life.'

South Korea's Economic Planning Board calculated that strikes reduced industrial production and exports for the first three months of 1989 by more than US$3 billion in lost production and delayed shipments. Industry had to choose between losing a lot of money and losing some money. They chose the latter. In 1987, wages rose 12 per cent, followed by increases of more than 20 per cent in 1988 and 1989. As a result, the *Chaebol* have rethought their strategies. Rising labour costs forced no fewer than a hundred medium-sized Korean companies in labour-intensive fields to relocate to Southeast Asia in the first half of 1989. Another 150 had relocated by the end of 1989.

Workers in labour-intensive industries like textiles and toys, not technology industries, were the engine of Korea's economy until the mid-1970s. Now it is more dependent on heavy industry, but Korea has imported many parts and technologies — from electronics components to car parts — from Japan. By Japanese standards, some Korean production methods are primitive. For instance, at a Japanese Matsushita VCR plant built in the early 1980s, robots do 80 per cent of the work. At a Korean Samsung plant built a few years later, the work was done by young women whose small incomes were supplemented by ten cent meals at the company cafeteria and free lodging in company dormitories.

As labour costs rise, South Korea is beginning to be priced out of industries like clothing and shoes. It must begin to move into more advanced fields. It must rely more on itself and less on Japanese and American technology and financing. This is happening already. In 1989, for the first time, electronics became the biggest export earner. South Korea wants a 10 per cent share of the computer chip market by the early 1990s. The nation has already stepped up research and development efforts.

To become technologically competitive, the *Chaebols* must pay off the loans which financed the building of their huge shipyards and steel mills. In the mid-1980s, South Korea was Asia's most heavily indebted country, and the fourth-largest debtor in the world after Brazil, Mexico, and Argentina. However, its debt-service ratio then ran about 20 per cent, far below that of problem debtors in Latin America and elsewhere. Additionally, by 1990, Korea's foreign debt had shrunk from US$45 billion to US$26 billion.

Even if South Korea continues to be plagued by the 'three highs' — the high won, high prices, and high labour costs — the country can probably sustain growth of 5–6 per cent annually without relying on access to foreign markets. Following policies set in the last decade, Seoul could resolve its problems and continue its economic progress. But South Korea's evolution into a fully developed country will depend upon more striking changes being made.

Some change has already arrived, whether the ruling class likes it or not. After a growth spurt, its economy is a little long in the legs and uncoordinated. Democracy has come to South Korea, but not in its final form. Industry has begun to restructure, but the process is nowhere near complete. Students have openly raised the questions of how much Western, and most importantly how much American, influence should be allowed in South Korea. The debates often flare to violence. Policemen get beaten up with regularity by demonstrators. Seoul has a real law and order problem. And as these issues are debated, policy will be marked by starts and stops, backtracking, and sudden moves forward. Like the adolescent democratic experience everywhere, it will be confusing.

The changes have started in the political arena. Politics set the tone for a nation. Since the Korean War ended with a ceasefire, South Korean politics have been heavy-handed — a series of coups, ruthless silencing of opposition organisations, and collusion between politics and industry. This should not come as a surprise. Korea has never cultivated a tradition of loyal opposition, not even in the limited sense that was developed in China, where Confucian philosophy instructed officials to raise questions about unjust policies, even if this meant risking their necks. In Korea, there has never been even a pretence of shared power. The military and the aristocracy — and in modern times, the government and the corporate leaders — have always made the big decisions.

President Roh started the process of political change in 1987 by announcing the most sweeping reforms that Korea had ever seen, including direct elections and guaranteed human rights. Still, as a former official in the repressive government of Chun Doo-Hwan, the Chun legacy clung to him like a bad odour. He won the December 1987 presidential elections, but two months later, the three opposition parties won a 55 per cent majority in the National Assembly.

The following two years were marked by confusion: demonstrations, divided opposition leaders, and a ruling party ever afraid of military backlash. Then came the merger announcement. It was, by all accounts, a political masterstroke, one which would keep political chaos at a minimum and give the government freedom to move slowly towards democracy. Roh announced that the ruling party would join forces with the parties of two opposition leaders who had once been banned from politics, so gaining an overwhelming majority in the National Assembly. Opponents have attacked the move as a consolidation of a one-party dictatorship. The alliance certainly brought together unlikely bedfellows. Roh, the consummate middle-road politician, joined forces with a radical democrat, Kim Young Sam, and a conservative militarist, Kim Jong Pil. But together, the three leaders have converged at the centre of the political spectrum.

The new strength of Roh's Democratic Justice Party gave the president the breathing space he needed to deal with labour strife, radical students, economic problems, and the relationship between the Korean Blue House and the US White House. It also gave him the freedom to consider significant constitutional changes. There was talk of turning from the current presidential form of government, in which charismatic figures are needed to draw votes, to a parliamentary form of government based on the British model, in which ideology is more important. The British system has obvious advantages. As a country where freedom to question has often degenerated into witch hunts, Korea has never had much success with American-style democracy. Roh was said to favour patterning South Korea's political system after Japan's. As a result, the new ruling party would be henceforth known as the Democratic Liberal Party (DLP), a slight variation on Japan's long-entrenched Liberal Democratic Party (LDP). Like Japan's LDP, the Korean DLP could be composed of several diverse factions, each jockeying for power but working within a system and reaching decisions by consensus.

The government has started to move away from the closed-door policies supported by the conglomerates. The South Korean stock market opened up in 1992, but certain strategic companies were kept off-limits. The maximum foreign shareholding in other companies was limited to 10 per cent, although, through certain specific mechanisms such as the purchase of international convertible bond market issues by Korean companies, these limits were later increased to 25 per cent. As was the case in developing Japan, the closed nature of South Korea's financial system is the last major hindrance to development. South Korea needs the rest of the world to build skyscrapers and factories in Seoul, not just to finance the loans for them. In the long run, foreign investment is needed by, and will benefit, Korea.

With the new economic picture come new rules. South Korean workers are demanding more equality, not just in pay but in attitude. Women are now protesting against sexism, insisting that bosses use their names instead of addressing them as, 'Hey, you'. Businessmen faced with union negotiators confide to visitors that they have never in the past had to deal with labour bargaining. It used to be that government just told business what to do. In stark contrast, Roh's government had begun to tell companies they were on their own. Then, in 1990, the government attitude changed again. The Blue House supported crackdowns on several strikes. The government introduced austerity measures, and exhorted citizens to restrain consumption and to avoid buying foreign goods. Once again, government became part of business negotiations. If democracy is to survive, this cannot continue; but if Korea is to survive, this intervention must not only be expected but be seen as necessary from time to time, until Korea has carved out a lasting role for itself.

Whatever solutions the Koreans choose, it seems likely that the Americans will not be the dominant partners that they have been in the past. Some now hold the United States responsible for inviting the North Korean invasion, saying that if Korea had never been partitioned by the two superpowers, there would never have been a war. For decades, the legacy of the American Korean War effort and the day-to-day reality of anti-communism produced genuine warmth towards, and dependence on, the United States. When students rebelled against President Rhee in 1960, the American ambassador publicly stated his support for democracy and virtually ordered Rhee to step down. When President Carter announced a plan to withdraw troops from South Korea, most South Koreans opposed the withdrawal. Even when President Park declared martial law at various times, these actions were viewed more as reactions to US policies — President Nixon's 'opening' to China or the collapse of the Saigon government, for example; most did not see them as moves directly supported by Washington.

The political crisis in 1979 marked the first signs of a change in this sympathetic attitude. After President Park's assassination, there was widespread confidence that the Americans would support moves towards democracy. But in the late 1970s, the United States was reeling from its loss in Vietnam, the collapse of the Shah's government in Iran, the Sandinista revolution in Nicaragua, and the growing strength of revolutionary movements in the Philippines and El Salvador. In reaction to all these global setbacks, the Carter administration decided to strengthen its position in Asia. This strategy included integrating the American and Korean militaries, placing 80 per cent of the Korean army under the direct command of an American general. When Park's system collapsed, the United States had a deepened strategic stake in South Korea. To the consternation of Korean democrats, this stake would override concerns about human rights and democracy.

When Chun staged his coup, American representatives protested. American military officials complained about Chun's unauthorised troop movements. The State Department warned of further unrest if democracy was stalled by the military. But neither President Carter nor the American commander in Korea made a move against Chun as he consolidated his power. For this reason, student dissidents assumed that the United States tacitly supported the coup.

If the Chun coup is a sore point for many, the Kwangju incident is the rallying cry for those who have soured on American involvement in Korea. While the official government line is that the Kwangju incident was a rebellion, an insurrection, to many South Koreans it was a just revolution followed by a massacre aided and abetted by the United States. The troop movement from the Demilitarized Zone has left a legacy of bitterness. Many Koreans assume the American commander must have given permission for men to be withdrawn from the North Korean border and sent to mop up the mess in Kwangju. By giving this permission, the commander — and, by extension, the American government — became a knowing accessory to what many consider a crime. The United States has always denied knowledge of the events in Kwangju, although its explanations have been somewhat ambiguous. Regardless, many South Koreans now link the Americans with an ugly memory of student demonstrations, crackdown, citizen revolt, and official revenge.

By the mid-1980s, anti-Americanism was widespread. Many people concluded that under Chun, South Korea had become even more subordinated to US military interests. For the first time in nearly three decades, the cry of 'Yankee Go Home' was heard on South Korean campuses. Students questioned not only the American military involvement in their country, but also the American economic role.

Many felt betrayed by growing protectionism in the United States. In 1984, when the US Commerce Department charged four South Korean companies with dumping colour television sets on the American market, major Korean business groups called for retaliation, and suggested that perhaps the contracts for the next two nuclear projects should not be awarded to American firms. In 1987, students occupied the American Chamber of Commerce, calling it a centre of 'economic imperialism'.

Popular discontent with the United States has flared at a time when the erstwhile protector is most likely to accept a diminished role on the peninsula. While the two countries will probably continue to have a special relationship, the United States will not be as omnipresent as in the past. American presence had been justified by the Soviet threat. Now that East–West tensions have disappeared, and the United States is struggling with its trade and budget deficits, Washington finds it more difficult to justify massive outlays in Korea. With diminished American presence and new-found economic success, Korea will have the freedom to evolve into a new, independent culture.

The word 'reunification' for many South Koreans still carries connotations of heresy, but reunion with North Korea is in fact inevitable. Despite the very real barriers between North and South, reunification will help both countries to meet the challenges that face them. For the North, unity with the South will mean a higher standard of living and a greater international role. For the South, unification will provide supplementary markets, labour, and natural resources. For both, it will provide them, as a single country, with a sufficient critical mass to play an important role in the region.

Perhaps even more important than the practical reasons for reunification are the emotional reasons. The Koreans feel the stress of artificial division acutely. On a personal level, they want to stop the family fight. When they do, it will set the stage for Korea's next level of development — a situation not too dissimilar to the former East and West Germanys.

But for the politics, the nation has every reason to be unified. The Korean peninsula is one of the most culturally and racially homogeneous areas in Asia Pacific. It is almost as distinct as Japan. In Korea, there are no religious conflicts, and although regional loyalties remain strong, they don't completely divide the people. The Koreans speak one language, not dozens of mutually unintelligible dialects like the Chinese, or hundreds of dialects and languages like the Indians. And the Koreans share in a truly national heritage. As memories of the Korean War have receded, this national culture has given the issue of unification a growing emotional appeal in the South.

Since the Korean War de-escalated into a truce, the two Koreas have faced off across the Demilitarized Zone. There has never been a peace treaty, and in the Cold War between East and West, it has probably been the most volatile border in the world. There are hundreds of thousands of men on each side, and with so much power poised to pounce, minor incidents have become exaggerated. In the 1970s, two UN soldiers trimming a tree were hacked to death by North Koreans, who claimed the tree trimmers were violating the truce. Commercial aircraft in Seoul, only three minutes jet time from the North Korean aerial frontier, are careful to keep to established flight patterns. In the 1980s, the South Koreans nearly shot the tail off a Northwest Airlines jumbo jet that was mistaken for an attacking North Korean jet. Koreans don't go to the beach much because most of their coastline is strung with barbed wire to discourage invaders. The threat is very real. Speculation is rife that the North is working on a nuclear bomb.

In this tense atmosphere, except for relations with the Soviet Union, China, and a few other countries, the North has kept to itself in Hermit Kingdom style. Kim Il-Sung, the young soldier installed by the Soviets, has turned the North into a Marxist-Leninist monarchy. He has appointed his son, Kim Jong-Il, as his successor. The jury is still out on whether the son will be able to retain power after his father dies, but the cult-makers are hard at work on Kim Jong-Il's image, even going so far as to name a begonia — the Kimjongilia — after him.

The elder Kim calls his philosophy *juche*, stressing that all foreign ideas are secondary. He has taken some ideas from the Chinese and some from the Soviets, but he has been careful not to commit to one model or the other. The land is rich in coal and iron ore. Agriculture is mechanised and sophisticated. Resources, combined with an industrial infrastructure left by the Japanese, have brought the North Koreans some success in manufacturing, steel, heavy machinery, and arms.

Relations between North and South have often been an absurd game of one-upmanship. The United States and the South might build an office building on one side of the border. To keep up appearances, the North will then build one higher and wider on the other side, but its foundations will only be six feet deep. The South has put a bounty on the enormous flag which the North Koreans fly just for spite.

In the past, these attitudes have turned the talks between North and South into a quest for advantage rather than a genuine desire to reach an agreement. The stronger one side is, the more conciliatory it is; the weaker the other side is, the more intransigent it is. In the 1950s and 1960s, the North was more developed and tried to woo the South with offers of aid and assistance. The South responded by denying any possibility of contacts or co-operation. As the South grew stronger in the late 1960s, the North began to talk of revolutionising workers in the South. By the 1970s, the South was strong enough not to be threatened by dialogue. The two sides met for talks which stretched into the 1980s.

The South proposed that 'either-or' diplomacy be stopped, allowing Moscow and Beijing to recognise both Koreas instead of having to choose one or the other. In the early 1980s, the North proposed that a confederation of North and South be declared, preserving the existing political regimes. But neither side would accept the other's plans. Long silences punctuated the dialogue and prospects of a resolution grew ever more vague. The world lost interest in Korea's bickering.

Yet it is largely the world's fault that the Koreans have failed to resolve their negotiations. When the world was divided up between the two superpowers, Korea was a pressure point. The Soviet Union and China could not allow a capitalist stronghold in their own backyard. They made sure the North didn't budge. Japan did not want the peninsula, only 145 kilometres away, to be wholly communist. The United States, in the interest of anti-communism and in support of Japan, spent billions propping up the South.

All this is changing. The success of the 1988 Seoul Olympics, coupled with the social and political changes in South Korea, have shown the world that South Korea is a less dogmatic, more reliable partner. However, it has still some way to go. In the area of intellectual property rights, Korea has a long record of pirating technology, which has discouraged foreign firms from investing in Korea. Foreign high-tech-related investments eligible for tax incentives dropped 90 per cent over the period 1988 to 1991. Other factors, such as the labyrinthine approval process for foreign investments, the high cost of real estate, and an over-strained infrastructure, all combine to provide a collective strong disincentive for foreign investments. The Japanese are even more negative because they claim that, on top of all these problems, the Koreans have an increasingly stronger racist bias towards them — Japan's direct investment in Korea declined more than 70 per cent over the period 1988 to 1991.

The government claims that it is addressing these problems and that genuine reform will be forthcoming. There is also a general belief, even by the government, that the economy is over-regulated and so change should come, albeit in fits and starts. However, there is general scepticism as to how real such reform will be and when it will take place. At the same time, the United States and the EC have begun to take protectionist steps against Korean steel and textiles, and action has been threatened over a range of electronic goods. In the meantime, one partial solution is for South Korea itself both to develop better foreign relations and to invest abroad, harnessing the increasing assertiveness and aggressiveness of its businessmen.

After moves were made to democratise society in 1987, national unification became a focal point of South Korean politics. At his inauguration, Roh said he would give top priority to 'paving the way to peaceful unification through the promotion of reconciliation and cooperation between the two Koreas.' In July 1988, flushed with Olympic success, he announced that South Korea would no longer avoid contact with the Eastern bloc, nor would Seoul oppose Pyongyang's overtures to the West. And in September 1989, Roh outlined a new plan for unification beginning with a Korean 'Commonwealth', in which the South and North would remain sovereign states yet their relations would not be international but something closer. This interim state would be followed by a gradual merging of the two political systems. This would be a two-stage process, whereas the North wants to unify in one fell swoop.

For the first time, Seoul had spelled out the principal structural components of an interim stage on the road to unity. Roh's proposal also described the contours of a unified Korea, including a democratically-elected bicameral parliament. President Roh has said it would be possible to achieve unification by the year 2000. But as long as the ageing Kim Il-Sung leads the North, all the South's diplomatic gymnastics are probably for naught. Pyongyang responded by saying that what Seoul really meant was a unification in which communism is obliterated. It dressed down South Korea in old-fashioned Marxist-Leninist fashion, accusing Seoul of 'flunkeyism' for referring to the model of reunified Germany.

In 1991, per capita GNP in the North was US$500 a year, while in the South it was US$6,498. The gap is growing. The North is spending an estimated 25 per cent of its GNP on the military, compared to 6 per cent in the South. And the North has no computer chips, no technology transfers. It is missing out on the high-tech fields that will be so important in the future. Although accurate information on the North Korean economy is sparse, budgets and public announcements suggest that the country's economic woes remain serious. There are apparent shortages in food, housing, and clothing.

Under economic and diplomatic pressure, Pyongyang has moderated its stance. Its own proposals are no longer predicated on the demise of the Republic of Korea or upon the withdrawal of American troops from the South. Unofficial contacts between North Korea and the United States have been made. The North's criticism of inter-Korean contacts in non-political spheres has grown weaker. The main focus now is not to allow such contacts to grow into political recognition.

The North seems to recognise that the two sides are likely to come together economically before political or diplomatic union can follow. Both stand to benefit from such a course of events. Under pressure from competing economies in Southeast Asia, South Korea needs the North for cheap land and labour. In South Korea, there is widespread belief that it is necessary to help their 'brothers' in the the North to improve their living standards. Since October 1988, South Korean firms have been allowed to develop direct trade with their North Korean counterparts. In January 1989, Hyundai Group founder Chung Ju-Young visited Pyongyang to discuss joint ventures and various other projects, including economic co-operation of the Koreas and the Soviet Union in the Soviet Far East. In 1990, the North also made tentative, but crucial, steps towards ending its isolation from the capitalist world. The North Koreans declared themselves willing to release two Japanese sailors whom they had imprisoned on spy charges. The Japanese hailed this decision as removing the most significant remaining obstacle to the establishment of normal ties with North Korea.

However, despite this apparent thawing of North Korea's position, it must not be forgotten that Kim Il-Sung and his son Kim Jong-Il have ruled their country with a despotic iron fist. They have also evinced extreme paranoia over any outside influences to such an extent that, in many respects, China's Cultural Revolution resembled a genteel picnic by comparison. President Kim has obviously modelled himself after Stalin. This regime has thus reduced the country to a state of absolute penury and the people to a state of terrified robotic automatons. This makes North Korea unpredictable and therefore potentially very irrational and dangerous. There was dramatic evidence of this in early 1993 when North Korea put the entire country on a semi-war alert in protest over South Korea's and the United States' joint military 'Team Spirit' exercises.

All this being said, a key strategic benefit to both Koreas is that the reunited Korean peninsula could provide a gateway to Manchuria in northeastern China. This could be the beginning of a rejuvenated economy in North Asia, including Asiatic Russia. Geography, history, and economics point in this direction. During Japan's brief attempt at building an empire, Manchuria became an economic powerhouse and it could become so again. China would welcome the economic help. The fact that China and South Korea, to the consternation of Taiwan and North Korea, formally recognised each other in September 1992 gives evidence of this. The South's *Nordpolitik* has led it actively to seek economic and diplomatic co-operation with China, Russia, and Eastern Europe, all of which initiatives are forcing North Korea to moderate its position. South Korean trade with China has steadily increased. A modest US$19 million shunted through Hong Kong in 1978. Thirteen years later in 1991, two-way trade had grown to more than US$5.8 billion. China has became South Korea's fourth-largest trading partner in terms of volume after the United States, Japan, and the EC. South Korea and

China agreed in October 1992 to establish a huge industrial complex in Tianjin for South Korean companies to set up factories there. Similarly, in late 1992, Boris Yeltsin discussed with Kim Woo-Choong, chairman of the Daewoo Group, a project to lay a 5,000-kilometre gas and oil pipeline from Asiatic Russia to South Korea and Japan via China and North Korea, who both indicated a willingness to co-operate.

The Korean economy complements that of China and Asiatic Russia. South Korea is poor in natural resources, and even a united Korea lacks many natural resources. China and Asiatic Russia are rich in resources but underdeveloped. In the 1980s, Korea exported electronics, iron and steel, synthetic fibres, and imported silks, cotton, animal feed, and coal. The trade reflects a natural division of labour. Ports on the mainland's coast are strategically located to buy raw materials and export manufactured products. With lower freight charges, it makes more sense for Korea to import iron ore and coal from China than from Australia and oil from Siberia rather than from the Middle East.

Despite the Tiananmen Square incident, Korean businessmen have continued to invest in China. Of nineteen South Korean projects in communist countries in 1989, sixteen were in China. Korea has been more successful than any other country at penetrating the mainland's electronics market. Korea's four leading electronics giants — Goldstar, Samsung, Daewoo, and Hyundai — have set up or will set up joint-venture manufacturing plants in China. In late 1989, the Korea Institute for Economics and Technology and the Korean Import-Export Bank reported that more than a hundred Korean firms had expressed interest in operating factories in the People's Republic. Increased investment in China can help to maintain the dynamism of the Korean economy in the 1990s.

Precedents exist for an expanded China–Korea relationship. Korea has been linked to China since the very earliest times. Furthermore, between the period 300 BC and AD 300, the Kingdom of Ancient Korea incorporated not only the entire Korean peninsula but also all of Manchuria. The Chinese introduced agriculture to Korea and then, considerably later, Chinese monks brought the Buddhist sutras to the peninsula around the time of Christ. The ancient kingdom of Silla organised government administration, a land and taxation system, a national university, and government exams along Chinese lines. Since Korea did not have a written script, the documents which tied together these institutions were written in Chinese. Chinese remained a *lingua franca* of the educated classes until the twentieth century. The tenth-century kingdom of Koryo borrowed even more from China, reviving the civil service, giving each farmer a piece of land for his lifetime, and providing universal education. When the Japanese invaded in the late sixteenth century, only the arrival of Chinese support troops, and some brilliant naval victories led by a Korean admiral, saved Korea from complete defeat.

In the 1880s, China's Qing dynasty decided to allow a small number of poor Koreans from the North to live and farm in the Chinese area of Yanbian across the Tumen River. Other Koreans crossed the Yalu River to settle in the southwestern region of Manchuria. An increasing number of Manchurian and Chinese landowners relied upon Korean tenant farmers in order to develop irrigation systems and to expand rice paddies.

Many Koreans helped in the Chinese resistance against the Japanese during the 1930s and 1940s, and stayed on in China after World War II. During the Korean War, the Chinese government gave autonomous status to Korean villages, resulting in five autonomous districts, 101 autonomous villages, and six Korean counties within China. Today, about 3 million ethnic Koreans live there, 1.75 million of these in southern Manchuria adjacent to North Korea. Koreans amount to 40.3 per cent of the population in the Yanbian area. They have had to adapt to the unpredictable winds of Chinese politics, but they have preserved their cultural identity. Political hardship in times of Chinese xenophobia has reinforced their appreciation of their Korean heritage as a form of psychological self-protection.

If a vibrant Korean-Manchurian economic zone develops, this could spur development in Asiatic Russia. Trade liaison offices were established in Seoul and Moscow in 1989, and South Korean business conglomerates have been invited to bid for construction projects in Siberia, including the construction of a trade centre in the Siberian city of Nahodka.

O verall, South Korea lags substantially behind the Japanese, Taiwanese, and other Overseas Chinese in penetrating Southeast Asia. It is likely to continue to do so. The same is also likely to apply to the penetration of India in the future. With the exception of Vietnam, the Koreans are temperamentally less able to deal with the softer, more subtle, and non-confrontational cultures of Southeast Asia. The Koreans' natural character, iron discipline, and determination have a much more natural match with the character and cultures of the people to the north of Korea. In racial or tribal terms, the Koreans have a great deal in common with the Mongol races of Manchuria and Asiatic Russia. This fact will considerably facilitate their future dealings with these peoples. It thus makes more sense for a united Korea to push north into China and Asiatic Russia than doggedly to attempt to follow the Japanese and Overseas Chinese into Southeast Asia and India where these two latter races possess so many cultural, financial, and technological advantages over the Koreans in penetrating these regions.

South and North Korea must resolve their differences if they are to survive over the medium term. North Korea must also give up its nuclear power pretensions if it wishes to survive *at all*. Should such economic developments come to pass, and if, for the first time in many centuries, an independent, unified Korea emerges, it should become a significant force in Asia Pacific.

The possibility of this happening was improved by the results of the December 1992 general elections, when Kim Young Sam, the new head of the ruling LDP, was elected to the Blue House with 42 per cent of the vote; the other two contenders, Kim Dae-Jung and Chung Ju-Yong, received 34 per cent and 16 per cent respectively. Kim is the first president without any military background and, because of his affluent background, he is untainted by any of the corruption scandals that have affected so many politicians in South Korea. He is therefore likely to be viewed more positively by North Korea.

Kim has also espoused non-violent opposition to the previous governments and has thus also avoided any association with any radical groups. His new leadership should therefore meet the South Korean people's requirements for a cabinet untainted by past corruption, and for a non-military, democratically appointed government, which will hopefully provide some respite from the corruption and violence of the past. In turn, with a more united country behind him and again without any military association, this should also facilitate his and his government's dialogue with North Korea.

However, even if North Korea were to remain intransigent on the subject of unification, given South Korea's *rapprochement* with China, given the Han Chinese of China's historical attitudes towards Manchuria, both of superiority and irrelevance, and given the Korean population in Manchuria, there is an interim solution. Specifically because of these factors, it would be perfectly feasible for South Korea to economically leap-frog over North Korea and start participating in, if not leading, the economic development of Manchuria. North Korea would then become squeezed between the two zones and there would be even more pressure for North Korea to acknowledge reality and rejoin the world by uniting, under realistic conditions and in due course, with South Korea. In the near term, this is possibly South Korea's best option.

An early 1990s report by a Korean Development Bank affiliate estimated that the cost of reunification, in particular the cost of bringing North Korea's economic development up to the level of South Korea's, would be in the region of US$200–400 billion over a ten-year period. This is hardly a sum that South Korea is able to afford just now, no matter how compelling any other reason may be. In such a time frame, if North Korea's economy were to crumble or there were to be succession or other problems, South Korea's economy is unlikely to be able to take the strain of unification. The West–East German example is very much a case in point — those in South Korea who aggressively advocate such immediate unification should bear this example in mind. Generally, though, the consensus in South Korea seems to be to live with the current division between North and South, and to make incremental advances on a broad front towards a general *rapprochement*.

However, in the future, a united Korea, with a population of more than 60 million people, and an add-on population of 3 million in Manchuria, could provide an independent source of political and economic regional initiatives and play an important balancing role in bringing together, and maintaining together, the countries of Asia Pacific. Similarly, Asia Pacific needs such a united Korea —if not at least because such a development presumes a resolution of the North Korean nuclear problem. Despite being a member of the Nuclear Non-Proliferation Treaty (NPT), and despite signs of co-operation in 1992, in early 1993 North Korea refused the International Atomic Energy Agency (IAEA) inspection of two suspected nuclear sites. This has caused considerable international concern. The IAEA was then put in the position of considering whether or not to demand 'a special inspection'. Such a step would be unprecedented in that this extraordinary procedure has never before been used to insist on visiting a suspected nuclear site in a country which has not confirmed that it has one. If it decided to go ahead, the IAEA could only refer the matter to the UN Security Council, which itself has no precedent for taking action.

In the meantime, North Korea suddenly announced in March 1993 that it was withdrawing its membership from the NPT. It also announced that it would take (unstated) strong defensive counter-measures if the UN imposed any sanctions on it as a result of its withdrawal. This move caused considerable surprise and shock worldwide, but fortunately China, probably North Korea's last-remaining 'friend', immediately announced that the problem should be resolved within the framework of the NPT. This new equation and its resolution has considerable regional, if not global, ramifications. If this problem is not resolved, it could have specific and highly negative domino consequences elsewhere in North Asia.

In the context of establishing a more participatory role for itself in the region, another initiative that should be seriously considered by South Korea is the question of whether it should apply for membership in ASEAN. ASEAN should welcome this, as it would give greater credibility and substance to ASEAN's role within the region, as well as give greater impetus to the inclusion in the medium term of the region's bigger players — namely, Japan, China, India, and Australasia.

The less developed Asia Pacific countries need all the capital and industrialisation help they can get in order to provide support for their much-needed domestic economic and social development. Thus, another aspect of this general theme could be a unified Korea's focus to the north, i.e. North China and Asiatic Russia, as this could assist greatly in the economic development of these two areas, the latter in particular. This, in turn, would assist in ensuring the future peaceful and co-operative participation of these areas with the rest of Asia Pacific.

All this is all very well in theory, but a new, totally reasonable, but disquietening all the same, change is taking place in South Korea. Specifically, the Koreans have responded historically to authoritarian rule and/or periods of crisis by showing their discipline and determination to get the job done, no matter what the cost. However, in the South Korea of the early 1990s, with the advent of considerable economic success and a more democratic form of government, the ordinary people of Korea quite reasonably want more out of life for themselves. They no longer want to perform the dirty, arduous, and sometimes dangerous labour that brought their industry to its current position. They want, instead, the benefits of a modern consumer society and have accordingly indulged themselves in a mad binge of consumerism, to the point that Rho's government exhorted its people to exercise restraint — the very Korean economy was being affected! Will, therefore, these 'new' Koreans be up to the task of further discipline and sacrifice in order to carve out a real and lasting place for South Korea in the new world order? Will they be up to their publicly stated determination to become a member of the industrialised world? I believe that they could do so, provided they harness the resources of their greatest asset — namely, their strong belief in their 'Koreanness' and in using their new-found freedom, after centuries of existing at the whim of their various colonial masters, to become at last 'something'.

Additionally, without the support of an Asia Pacific regional community, South Korea, with even fewer friends than Japan, will find it difficult to make much further progress. It needs help, in particular from its regional neighbours, *vis-à-vis* both North Korea, its own better integration within the region, and with its negotiations with the EC, the United States and, in future, NAFTA. North Korea needs the same form of help from the region, but to a much greater degree. A constantly divided Greater Korea, an increasingly frustrated and angry South Korea, and a wild-card nuclear North Korea would be in no one's best interests.

SOUTHEAST ASIA
A Catalyst for Regional Unity?

INDONESIA
MALAYSIA
THE PHILIPPINES
SINGAPORE
THAILAND
BRUNEI
INDOCHINA
BURMA (MYANMAR)

SOUTHEAST ASIA
A Catalyst for Regional Unity?

If Asia Pacific is to create a regional forum, as I have already alluded to, Southeast Asia must and will play a pivotal role. Today, Japan is the most important economy in Asia Pacific by far; without Japan, an economic grouping encompassing the countries of the western Pacific rim is inconceivable. The Japanese can, in the near term, singlehandedly prevent it from happening. But they cannot initiate the process. Nor can China or India, as they are both too involved in the rapid evolution of their own domestic societies. Through APEC, Australia tried and failed. I believe this can only be done by the ASEAN. In turn, it must ensure that Japan, China, India and Australia are at least brought into ASEAN, however nervously or reluctantly.

Japan remains politically stunted. And Asia Pacific remains haunted by Japan's attempt to establish by force a Greater East Asia Co-Prosperity Sphere in the 1940s that would stretch from Hokkaido to Mandalay and Sydney. The Japanese are not prepared to assert themselves again, no matter how peaceful their methods may be. Nor are Japan's Asia Pacific neighbours likely to follow the lead of their former oppressor. The initiative will have to come 'from the middle up', so to speak.

In Asia Pacific terms, this means Southeast Asia, because it provides the geographical 'swing factor' between Japan and China on the one hand and the Indian subcontinent and Australasia on the other. Southeast Asia bestrides the sea routes between the Middle East and North Asia. It is rich in natural, and not least in human, resources. But above all, it has already set an example of regional co-operation in a part of the world notably lacking in good-neighbourliness.

At this stage, the ASEAN countries that are co-operating together comprise only six of the ten countries that make up what is now called Southeast Asia. The six — Indonesia, Thailand, the Philippines, Malaysia,

Singapore, and Brunei — form the Association of Southeast Asian Nations (ASEAN), a quarter-century-old club that is now beginning to organise this co-operation. The remaining four countries are Vietnam, Cambodia, Laos, and Burma (Myanmar).

Since a fragile peace was achieved in Cambodia in October 1991, the prospects for eventually widening the ASEAN community to the three countries of Indochina — Vietnam, Cambodia, and Laos — have improved significantly. Mountains still need to be moved, that Southeast Asia should be seen in this light shows how far this disparate collection of countries has come in the past few decades. But this transformation is the whole point: these countries show what can be achieved within a short time. Southeast Asia is a microcosm of the Asia Pacific macrocosm. It is the nucleus of a larger community forum in the future.

The term 'Southeast Asia' came into use during World War II, when the Allies were working out how to dispossess Japan of its military gains. Previously, the region was defined by colonialism of a different kind. The British held sway over Burma and Malaya, the Dutch over Indonesia, the French over Indochina, and the Americans over the Philippines, while the Portuguese had half an island: East Timor. Only Thailand escaped formal colonisation. Each of the colonies looked in different directions, and often the last place they looked was towards their neighbours. Imperial lines of communication determined the direction of decision-making, the flow of people, and above all the flow of goods. The ultimate masters of their fate resided in Paris, London, The Hague, Lisbon, and Washington.

It was not always so. During the so-called classical period of Southeast Asian history, from the seventh to the thirteenth century, two great regional empires and several lesser ones laid claim to large swathes of territory. The empire centred on Angkor in Cambodia, which controlled not only the modern nation of that name, but also a number of vassal states in Thailand, Laos, and Vietnam's Mekong Delta. By contrast, the trading empire of Srivijaya reached a dominant position in the region by effectively mastering the Straits of Malacca and thus the sea lanes between West and East Asia.

But by the early sixteenth century, these empires had disappeared, leaving a host of smaller states that were no match for the Europeans. Within two hundred years, there were forty states in what is now called

Southeast Asia. By then, the only coherence in the region came from religion and trade. Buddhism travelled eastwards across the land mass from India. Islam worked the maritime routes, marking the coasts and seeping up the rivers. Trade flowed from West Asia, but more particularly from China, whose merchants and wayfarers settled throughout Southeast Asia long before Europeans ever set foot in the region.

Southeast Asia has always been highly pervious to foreign influences. The region is wedged between the two great civilisations of the Asian land mass, India and China. But this vulnerability to the whims of the bigger powers has made the countries of the region peculiarly resilient. They can bend with the wind. Thailand, for example, has proven flexible enough to absorb a heady concoction of races, whether they be the Lao (whose numbers in Thailand exceed those in Laos), the Khmers, or the Chinese.

Now that the colonial interlude is over, perhaps Southeast Asia will return to its ancient role, as the smaller cog between two giant wheels, India and China. If India turns eastwards, and as China becomes more adventurous economically, the lands between them, together with Japan, will play an important role in balancing one against the other. In particular, ASEAN should play a key role in this process. Its newly created AFTA should greatly facilitate the economic integration of the ASEAN countries, as well as provide an incentive for the other regional countries to join AFTA as an intermediate step (possibly first taking 'associate' status), prior to eventually joining ASEAN itself. Additionally, ASEAN's security forum has been enlarged to include Vietnam and Laos, both with observer status. ASEAN also consults with certain external powers, such as the EC, the United States, Russia, and China on security issues. This security forum could provide an important regional catalyst for closer general regional co-operation, as well as on security-related issues.

For reasons of time, space, and constraints imposed by the publisher, I regret that the following chapters provide only an outline, rather than a detailed analysis, of the history and culture of the countries of the region, together with an indication of the geopolitical trends that are taking place in those countries. However, despite these constraints, I believe that the ASEAN countries must and will play a major role, if not the central role, in the development of an Asia Pacific community forum.

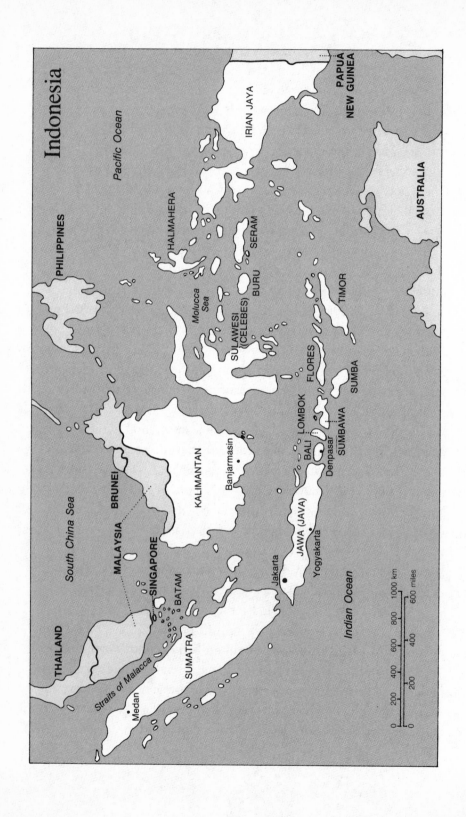

INDONESIA
Can Real Unity be Forged from Such Diversity?

If the ten countries of Southeast Asia are, in their diversity, symptomatic of the the rich variety of peoples making up Asia Pacific, then Indonesia perfectly expresses this profusion, albeit under one national roof. But what a huge, rambling mansion.

Indonesia is the fifth most populous country in the world, after China, India, the United States, and Russia. Its 180 million people speak 250 regional dialects and languages and are scattered over some 13,700 islands that stretch for 5,120 kilometres, like a necklace of pearls scattered on the sea. In sheer numbers of people and geographical expanse, Indonesia dominates Southeast Asia.

The bald numbers are not the only factor which makes Indonesia the most important country in Southeast Asia. Its geographical location buttresses the point. It comprises the entire southern flank of all the main waterways between the Indian Ocean and the South China Sea. If ships were to avoid Indonesia on their way between the two, they would have to sail through treacherous seas to the south of Australia.

But Indonesia is not one to flex its muscles, preferring to assert its authority in a more subtle manner. It is too big to be ignored, but too small, or rather too dispersed, to throw its weight around in the way that China and India have done in the past. The Javanese, the dominant ethnic group, believe that resorting to violence in word and deed is a sign of weakness. Strength is derived from the absence of self-assertion. This has its advantages and disadvantages. For its size, Indonesia is probably the least reported country in the world. The country's president, Suharto, who came to power following a failed communist coup in 1965, likes it that way. Indonesia's human rights record, which is little better than China's, has been placed under far less international scrutiny. When scores of demonstrators were killed by government troops on the eastern part of the remote island of Timor in November 1991, few donors halted their aid and there were no material outcries in the US Congress. However, with the Clinton administration, this could change.

But this apparent lack of foreign interest has some drawbacks. After years of patient lobbying, Indonesia was elected to the chairmanship of the 103-nation Non-Aligned Movement in September 1991, at a time when the Movement's influence in world affairs had long passed. Indonesia wanted to play the role of peacemaker in Cambodia, but the settlement agreed upon by the warring factions in October 1991 virtually ignored Jakarta's views.

Indonesia is rich in natural resources, particularly oil, gas, timber, and tin. It is the largest country by far in ASEAN and has long considered itself *primus inter pares* — first among equals — within the grouping. But it has failed to take a leading role in working out new ways for the ASEAN countries to co-operate economically. Instead, it has been Malaysia and Thailand which have made most of the running.

Indonesia may be the leader of the Non-Aligned countries, but this has not stopped it from developing an extremely close relationship with the United States, both economically and militarily. Indonesia's strategic position and its role from 1965 to 1990 as a bulwark of anti-communism help to explain why Washington has rarely been very strident in calling on the Jakarta government to become more democratic.

There are other reasons why Suharto's military-backed rule has not been questioned more searchingly by the West. One reason is the largely implicit view that keeping such a diverse archipelago within a single nation has required strong central control, with the full support of the armed forces — an argument that should be equally applied to China *vis-à-vis* its large and diverse population and its huge land mass. Since independence, central control has meant that power has resided among the Javanese, the inhabitants of the most populous island in Indonesia, comprising 60 per cent of the total population.

Indonesia was largely the achievement of Suharto's predecessor, the vain and flamboyant Sukarno, who brought the archipelago together in a modern nation-state, following the declaration of independence from the Netherlands in August 1945. It took another five years before the Dutch gave up trying to reimpose colonial rule, and it was not until 1963 that the last remnant of the Dutch East Indies, called West Guinea or Irian Jaya, was incorporated into Indonesia. The territory of East Timor was seized by force in 1976, following the withdrawal of the Portuguese from one of the last remnants of their colonial empire. Portugal had ruled a great deal more of Indonesia in the sixteenth century, until the Dutch took over a hundred years later.

By having to fight for its independence after World War II, Indonesia's decolonising struggle differed markedly from the more peaceful experience of the British colonies, such as Malaysia and Singapore, or of the Philippines, under the United States. In this respect, Vietnam was the closest thing to a kindred spirit in Southeast Asia, but it eventually went communist from head to toe. Indonesia merely flirted with communism.

In struggling to weld together so diverse a nation as Indonesia in the 1950s and early 1960s, Sukarno neglected the economy after he had nationalised the commanding heights of industry. As time went by, Sukarno played the foreign card in order to shore up his increasingly precarious position. He cosied up to Maoist China and to the Indonesian Communist Party. And he engaged in a disastrous campaign of military confrontation with Malaysia in the early 1960s. Both rebounded badly against him and he was effectively deposed by a group of generals led by Suharto, following the failed communist coup of September 1965. The armed forces seized the opportunity to purge Indonesia of leftists once and for all. Some accounts say that more than half a million people were killed and thousands imprisoned, as the native Indonesian ethnic communities took the opportunity to settle old scores. The chief sponsors of the Indonesian Communist Party were the Chinese, who bore the brunt of the violence. Many of those that survived had to go into hiding.

Suharto followed the opposite policy to that of his predecessor. He relied on economic progress rather than political rhetoric to ensure national unity. He is as colourless a public speaker as Sukarno was outspoken. Suharto promulgated a creed called *pancasila* (belief in God, national unity, democracy, justice, and humanitarianism) that was both sufficiently idealistic, yet sufficiently vague, for the entire population to espouse it without being either completely vacuous or too specific.

Pancasila was not a concept that was conjured up in one man's mind.

It was a political adaptation of Indonesia's culture. Although it is the most populous Islamic country in the world, the influence of Hinduism and Buddhism in the popular mind remains strong. Borobudur, one of the world's great monuments, which was built in the late eighth century in central Java, is entirely Buddhist in inspiration. Dotted around the same island are a host of Hindu temples. When Islam began to take over in the fourteenth century, the Indian Hindu religion retreated until it is now found only on the island of Bali. These three streams of religion also course their way through India. Unlike in India, however, where many ethnic groups jockey for position, one native Indonesian ethnic group, the Javanese, is so preponderant that it has been able to impose a unitary, rather than a federal, state on the archipelago. The motto on the national crest, *Bhinneka Tunggal Ika* ('Out of many, one'), is as much a declaration of intent as a statement of fact. That said, the power of Islam should not be underestimated in Indonesia. It forms one of the two main pillars of society, the other being the armed forces. By virtue of its history and culture, Indonesian Islam, which forms part of the Sunni sect, has been tolerant of other religions and beliefs.

One of the three authorised political parties in Indonesia's highly choreographed political scene is Islamic-based. Additionally, the main Islamic organisation, the 35 million-strong Nahdlatul Ulama, is a political and social force in its own right. However, Suharto has proven adept at preventing Islamic radicalism or fundamentalism from taking hold politically, by intimidating its leaders, yet burnishing his own Muslim credentials. The result has been a steady marginalisation of Islam from political power in the past twenty-five years under Suharto's Golkar Party. Only in the northern tip of Sumatra is Islam a potent force, bound up as it is with separatist ambitions.

If Islam is the warp of Indonesia's cloth, the armed forces are the weft. Their legitimacy is derived from the independence struggle, when their role was seen as both military and political, a dual function that survives today, almost as strong as it was in the 1950s. There is no sign of the military relaxing their grip on the body politic; despite having been (automatically) re-elected in March 1993 for another five-year term, at some point the seventy-one-year-old General Suharto must step down. When he does, it is assumed that he will be replaced by another officer. The top brass occupy key ministerial positions, and a sizeable number of seats in the national assembly are set aside for the armed forces.

Conversely, their grip on the body economic is slipping slightly, largely as a result of the reforms Suharto has introduced since the early 1980s. The Indonesian military have traditionally been paid what amounts to protection money by ethnic-Chinese businessmen. The practice goes on today, but a growing middle class has made it somewhat less necessary.

Suharto's widely-praised reforms have opened up the economy to much greater international competition. Import tariffs have been cut, foreign-investment regulations relaxed, and the licensing system has been reduced. The financial markets have been completely overhauled. The result has been the emergence of a new entrepreneurial class of young Indonesians, still predominantly ethnic Chinese, but more integrated into the local community than their parents. As the stock market has opened its doors to foreign investors, the amount of publicly available information about Indonesian companies has increased.

The need for economic reform has been largely driven by the weakness of oil prices since the early 1980s. The oil glut did Indonesia a big favour, forcing it to reduce its dependence on revenue from oil exports and to invest more in resource-based exports, such as pulp and paper, as well as to sell more manufactured goods abroad, such as footwear. The strategy has worked. In 1982, oil and gas exports comprised 82 per cent of the total, but today, the proportion has fallen to around 40 per cent.

Much of the credit must go to the technocrats, to whom Suharto gave a relatively free hand in restructuring the economy. But much of the credit is also due to Suharto for his acumen in ensuring that the various power groups (not least the army) were not in a position to block the reforms. The president's main achievement has been to balance one block of interests against another in order to produce the political stability needed to grow rapidly. The economy's rate of expansion, which averaged 6 per cent a year during the period 1975–1991, compares favourably with other countries in ASEAN.

Capital has flowed in from other countries, especially Japan. Outside the oil and banking industries, Japan is by far the largest investor, with US$10 billion worth of investment approvals between 1967 and 1990. As might be expected of such a resource-rich country, most of that investment has gone into extractive and primary industries, such as aluminium, palm oil, and timber. However, considerable investment has also gone into the manufacturing sector, such as textiles and automobiles.

At the government and business establishment levels, the effect of this close relationship is that the Indonesians feel ambivalent towards Japan. Japan has played a crucial role in helping the development of the new Indonesia which arose from the upheavals of the mid-1960s. President Suharto has visited Tokyo more frequently than any other non-ASEAN capital. Yet Indonesians, particularly the older ones, are suspicious of Japan's intentions towards the region.

The man on the street is more concerned about domestic factors that affect the country's long-term prospects than about foreign ones. One particular preoccupation is the future of the Indonesian presidency. By ensuring the stable development of his country, Suharto has succeeded in attracting steady inward investment. Indonesia has become self-sufficient in food during his years in office and has achieved an enviable record in curbing the growth of its population. But Suharto has a blind spot. He has shown excessive favouritism towards his family and their business dealings. Few major industrial contracts are awarded without the 'help' of one of Suharto's relatives. Whether it be telecommunications or naphtha crackers, a Suharto offspring or relation somehow gets in on the act. Foreign businessmen are finding it increasingly difficult to invest in Indonesia without bringing one member of the 'first' family into the deal.

Some Indonesians defend such nepotism, saying that it is better to award the contracts and licences to *pribumis*, such as Suharto's kin, than to allow the ethnic Chinese businesses to control still more of the economy. Others say that indigenous entrepreneurs will remain stifled if only a tiny handful of them receive special treatment from the government.

How Indonesians will respond to the excessive concentration of economic power in the hands of the ethnic Chinese is one of the two unanswered questions of Suharto's presidency. The other is the question of who will succeed him, a point that is related to the first. For if Suharto can display such a lack of judgement over such a crucial matter, some observers ask whether he can be expected to handle effectively an even more delicate issue, namely the inevitable transition to a new regime.

Suharto has shown no sign of wanting to hand over the reins in the immediate future. It is said that Javanese kings do not retire, and Suharto seems no exception. Whatever happens, Indonesia is in for a bumpy ride over the next few years. Indonesia's challenge is to harness its human and natural resources into a collective whole, a Herculean task given its geographical spread and different ethnic groups.

However, once this unity is more or less achieved — or, better yet, achieved in parallel to this process — Indonesia must develop the vision to play a larger regional role more commensurate with its potential contribution. It will require the region's support and general involvement, particularly if it wishes to prepare for the inevitable diminution of support from the West, in particular from the United States. It will also need to be less prickly about its own perception that it is the elder brother of the other Southeast Asian countries. It needs to be more collegiate and proactive in its relations with these neighbours — after all, Malaysia, Singapore, and Thailand have achieved great successes too. In turn, the Asia Pacific region cannot ignore Indonesia, due to its geographical position, population size, and resources. The region needs its active participation and support for a regional forum.

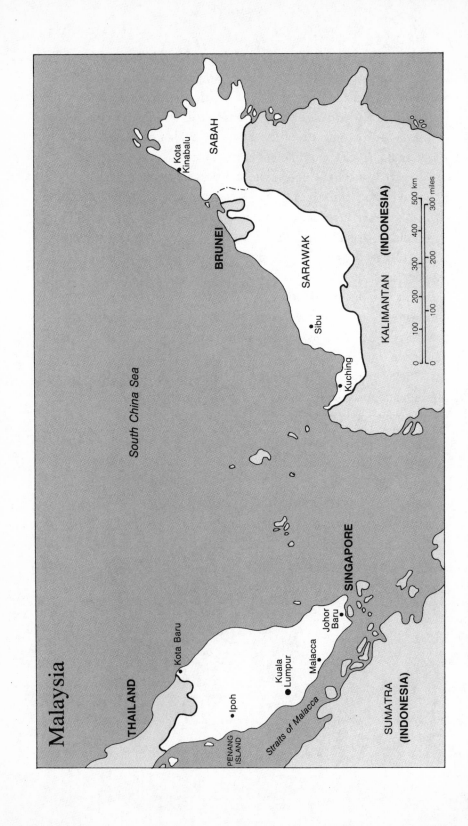

MALAYSIA

A Geopolitical Vision versus an Ideological Risk

Malaysia is finding a place on the diplomatic world map. Its prime minister, Datuk Seri Dr Mahathir bin Mohamad, is regarded as something of an international statesman. However, closer to home, he has ambitions of leading ASEAN, and in the process has possibly rubbed some of his neighbours up the wrong way.

It is probably more than a coincidence that Mahathir raised his profile after Singapore's Lee Kuan Yew stepped down as prime minister in 1990. Mahathir then came into his own in December 1990, when he proposed the creation of a trading community called the East Asian Economic Grouping (EAEG), to include the six ASEAN nations, China and Japan and, possibly, Taiwan, Korea, and Hong Kong. The idea was deliberately general, but the essential aim was to create a bloc that would be the Asia Pacific response to the emerging economic blocs in the West.

The initiative came only days after a meeting of world leaders in Brussels failed, once again, to achieve a breakthrough in the Uruguay Round of talks convened under the auspices of the GATT. If East Asian nations do not join together, said Mahathir, 'we will not be able to protect our trade share, as individually we don't have the strength.' Unfortunately, the idea received a cool response from other potential members, China and Japan included. The grouping has since been watered down to an agreement among potential members to form a caucus, or a group which will meet occasionally to discuss matters of common interest.

If Malaysia's leader is somewhat abrasive, albeit with considerable vision, the country itself is charming. Its five thousand-kilometre coastline is dotted with casuarina-lined, sandy beaches and extends from the Andaman Sea at the country's westernmost point south to the Strait of Malacca. Much of the country is mountainous, with dense tropical jungles and swamps, but most of western peninsular Malaysia has been cleared and developed, with picturesque plantations of rubber, pineapple, and sway-ing oil palms. It is this surfeit of natural resources, including tin, that has made the nation rich. In fact, it was these resources that first drew Chinese and Indian immigrants to its shores. By 1990, GNP per capita was US$2,320 per annum, less than a quarter of Singapore's, but nearly half as much again as Thailand's.

Malaysia itself is a federation of eleven states on the Malay peninsula, and Sabah and Sarawak on the nearby island of Borneo to the east. The peninsular states were dominated by a series of European rulers. The first were the Portuguese who colonised Malacca in 1511, to be replaced by the Dutch in 1641. Then the British took control of Penang in 1786, and less than a decade later, spread their control over much of the peninsula's west coast. It was during the period of Britain's colonisation that the basis of Malaysia's prosperity was laid: rubber and tin.

In World War II, Japanese forces occupied the country from 1941 to 1943. If anything good could be said to have come out of Japan's brutal reign, it was that Malaysians were left wanting to be their own masters. This was the beginning of the end of British colonial rule. The twelve-year communist insurgency after the war led to Britain granting independence to Malaya's eleven states in 1957. The federation of Malaysia was formed with Sabah, Sarawak, and Singapore in 1963. Two years later, Singapore was excluded from the cosy arrangement. The main reason for this was racial. While both Malaysia and Singapore call themselves multi-racial, Singapore's version is predominantly Chinese and Malaysia's predomi-nantly Malay.

It was the flow of Chinese and Indian immigrants to Malaysia that was to give the country its multi-racial flavour. But theirs has not been an easy existence. In particular, the relationship between the Malays and the Chinese is delicate, to say the least. The country's indigenous *bumiputra* (translated literally as 'sons of the soil'), almost all of whom are Malays, make up nearly 62 per cent of the total population of 17.7 million, the Chinese almost 30 per cent, and the Indians some 8 per cent. Yet the nation's largest racial group had a disproportionately small stake in the economy. The indigenous Malay was no match, commercially speaking, for the Chinese merchant.

Resentment over the effective control of most of the economy by the ethnic Chinese eventually spilled over into five days of violence in May 1969, during which dozens of people were killed. Since independence twelve years before, the implicit assumption underlying the state was that the Malays would govern while the Chinese would be left to make money. The blood-letting of 1969 showed that such an arrangement was no longer tenable; Malays would have to be allocated a bigger share of the economic pie so as to avoid similar events in the future. This conclusion lay behind what became known as the 'New Economic Policy'. The twenty-year policy, which expired in December 1990, was to put wealth into *bumiputra* hands through a package of economic measures, including preferential share allocations, government handouts, and educational concessions favouring the native Malays.

The New Economic Policy has been succeeded by the 'New Development ment Policy', covering the decade from 1991 to 2000. The goals of the two policies are similar, with some revisions. For example, a revised goal is the eradication of 'hardcore' poverty, especially among palm-oil and rubber plantation workers, as well as the small aboriginal population. The redistribution of the country's wealth continues to be a goal. But the emphasis will be on strengthening the capacity of the *bumiputra* to manage, operate, and own their own businesses, rather than on achieving a numerical target for *bumiputra* control.

Malay-Chinese acrimony is likely to remain a feature of Malaysian life. In 1991, the Malaysian Chinese Association (MCA) proposed spending M$5 million on a Chinese cultural centre and depository for Chinese literature and artifacts. The United Malays National Organisation (UMNO), Mahathir's party in power and the stalwart of Malay dominance in Malaysia, protested against this proposed elevation of Chinese culture. The MCA gave in and abandoned the idea. But the affair has left a bitter taste in Chinese mouths. Islamic radicalism, too, is enjoying something of a renaissance, much to the chagrin of Malaysia's Chinese citizens and Chinese neighbours in nearby Singapore. It is also causing concern amongst the more moderate Malays.

Further afield, Malaysian sensitivities were upset in 1990–1991 by an Australian television drama series portraying life in an Australian embassy in a fictitious Asian country. The Malaysian government thought that the series made the country look like a corrupt, lazy stereotype of a Third

World country where human rights are shown scant respect. In yet another case, the government objected to an Australian film depicting a boatload of Vietnamese refugees landing on Malaysian shores to a hostile reception. This may sound petty, but it put relations with Canberra into the deep freezer for a while and the rift had to be resolved by the countries' prime ministers.

On the economic front, Malaysia is on a roll, breaking new records in spite of economic slowdown in the rest of the world. The country's GDP grew by a record 9.8 per cent in 1990, and 8.7 per cent in 1991. In 1990, too, a record US$6.5 billion was invested in the manufacturing sector by foreign industrialists, especially from Taiwan and Japan. Domestic investments that year reached US$3.8 billion, three times the level of the previous year. According to *Time* magazine of 14 September 1992, Malaysia had become the world's leading exporter of computer chips and the third-largest producer of semiconductors after Japan and the United States. It is investments such as these which are expected to see the economy through the hard times being suffered in the developed world.

The huge foreign and domestic investment has unfortunately led to a worsening labour shortage. This, in turn, has resulted in wage increases and fuelled inflation. Infrastructural strains are also beginning to be felt. Foreign investors are beginning to think twice about putting yet more money into the country. In the meantime, Japan continues to be the country's leading source of foreign aid and its most important trading partner. Japan has played a prominent role in Malaysia's economic development. Mahathir, more than any other Asian leader, has tried hard to put behind the country its wartime experiences and to court Japanese economic leadership. It was Mahathir who came up with the 'Look East' policy in 1981, exhorting his countrymen to turn away from the West, and in particular from its former British colonial masters, and look to a more Asian future. He proposed that Malaysia model itself along the lines of the successful economies in the East, such as Japan.

This policy has certainly reaped benefits. Japanese investment poured in from 1986, when investment laws were liberalised to allow foreigners to own up to 100 per cent of certain manufacturing ventures. The

Japanese received investment approvals in Malaysia totalling more than US$3.7 billion between 1987 and 1991. For their part, the Taiwanese seem to be competing with the Japanese to see who can put more money into the economy. In 1990, they overtook Japan as Malaysia's top source of foreign investment.

Japanese industrialists are getting on just fine in Malaysia, not least because of a special relationship they appear to have nurtured with Mahathir's ruling UMNO party. For example, when UMNO lost the states of Sabah and Kelantan in the October 1990 election, the Japanese were instructed to cancel an aid mission to these renegade states. Japanese investors with big stakes in the country often go directly to Mahathir to get their plans approved. And major projects often go to the Japanese. But the relationship is not in balance, being too weighted in favour of Japan. Malaysia's trade deficit with Japan is widening — Japan accounted for 20 per cent of Malaysia's total trade in 1989, leaving Malaysia with a substantial trade deficit. On top of that, Japan buys mostly oil and commodities and little in the way of manufactured goods. Too little technology is being transferred to Malaysia, and Japanese companies are not keen even to embark on major staff training projects. It has also been said that the Japanese use their soft loans and so-called untied grants to get business in Malaysia. And all the while, Malaysia is becoming more dependent on Japanese investment and technology.

Malaysia is also taking on other more fundamental risks, which could have severe consequences in terms of both its domestic development and how it is perceived by the outside world. Fundamentalist Islam as practised by Iran since the Shah's downfall and as advocated by extremist groups throughout the Middle East, North Africa, and Asia, has caused economic and social mayhem in these countries. In a world beset with extreme change, which is often followed by chaos, the thought of extreme fundamentalist Islam taking hold in Malaysia causes, rightly or wrongly, considerable concern, if not outright aversion on the part of traditional Malays, let alone on the part of the minority ethnic groups. Even more specific and negative reactions are likely to be evidenced by other countries and would-be foreign investors. The state of Kelantan's aggressive policy of implementing an Islamic state to the extent of introducing the Islamic criminal code know as *hudud* law, involving the mandatory amputation of limbs for certain offences, will further exacerbate these internal and external perceptions. Unfortunately, the more subtle reasons for this development are lost on the outside world. Thus Mahathir's government and the people of Malaysia will have to monitor this process carefully, if they are to avoid being tarred with the general Middle East brush.

A further destabilising factor arose in 1992 and early 1993. As a result of the view held by many in Malaysia — including, in particular, Mahathir's government and his UMNO party — concerning abuses by some of the nine Malaysian hereditary sultans (rulers) of their immunity-from-prosecution privilege, Mahathir launched a major initiative in January 1993 to curb these privileges. Under Malaysia's constitution, the nine rulers, in rotation, elect one from their group to take up the position of Malaysia's 'king', who will be Malaysia's head of state for a five-year period. The constitution also provides that no government bill affecting the rights and privileges of the rulers can be passed into law without their consent. Mahathir claimed that sovereign immunity was a feudalistic principle which had been abolished in the West. The opinion of one Malay businessman may be typical: 'We want to modernise the monarchy. We reject their feudal ways. But we still need the monarchy to maintain Malay dominance and a Malay as head of state. But we must discipline them.' Others believed the confrontation was carried out with indecent haste, which is not the usual Malay or Muslim way of solving a problem. Some went so far as to say that in certain states they would support their sultans come what may. In the event, the nine rulers caved in and have basically accepted Mahathir's amendments, with some concessions being made by the government. As a consequence, many Malays are now saying that a similar public scrutiny of what critics call Malaysia's new *rajas* is also now called for — referring to the activities of some senior government officials! Should this initiative and its result turn sour over time by pitting the rulers and their supporters against the government, it could split the Malay community into opposing factions. This would, in turn, give rise to further questions about Malaysia's general stability, and foreign investors would have even more cause for concern.

These are real concerns, but, so far, they are not sufficiently serious to warrant taking any evasive action. On the positive side, Mahathir has recently come up with a new initiative for Malaysia as a whole which he terms 'Vision 2020'. In essence, he is exhorting the Malaysians to make every effort in terms of, *inter alia*, creating a sense of common purpose and shared destiny, developing a mature democratic society where Malaysians of all colours and creeds are free to practise and profess their customs, cultures, and religious beliefs, yet feel they all belong to one nation, ensuring that there is an equitable distribution of the nation's wealth and the removal of any racial identification with wealth and economic function, and, finally, to establishing a prosperous society with an economy that is fully competitive, dynamic, robust, and resilient. If the Malaysian people can work together to achieve these goals, Mahathir feels that by the year 2020, Malaysia should be able to join the ranks of the world's developed countries.

In the final analysis, Malaysia needs to deal with the dynamics of its own society in its own way. Yet, if it wishes to play an important regional role and continue to attract outside interest, it needs to do so in a way that more or less fits into the framework of the perceived reality of its regional neighbours and foreign investors. Fortunately, Mahathir is committed to his 'Look East' policy. More than any other Asian country, Malaysia is prepared to envisage a broader Asian community and for Japan to be a 'sort of' regional and economic leader. But two things are needed. First, Southeast Asia and the region needs leaders of Mahathir's stamp. Without his type of vision — that is to say, a pragmatic assessment of how the world is evolving economically and geopolitically — and a willingness to press for change, the ASEAN countries risk remaining little more than a 'soap box' for endless debate. Secondly, Japan has to iron out the bumps in its investments in Malaysia and elsewhere in the region. Japan also has to want to wear a co-leader's hat. However, less obvious, perhaps, is the real need for Mahathir, and ASEAN, to review the question of India's and Australasia's participation in this vision. Pursuing it without them will, I suspect, prove unfruitful in the long run.

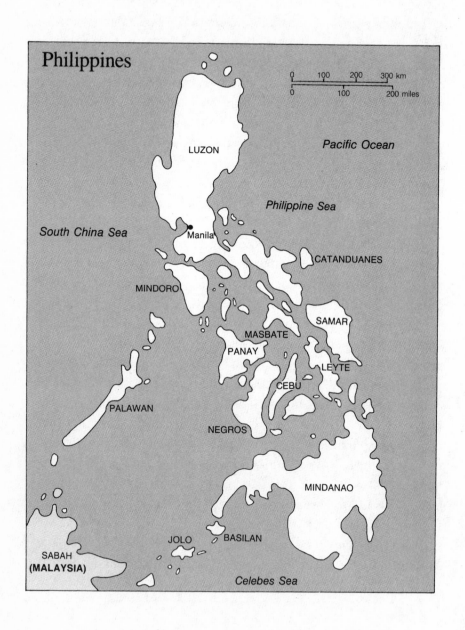

Philippines

0   100   200   300 km
0   100   200 miles

LUZON

Pacific Ocean

Philippine Sea

South China Sea

Manila

CATANDUANES

MINDORO

SAMAR

MASBATE

PANAY

LEYTE

CEBU

PALAWAN

NEGROS

MINDANAO

JOLO   BASILAN

SABAH
(MALAYSIA)

Celebes Sea

THE PHILIPPINES

A Sad, Anarchic Teenage Farce — When Will They Grow up?

The Philippines can never mature until the country cuts the political, psychological, and cultural umbilical cord connecting it to the United States. After three centuries spent in a Roman Catholic monastery, followed by fifty years in Hollywood, it is still groping to find an identity. Discovered by Ferdinand Magellan in 1521, the Philippines became part of the Spanish empire in 1565. Independence was achieved more than three hundred years later in 1898, the first country in Asia to win freedom — only to be lost to the United States two years later. Following the Japanese occupation of 1941–1945, the Philippines was granted independence in 1946.

In many ways, the Philippines has more in common with Latin America than with Asia. It is the only Catholic country in the region, and it suffers from social inequality to a Latin degree. The armed forces cannot seem to stay in their barracks, although in Asia this is not a phenomenon unique to the Philippines. The Catholic Church and the armed forces are the twin pillars of Philippine society, in the same way that Islam and the military hold together the neighbouring archipelago of Indonesia. In both countries, they are a source of weakness as well as strength.

For the Philippines, the Catholic Church has provided a social discipline, but not an economic one. Filipinos are hard-working, but they lack the consistent focus and diligence that Confucianism instils in the Overseas Chinese, the South Koreans, the Japanese, and other Asians, and which helps make these latter races so successful economically.

For their part, the Americans gave the Philippines two things: democracy and an education system. The result is that most people speak English, an inestimable resource in a region with a generally low level of proficiency in the world's business language. Three-quarters of those eligible attend secondary school and a quarter are enrolled in some form of tertiary education, an astonishingly high level for such a poor country. Such high levels of enrolment are only otherwise found in countries with at least two-and-a-half times the income per head, such as Chile and Poland.

One reason why this strong educational base has not helped turn the Philippines into an affluent society is the political system. American-style democracy has provided a recipe for corruption and mismanagement. In the 1950s, the Philippines had one of the strongest economies in the region. It was the envy, if not the ideal, of many other Asian countries, all of whom were trying to cope with the aftermath of World War II. For example, it sent its economic advisers to South Korea to help the country get back on its feet. But as time wore on, its neighbours overtook the Philippines. In some strange, perverse way, the Philippines could not deliver on its early promise. In 1980, Thailand and the Philippines shared the same living standard. However, by 1990, the Thai GNP per capita was more than US$1,420, almost double that of the Philippines.

There are two élites in the country. One is the Spanish *mestizo*, or landowning class, descended from the colonisers who came via Mexico in the seventeenth and eighteenth centuries in search of gold and silver. The other élite is the ethnic Chinese, who started arriving during the Spanish occupation and carved a niche for themselves in commerce. As with their fellow Chinese in Indonesia and elsewhere, they have had few political pretensions, being content instead to make money, buy themselves political insurance, and maintain a very low profile.

In contrast, for the (originally) landowning class, things were different. Since World War II, a small number of families have controlled both the political and economic systems, taking it in turns to push around the other members of the élite. Among the oligarchs, perhaps the most powerful and durable has proven to be the Cojuangco clan, from Central Luzon, north of Manila. This family was split by President Ferdinand Marcos, who ruled the country from 1965 to 1986 as a virtual dictator.

One side, led by Eduardo 'Danding' Cojuangco, allied itself with Marcos. Danding enriched himself in the process, by turning the market- ing of coconut, a crop which is the country's main employer, into a monopoly, with himself at the helm. From this pad, he launched into banking and industry. He went on to build a substantial business empire with allegedly substantial support from Marcos.

The other side was led by Benigno 'Ninoy' Aquino, the husband of Danding's cousin Corazon. Ninoy was the most painful thorn in Marcos's flesh, a consummate politician in the true Filipino tradition. He would have made a powerful president, perhaps too much like Marcos, the man he opposed. The Philippines never found out, because he was assassinated at Manila airport on his return from exile in September 1983.

The Philippines' industrialisation took a wrong turn early in the 1960s by emphasising import substitution rather than export promotion. This appeared to work for a while, because the economy received a fillip from the United States, which imported sugar under preferential terms. Direct investment from American multi-nationals flowed in, and the US military spent tens of millions of US dollars upgrading its huge bases at Clark and Subic Bay, north of Manila, during the Vietnam War.

This flow of capital and aid from Uncle Sam petered out in the late 1970s, following the end of the Vietnam War, when American business-men began searching for new Asian pastures. The Philippines was becoming a growing political risk. The emergency powers Marcos arro-gated to himself under martial law were ostensibly intended to help him curb communist and Islamic insurgency movements. The latter was gradually brought under control by the late 1980s, but the communist New People's Army stubbornly kept up its attacks on the government. It remains a running sore on the body politic, despite the demise of communism in the West and lack of Chinese support.

Marcos's presidential powers were more effective in attacking his constitutional opponents than the Communists. Politicians such as Benigno Aquino were imprisoned and the press muzzled. Only the Catholic Church was strong enough to voice its dissatisfaction. By February 1986, Filipinos had had enough. Marcos's attempt to stage-manage yet another presidential election was the last straw and he was toppled in a largely bloodless 'people-power' revolt which saw Aquino's widow, Corazon, reluctantly assume the presidency and Marcos driven into exile.

Aquino introduced a number of economic reforms which should have provided a reasonably firm foundation for her successor. But she failed to push through their implementation. She also made only a half-hearted attempt to dispossess and punish the cronies who grew fat during the Marcos years. The most notable of these was Danding, her cousin. The Presidential Commission on Good Government, established by Aquino, sequestered almost all of his assets, but in a series of legal reverses he was able to claw most of them back, including his shares in the San Miguel brewery. Although not corrupt herself, Corazon Aquino did little to break the power of the oligarchs, some of whom, such as the Lopez clan which controls a big power utility and media empire, emerged from her period in office stronger than ever. Indeed, her nephew, Antonio Cojuangco, has come out of the May 1992 election as possibly one of the most powerful businessmen in the Philippines. The tragedy is that the government, its cronies, and the powerful clans have a penchant for large aid-assisted projects and for looking after themselves. Little effort is seemingly made to help the majority of Filipinos, namely the hard-working poor, who have a surprising capacity to make something out of very little. All they need is a small loan to get started. In this area, the *Tulay sa Pag-unlad* (Bridge to Progress) agency has made significant progress in helping the micro and small entrepreneurs. More funding should be made available for this type of support. If properly supported, this huge reservoir of talent and effort could ultimately make a significant impact on the economy, the maturity, and the stability of the Philippines.

When Cory Aquino was seen to be lacking in the 'right stuff', disaffected army officers tried to topple her — on no less than six occasions. Although each time they were unsuccessful, and almost Chaplinesque in their efforts, it hardly enhanced the Philippines' image as either a sufficiently serious or stable place in which to invest. The armed forces had been politicised by their experience in combatting the Communists and the Islamic separatists in the south of the archipelago. They felt it natural that they should step in if the civilians were not, as they saw it, up to the job. The foreigners that were most disillusioned by the country's halting progress were the Americans. Sometimes called the sentimental imperialists, the United States during its forty years in control had tried to mould the Philippines into a God-fearing, Coca-Cola-drinking democracy. Even after independence, the Americans were deeply involved in the country, helping to defeat the communist *Hukbalahap* rebellion of the 1940s and 1950s (with tactics they tried later to adapt to Vietnam). And during the last coup against Aquino in December 1990, American air force pilots played a crucial role in foiling the rebels by buzzing Manila in their Phantom jet fighters.

The Philippine Congress repaid the Americans for their help by telling them to clear out of the military bases before the end of 1992, following long and unsuccessful negotiations to renew an agreement that would have enabled the United States to continue to use the installations. Much to Manila's chagrin, the US forces took everything movable with them, including some of the best floating docks in the world. Such is the pain of maturation. Although with the winding down of the Cold War, the US bases' days in the Philippines were possibly numbered anyway. However, there is no question that denying the United States further use of these facilities has diminished the US government's degree of commitment to its future participation in the region's security equation — something which has caused and continues to cause, considerable concern amongst the other countries of the region.

Now Manila is looking for a new general benefactor and with the one obvious candidate being Japan. Taiwan, however, is not far behind. It agreed in February 1993 with the Philippine government that it will put together a consortium to invest up to US$20 million to develop a new industrial site out of Subic Bay, the old US military base.

Japan is clearly concerned to help ensure a stable and prosperous neighbour to the south. It will probably continue to provide the lion's share of economic assistance to the country (well over half since the early 1980s), but investment is another matter. Out of a total of US$26 billion invested by Japan in Asia between 1987 and 1991, less than 3 per cent found its way to the Philippines. Whether that proportion will rise will depend upon the effectiveness of President Fidel Ramos. Despite early positive signs, the prognosis is uncertain.

Another support alternative is Taiwan, which has already made a considerable investment in the Philippines. As of March 1992, the Philippine Central Bank reported the cumulative total of Taiwanese investment to that date was US$35 million, which made it the fourteenth-largest foreign investor. However, reliable estimates from businessmen put the figure at well over US$1 billion. This is because Taiwanese investors are known either to invest through local partner companies or individuals as 'frontmen', or to invest through 'informal' remittances. Yet the Chinese community in the Philippines is not always sure of how it will fare. Certainly, the spate of kidnappings of members of wealthy Chinese families in 1992, some say with the active connivance of some members of the police force, did little to allay their concerns. Their declining commitment to the Philippines over the last thirty years, the endemic problem of 'cronyism', and the immaturity of the Philippine society as a whole, with their almost teenager-like excesses and enthusiasms, have resulted in the rest of Asia (and, for that matter, the rest of the world) being somewhat sceptical as to whether or not investment in the Philippines is advisable over the medium or long term. This result is exacerbated by the fact that so many more attractive and/or stable alternatives exist elsewhere in Asia Pacific.

Since Marcos was kicked out of office, little has been done to dent the wealth and power of the main clans that control Philippine life. But perhaps this was too much to hope for from somebody such as Aquino, a member of the élite herself, who never wanted the highest office but had it thrust upon her by virtue of being the wife of a martyr. However, her six years in office restored a surprisingly robust democracy to the country. The big test of the system came in May 1992, when her anointed successor, Fidel Ramos, a former general and a Protestant, was elected president in a more or less orderly, more or less clean ballot.

This leaves Ramos with the Herculean task of overcoming the problems that beset the country. He cannot quickly break the economic grip of the country's political élite, even if he wants to, which is a moot point. But he can gradually loosen its hold, by modernising the economy. His bold step of removing, on 1 September 1992, all the country's foreign exchange regulations on moving the peso in and out of the country was well received. The peso, to everyone's astonishment, actually strengthened as a result. Whether or not he can effect the more important and radical land-reform programme is another moot point. It worked in Japan, South Korea, and Taiwan, after all. Aquino introduced land reforms, but they have been far too slow to take effect, partly because the government has not had the money to finance the transfer of much land to impoverished farmers. Problems in the rural economy seem intractable. Changes are more likely to come by liberalising the economy still further, by introducing competition into, say, telecommunications, aviation, and manufacturing.

While the Philippines is part of ASEAN, it is probably the most insignificant member, other than tiny Brunei, in terms of clout and general relevance. Therefore, the development of an Asia Pacific community forum would probably be of enormous benefit to the Philippines, as without its participation in, and support from, such a forum, it is difficult to foresee the Philippines becoming anything less than irrelevant to the world as a whole—unless, of course, under Ramos, it finally begins to grow up. Conversely, it could be argued that, in this rare case, an Asia Pacific community forum would not necessarily gain a great deal from the Philippines' participation — other than more talk and confusion. However, that being said, it is part of ASEAN and therefore by virtue of this fact alone it should continue to be included.

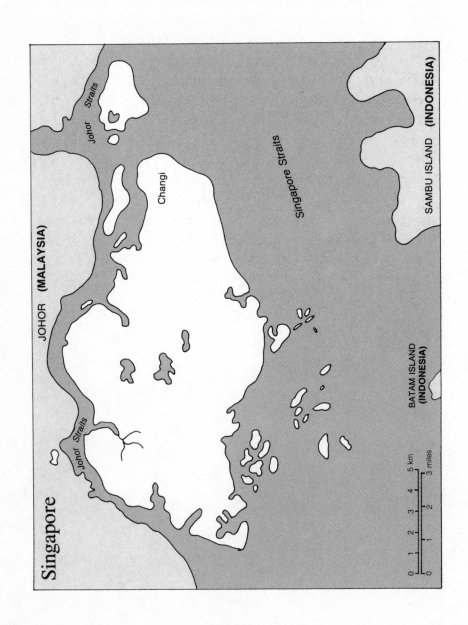

SINGAPORE

The New Regional Community's Centre,
or an Increasing Struggle to Maintain its Niche Role?

A short car ride on a causeway over the narrow Johor Straits joins Singapore island to mainland Malaysia. Singapore is a geographical afterthought on the tip of the Malaysian peninsula, the southernmost point on the Asian continent. It has no natural resources except its geographical position and the vim and vigour of its population. But this diamond-shaped island glitters as one of Southeast Asia's brightest economic gems.

When Sir Stamford Raffles in 1819 took a sandbank off a local rajah, his purpose was clear: to establish Britain's East India Company astride the narrowest point in the trade route between East and West Asia. His expectation was that eventually it might be possible to start some commerce with 'a race of people remarkable for freedom of manner and disposition, for intelligent enquiry...in a climate where European manufactured goods are almost a necessary comfort.'

When Raffles founded Singapore, it was a small village with fewer than two hundred Malay fishermen. Now, it is a thriving city-state which has a highly effective and motivated government, the third-busiest port in the world, after Rotterdam and Hong Kong, a strong financial centre, a government pension and healthcare scheme that is the envy of the region, and an excellent educational system. It has a first-class international airport and national carrier. Today's government has effectively set up the country as the Switzerland of the East. There is much to be said for this. The island nation has the third-highest standard of living in Asia, after Brunei and Japan.

What makes the country tick? There are no metals to be mined here and no rubber to tap. It is not self-sufficient in food, nor do its three reservoirs collect enough water for the population of 3 million — it has to supplement its water supply from Malaysia. In the early days, its success was due to its natural deep harbour, situated in the middle of the trade routes. But what was to propel the island into the twentieth century were its people, and a stable, honest government which leaves little to chance. The country works like a well-managed small business, epitomising the best of the Chinese character, and one that is quick to respond to changes. Its English-speaking workforce is one of the best-educated in the region.

Its achievements have come in just one lifetime, that of Lee Kuan Yew, who was the city-state's first prime minister. Lee shaped the country, and gave it a distinctive flavour. Until he resigned in late 1990, Lee was the longest-serving head of government in the British Commonwealth.

Although Singapore is a democracy in a formal sense, Lee has often been referred to as a benign dictator. He ruled with an iron hand from 1959, when the former British colony won the right to be self-governing, until 1990 when he relinquished his position to Goh Chok Tong. Lee remains in the cabinet as the 'senior minister' and continues to exert great influence both in the running of the country and in the ruling People's Action Party (PAP), which he founded. For that matter, he also has considerable influence in Asia as a whole.

When the PAP first came to power, it set out to rid Singapore of communists and *triads* (criminal gangs), to give the people a decent roof over their head, clean water, a good health service and education for all, and to build good roads. Today, 84 per cent of Singaporeans own their own homes. Compulsory savings with the government, financed by the wage earner and the employer, are used for buying property and for hospital care. Singaporeans have a stake in their country.

Things hum in Singapore. The place is clean, orderly, and prosperous. More than that, it is highly disciplined. Dissent is not entertained. The local press is obedient, often censoring itself. Foreigners are allowed to operate freely, so long as they obey the local 'rules', because that benefits Singapore. The same is true for local people, but for them the 'rules' are slightly different. A few years ago, a senior minister said in an interview, 'We welcome constructive criticism, but then we have that within the party. As for people who criticise just for the sake of criticising, they know what they can expect.' Indeed they did; anyone who dared take on the government was apt to find himself, if a local, either facing a lawsuit or gaoled as a subversive and, if a foreigner or a foreign firm, expelled as an undesirable alien. Today, however, the government has begun to accept that constructive criticism is an essential part of an evolving society. Such criticism is thus now beginning to play a useful role.

The PAP has dominated the government, winning every election since the country's first in May 1959. At the snap election held on 31 August 1991, the opposition won four out of eighty-one seats. The government's share of votes fell to 59.7 per cent from 61.8 per cent at the previous election in 1988. The 1991 result would seem like a ringing endorsement, something most governments would dearly love to achieve in a corruption-free election such as Singapore's. But not in the city-state, where the ruling party ruminated for months on its 'poor' showing. Why the neurosis? Quite simply, because nobody, not even the far-sighted Lee, ever intended Singapore to be a nation. It was meant to be part of Malaysia, and indeed was between 1963 and 1965. But irreconcilable differences, not least between Lee and Malaysia's first prime minister, Tunku Abdul Rahman, severed the relationship. Singapore was out on its own.

One reason why Singapore is an autocracy is that its rulers feel themselves and their country to be constantly under threat from abroad and at home. For years, communism menaced the region's stability. And the Singaporeans are regarded with something close to suspicion by their neighbours, partly because they are predominantly Chinese and partly because they are so infuriatingly successful. There is little outward sign of racial tension, but there is an awareness that racially insensitive policies could divide a society in which the Chinese predominate, with nearly 78 per cent of the population, followed by the Malays at 14 per cent and the Indians with 7 per cent. The remaining 1 per cent is made up mostly of Eurasians. Christianity, Buddhism, Hinduism, Taoism, and Islam are the main religions. What is threatening is that this predominantly Chinese isle sits in a sometimes hostile Muslim–Malay sea. Animosity towards the Chinese goes back as far as the hills in the larger neighbouring countries of Malaysia and Indonesia.

The final reason for the government's sense of insecurity is the fear that if the people are not disciplined, they may relapse into either the passive inertia or corrupted chaos that was so long the curse of Chinese people everywhere. But the more successful Singapore becomes, the less vulnerable its people feel. The result is that Singaporeans are getting fed up with the way the government continues to meddle in their lives. Nothing, it seems, is sacred, not even how many children one has or who one marries. The country is a land of campaigns. Singaporeans have been exhorted to do one thing and not another for as long as they can remember — to keep the country clean and green, not to litter, to speak Mandarin, not to chew chewing gum. And these campaigns work, sometimes too well.

A previous family planning effort to get people to 'stop at two' has had to be reversed. Singaporeans took the advice so much to heart that they ended up with the lowest procreation rate among the Overseas Chinese. The government, worried about dwindling numbers, has had to intervene again, by providing generous tax incentives to encourage Singaporeans who have the means and education, to have three or more children.

There was another concern here. The Chinese and other better-educated people were having fewer children, while the Malays and the less well-educated continued breeding. This sparked off a 'nature-versus-nurture' debate in Singapore in the early 1980s, in which Lee made his eugenic views abundantly clear. Singapore's latest drive is to get graduate women to marry graduate men and produce a new breed of intelligent Singaporeans. The country is obsessed with educational qualifications. The civil service and the government are run by technocrats. Lee himself, like his wife, scored a double first at Cambridge University in England.

Because of the underlying racial tension, and because it is so small, Singapore needs to belong to a greater community. Economically, too, it needs a hinterland, for it has run out of space on which to build factories and the people to work in them. There is a limit to what can be achieved by 3 million people on a small island. The double-digit economic growth rates of the late 1980s are over. The 1992 growth rate was officially forecast at 5–7 per cent. The economy is more heavily dependent on trade than any other country in the region; the value of its total trade is three times its GDP. So when Singapore's largest trading partner, the United States, suffers a slowdown, so does Singapore.

The other potential problem is that the economy is one of the most dependent on foreign labour in Asia; the government has made provision to allow overseas workers to make up 20 per cent of the 1.3 million workforce. In fact, this problem could be an advantage as it could provide Singapore with a much greater degree of economic flexibility. Specifically, when the labour market is tight, more foreign workers can be brought in to alleviate the problem, while during a period of economic slowdown, such foreign workers could be repatriated.

Singapore's way out of the doldrums runs in two directions: to tie its economy more closely to those of its neighbours, and to aim to be the region's equivalent of a blend between Switzerland and what Brussels is to the EC. The first option, a search for a hinterland, has been going well. A Singapore-sponsored 'growth triangle' of economic opportunity is opening up in the Malaysian state of Johore to the north, and to the south in Batam in the Indonesian Riau archipelago. However, Batam's land and labour costs are 40 per cent higher than in China's similar special economic zone, Shenzhen. Industrial estates, oil exploration depots, and even tourist resorts are being established on Singapore's doorstep. The second option is largely an extension of Singapore's old role as an entrepôt, capitalising on its location in the heart of Southeast Asia. Singapore's infrastructure is excellent and it is easy of access. The races have lived together relatively well. Civil unrest is unlikely. It is an attractive place in which, or from which, to do business. Even the punctilious Japanese think of Singapore as the hub of Southeast Asia.

The Japanese were first lured to this island, along with other foreign investors, in the late 1960s, when the Singapore government offered attractive tax incentives, aimed at foreign multinational investors, to set up shop. The number of Japanese living there has since mushroomed, from only 200 then to over 20,000 today, making them the single largest expatriate group in Singapore. Sony, Fujikura, Omron, Matsushita, Hitachi, Toshiba, and NEC all have their regional headquarters in Singapore. In 1990, Japanese industrialists invested a record S$708 million in Singapore manufacturing, or 32 per cent of all foreign investment. There are about 1,500 Japanese companies in Singapore, employing 70,000 people.

Unfortunately, the relationship is unequal. Singapore needs the Japanese more than the Japanese need Singapore. Singapore has always suffered a trade deficit with Japan, nearly trebling from S$6.3 billion in 1990. And three decades after Japanese industrialists first came to Singapore as pioneer foreign investors, the transfer of technology that was part of the deal has still not really come about. In 1989, a Japan–Singapore

Economic Advisory Group was set up to right the situation. It should also be said that there are several factors which mitigate this superficially viewed problem. Specifically, Singapore re-exports to neighbouring countries most of the Japanese finished goods it imports from Japan. Japanese-made components are often essential for the manufacture and export of many high-tech Singaporean industrial products. Finally, the surpluses in its tourist trade and capital accounts with Japan are large enough to cancel out its deficit in merchandise trade.

The other hurdle for the Japanese in Singapore is the memory of wartime atrocities. Singaporeans, and the Chinese in the region as a whole, suffered appallingly at the hands of Japanese troops. Japan has to heal these wounds if it wants to play a greater role in Asia Pacific.

Singaporeans pride themselves on being a pragmatic people. They are forward-looking, and do not harp on the past. But my question is, what will they do next? Singapore has succeeded beyond all initial expectations by cleverly and imaginatively developing and exploiting various niches — providing a transshipment hub for Southeast Asian raw materials, for goods, and travellers, providing an efficient manufacturing centre, as well as an efficient financial services centre and a base for corporate regional head offices. However, its neighbours have caught up, or are about to catch up, in all these activities, either by taking upon themselves those functions they previously relied on Singapore to provide, or by coming up with alternatives. For example, in terms of the Singapore stock market versus the region's other stock markets, the government has placed a high priority on Singapore's market and has invested a good deal of time in it. At one time, it was a major investment focus in the region. Today, however, in just the ASEAN countries, Malaysia, which used to trade all its public corporations' shares on both the Singapore and Malaysian exchanges, decided in 1989 to trade such shares only on its own Kuala Lumpur exchange. Malaysia's share market capitalisation is now almost twice that of Singapore. Thailand's market capitalisation is about 40 per cent larger, but its daily trading turnover is often more than 600 per cent greater than Singapore's. The problem is not quality or effort, but that there is ultimately a limit to what 3 million people can do on a small island.

However, as long as it maintains its discipline and focus, Singapore will no doubt continue to surprise the world by adapting to new conditions and finding new solutions — its government-sponsored 'growth triangle' is a good example of its endless, imaginative search for new solutions. One such initiative that should be given a high priority is to encourage Singaporean government agencies and corporations, as well as private-sector corporations, to take an active investment role outside Singapore and thus enlarge its economic base. This process has already begun and bodes well for the future. Given its small, stable, and highly educated population, it could also provide a safe, neutral haven and/or jumping-off point in a variety of ways, while its neighbours, including China, go through the often wrenching changes necessitated by coming to terms with the new world order. However, there is also an underlying problem in that, because of Singapore's successes, Singaporeans are now much more concerned about having a secure career. And they like an orderly life with its proper creature comforts. It thus may become increasingly difficult for them to compete in the general hurly-burly of the Asian market, where entrepreneural talent is required, along with the ability to take major risks and to be very flexible.

Singapore, of all the countries in Asia Pacific, could best benefit by espousing the cause of a regional forum and becoming an amalgam of Brussels and Switzerland, both geopolitically and economically. Given Lee's regional and international prestige and Singapore's reputation for being corruption-free, efficient, and stable, it could with great credibility make a major contribution to the bringing together of the region.

Without such a role, Singapore risks becoming less central to the region's political and economic affairs. This may not necessarily be a bad thing, as it will no doubt continue to enjoy a disproportionate share of the region's economic growth. However, such a state of affairs will not necessarily satisfy either the young government technocrats or their private-sector opposite numbers. If they cannot collectively keep creating a sufficiently interesting arena with Singapore at its centre, the problem that Singapore as a whole will face is to keep such talented people from moving on to bigger and better challenges outside — particularly with the further opening up of China. Conversely, the region would need a neutral, highly respected, geographically central *locus* for its new community forum, in addition to Singapore's considerable current influence.

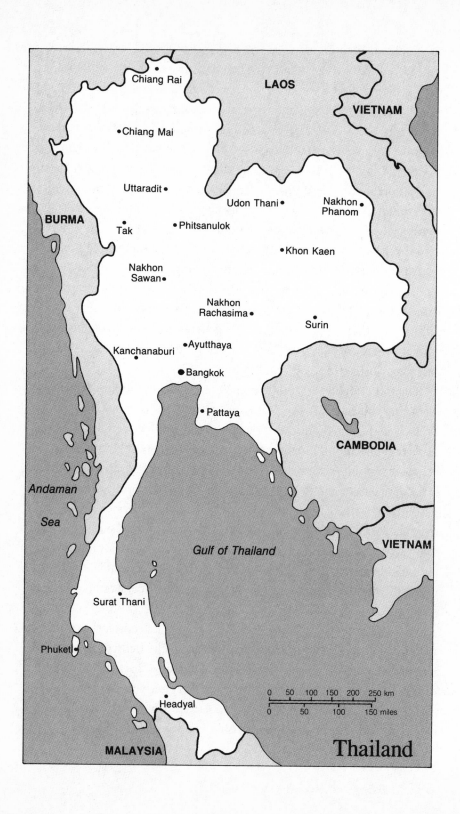

Thailand

THAILAND
Stability amidst Constant Change — a Fascinating Enigma

W hich is the most stable country in Southeast Asia? Malaysia is strained by ethnic tension. Indonesia is preoccupied with political succession. Philippine society is deeply divided. Singapore's government has created a climate of intimidation. And Vietnam is still an impoverished one-party state.

It is quite clearly, Thailand. This may seem a surprising choice, given that it has experienced seventeen attempted or successful coups since the country became a constitutional monarchy in 1932. But let not appearances deceive, for Thailand is a stable country, both economically and socially. Governments may come and go, but Thais go about their business in a remarkably harmonious fashion.

Or at least they used to. In May 1992, the streets of Bangkok were wracked by violence and bloodshed, as demonstrators sought the removal of General Suchinda Kraprayoon as prime minister. Thousands of protesters brought life in the capital to a standstill for days, demanding that parliament introduce a constitutional provision preventing non-elected people from becoming prime minister.

In essence, the conflict is between civilians and soldiers as to who should be calling the shots in Thailand. Since 1932, the country's much-vaunted social harmony has been based on three institutions: the royal family, the armed forces, and the bureaucracy. Four, actually, if the Buddhist church is included. And five if one includes the Thai-Chinese merchants who would prefer, as elsewhere in Asia, to remain neutral if not invisible.

Until now, it has been Thailand's élite breed of technocrats which has governed the country. As the corrupt political parties forever coalesce and dissolve, it has been the bureaucrats who have maintained continuity. But the army has not been content to leave things that way. It sees itself as the true guardian of social stability and national integrity. Whenever the top brass has reckoned the civilian politicians and, to a lesser extent, their bureaucrats have dipped too deeply into the trough, they have intervened to suspend normal political activity. A notional cleansing of the Augean stables then took place. This was followed by the military-turned-politicians feeding at the same trough. They and their new friends, the other politicians, subsequently resumed the usual games. Throughout this process it has been the royal family that has been the balancing factor or catalyst for change; as in the case of the peaceful resignation of Suchinda, always attempting to maintain a balance between the interests of the military, the bureaucrats, the politicians, and the Thai people as a whole.

This has been the pattern of Thai politics since King Bhumibol Adulyadej ascended the throne in 1946. But the pattern appears to be changing, primarily because the economy has developed too far and too quickly to accommodate the sort of musical chairs played by an élite few.

When the corrupt civilian government of former prime minister Chatichai Choonhavan was overthrown in a bloodless coup in February 1991, the world — indeed most Thais — regarded it as business as usual. In fact, on a governmental level, things worked much more smoothly than under Chatichai. In their wisdom, Suchinda and his military junta appointed a top technocrat and businessman, Anand Panyarachun, as prime minister and gave him a surprisingly free hand to introduce long-delayed economic reforms and to resolve some of the legislative and infrastructural bottlenecks plaguing the country.

But the Thais became increasingly uneasy about two separate developments. One was the weak attempts to purge the political parties of corruption. Chatichai himself was prosecuted, but there was a widespread perception that things would continue much as they had done before. This was hardly surprising in view of the fact that many military men, figures who would not have looked out of place in European tales of medieval chivalry, were themselves as deeply corrupt as the politicians they were supposedly cleansing. Unlike the largely professional army in neighbouring Malaysia, but in common with its counterparts in Indonesia, the Thai military takes its civilian involvement far more seriously than its duties as a professional organisation. Indeed, as a fighting force, the

Thai military has become something of a joke among Southeast Asian defence analysts. The armed forces are top-heavy to an almost comical degree: 500 generals out of a total complement of 280,000 troops. Almost all of these top officers spend most of their time pursuing their business interests. The priorities show up on the battlefield. When the Thai army tried to dislodge their Lao counterparts from a contested border position in 1988, it was the better-equipped Thais who came off the worst from the encounter. Notwithstanding this, it should be noted that, by the early 1980s, the Thai army had played a crucial role in stamping out communist insurgency.

The other development that concerned the Thais was the position of General Suchinda. Initially he said that he had no ambitions to become prime minister. This claim looked increasingly threadbare as time wore on. When the political parties were unable to agree on a candidate for prime minister after the March 1992 election, Suchinda was asked to step into the breach. This outraged the opposition parties and the Bangkok masses.

Following the strong, well-organised, middle-class demonstrations against Suchinda and the 'old Thai system' and the subsequent bloodletting, parliament shamefacedly acceded to the first of the demonstrators' demands. They introduced the constitutional provision to ensure prime ministers would in future be elected rather than arrive, effectively self-elected, from the military. Due then to the extraordinary, adept (and very rare) intervention by King Bhumibol, Suchinda stepped down, thus acceding to the second of the demonstrators' two main demands.

With the election in September 1992 of Prime Minister Chuan Leekpai, there is some slight sign that the fundamentals of the Thai system have changed. But will the military merely lie low until the fuss blows over, and will the political parties resume their usual activities? Leekpai, a lawyer by training and a seasoned civilian politician with many terms of office behind him, could be the right man to harness, with credibility, the people-power of the new Thai middle classes in order to reduce corruption and restrain a resurgence of military interference in politics. Thailand must still resolve the conundrum: if it has outgrown the old system, what should replace it and how should this be achieved? Switching to a civilian form of government is necessary, but not sufficient, for the checks against politicians abusing their powers are not yet demonstrably strong enough.

One reason why the political system is difficult to alter lies in the huge disparity between urban and rural life. To be precise, the cleft is between Bangkok, where almost one-fifth of Thailand's population of 56.7 million (in 1990) live, and the rest of the country. During national elections, opposition parties regularly sweep the board in Bangkok, but the pro-military parties usually find it easy to 'win' enough rural votes to assure themselves of a majority in parliament. And vote-buying is endemic in the rural areas.

Government planners themselves admit that there has not been enough effort made to decentralise the economy. Only Chiang Mai in the far north has received the money needed to develop into an economic and intellectual centre. Much of the rest of the country remains a backwater, a huge reservoir of controlled stability, perhaps, but also a drag on Thailand's political evolution. The government has clearly recognised this general disparity, and considerable resources are being directed towards the development of other regional centres — namely, Phitsonulok in the north, Khon Kaen and Nakhon Ratchasima in the northeast, and Songkhia in the south. Additionally, substantial effort has already been made to develop the eastern and southern seaboards.

There is also a growing general, economic liability. This is due largely to the over-concentration of investment in and around Bangkok which has led to severe infrastructural bottlenecks. The city's world-famous traffic jams are only one symptom of the predicament. The ports are choked. There are not enough telephones. And pollution is making life hell for the people of Bangkok. Provided the infrastructural problems of access, telecommunications, and so on can be addressed in parallel, these diversification initiatives should assist in spreading industry, wealth, and social support throughout the country. This, in turn, will have a considerable impact on the rural voters' sophistication and, in time, the current vote-buying abuses should be greatly minimised.

Many of these problems come with economic success. The Thai system, in which the élite compete for power among themselves, has left the economy largely to its own devices; in fact, it is one of the freest in the world. The result has been a highly diversified economy that has grown more rapidly (by about 8 per cent annually) since the early 1980s than that of almost any other country. An open regulatory environment and an open society are other reasons. Thailand has allowed the most active economic group, the ethnic Chinese, to integrate more successfully than anywhere else in Southeast Asia. The Thais are a tolerant people — more so, it appears, than their fellow Buddhists in Burma and Sri Lanka.

Their tolerance of the Japanese is high, too. Historically, the Thais have been able to prevent any state stronger than them from exerting too much control over their destiny. For many years until the beginning of the seventeenth century, trade flourished between what was then Siam and Japan. A sizeable community of Japanese merchants lived in Ayuthya, the country's capital at the time. They were eventually kicked out of the country for meddling too much in internal affairs, but the precedent had been set. And in the eighteenth and nineteenth centuries, the Thais successfully played off the British against the French colonisers.

Japan was by far the biggest investor in Thailand; in 1992, at least one Japanese factory opened each week. Japan is the largest source of aid and the biggest supplier of imports. Prominent Japanese say there are three reasons why the two countries get on so well: they share the same Buddhist religion, they have never gone to war with each other, and both countries have monarchies, with increasingly frequent royal exchanges. However, in early 1993, many Japanese believed that Japan's direct capital investment had peaked. Part of the reason was the increases in both wages and infrastructural bottlenecks. But another increasingly important reason was the shortage of mid-level managers, technicians, and other skilled human resources. Thailand is believed to lag even the Philippines and Indonesia in education. And if it wishes to continue to enjoy its very real successes to date, it must address this serious lacuna.

In fact, the royal families in both countries share the same function, which is to act as a focus for social stability. The Thai king now plays a considerably more important role than the Japanese emperor, whose powers were taken away by the US-imposed peace constitution after World War II. By contrast, King Bhumibol has always worked hard to ensure Thailand's stability, intervening in moments of crisis to bring opposing interests to a compromise. Indeed, the question of a successor to the man who has ruled Thailand so well since 1946 will loom ever larger during the 1990s.

The third long-term issue Thailand must address, along with the royal succession and the future role of the armed forces, is its relations with its neighbours. During the Vietnam War and the Vietnamese occupation of Cambodia, there were fears that Thailand would be the next domino to fall. Thailand triumphantly proved them wrong. Now the worry is that the tables may have been turned, to an uncomfortable degree. Prime Minister Chatichai vowed to help turn Indochina from a battlefield into a marketplace and, after the late 1980s, Thai businessmen took him at his word. They have focused their activities on extractive industries such as gem mining and logging in Laos and Cambodia to the east, as well as in Burma to the west.

In particular, there is much regional and international resentment and frustration at the Thai government's indirect, tacit support of the Cambodian Khmer Rouge. In early 1993, there were some sixteen Thai companies, including the Thai government-owned Forest Industry Organisation (FIO), which from 1989 granted three- to five-year logging concessions in Khmer Rouge-controlled territory. Despite the imposition of a logging ban by Cambodia's Supreme National Council in September 1992, the Khmer Rouge, although a member, ignored it. A late 1992 Thai intelligence document estimated that the Khmer Rouge could earn more than US$1 billion, if all the Thai companies fully utilised their concessions. In addition to logging, there are a number of Thai interests in gem mining in Khmer Rouge territory, which activities are estimated to add significantly to the revenues being earned by the Khmer Rouge from the logging concessions. This stew has an additional ingredient, the murky participation of the ubiquitous Thai military. All this takes on an even greater significance, as it appears that the Khmer Rouge are unlikely to support, and participate in, the UN-sponsored general elections. Further, it appears the only way that the Khmer Rouge can be persuaded to conform for the good of the whole country will be by the use of a UN-sponsored military force.

Finally, from a broader perspective, there is the serious environmental cost of these nefarious exercises, particularly with regard to logging. In 1989, the Thais themselves banned all further logging in order to try and stop the dangerous rate of deforestation in Thailand. They now also have major logging operations in Laos and Burma, with similar rather questionable deals being struck between the contracting parties concerned, with questionable benefits for the countries of Laos and Burma, and with an unquestionably serious negative environmental impact on both countries. However, to be fair in the case of the Thai FIO, they are probably much more discriminate in their cutting and they have offered a reforestation programme similar to that which they commenced in their Burmese logging concessions. For example, an April 1992 UN Development Programme study indicated that Cambodia has some 7 million hectares of remaining forest out of Cambodia's total land area of 18 million hectares. The study states that Cambodia has one of the world's highest deforestation rates, which in turn affects agricultural and fishery productivity — in short, the basic, future sustainability of economic development in Cambodia.

Another major criticism from its Indochinese neighbours is that Thailand disregards their concerns about the unfettered, modern Thai cultural influences on their respective countries. For example, in Laos, anyone living within fifty kilometres of the Thai border (this includes Vientiane, the capital) can easily receive all four of the Thai television stations' broadcasts. As the Lao and Thai languages are similar (most people from Northern Thailand are ethnically Lao), this results in, for example, many Lao children being inculcated with Thai cultural influences (from Thai boxing, to glossy advertising, entertainment, and so on) to the detriment of their ability to learn about their own culture.

This kind of excessively commercially driven activity has rekindled fears among its neighbours that Thailand wants to 're-colonise' them, as it partially succeeded in doing before the Europeans came on the scene in the sixteenth and seventeenth centuries. Much of this fear is exaggerated, but if Thailand is to take its rightful place as a regional power in Southeast Asia, it must treat its sensitive neighbours with more respect.

Thailand, with its centuries of experience at juggling and off-setting the territorial ambitions of various outsiders, its general political prestige in the region, and its membership of ASEAN, could make a material contribution to the development of an Asia Pacific community. Its advocacy could carry considerable weight and, in taking a proactive role, it could enhance its own leadership ambitions in the Indochinese region. The region, in turn, needs its fundamental stability and serene self-confidence — unusual characteristics in Asia Pacific.

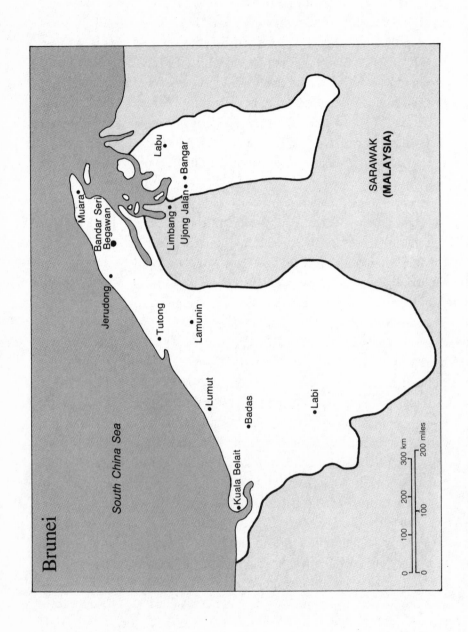

Brunei

South China Sea

Muara

Bandar Seri
Begawan

Jerudong

Tutong

Lamunin

Lumut

Badas

Labi

Kuala Belait

Labu

Limbang

Ujong Jalan • Bangar

SARAWAK
(MALAYSIA)

| 0 | 100 | 200 | 300 km |
| 0 | 100 | 200 miles |

BRUNEI
An Efficient Oddity

Brunei is ASEAN's odd man out; a small, wealthy sultanate which seems like a bit of the Middle East stuck in the centre of Southeast Asia.

This country, with only 264,000 people, struck it rich on oil and gas; it has a GNP per head of over US$17,000. Its ruler and absolute monarch, Sultan Hassanal Bolkiah, is reputed to be the world's richest man. It is one of very few countries to have no financial worries for the future. If the flow of oil and gas ceased tomorrow, Bruneians could still live quite comfortably off the investment income from its foreign exchange reserves. It is a sizeable exporter of hydrocarbons to Japan, its largest market.

The people of Brunei had enormous respect for Hassanal's father, Omar Alil Saifuddin III, whom they credit with ensuring the sultanate remained independent and rich. Modern-day Brunei is only 5,765 square kilometres on two small fragments on the north coast of Borneo. Five centuries ago, Brunei's trading empire stretched from the island of Borneo to Luzon in the Philippines and down to the Sulu archipelago. But territorial chieftains sold off large tracts of the empire to foreign interests, such that there was not much left of Brunei by the time they sought protection from Britain in 1888.

The tide of decolonisation swept across Southeast Asia after World War II. The British tried to persuade Sultan Omar that the region was too dangerous for him to go it alone and that his best bet was to become part of the Malaysian federation on its formation in 1963. Omar decided otherwise, fearing that the federation would seize Brunei's growing oil and gas revenues. Instead, he tried his hand at democracy. And the country's first election was won by a socialist party on an anti-Malaysia and anti-British campaign. But Omar would not allow the party to take power, and he called in British troops to put down a rebellion. Omar ruled, and even after passing on the throne to his son Hassanal in October 1967, he remained the power behind the throne until his death in September 1986.

The sultanate has come a long way since it became a sovereign independent country in January 1984. Bruneians enjoy the second-highest standard of living in Asia. There is no personal income tax; medical services and education to tertiary level are free; pensions are non-contributory; and there are subsidies for rice and housing. Almost every family owns a car and a television, even those living in longhouses; the traditional dwelling of many Bruneians.

Brunei is now a full member of ASEAN. It has a modern form of government, with a prime minister presiding over a cabinet. One of the first things that Hassanal did after his father's death was to form a new cabinet, increasing its members from five to eleven, splitting ministerial responsibilities, and broadening the base of his government to the point where aristocrats and commoners now outnumber the royal family in the highest tier of government.

Another theme of Hassanal's reign is to emphasise Malayness in the already Malay-dominated sultanate. Further reflecting the government's bias against the Chinese, in July 1990, Hassanal outlined the principles of *Melayu Islam Berjaya*, which translates as 'Malay Muslim monarchy', as the basis of the state. This was a further blow to 50,000 ethnic Chinese in Brunei who have been steadily squeezed out of jobs (and contracts), despite the fact that Brunei is chronically labour short, and who are being inexorably squeezed out of the country. The estimated 36,000 foreign workers in Brunei make up nearly 40 per cent of its workforce.

Over the next few decades, it will be interesting to see what will happen to the role of the sultan, and indeed the sultanate. How will this constitutional oddity survive, surrounded by the very different regimes in Malaysia, Indonesia, and the Philippines? Of late, Brunei has increasingly clung to Singapore, identifying with its smallness and affluence. If it wanted to, Brunei could set itself up as the Monaco of the region, Asia Pacific's tax-free playground. Even though it is predominantly Malay and Muslim, its wealth makes it feel threatened by its larger Malay neighbours. It could also, if it so wished, run its economy solely off the earnings from its foreign exchange reserves.

If Brunei felt more secure, it could provide a small but strong link in the region. It has certainly put itself on the right track by joining ASEAN and setting up the workings of a good government. It has also recognised, in theory at least, that it should develop a more balanced economy, rather than relying solely on its oil reserves. However, in this regard, nothing tangible has yet been put into effect. Alternatively, in a worst case scenario, with increasing geopolitical and trade friction pitting neighbour against neighbour and without there being an international framework to provide sanctions against excesses of territorial aggrandisement, Brunei could be an easy takeover target. Its support, therefore, of a regional forum would provide it with some insurance against such an eventuality.

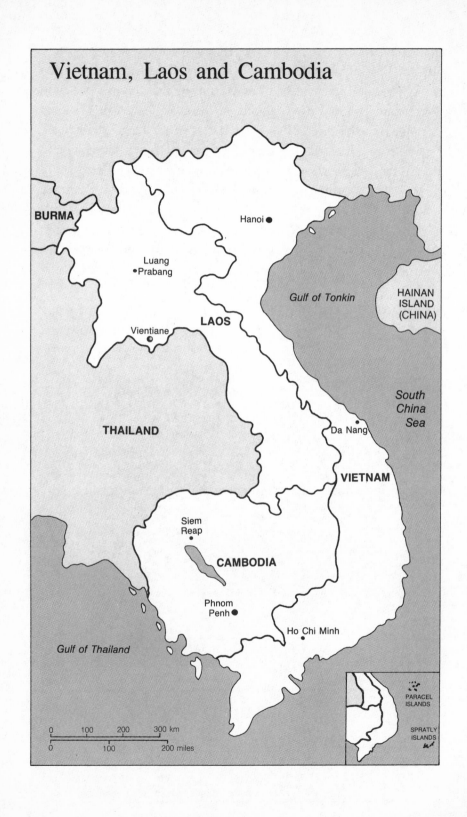

Vietnam, Laos and Cambodia

BURMA

Hanoi ●

Luang
● Prabang

Gulf of Tonkin

HAINAN
ISLAND
(CHINA)

LAOS

Vientiane ○

*South
China
Sea*

THAILAND

Da Nang ●

VIETNAM

Siem
Reap ●

CAMBODIA

Phnom
Penh ●

Ho Chi Minh ●

Gulf of Thailand

| 0 | 100 | 200 | 300 km |

| 0 | | 100 | | 200 miles |

PARACEL
ISLANDS

SPRATLY
ISLANDS

INDOCHINA
Historically Fascinating — Currently a Madhatter's Tea Party

Amid the jigsaw puzzle of Asia Pacific, the pieces that make up Indochina do not quite fit. The area known as Indochina denotes a geographical area consisting of three countries: Vietnam, Cambodia, and Laos. On the eastern side, it is rimmed by the South China Sea. To the north, it is bordered by China, and to the west by Burma and Thailand. The pieces were forced to fit together by France, which colonised the area in the mid-nineteenth century; prior to that, Indochina had not existed, since the Lao and the Khmer peoples had been buffers between the Vietnamese and the Thais for the previous four hundred years. In the tumult of decolonisation that began after World War II, Indochina took on a new importance by becoming the frontier states of communism during the Cold War.

Now, as the new world order slowly takes shape, the three Indochinese states are struggling to find their place in the scheme of things. Two of them, Vietnam and Laos, are still run by communist regimes. The third, Cambodia, is caught betwixt two, or even three, worlds: the pragmatic Marxism practised by China and Vietnam; the xenophobic, mutant Maoism of the Khmer Rouge; and the freewheeling capitalism of Thailand. Indochina looks as though it will continue, for some time to come, to be a source of instability for the wider region.

France was not the only country that tried to impose its pattern on Indochina. After Vietnam was unified in 1975, Hanoi attempted to establish its sway over the much weaker states of Laos and Cambodia. All three were communist, with regimes that had won power with the help of China and the Soviet Union. Vietnam had by far the largest population (it currently numbers 66 million, compared with 8 million for Cambodia and 4 million for Laos) and, although its economy was weak, it tried to knit the three together in a scaled-down version of Comecon, the economic counterpart to the Warsaw Pact.

Economic and political co-operation never bore much fruit. Then, in 1978, Vietnam invaded Cambodia in order to drive the Khmer Rouge from power. Hanoi's campaign was never completely successful. Backed by Thailand and China, which had fallen out with Vietnam in the mid-1970s, the Khmer Rouge was able to sustain itself on the Thai border. Even after Vietnam withdrew and a peace accord was agreed upon for Cambodia, the Khmer Rouge was able to ignore the settlement, largely because it was able to finance itself by the sale of timber and mineral rights — primarily to the Thais.

When the Soviet Union abruptly ended its aid to Indochina in 1990, it was a case of 'every man for himself'. Vietnam moved swiftly to open up its economy. It is now poised to enjoy an economic revival, particularly as it benefits more and more from the increasing foreign aid and investment coming into the country — primarily from Asian sources. In stark contrast, Cambodia remains deeply mired in tension, confusion, and conflict, even as it tries to take a giant step towards stability, with general elections planned for 1993. Laos has reverted to its old game of playing off China, Vietnam, Thailand, and Burma against each other. In the early 1990s, its main diplomatic advances were towards China, to stress its independence from Vietnam and to try to keep Thailand at arms' length — although such efforts are, at least for the time being, probably in vain.

There is perhaps no other part of Asia Pacific where economic development could have so dramatic an effect as in Indochina. Yet the prospect of take-off remains distant, because the wounds of post-colonisation are taking so long to heal. The southern part of Indochina has a near-perfect route to the open sea in the shape of the Mekong River, yet its development remains dogged by the political instability of the area. The northern reaches would benefit greatly from more open links with southern China's booming economy. But northern Vietnam and Laos fear being dragged into China's economic — and ultimately political — orbit.

If Indochina is to be made to fit into the Asia Pacific jigsaw, it will require a concerted effort on the part of ASEAN, China, and Japan to overcome the many problems facing the area. Any success in helping the three Indochinese states to get on their feet would represent a big step forward for regional co-operation.

VIETNAM
A Disciplined, Focused New Player with Great Potential

If the United States had not gone to war with Vietnam and the latter had been unified peacefully, Congress in Washington would now be clamouring for protection from cheap Vietnamese exports. Vietnam would be regarded as the fifth 'Asian dragon', and mobile phones would be as common in Hanoi as they now are in Hong Kong. It has not yet happened, of course, but something like this will occur in the not-too-distant future. Vietnam is, indeed, a newly-industrialised country (NIC) in-waiting. It has a highly educated and disciplined workforce, whose members display a seriousness of purpose matched only perhaps by the South Koreans — but at one-tenth the pay. One day, Vietnam's competitiveness will pose a threat to many of its prosperous neighbours, notably Thailand, whose similarly-sized population is considerably more relaxed and fun-loving than the Vietnamese.

It will not happen, though, until Vietnam first jettisons a lot of its ideological and historical baggage. The reason for this is simply that, more than any other country in Asia, Vietnam is scarred by war. It's a common misconception that the wars began when the Vietnamese tried to kick out the French colonists in 1945, but Vietnam has been fighting the Khmers, the Thais and, above all, the Chinese, for centuries.

China has menaced the Vietnamese from the beginning of recorded history. The Koreans along China's northeastern border got along remarkably well with their bigger neighbour for hundreds of years, paying their dues, but being left alone for the most part. By contrast, the Annamites and others who inhabited the lands to the south of what is now the Chinese border province of Guangxi were never able to find a *modus vivendi* with China for very long before a fresh conflict would break out. In the nineteenth century, as Chinese power receded, European expansionism came to take its place. For Vietnam, the primary Western interloper was the French, who took over the entire country in stages between 1858 and 1883. France's hard-won supremacy was not undisputed for long. Vietnam's revolutionary movement was founded in 1905, though it was suppressed and splintered several times thereafter.

But as early as 1925, Vietnam had a Marxist independence organisation founded by Ho Chi Minh, who went on to become the father of the modern Vietnamese state. The movement to free Vietnam from colonial rule became one of the most convulsive in Asia, leading to wars first with the French (1945–1954) and later with the United States (1960–1973).

But then Vietnam's geographical position made it feel a lot more vulnerable. The Koreas occupy what is effectively a large peninsula surrounded by water on three sides, a relatively easy territory to defend. Vietnam is a very different shape, being a long, thin country (only 50 kilometres wide at one point), occupying the entire eastern rim of Indochina. It was therefore exposed to attack from the sea on one side and from hostile peoples, such as the Khmers, on the other. And all the time there was China, towering over it.

Vietnam's invasion of Cambodia in December 1978 should be seen primarily in this light. After two years of attacks from the Khmer Rouge along Vietnam's southwestern flank, Hanoi lunged into Cambodia and ousted the China-backed regime. Vietnam knew that this would earn it universal opprobrium, but national unity was at stake. Here was a Chinese client trying to destabilise, possibly even take over, southern Vietnam. Ho Chi Minh City (formerly Saigon) was less than a hundred kilometres from the Cambodian border. Vietnam was not going to allow a bunch of genocidal Cambodian fanatics to undermine the national unity it had fought the French and the Americans to achieve.

Vietnam is especially vulnerable because its southern half is only tenuously connected to the northern half. After all, the two halves were at war with each other from 1954 to 1975. The country's poor infrastructure makes communication between the two halves painfully difficult. Even today, it takes almost a week to make the train journey from Hanoi to Ho Chi Minh City. The two cities are as different as chalk and cheese. Hanoi is like a beautiful orphan of rich parents, fallen upon hard times. Its elegant and impressive colonial architecture is unique in Southeast Asia, perhaps the world, a remnant of a bygone era when the French colonisers were intent on tailoring a city to the requirements of their own civilisation. But beneath the colonial carapace is a Confucian city, austere and grand, with its lakes and temples. While Hanoi cannot avoid displaying its Chinese influence, Ho Chi Minh City is much more Southeast Asian in inspiration. The climate is balmier, the people more relaxed, the amosphere more free-wheeling. And there in the heart of it all is Cholon, a teeming, bustling Chinatown, far bigger than those to be found in cities such as Manila or Bangkok.

The differences between north and south are immense. Hanoi and the Red River Delta is the land of the Vietnamese-style mandarinate, the hub of the country's communist ideology and state-directed planning. Ho Chi Minh City and the Mekong Delta is the land of the entrepreneur and one of the richest agricultural regions in Southeast Asia — a similar contrast to that found between north and south China. No wonder Hanoi feels vulnerable. If it is not careful, the economic dynamism of the south could undermine the communist superstructure so carefully erected in the north. Indeed, the *yin* of Vietnam's one-party state and the *yang* of its increasingly vibrant capitalist economy are locked in combat, competing rather than complementing each other.

However, although Hanoi's communists may be totalitarians, brooking no hint of political opposition, they are pragmatic nonetheless. After the country was reunified in 1975, the government, flushed with victory, set about building a socialist utopia. Projects on the grand scale were embarked upon, as aid began to flow in from the West. But when Vietnam invaded Cambodia three years later, the flow of foreign capital slowed to a trickle and the government was forced to change tack. It did so with an alacrity found elsewhere only in China. Indeed, the economic reforms introduced by Hanoi, particularly the agricultural ones, were remarkably similar to those north of the border. Peasants were allowed to sell an increasing proportion of their produce on the free market, and business-men were allowed to set up their own enterprises. But Vietnam made only slow progress down the road of economic liberalisation, much slower than China. The government, perpetually insecure, launched periodic crack-downs on private businesses in the 1980s, when they feared things were getting out of hand. Small firms were often forcibly closed down or run out of business by being charged punitive taxes. In addition, after its occupation of Cambodia, foreign aid was all but cut off, and there was virtually no foreign investment in Vietnam.

Economic assistance started to trickle back in after the troops completed their withdrawal from Cambodia in 1989, but this could not make up for the decline in aid from the Soviet Union, whose break-up brought to an end the chief source of financial help for Vietnam (as well as for Cambodia and Laos). All along, the United States maintained its economic embargo, forbidding trade with, investment in, and aid to, its former adversary. It has also blocked the World Bank and the International Monetary Fund from helping Vietnam's economy get back on its feet.

As the Hanoi government has gained in self-confidence, so the Communist Party has felt able to relax its socialist grip on the economy and its economic reforms have grown bolder. It has now become one of the most liberal foreign-investment, developing country regimes in the world, allowing foreign companies to hold as much as 100 per cent of the equity in Vietnamese ventures, with the ability to repatriate all their foreign-currency earnings. Investors have entered in larger numbers, particularly from Taiwan, Hong Kong, and South Korea, though they continue to complain about the stifling bureaucracy, incompetent or corrupt officials, and frequent regulation changes.

But matters will improve and the country which stands to do most for Vietnam economically — Japan — has been patiently laying the groundwork. Tokyo has a twin agenda, commercial and geopolitical. Vietnam (indeed, the whole of Indochina, Laos and Cambodia included) offers a copious supply of natural resources, and an economically regenerated Vietnam would represent a lucrative new market. On the diplomatic side, Japan has been very active in trying to influence Vietnam to push for a peaceful settlement of the conflict in Cambodia, the first stage of which goal was attained at the end of 1991 when Vietnam withdrew its forces. Indeed, Japan appears to regard Vietnam as one of the most important factors for stabilising Indochina.

Like so many of its neighbours, Vietnam's attitude towards Japan is ambiguous, fearful of being swamped by the region's most powerful economy and yet anxious to partake of its largess. Early this century, some

Vietnamese nationalists, inspired by the Japanese defeat of Czarist Russia in 1905, looked to Japan as a potential ally in their fight against French colonial rule. But others, including Ho Chi Minh, the father of the modern Vietnamese state, rejected such a relationship, fearing Japanese imperialism as much as the French version. At the outset of World War II, when many Southeast Asian nationalists rallied to the Japanese side, Ho sided with the Allies, believing they would ultimately defeat Japan.

Nowadays, Vietnam looks to Japan as a counterweight to China, its old adversary. Japan resumed its aid to Vietnam in November 1992 and it is likely that Japanese private-sector investment will soon follow. The collapse of communism in Eastern Europe and the Soviet Union has pushed Vietnam and China closer, and the two countries normalised relations in November 1991. But the generation of a new, comfortable, ideological mutuality of interest will continue to be tempered by Vietnam's fear of becoming a client state of China, as in the past.

Vietnam's current major impediment to future growth is the US embargo and other indirect sanctions. It is curious that, in the role of a victor, the United States has been magnanimous (viz., its behaviour after World War II towards Germany and Japan), and yet in the role of a loser (its loss of the war in Vietnam) it can be petty and vengeful. There is no broadly-based reason for continuing its embargo on Vietnam and especially in its influencing others to follow suit. It is more than time for the United States to put its loss and humiliation behind it and to let Vietnam go free.

The main excuse offered up by the United States for not lifting the embargo is that it feels the Vietnamese have not been fully honest with regard to their records on the US military's 'Missing in Action' (MIA) and 'Killed in Action' (KIA) personnel. It could be argued that the Vietnamese have in fact done their best to assist the United States in this regard. Therefore, it could also be argued that the US refusal is more indicative of the 1992 US domestic election campaign's frantic search for more voter support, however proportionately insignificant the contribution of such voters. It is obviously reasonable, and very important for the relatives concerned, to insist on such disclosure — and the Vietnamese have agreed. However, it is now time for President Clinton to make this a separate issue and to begin the process of lifting the embargo.

Vietnam has achieved some real, albeit tenuous, successes. The country achieved an estimated trade surplus for 1992 of some US$70 million — no mean achievement when ten years previously its exports were a paltry 25 per cent of its imports. Inflation was brought down to around 18 per cent from 70 per cent in 1990 and 1991. Its currency, the dong, actually appreciated by some 15 per cent against the US dollar. However, its economic base remains weak and too narrowly focused on oil and unprocessed agricultural products, both of which account for some three-quarters of its exports. It also has around 25 per cent unemployment.

Vietnam's steely resolve and well-educated population of 70 million could provide an interesting, albeit minor, off-set to China, and to the Greater China of the future. It could also balance Thailand's rather excessive ambitions in Indochina, particularly those of its businessmen. In so doing, it could make a useful contribution to the overall balance of the region. In turn, with the support of the region, Vietnam could considerably accelerate the pace of its economic, and hopefully social, rebuilding programme. It is encouraging that ASEAN is already taking steps to bring Vietnam into its fold. On an individual basis, most of ASEAN's member countries are actively promoting political, trade, and investment ties with Vietnam, with Singapore being particularly active in this respect. Vietnam's future involvement with ASEAN will give ASEAN even more muscle and thus more impetus for the development of a regional community forum.

CAMBODIA

A Horror Story — Hardly Understood and Yet to End

The past twenty years have been far more traumatic for Cambodia than for Laos. Between 1953 and 1970, King (later 'Prince') Norodom Sihanouk, a mercurial, tragic figure, had tried to keep Cambodia neutral, in an effort to avoid being caught up in the anti-communist war in Laos and Vietnam. He ultimately failed and was ousted by an American-backed junta, only to find himself in alliance with the communist Khmer Rouge, led by the dreaded and infamous Pol Pot.

In April 1975, the same month that the Communists took control of Saigon, Pol Pot's forces captured the Cambodian capital of Phnom Penh. His rule, during which Sihanouk was kept a virtual prisoner, was a nightmare. In Pol Pot's drive to reach what he called 'Year Zero' before rebuilding the Cambodian society, he tried to erase an entire culture; his purpose was to create a classless society based on agriculture. All towns and cities were emptied. Out of a population of 7 million people, more than 2 million were killed by the Khmer Rouge or died from hunger and disease as a result of Pol Pot's insane policies.

Even when the Vietnamese drove out Pol Pot in 1978, forcing Sihanouk into exile, the nightmare did not end. A civil war ensued, which went on until October 1991. Peace has returned to Cambodia, but the truce between pro-Sihanouk forces, the Vietnam-backed regime of Hun Sen, and the Khmer Rouge is an uneasy one. The formerly warring groups now comprise a Supreme National Council, which is intended to govern the country until the next general elections are held. Sihanouk is the provisional head of state.

Overseeing the process is the UN Transitional Authority in Cambodia (UNTAC), charged with the seemingly insurmountable task of disarming the rival factions, defusing tens of thousands of land mines, and bringing home some 350,000 refugees and registering them for the proposed general elections in 1993. It is the largest and costliest operation the UN has ever undertaken and success is far from assured.

Private businessmen, though, go where angels fear to tread. Thai entrepreneurs, often backed by Thai generals, have moved in to buy land, build hotels, cut down trees, and dig for gems. The Khmer Rouge itself, claiming to have dropped Marxist-Leninist ideology, is also heavily involved in logging and mining, thus providing them with much-needed funding. After international protest, the Thai government announced in January 1993 that it would enforce an embargo on all such trade, but whether it will in fact do so is a moot point. In many parts of the country, the government is the best-organised force, as it prepares to fight in the national election. Meanwhile, the UN, in its haste to secure a peace settlement, has done little to prevent the Khmer Rouge from seizing power again in part of the country. In early 1993, although having previously agreed to participate in the UN-sponsored general elections, the Khmer Rouge threatened to boycott the elections. Fortunately, China, in an interesting display of its willingness to start playing a more responsible role in the region, subsequently announced that it would support the results of these elections — even if the Khmer Rouge did not participate.

Cambodia's role in the future Asia Pacific community in the near and medium term should be largely irrelevant. However, its complex mix of factions, its confused and conflicting goals, the murderous nature of some of the factions, and the involvement of Vietnam (now in the wings) create a disproportionately destabilising influence. And, in resolving this problem, Cambodia risks absorbing a disproportionate amount of the region's political and economic energy. It is also proving to be an enormous and costly headache for the UN. During the whole process, the wretched Khmer Rouge play frighteningly realistic games — for instance, they regularly kidnap UN officials and then later release them. It would appear that the ruthless and pointless killing may continue.

On the other hand, Cambodia has been, and could continue to be, an interesting, albeit costly, catalyst in the development of a regional partnership aimed at dealing with this problem. After all, the original Cambodian security issue *vis-à-vis* Vietnam provided the catalyst for

ASEAN's greater concern over regional security issues. More recently, Cambodia became the catalyst for Japan's first post-World War II military involvement outside of Japan, and now China is playing a regional statesman-like role *vis-à-vis* the country's affairs.

There is no doubt that sorting out, and introducing some form of democratic government to, Cambodia will be a long and expensive proposition. In some senses, the most effective solution would be simply to cordon off and then embargo the Khmer Rouge, but is there sufficient regional discipline and will to do so effectively? Time will tell, but one should not be too optimistic.

LAOS
A Thai Vassal State?

Laos, too, has had its share of tur-
moil. Its own civil war ended with the communist Pathet Lao finally in
control in 1975. The new rulers allied themselves with Vietnam and the
Soviet Union and moved quickly to collectivise agriculture and shut down
private traders. These policies brought the economy to the brink of
collapse, forcing the Communists to introduce market-style reforms in
the mid-1980s and to improve their relations with Thailand, China, and
the United States. As with Vietnam and China, the government retains a
monopoly of political, but not economic, power.

The collapse of the Soviet Union in 1990 has created a much more
fluid diplomatic situation for Laos. Senior politicians from both Thailand
and China have exchanged visits, and Laos has stepped up trade with its
two neighbours. Residents in the capital, Vientiane, are so close to the
border with Thailand that they pick up all the Thai television. Additionally, by a process of natural domestic market attrition, it is becoming an
extension of the Thai economy. Already many Vientiane shops prefer
payment in Thai baht rather than new Laotian kip, partly, of course,
because they purchase their merchandise in baht. However, despite all
this, the Laos government has not abandoned its longstanding 'special
relationship' with Vietnam — no doubt, because this relationship provides an insurance policy against domination by Thailand.

As long as the Communists in Vientiane do not face any serious threat
to their grip on power, they have been content to allow much of the
economy to go its own way. The country is poor and land-locked, and
most of its 4 million people are subsistence farmers. Its physical infrastructure is rudimentary, and thus central government control over many of its
provinces has always been tenuous at best. This is not helped by the fact
that there is no modern road running the length of the country. But then,

the pace of life is commensurately slow. As writer and journalist Dennis Bloodworth once observed, Laos makes *mañana* sound like *achtung*!

Despite the fact that Laos has a hardline communist government, it has never suffered the pariah status of Cambodia or Vietnam. Western and Japanese aid has continued to flow into Laos since 1975. Now, development assistance will also go into Cambodia, but while prospects may look brighter for these two buffer states, they are also entering a period of heightened uncertainty. In the overall scheme of things, Laos, with its minute, multi-ethnic population and lack of any meaningful resources, is likely to remain largely irrelevant to the activities of the Asia Pacific region for a long time to come.

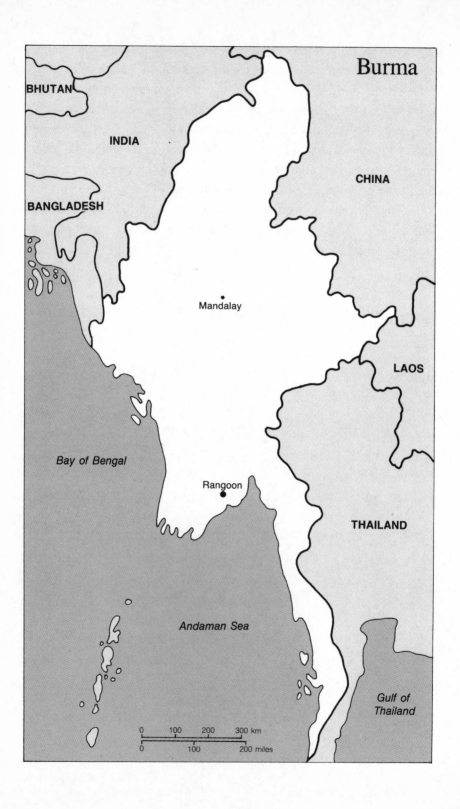

BURMA (MYANMAR)
A Tragic Exercise in Futility

One of the most remarkable contrasts to be found between neighbours is that between Burma (now called 'Myanmar') and Thailand. They are both ethnically diverse, Buddhist, and resource-rich. They have a roughly similar size of population, similar resources, and even a similar shape, yet something has gone seriously wrong with Burma.

Most commentators say the two countries started evolving in different directions in 1962, when General Ne Win toppled the regime of U Nu in a military coup, ending a democratic era that had lasted since independence in 1948. What followed was Burma's modern equivalent of the 'Dark Ages' or a longer version of China's Cultural Revolution. Ne Win sealed off the country from the outside world and promulgated the 'Burmese Way to Socialism'.

When Ne Win's long reign began, Burma was among the richest and most charming nations in Asia, with a living standard on a par with Thailand. Thirty years later, Burma was one of the poorest, most isolated, most corrupt countries in the world. In 1990, its generally estimated GNP per capita income was around US$195; Thailand's GNP was seven times that figure.

In 1988, amid mounting protests at one-party rule, Ne Win officially stepped down as chairman of the Burma Socialist Programme Party, although he continued to exert absolute control from behind the scenes. Hundreds of unarmed civilians were killed in the crackdown. As a sop to international opinion, a general election was held in May 1990, which was won handsomely by the opposition 'National League for Democracy' party. The result was ignored by the military junta, which used the opportunity to round up the remaining opposition figures who had not been imprisoned in 1988. From there the generals went after the Buddhist clergy, the last remaining redoubt of independent thinking in Burma, and imprisoned many senior clerics. The civil service was cowed into quiescence and the students were brutally repressed.

Since the 1990 election, the junta has gone on a spending spree, purchasing armaments from China, its closest ally, with money raised from the sale of oil and timber concessions and from gem mining. The military is also widely said to have raised revenue from heroin exports. The armaments are being used to prosecute a campaign against rebel insurgents and others who represent a threat to the regime. From a military point of view, things went well. The Communist Party of Burma collapsed in 1990 and several other resistance groups made peace with the Rangoon (now called 'Yangon') government. One of the most stubborn independence movements, the Karen National Union, was wiped out in many places along the border with Thailand. And on the western border, thousands of Burmese Muslims were forced to leave their homes and seek sanctuary in Bangladesh.

How did Burma come to such a pass? For one thing, it was not able to escape the clutches of colonisation in the way that Thailand did. It was annexed by Britain and made a province of British India in 1895. It had to fight for its independence for many years until it was granted limited internal self-rule in 1937, only to have it snatched away by Japan four years later. When it finally gained its freedom in 1945, doctrinaire socialism was the coming thing in India and Britain, not to mention Burma. Left-wing policies became fossilised under Ne Win, who nationalised the banks and major industries.

Unlike Thailand, Burma has two big powers as neighbours, India and China, whose peoples had settled throughout the resource-rich country over the years. After the British left, it was the Indians and Chinese who controlled Burmese commerce. Ethnic Burmans felt like the dispossessed in their own country, an attitude which led to their long isolation; it was considered better to keep all foreigners out than to open the gates and allow the Indians, Chinese, and others to flood back in. Isolation has trapped Burma in a time-warp of the 1950s.

A further problem was the question of the ethnic minorities. In the fruitless search for a federal formula that would reconcile the former's desire for autonomy with the latter's desire for security, negotiations between them and the politically dominant Burmans dragged on after independence. It was at this point that Ne Win stepped in to decide matters once and for all, introducing a draconian government and forcing the different ethnic communities to flee to the hills, where they have been fighting a guerrilla war against the central government ever since. Finally, there is the character of Ne Win to consider. A deeply superstitious, iron-willed figure, he felt that the only way to maintain Burmese unity was to suppress the ethnic minorities through military means. National coherence has been the *leitmotif* of his rule since 1962.

Eventually, Burma will have to open itself to the outside world, to the point where the regime will crumble. But this could be many years away. Ne Win has no single, chosen successor, but has prepared a group of hardline generals to take over after his demise.

There is almost nothing the world can do to pressure the junta to give up power, because Burma is largely self-sufficient in food. By the early 1990s, industry had been run into the ground and energy supplies were running out, but there was no sign that these weaknesses would prove to be the regime's undoing.

Japan mistakenly regards itself as having a special relationship with Burma, by virtue of the fact that, during World War II, a small band of nationalists including Ne Win were trained in Japan. It is true that Japan was by far the largest aid donor, until 1988 when all fresh assistance programmes were stopped after the massacre of civilians in Rangoon by the army. This has weakened the economy, but not fatally so. More important are the recent ASEAN reactions. For example, in 1992, the ASEAN foreign ministers advised their Burmese counterparts during the September UN General Assembly that the Burmese government's behaviour was generally unacceptable.

However, the country with the most influence on Burma is probably China, which itself has a poor human rights record. It appears also that China is gradually working to make Burma a client state, as it was for centuries before its colonisation. There is some real evidence of this trend. Rangoon is full of Chinese products. The ruling junta has purchased hundreds of millions of US dollars worth of military equipment from China. There is the view that the government has received Chinese construction assistance for the Haing Gyi island naval facilities. All this causes considerable concern amongst Burma's Southeast Asian neighbours and even further afield. If the current Rangoon government is not prepared to make any material, lasting change, as a regional and world pariah, it might have little choice but to fall into China's embrace. If this happens, Ne Win and his colleagues will have paid a high price to preserve a farcical semblance of national unity and independence — tragically, the cost to the Burmese people will be vastly higher.

Once again, as the ASEAN member states have begun to demonstrate, the Asia Pacific community is not likely to tolerate this cancer forever. Furthermore, one of the more humanitarian benefits of having a regional forum is to bring the entire region's weight to bear on this pernicious regime. Such pressure, coupled with the existing general worldwide approbation, could probably tip the balance. A changed Burma with all its resources could make a useful contribution to the region. As importantly, it could provide a counter-balance to Thailand and, in the future, to Vietnam.

PART THREE

The Arguments
and a
General Blueprint
for a
Regional Forum
in Asia Pacific

INTRODUCTION

If one wants to anticipate the future, one has to ignore short-term accidents and look instead at long-term trends. If one concentrates on these, one can see that the only way the countries of Asia Pacific can solve their common problems *vis-à-vis* the rest of the world is by coming together as a regional community. This would also have the likely effect of resolving, or at least addressing, many intra-regional problems.

I do not wish in any way to suggest that the Asia Pacific region is an economic community waiting to happen; a natural confederation longing to launch itself on an unsuspecting world. Just as it was difficult for the EEC to get started or for NAFTA to get bedded down, so will it be for the countries of the Asia Pacific region to take not only the bold, but also the cautious, various steps required to nail their respective flags to the regional community mast. There will be many false starts, many compromises, much debate, and yet there are faint signs of a gathering momentum. However, despite all these provisos, I am convinced that the ingredients are there for a regional forum to happen. And that in due course it will and must happen.

In this connection, I should reiterate that not all the countries of the region will start this process simultaneously. Some will obviously take longer than others; some, indeed, would not be suitable members of the first, or even second, round of membership discussions. One should not forget the origins of the EC and the tortuous road it has trodden to get only as far as it has today. Yet even in February 1993, despite the difficulties over the Maastricht Treaty in late 1992, the EC announced that it had commenced official discussions to bring Sweden, Finland, and Austria into the EC as full members.

In Part One of this book, I have tried to show, in an overview of the Asia Pacific region, how much the different countries have in common with one another. The region's varied geography and climate have in the past posed fundamental barriers to its unified development. In today's technological world, these factors are no longer as relevant. Far from being sharply autonomous, the region's peoples have taken part over the last thousand years or so in a gradual mixing of ethnic groups. In the broad sweep, the early history of Asia was similar to that of Europe, a never-ending succession of invasions, empires, and cultural mixing.

Despite their variety, religions in Asia Pacific have moulded societies which share ideas about kinship, religious/philosophical tolerance, discipline, and death. With the advent of colonialism, Asia Pacific's history became fundamentally different from that of Europe. Orthodoxy says Western influence in Asia Pacific has been divisive. But there has been unity in the struggle, and in the legacies left by that struggle. The region may also prove the adage that 'the student becomes the teacher'.

As with the rest of the world, Asia has suffered an endless succession of wars. But unlike Europe and North America since the end of World War II, the peoples of Asia Pacific have continued to suffer, not only from floods, famines, earthquakes, and poverty, but also from continuing regional wars, all of which have provided a continuous experience of what I call the 'pain' factor. Pain has taught the people of Asia to focus, plan, sacrifice and exercise discipline. These skills are essential for understanding 'reality', and, by extension, for economic and trade success. Thus, Asia Pacific's experience of pain has made it uniquely prepared to face a future of possible economic and trade warfare. History, culture, and pain have all taught the peoples of Asia Pacific how to adapt quickly to the vagaries of life — what I call the 'wild card' factor. The world must be prepared to accept that an Asia Pacific community will itself represent a new wild card.

In Part Two, I have examined each of these countries in an attempt to demystify these very different and often misrepresented societies. I have also tried to demonstrate how much each individual country has to gain by participating in some form of union with the rest of Asia Pacific.

In Part Three, I will argue that global forces — rapid change and development in technology, ideology, economics, and 'people-power' — are all pulling in the same direction. Despite the chaos surrounding the changes in the former Soviet Union, brought about by historical factors and the way in which the Soviet government has managed its own demise, and despite the setbacks concerning the Maastricht Treaty, the tendency everywhere, but particularly in the Northern Hemisphere, seems to be for countries to coalesce in supra-national, regional groupings. This process is very likely to result in the evolution of a tri-polar world of Europe (or Greater Europe), North America, and Asia Pacific, with each regional grouping having multi-polar leadership. A historic opportunity presents itself for Asia Pacific to come together, to redress the imbalances within the region, and to restore the balance between the region and the outside world.

In the final chapter of Part Three, I shall examine the attempts made to date to form links between the region's countries, and I shall suggest a general blueprint to show how a new Asia Pacific regional community forum might evolve in the future. The addition of such a forum would create a more balanced global community and a strong support for the continuance of free trade, while itself creating the foundation for a vibrant and prosperous region. Further, I hope to show that if the global, political, and economic environment were to become even more negative in the future, such a forum would be likely to assist materially in reducing any potentially belligerent behaviour by countries in the region. Thus, the result will be advantageous, not just for the peoples of Asia Pacific but, I believe, for the world as a whole.

THE NEW GLOBAL POWER EQUATION

In the days of the Cold War, two opposing ideologies, communism and capitalism, dominated the world. Lest they end up victims in the middle, most of the world's countries were forced to take sides. Which side a country chose sometimes depended upon ideological affinity, sometimes upon economic convenience, sometimes both. In the Third World, it was all too often brute force that tipped a country in one direction or the other. Western Europe and the United States threw in their lot with each other in the NATO alliance, as a result of shared values and a perceived common threat from the Warsaw Pact. Japan, dependent on the United States for defence, supported the West in the Cold War while busily selling its products to everyone. Eastern Europe and Mongolia had little choice but to align with the Soviet Union. In Central America, warring factions in El Salvador and Nicaragua played on the superpowers' fears to get the United States and the Soviet Union to help further their national ambitions. Leaders in South America and Africa used the same technique. Some countries — India and Finland, for instance — tried to remain neutral in the Cold War stand-off. But even these neutral parties tended to lean towards one camp or the other.

The US Reagan administration, whether it meant to or not, expanded its defence expenditure to the point where it effectively bankrupted the Soviet bloc — for that, and for all the efforts of the United States to lead the democratic/capitalist side during the Cold War, we all owe a great debt of gratitude to the United States. Under pressure from the American military build-up and from problems within the Soviet Union, President Mikhail Gorbachev finally admitted that the Soviet Union could not even feed and house its people. By doing so, he provided a catalyst for change throughout the world.

The momentous changes set in motion in 1989 seem to have altered the balance of power for good. In all its variant forms, democracy, with its attendant capitalism, has emerged as the world's dominant ideology. Change has been so momentous and so fast, it has been difficult to keep track of it. After seventy years of the Iron Curtain, the 'evil empire', 'capitalist imperialism', proxy wars, and spy trades at Berlin's famous Checkpoint Charlie, Warsaw Pact members pronounced, in June 1990, an end to the notion of the West as 'an ideological enemy'. Checkpoint Charlie no longer exists, along with the Berlin Wall and, indeed, the Warsaw Pact itself!

According to Francis Fukuyama, author of *The End of History and the Last Man*, 'What we may be witnessing is not just the end of the Cold War, or the passing of a particular period of post-war history, but the end of history as such: that is the end of mankind's ideological evolution and the universalisation of Western liberal democracy as the final form of human government.'

For some, it is too early yet to say whether Fukuyama is right or wrong. I personally think he is being too simplistic. But, in any event, one can say definitely that the Cold War is finished, and that the world is now decisively different. One can also say that the countries of Asia have some way yet to go before they achieve Fukuyama's definition of the end of their respective histories! However, the old politics — under which all the world's countries were divided according to whether or not their governments subscribed to the ideas of the nineteenth-century German philosopher Karl Marx — appear to be gone for good. People are no longer threatened by a balance of superpower-organised nuclear terror.

The American president's staff have tutored the former Soviet president and his staff in administration and bureaucratic policy. For the first time in forty years, students at the US Naval War College no longer play war games against the Soviet Union. Instead, cadets play against the possible threats posed by Muslim extremists, hardliners in China, and the risk of extreme nationalist movements obtaining nuclear warheads. In Asia Pacific, as in other parts of the world, barriers erected during the Cold War conflict have been dissolving, freeing nations to develop more natural ties dictated by blood ties, trade, and geography. Taiwan, for example, has allowed its citizens to visit a China ruled by what it has long called 'an illegitimate regime'. A Chinese table tennis champion now plays exhibition matches in Taiwan. Taiwanese industrialists have set up plants in China. Indonesia, which brutally repressed a Chinese-backed communist uprising in 1966, has now re-established relations with China. In Indochina, which endured some of the most painful hot flushes of the Cold War, the shooting has largely stopped. In 1988, the year that Gorbachev stunned the West by declaring that class warfare on an international scale was obsolete, Vietnam started searching for olive branches rather than arms as ways to resolve the Cambodian conflict and rejoin the Asian community. Two years later, in 1990, the president in charge of the once staunchly-communist Vietnamese government told reporters that reforms were essential if the country was to avoid collapse.

In Cambodia, a country even more traumatised than Vietnam, it seems that at last peace may be more or less achieved, supervised by a multinational UN peacekeeping force (UNTAC) which now includes a six hundred-strong contingent from Japan's armed forces. All this is in stark contrast to the former positions of the United States and the Soviet Union, which supported various factions in the Cambodian civil war in order to further their own Cold War interests. In effect, they kept the civil war simmering. But now the superpowers have lost interest in their old priorities. When China indicated that it would be willing to abandon its support for the reviled Khmer Rouge, Vietnam promised to withdraw all its troops from Cambodia.

Although not all nations took Vietnam at its word, the withdrawal — or partial withdrawal — has changed the political landscape of Indochina. For a decade, Vietnam's border with China was marked by bloody clashes. Since the withdrawal, markets have sprung up along it. Vietnamese officials are now actively pursuing their own version of Gorbachev's economic restructuring programme. While the government has allowed some economic reform, like the Chinese government, it still clings to the Communist Party structure as the only means of controlling the economic and political evolution of the country.

Other governments have also relaxed. The new atmosphere has given an opening to Thailand, which has been hailed as Asia's next growth economy. The Thai economy thrived in the late 1980s. A broad spectrum of industries grew, foreign investment was strong, and tourism boomed. Traditionally, Thailand has been preoccupied with its internal military coups and with fighting the communists in Indochina. However, in the belief that East–West relations would soon normalise and usher in a new era of peace, the country's former prime minister Chatichai Choonhavan announced in 1990 that he would like to turn Indochina from 'a battleground into a marketplace'. Bangkok began to set itself up as the hub of a new Southeast Asian sub-region of economic prosperity. In Cambodia and Laos, the Thais have forged joint ventures and offered manufactured goods in exchange for Cambodia's and Laos's forest products, minerals, and other commodities. Thai projects in Vietnam and Cambodia are playing a major role in opening up these countries' economies.

Several thousand kilometres to the northeast, neighbours with far more profound differences have also begun to patch things up. In 1990, South Korea, a country created and sustained by the Cold War, established diplomatic relations with the Soviet Union. This announcement was the end-result of a diplomatic flirtation with the Eastern bloc, which officials in Seoul hoped would help resolve a more painful conflict: that with North Korea. Seoul began its Eastern bloc courtship — jokingly called *Nordpolitik* (a reference to Willi Brandt's *Ostpolitik*) — with the 1988 Olympic Games in Seoul, attended by athletes from the Soviet Union, China, and every other important communist country with the exception of North Korea. South Korean leaders believed that expanding economic ties with the Soviets would slowly draw political concessions from the Eastern bloc, further isolating North Korea's leader Kim Il-Sung. Within two years, Seoul was exchanging contracts and ambassadors with all the Eastern European countries save isolationist Albania. The South's strategy seems to be working. In September 1990, in the highest-level meeting since the Korean War, the prime ministers of the two Koreas met in Seoul. Since then there has been further progress, albeit sporadic, towards normalisation of relations. In 1992, South Korea and the People's Republic of China, previously bitter enemies, established formal relations and a number of important new economic ventures. This has put further pressure on North Korea both to reassess its isolationist position and to rejoin the Asian community.

Meanwhile, the Philippines — long the forward position for the United States in Asia — began to reassess the desirability of having enormous American naval and air force bases in the country. No longer afraid of the Soviet threat in the Pacific, Philippine nationalists argued that the 1947 agreement allowing American military bases was an extension of the 'colonial relationship' with the United States. Conversely, many other Filipinos supported the bases because they pumped an estimated US$1 billion into the economy every year. But in May 1990, the Philippine government formally told the United States that the agreement would not be extended and the bases were closed.

In this new, warmer atmosphere, countries like Vietnam, North Korea, Cambodia, and even China can all come in from the cold. Regional disputes that once seemed to threaten war — like those over the Spratly and Kurile islands — assume their proper significance and, hopefully, may now be resolved. After years of frigid relations with the Soviet Union, Japan welcomed President Gorbachev's visit to Tokyo in April 1991. Nevertheless, succession of efforts have so far failed to resolve a territorial dispute over the Kurile Islands, previously a Japanese possession. The dispute dates back to the last days of World War II and has kept Tokyo's diplomatic relations with the Soviet Union in an uneasily frozen state. As a matter of national face, Japan wants to regain its islands. Land is precious to a populace crowded on to a tiny land mass. Russia wants, and must have, Japanese aid, both economic and humanitarian. Unlike Europe and the United States, which have begun to pledge aid to countries of the former Soviet Union, Japan has so far refused to provide any material economic aid until the Russians return the Kuriles. Like the other potential donors, the Japanese are also concerned about whether money they might send will end up in the wrong hands. They see it as a European problem. On the other hand, they are willing to make a gesture, but they want a *quid pro quo*. In September 1990, the Russians agreed at least to talk about giving back the islands. One solution might be to ask Japan to buy back the Kuriles, just as their nineteenth-century predecessors sold Alaska to the United States. However, when President Boris Yeltsin cancelled his much-heralded visit to Japan in September 1992, due to domestic conservative and nationalist pressure about not handing back the islands, the Japanese felt insulted. The result is a stand-off, particularly as Japanese big business is showing little interest in pushing the government to make any material concessions for purely business reasons.

The victory of capitalism and representative government sets the stage for a new world in which people will be able to reassert power over their governments. Military considerations will become less important. What remains is the so-called new world order, with the United States as the only power potentially strong enough to act as the world's policeman, but without sufficient funds to do the job on its own. But America is rightly reluctant to act to resolve regional conflicts without the consent and economic support of others. Although the unity the world has been able to demonstrate in its approach to the Gulf War, for example, has been impressive and unprecedented, the subsequent results in Kurdistan and Yugoslavia have shown the limitations of superpower intervention and collective purpose. Some future immediate questions will include whether or not the United States, with or without UN support, will ultimately be able to deal with Iraq's refusal to comply with UN directives; whether the EC, the United States, and/or the UN will be able to stop the appalling horror of the break-up of Yugoslavia; and whether the UN will be able to resolve the Somalian problem.

Within the United States, there is increasing indifference, or even hostility, to the outside world. America is withdrawing, psychologically and physically, from much of the world, particularly Africa and Asia — despite its aid involvement in Somalia and Yugoslavia. In the future, it is likely to focus increasingly on its immediate neighbours, Canada, the Caribbean, and Latin America. President Clinton's January 1993 announcement of the need for a 'Western Hemisphere Community of Democracies', encompassing North America to the Caribbean and Latin America, is indicative of this. No longer involved in a global struggle with the Soviet Union, America is diverting its resources — bringing home the troops and cancelling aid — in order to deal with its own burgeoning social problems. Although theoretically the world has been made safe for democracy and market economy capitalism, in Asia Pacific, as elsewhere, a vacuum is appearing.

Japan is being pulled by regional forces within Asia Pacific and is also beginning to assert itself within the region. Thus, it is beginning to take on a co-leadership role in the region. Because of sensitivities from the past, this is being done quietly, but nonetheless effectively. Japan was the first country to continue to supply aid to China after the events in Tiananmen Square in 1989, despite American disapproval, and it pressed other nations to lift sanctions. It has started providing aid to Vietnam despite the continuing US embargo and it has committed peacekeeping troops to UNTAC in Cambodia.

As the most important aid donor and investor in the region by far, Japan has been able to exert influence behind the scenes. When demonstrators in East Timor were killed by Indonesian security forces in November 1991, Japanese pressure was instrumental in ensuring that a government report assigned partial responsibility to Indonesian security forces. Japanese aid to Indonesia totals US$1.15 billion (1989 figure), 67 per cent of all aid received by it. Japan has also tried to put pressure on the Burmese government to relax its iron grip on the country. In September 1988, nine days after the military junta took power, the Japanese government made public its conditions for the resumption of aid: a political settlement reflecting the general will of the Burmese people and the opening up of the economy.

Many of the other countries in the region have, in the past, been suspicious of Japan's intentions. This is not surprising in view of the events that led up to, and Japan's behaviour during, World War II. However, in the recent past, these views have changed considerably. Most countries now view the EC and the evolving NAFTA community in North America with more suspicion. A leading Chinese official, in a statement made in Tokyo in October 1992, recognised the need for Japan to become more integrated into the region — a dramatic change from its previous position. More specifically and as reported in the *Far Eastern Economic Review* of 13 August 1992, party leader Jiang Zemin, during his visit to Tokyo in mid-1992, stated, 'The friendly relations between China and Japan are ... an important contribution to the peace and development of the Asia Pacific region and the world. The Chinese Government and people ... support Japan in playing a positive role in the defence of peace in Asia and the world and in promoting the common prosperity of all countries.' Additionally, Jiang hinted that China would not oppose Japan's Peace Keeping Bill which would allow it to participate in the UN-sponsored peacekeeping forces in Cambodia. This tacit support was vital in getting the related Bill passed by Japan's Diet.

Today, the common perception in Japan and elsewhere that the rest of Asia is terrified of any Japanese military involvement outside Japan, is generally not true. Japan is far too vulnerable to an attack using modern military technology, even without nuclear weapons, to attempt realistically to be a new military superpower, let alone embark on a new military-driven, empire-building exercise. One should not forget that the Japanese population is concentrated in only 20 per cent of its small land mass; the remaining 80 per cent is mountains, thus creating extremely densely packed, military, industrial, and civilian targets.

Asia Pacific needs a system of collective security in order to counteract the military adventures that will no doubt occur in the future, and Japan must be involved in order to balance China and India. China itself has a large standing army numbering 3.2 million, and a nuclear capability, as well as a substantial arms exporting industry. Given the inherent difficulty of maintaining central government control due to China's geographical size, poor infrastructure, and immense, diverse population, it could be argued that its large army is more or less legitimate. However, China may well prove to be unstable in the next century, which would make it all the more necessary for Japan to make a substantial military, peacekeeping commitment to the region. The same arguments may be applied to India. There is also the reasonable possibility that the region could, over time, develop its own permanent peacekeeping force along NATO lines. I believe that other countries will come to accept Japan's emergence as a regional military partner, particularly if it agrees not to act except in concert with the UN/ASEAN in the region or with the UN globally.

Thus, while the demise of the former global superpower security-driven stand-off has led to these changes, the evolution of both the new global community and an Asia Pacific community will now be driven more by economic and trade considerations and not by the old superpower-supported security ones. The world is already dividing into north–south trade-driven axes, as is already being evidenced in Greater Europe and North America. Faced with this emerging reality, it would be prudent for the countries of Asia Pacific to take steps towards creating a regional forum. This forum could subsequently evolve naturally into a more tightly knit form of community, say a confederation, or be forced to do so as a reaction to protectionist pressures from the West. At the same time, such a forum would enable the region to cope more effectively with the last major 'wild card' in the regional equation — namely, how to deal with the rapidly evolving and constantly changing question of 'security' within the region.

Inter-regional Trade Wars
Replace the Superpower Cold War

The struggle for power is now focused on the arena of trade and economics, rather than on military strength. It is significant that two of the most powerful players in this new game, Germany and Japan, are the two nations demilitarised after the last world war. The battle is one between attempts to dominate markets, now that the ideological barriers are down almost everywhere, and those aimed at ensuring that free trade can flourish. Some issues, such as the environment and Third World aid, require global action. However, countries are not necessarily going to beat their swords into ploughshares; the relaxation of East–West defence/security-driven tension does not mean the end of disagreement. But a fundamental change has occurred. More power is now likely to flow from the boardroom than from the war room. The rise in foreign direct investment has already reduced the freedom of governments to determine their own economic policy. If a government tries to push tax rates up, for example, it is increasingly easy for businesses to shift production overseas. Equally, if state or regional governments fail to invest in roads, education, and other forms of infrastructure, domestic entrepreneurs are likely to migrate. In short, the need for private-sector investment and business flexibility is forcing governments to compete — not only for voters but for investors and businessmen.

The disputes likely to arise from this increasingly complex equation will all have their roots in a fundamental paradox: people and companies want to be able to buy goods from the global market at the lowest price — yet people want to protect their own jobs, and companies their own markets. These two opposing sides of any economic equation inevitably lead to friction, and will probably lead to the next form of cold war — namely, trade wars on a global scale replacing the previous balance of military tension between the Pentagon and the Kremlin.

What is now palpable is the change from the old global East–West defence axes to the new regional north–south trade axes. Until recently, military considerations inhibited the egalitarian effects of trade. Ideological disputes that fuelled the nuclear stand-off kept nations from trading freely with one another. Bulgaria would not buy South Korean electronic components, even if they were better and less expensive than the Eastern bloc alternatives. IBM, a symbol of American capitalism, was prohibited from seeking contracts in the Soviet Union. These barriers are now eroding, or have disappeared altogether. The collapse of communism and the abolition of controlled, centralised economies, have enabled the expansion of trade to almost every corner of the globe. The world appears to have adopted the concept of 'free-market economy capitalism' as its new standard. Even the staunchly communist Chinese are now advocating their version — which they call 'socialist market economy capitalism'. This, of course, means competition at a global level. As Lester Thurow, author of *Head to Head: The Coming Economic Battle among Japan, Europe and America* (1992), puts it, 'future historians will see the twentieth century as a century of niche competition and the twenty-first century as a century of head-to-head (trade and economic) competition.'

But there are new barriers going up between regions as countries reorganise themselves according to regionalism or tribalism, rather than ideology. A crucial factor here is the ever-increasing Japanese economic challenge to American hegemony, and the resentment it generates in the United States. Japan, and other countries in the Asia Pacific region, such as South Korea, Taiwan, and now even China, have a huge balance-of-payments surplus with the United States; this imbalance has a destabilising effect. Japanese investment in America is seen as particularly threatening, despite, for example, the fact that, although British investment is higher, the reactions against this have been much more muted. America looks set to become increasingly isolationist, withdrawing behind tariff walls and concentrating its trade increasingly on its neighbours, Canada and South and Central America.

A United States–Canada Free Trade Agreement was signed in 1988; and in December 1992, Mexico, the United States, and Canada signed agreements on a North American Free

Trade Association (NAFTA), which will now need to be ratified by the legislatures of the three countries. Once ratified, the pact will eliminate tariffs on North American goods over fifteen years. It will create the world's largest free-trade area, with an estimated annual output exceeding US$6 trillion and with over 360 million consumers. It is likely that NAFTA, and the United States in particular, will want to expand this free-trade zone to incorporate other Central and South American countries. Conversely, it is highly unlikely that any countries from Asia Pacific will join NAFTA, despite suggestions that it be expanded to include such countries, and indications that Australia and New Zealand might also seek membership. The conflicts of interest, economically and geopolitically, would be enormous if such developments were to occur. To extend the argument further, if nations from Asia Pacific and elsewhere were to join NAFTA, not only would the conflicts of interest be impossible to manage, but NAFTA in such a global form could directly undermine the purpose and function of GATT. This, in turn, would probably cause its collapse and 'trade-blocism' could be upon us with a vengeance.

This confusion is being further compounded, possibly dramatically so, by President Clinton's statement in January 1993 that he wanted to join with the nations of Latin America and the Caribbean to form a 'Western Hemisphere Community of Democracies'. Where does that place NAFTA and such enthusiastic would-be non-regional members?

In the 1980s and early 1990s before Clinton's election, something in the once-indomitable American spirit seemed to have lagged. A popular T-shirt depicting the American television anti-hero Bart Simpson bore the telling slogan, 'Underachiever and Proud of It'. Internal problems were dogging the United States from every angle. Hundreds of billions of dollars were needed to bail out its savings and loan industry. The administration and Congress have been reluctant to approve either major tax increases or large spending cuts, two obvious ways of bringing about a major drop in the country's budget deficit. In October 1990, the US government had to shut down for a few days because the president and legislators couldn't agree on a federal budget package which called for cuts of US$500 billion over five years — the government was incapable of making the necessary decisions. It could be argued that earlier Defense Department investments in programmes such as the interstate highway system and the National Defense Education Act improved the performance of the economy. Thurow holds that the faster, cheaper transportation permitted by America's interstate highway system was responsible for a substantial part of the high productivity gains recorded in the 1960s. But infrastructure investments are now running at less than half the rates they were then; as a result, little has been done to improve the productive base of the economy through education, public works, and innovations — let alone to properly maintain the current infrastructure. Stagnant productivity growth, low national saving, and heavy indebtedness to foreigners threaten the future standard of living of Americans. While spending trillions of dollars to buy sophisticated weapons systems, the United States has neglected even to adequately maintain its roads, bridges, and subways. In 1990, the *New York Times* called the New York area 'one big road repair'.

America's social problems are legion. Education has proved inadequate, and the workforce has suffered. In poor families, single mothers are now the norm rather than the exception. Drugs and poverty are creating an underclass which can only aspire to success through cocaine or other drug dealing. Insurance and healthcare costs have skyrocketed beyond all reasonable levels. Legal anarchy means that vast sums of money are needed to protect business and individuals against absurd lawsuits. America has more than one-third of the world's lawyers — some say as many as seventeen times the number per capita in Japan, and that US tort costs as a percentage of GNP are six times as high as in Japan.

The United States may be loath to give up its role as a world leader, but the mounting burden of its problems may leave it no choice. It just doesn't have the money that Eastern Europe needs for its development, for example. A nation in arrears on its dues to international organisations such as the UN, and pleading poverty at every turn, cannot hope to continue indefinitely to play the leading role in world affairs without first putting its own house in order.

However, the United States has reason to maintain good relations with Canada and Latin America. It has an enormous stake in a prosperous and democratic Latin America. There is no hope of stemming the tide of either immigrants or drugs, together with their associated social problems, so long as the wages of Mexican workers are so low and the farmers in the

Andes have no viable alternative to growing coca. The United States will still need natural resources such as oil to maintain its own economy. It will still need markets for its products. For these, it will be more likely to look to Canada and Central and South America. Meanwhile, American companies have been moving factories into Mexico, both before and after government negotiators concluded the NAFTA agreement. In 1990, President Bush launched his 'Enterprise for the Americas Initiative'. Bush indicated that his government would be willing to forego some of the debts it is owed by Latin American countries, and promised to foster new investment as they liberalised their trade and their economies. Bush's vision of a trading zone from Alaska to Cape Horn is being built on the rubble of half-a-dozen failed Latin American attempts at regional integration. But unlike previous plans, most of which limited participation to the countries of Latin America, Bush's idea includes the rich north as well as the poor south, and could benefit both.

Self-interest is likely to encourage this continued evolution. An economic community in the Americas would help to provide a sustained solution to the Latin American debt crisis. Latin American countries need to trade with rich countries like America and Canada, not with their fellow poor countries. Likewise, poorer Asian countries need to trade with richer ones. However, as the statistics (stated below) show, intra-Asia Pacific trade is expanding rapidly and now overtaking trade volumes with the EC and the United States.

At the same time, there are also powerful motivations for this developing community to be a protectionist bloc. While the United States has long preached the value of free trade and has kept its markets open, this has frequently been to the detriment of its own economy. This was fine when the American economy was the strongest in the world. But now that, as Thurow puts it, 'the great wall is down, American industry is looking increasingly uncompetitive.' Patent registrations bear this out. In 1980, seven out of the top ten patent winners registered in the United States were American; at the end of the decade the figure was only three out of ten, and the best-placed American firm was fifth. When a survey asked the Japanese which imported cars they wanted to buy, no American cars appeared on the list (Thurow, pp. 158 and 162). In April 1992, the United States passed anti-trust laws which were widely regarded in Japan as potential weapons against Japanese companies.

As American industry falters, protectionist sentiment is rising in the US Congress. Threats of protectionism often have more to do with politics than with economics. Washington is constantly threatening China, and thus effectively Hong Kong as well — both of which have rising trade surpluses with the United States — with the removal of China's 'Most Favoured Nation' trading status. Indonesia has received similar threats, as has Malaysia. South Korea, Taiwan, and Hong Kong, amongst other Asian countries, have all been accused of dumping (selling exports below cost). Thailand and Taiwan are threatened with retaliation for not participating in, and complying with, international agreements on intellectual property rights. The irony of American trade policy in the 1980s is that President Reagan, the post-Cold War chief executive with the most passionate love of *laissez-faire*, presided over the greatest domestic American people's swing towards protectionism since the 1930s.

Despite this gloomy recital, one must not underestimate the energy and talent of the American people. The election of President Clinton, which united the administration and Congress under the Democratic Party banner, together with Clinton's stated objectives during, and immediately after, the election period, may bring a new sense of purpose, discipline, and focus to the United States. However, even if this proves to be true, the task still remains an enormous one.

Across the Atlantic, another bloc could be developing. Europe, too, threatens to build a fortress, creating an even more powerful and intimidating economic community. The EC has the potential to embrace not only the European Free Trade Association, or EFTA (Austria, Switzerland, Liechtenstein, Sweden, Norway, and Iceland), and Eastern Europe, but also Russia and the other former member states of the Soviet Union, the Commonwealth of Independent States (CIS); indeed, ultimately the EC probably has no choice but to do so eventually, if it is to prevent massive westward migration and resentment boiling over into conflict (Thurow, p. 111). These countries will be able to exploit a huge market with an ease of access previously unthinkable. This prospect has probably given nightmares to finance ministers and commerce secretaries of countries outside the region, who fear the development of a 'Fortress Europe'. The *Financial Times* of 6 October 1992 reported that the countries of the EC had, for the first time, begun discussing controversial plans to give the EC greater power to push through 'commercial defense measures' to prepare for the EC's single market commencing on 1 January 1993. Such debate can only exacerbate the existing concerns about a protectionist Europe.

Europe currently represents the world's single largest, most integrated and sophisticated economic market, with, in the medium-term future, the free flow of goods, investment capital, and workers likely to be paid for with a unified currency. It would not be difficult to exclude outsiders. Indeed, part of the incentive for Europeans to join in ever-closer union is to gain special trading privileges unavailable to non-members (Thurow, pp. 66 and 69). With a combined population of more than 337 million — approximately 500 million more if former Warsaw Pact countries join — *in extremis*, 'Greater Europe' could survive, and possibly even power its own growth, while largely ignoring the rest of the world. Indeed, creating a Greater Europe will preoccupy the EC for decades. In late 1990, the president of the Asian subsidiary of a German chemicals concern told *Asian Business*, 'Our Far East plans have gone off the boil. Head office has become totally obsessed by the 1993 unified EC and it isn't interested anymore. We're just marking time here.'

Elements of this can be seen already. In 1990, for instance, the EC's policy-making arm, the European Commission, came up with standards for the development of products such as high-definition television which will keep the Japanese, its pioneers, out of Europe's domestic markets. With modern equipment, fertilisers, and agricultural technologies, it is possible that Greater Europe would become self-sufficient in food. Asian exporters have predicted that regulations on food preservatives and additives will be set at the level of the most demanding country, thereby acting as non-tariff barriers.

In the most controversial industry of all, automobile manufacture, European companies have suggested that when an EC quota comes in, the Japanese market share should be reduced from its 11 per cent in 1992, to 9.5 per cent. When the Japanese tried to respond to European import quotas by building European plants to assemble imported parts, the EC countered with local content rules. In its dealings with Asia, the European

Commission has been stretching the concept of anti-dumping to the limit; the way the Commission has set its rules, an Asian company's export price might be 50 per cent higher than its domestic price and the company could still pay penalties for dumping. Although the reactions of various member countries to the Maastricht Treaty and the partial collapse of the EC's European Monetary System (EMS) in August, September, and October of 1992, have collectively caused considerable confusion as to how the EC will evolve, there can be little doubt that the EC will continue to do so, even if only in fits and starts.

Economic self-interest will encourage people within these two regional trading communities to look inwards, not outwards. First of all, there won't be as much money to go around; the excesses of the 1980s have caused a major recession in the 1990s around the globe — including Japan, but excluding the rest of Asia. This trend will be accentuated by the capital demands of Eastern Europe — let alone Russia and the other CIS member states — to finance the reconstruction of its infrastructure and industry, and to clean up its environment. While inter-regional government aid will not disappear, its scale has already been drastically reduced. During the Cold War, the Soviet Union and the United States both tried to use vast amounts of economic and military aid to bribe developing countries into allegiance. Today, Russia is not only unable to provide aid to other countries, but is itself in desperate need of aid. The United States, with its growing economic problems at home and increased demands from its neighbours, will just not have enough capital and resources to continue to provide economic aid to countries such as Uzbekistan, Bangladesh, and Namibia.

The same is true of Europe. Struggling to fulfil the almost incomprehensible needs of the restructuring Soviet bloc, Europe will not be able to give much help to Asia, Africa, and South America.

What one is likely to see in the future is a new kind of superbloc rivalry, but taking place in the economic rather than the military sphere. Strong evidence of this process is the protracted, and highly complex, Uruguay Round of negotiations on GATT. In its simplest form, GATT strives to lower trade barriers and to seek freer trade between nations. It formulates agreements between nations for doing this. When possible, it referees disputes that may arise. Until the negotiations began on the Uruguay Round, GATT had been fairly successful. Tariffs are now lower than before, and there are many fewer barriers to trade worldwide than there would have been had GATT not existed.

Obviously, the primary defence against possible economic superbloc rivalry must be the whole world's general, ongoing support of the free trade principles embodied in GATT and its specific support for the finalisation of the Uruguay Round of GATT negotiations. Unfortunately, it is unlikely that such support will be ongoing, despite general agreement that it must be supported. The Uruguay Round of negotiations began on 20 September 1986 and was due to end in 1990. What was to have been the final meeting, on 7 December 1990 in Brussels, terminated in chaos. The negotiations slogged on.

More specifically, as special-interest groups became increasingly powerful, these GATT negotiations began to suffer serious strains. In 1988, disagreement between the United States and the EC over the long-term future of agricultural subsidies paralysed the negotiations. In 1989, 1990, and again in 1992, the issue of abolishing agricultural subsidies, which distort the world market for food, caused most of the leaders to backpedal. The United States wanted to abolish subsidies, as this would give its efficient agricultural sector a huge economic advantage. On the other side, Japan and the EC, particularly France, put the interests of their farmers at home first. They wanted the subsidies to continue to protect their agricultural sectors. In October 1992, Jean-Pierre Soisan, France's agricultural minister, stated that the concessions demanded by the United States could cause another peasants' revolt in France. Further, demonstrating the increasing emotional irrationality of the conflict, he said that the EC shouldn't be pressured into making a hurried agreement just to assist Bush in being re-elected.

Agreement in principle on agricultural subsidies, which had been deadlocked, was finally reached in late November 1992, but it had still to be formally signed. France soon pressed for modifications, and threatened that it would exercise its right to use its veto. The subsequent negotiations have not been without hindrance, including the announcement by the United States of trade sanctions against the EC on 5 November 1992, and as a result the negotiations were still not 'fully finalised' by January 1993.

There was still the hurdle of finalising the GATT agreement so that it could be presented to the US Congress in March 1993, which deadline was not met. The future outcome of the GATT is definitely unclear.

The Clinton administration's tougher stand on trade issues — evidenced by a series of tough new actions, such as the Commerce Department's imposition in February 1993 of temporary duties of as high as 106 per cent on US$2 billion worth of steel imports from nineteen countries around the world, and the US government's announcement that its future procurement of EC utility and telecommunications products would be blocked until the EC put a stop to its discrimination against similar US products — does not augur well for the future. It is actions such as these that will become the new weaponry in the future trade skirmishes that could presage possible future trade wars.

Indeed, GATT itself is bleeding to death from multiple wounds, and European integration provides, by implication, its death warrant (Thurow, p. 76). If GATT ever does succumb to regional self-interest, countries could begin abandoning hard-won multilateral trade agreements in favour of protectionist measures and/or bilateral trade agreements. With the possible exception of Japan, the new world of bilateral agreements will force the countries of Asia Pacific to recognise their limited national economic and political clout in taking on the EC and NAFTA. Their respective recognition of their weaker negotiating position with more powerful communities will no doubt force them to recognise the need to join together to create their own regional community forum. This forum would give them the economic and political clout to, at best, negotiate equitable treatment — or, at worst, simply to ensure their survival.

Whatever happens with GATT and other talks in the future, there is a clear indication in the statistics on Asia Pacific intra-regional trade and investment flows worldwide that investors within each region will start looking inward rather than outward. In the Asia Pacific region, this means investment by cash-rich countries such as Japan, Taiwan, Singapore, Hong Kong, and South Korea in underdeveloped countries such as China, Vietnam, India, and North Korea.

The threat of the horrors of a nuclear attack was a great deterrent against precipitate action during the superpower Cold War. This deterrent does not exist in the developing cold trade war and, as a result, there is likely to be a faster escalation of threats and action in this new global trade-oriented world; a situation which is hardly a positive indication of a resolution of the Uruguay Round of GATT negotiations.

The gradual unification of Greater Europe and of North and South America will galvanise the countries of Asia Pacific into banding together. Very few countries will be strong enough to get around protectionism by setting up offshore product development, management, and production operations. Thousands of Asian manufacturers and exporters are now giving more priority to the development of intra-regional trade. Previously, they may have lived by low-cost, high-volume trading to the United States and Europe, but increasingly they will be unable to compete in this way. In 1988, the newly industrialised economies of Asia — South Korea, Taiwan, Hong Kong, and Singapore — relied on the United States to take 31 per cent of their exports. This figure is expected to fall to 24 per cent by the year 2000. Exports to Europe currently make up 20 per cent of the total. In 1991, for the first time, intra-Asian trade volumes exceeded those to and from both North America and the EC.

Most countries in Asia Pacific are dependent upon exports for growth. Even if Thailand and Japan are in different economic leagues, they have a similar stake in preserving free trade, at the very least within their region. In 1989, the Asia Pacific countries began to export more to each other than they did to the United States. Trade between the nations of Asia Pacific in 1989 amounted to US$256 billion, 40 per cent of the region's total trade worldwide. This figure should increase to 55 per cent by the year 2000, according to estimates by the Nomura Research Institute of Japan. Should this happen, the nations of Asia Pacific will enjoy almost as much economic integration as the EC countries do today.

Japan is the largest single direct investor in the region. Everyone is investing in China. Korea is anxiously trying to make deals with China and Vietnam. Taiwanese investors are cutting a swathe through China, Thailand, Hong Kong, Vietnam, and the Philippines. Hong Kong companies are setting up manufacturing operations almost everywhere in Asia, except in crowded and expensive Hong Kong. The Thais are all over

Indochina. Even the Indians are setting up factories in China. In some cases, surplus cash is the principal motivation for these investments. In the case of Korea and Taiwan, a greater regional presence is part of a process of ending isolation and of buying legitimacy. In a few cases, it is an attempt to create economic co-prosperity spheres, as in the case of Thailand's economic ambitions *vis-à-vis* the rest of Indochina. Trade pressure is also playing a part. Japan's Asian neighbours are no less vocal than the United States in their criticism of the Japanese obsession with export and market protection. In response to this criticism and a need for cheaper production facilities, Japanese manufacturers are building factories across Asia. United States trade pressure is making all these countries realise that if the American market is ever closed to Asian companies, intra-Asian trade will be the only way to begin to replace it. Japan must become a large net importer, since only Japanese consumers have the purchasing power to replace the Americans (Thurow, pp. 213 and 214). Asia Pacific's export dependence on Japan is expected to rise from 12 per cent in 1988 to 18 per cent by the turn of the century.

Over-dependence on the US dollar as the main regional trading currency has led to serious discussions on the possibility of a 'yen bloc' in Asia Pacific. As in Europe, monetary union in the region could facilitate international trade by reducing the exchange risk and making it easier to control inflation. Because many countries in Asia Pacific are still suspicious of Japan, calls for a yen bloc are premature, if appropriate at all. The Japanese would be unlikely to welcome it, having seen the British and American governments 'lose' control of their currencies. An alternative could be to develop an Asian Currency Unit (ACU), based on the same principles as the European Currency Unit (ECU), in order to allay concerns about Tokyo exercising too much control. However, given the travails of the EC's European Monetary System (EMS) in 1992 and the gloomy prospects for its medium-term future, this is not likely to happen in the foreseeable future.

The Asia Pacific region would form a natural economic group. It has more than half the world's population, many of whom are highly disciplined and motivated to succeed. If its peoples grasp, and act upon, the opportunities presented, they will be able to build a new regional presence from a position of strength, while the other two economic regions of the world are retreating, retrenching, and rebuilding. As those regions make wrenching economic changes, so must the countries of Asia Pacific make cultural and attitudinal changes. Asia Pacific's need for change is widely recognised by its peoples. Many now recognise that unless they band together and negotiate as one, the countries of Asia Pacific risk being squeezed by these new economic superpowers. Even Japan is vulnerable, especially in the long term.

As the dominant economy in the region, Japan must play a leading part in the new Asia Pacific — but as a co-leader, not the leader. It must shrug off its inhibitions and demonstrate to other countries, who may be wary of a revival of Japanese power, its ability to play such a role. Japan must grow up. Its Greater East Asia Co-Prosperity Sphere may have been a disaster, but if Japan's leaders assume the role which history is now thrusting upon them, they can play a critical and constructive part in bringing Asia Pacific together. As the economies of India and, especially, China grow, it will also clearly be in the interests of those countries to play a part in this process.

No matter how each country plays out its objectives, the one constant, which must remain fundamental to all the parties' positions, is their support of GATT and their insistence on the continuance of free trade. To allow the protectionism skirmishing of the early 1990s to develop into a full-scale battle, let alone a war, could have incalculable negative consequences for the world economy as a whole.

Traditional National Borders Become Less Relevant

The growth of both intra-regional trade and global trade has been materially assisted by the fact that traditional national borders have changed dramatically in their definition. Historically, national borders have been natural boundaries dictated by defence considerations, or geographical barriers such as mountain ranges. Mountains surrounded Switzerland and cut off Spain and Italy from the rest of Europe. The sea surrounded Britain, Japan, and Australia. When geography allowed the creation of strategic borders, the cultural borders followed naturally.

But in many cases, people created borders consciously in an attempt to keep others out. The primary motivation for establishing a border was usually a military one. The Chinese built the Great Wall to keep out marauding Central Asian tribes. The Romans built two walls in Britain to protect its northern frontier. During the Cold War, the Berlin Wall dramatically defined the ideological line between capitalist and communist spheres of influence, regardless of the ethnic and cultural ties between the Germans it divided.

With the main exceptions of the newly liberated Soviet bloc countries and the endless agonies of the Middle East countries, today, in many countries, these considerations no longer apply. In a Western and Asian world now largely free from extreme ideologies, there is less reason to fear one's neighbours. The only exception is extreme Islamic fundamentalism, which in its most virulent ideological form has largely confined itself to the Middle and Near East, and Hindu extremism confined to the Indian subcontinent. In any case, technology has already rendered these old barriers irrelevant: missiles can cross the highest mountains; but more importantly, so can planes carrying tourists and businessmen, and global communications such as satellite television, fax, telephone, and publications. The speed and the ease of travel, and of international communication, is increasing all the time, while the costs are coming down, making them more widely available. Commercial 'multinational' organisations are now less tied to the country of their origin; indeed, many Western companies are creating advisory councils of international leaders and developing cadres of multilingual, multicultural employees to ensure that their directors and corporate executives do not take a parochial view of other cultures and economies. The same phenomenon will no doubt occur in Asia.

As a result, national differences are becoming less important. National borders have become a tiresome restriction, not a protection; keeping people in, not out. Mainland Chinese now travel to, and do business with, Taiwan, and vice versa. People can now travel freely throughout almost all of the Asia Pacific region, but as yet cannot easily live and work in other countries.

Education, too, is a factor. Language barriers are being broken down and traditional values undermined. Like it or not, we are approaching McLuhan's 'Global Village'. Today's cosmopolitan élite, ranging from businessmen to rock stars, travel the world and feel at home in many parts of it. In Asia Pacific, the Overseas Chinese and Indians have migrated across the region with considerable success; their presence is both a glue binding their new host countries to their countries of ethnic origin and an oil lubricating the overall process of bringing Asia Pacific together. Until recently, the region was divided by war and political dislocation. Today, however, there is a boom in intra-regional travel, driven by local businessmen, tourists, and dispersed families.

At the other end of the scale, people worldwide are demanding more autonomy at the local, grass-roots level. The Croats don't want to be part of Yugoslavia, the Kashmiris want no part of India, and the Tibetans don't accept Beijing as their capital. People are willing to go to war to defend their local concerns. They live not only in tribal groups in the old Soviet bloc and the Third World, but also in Europe and America. Extremists in Wales and Scotland, not to mention Northern Ireland, want to secede from the United Kingdom. Basques have long wanted to declare independence from Spain. Italy risks breaking in two, and Bavaria wishes to secede from Germany and have separate representation at the EC. Cree Indians, the people of Alberta and British Colombia, and the Quebeçois do not want to be part of Canada. The referendum held in October 1992 on the future of Canada could conceivably have resulted in Canada separating into either different countries or a confederation of ten separate sovereign states, with a central government authority controlling only foreign relations and foreign economic policies. The result of the referendum was a resounding 'no' from six of the ten provinces. This constitutional reform initiative is now deemed to be dead. The consensus of government and the private sector now seems to be that Canadians should focus on strengthening their economy in order to help it survive in the increasingly competitive, international economic environment. Such a focus would be further reinforcement for its involvement in NAFTA.

American studies released in 1990 show that the current generation of young Americans knows less, cares less, votes less, and is less critical of its leaders and institutions than young people in the past. The population's declining interest in the federal government was apparent in the autumn of 1990, when almost two-thirds of the electorate did not vote. It was estimated that, in 1990, for every US$5 in federal taxes owed, US$1 was evaded — mostly by sole proprietors and small businesses. Such localists do not care about national, let alone global, politics. Increased voter interest in the Clinton–Bush election campaign in 1992 will, I suspect, prove to be a temporary phenomenon, particularly once Clinton's government becomes deeply immersed in the reality of America's current malaise.

The complement to the evolution of real internationalism is the reassertion of power for local government. Not all issues rise to the lofty heights of the negotiating halls of Geneva and the UN. Bread-and-butter problems such as education, transport, housing, health, and even taxation, are best hammered out in municipal, county, or state halls where the government and the governed can easily keep in touch. The principle of 'subsidiarity' — of making decisions at the lowest possible practical level of efficiency — is being asserted everywhere, including in the EC following the Maastricht Treaty debacle. Thus the nation-state, which used to demand absolute obedience, is being undermined from both above and below. If one doubts the power of these forces, one need look only as far as Europe; there, one of the world's most powerful leaders,

Margaret Thatcher, found herself unable to resist the march towards the European union, although the bandwagon was halted, at least temporarily, by the surprise result of a referendum in Denmark concerning the Maastricht Treaty.

The break-up of the Soviet Union poses the question whether other large countries, such as the United States, or even India and China, will continue in their present, national form in the twenty-first century. People bound together by conquest or fear of outsiders may eventually learn to live together, but only if a national identity develops that is stronger than the sub-national identities. Although the divisive elements within Canada and the former Soviet Union — and, for that matter, within the United States, Belgium, Italy, and China — are nothing new, the secessionist argument has acquired new potency in the post-Cold War world. In this new political environment, the idea that governments exist to serve the governed has finally begun to gain some recognition. The logical next step is that people should choose not only their leaders, but also the units in which they will be ruled. Few nations are natural nation-states. Tens of millions of Chinese live outside China; millions of Hungarians outside Hungary. Millions of Turks call Bulgaria home; millions of Irish live in the United States. Some countries, such as India and Nigeria, encompass a patchwork quilt of tribes as nations. Other nations — the Basques, the Palestinians, and the Kurds — have no country at all.

National or 'tribal' feeling will survive longer than any artificial boundaries. Many countries were created artificially during the break-up of the great European empires. Paradoxically, the prospect of regional co-operation has given many of these countries' tribal, provincial, or state components the confidence to consider independence. Growing numbers of Walloon and Flemish nationalists, for example, want independence from Belgium but wish to remain within the EC.

As regional issues are likely to become more important than global concerns, national governments are likely to become less than the sum of their parts. This trend is evident in industry, where a number of huge conglomerates have been broken up because the individual components were more efficient and better integrated, and hence more valuable, than the enterprise as a whole. Corporations such as IBM and Sears Roebuck, which have been unable to manage their huge size effectively, have been forced to downsize in order to survive. A similar future might possibly be in store for the national governments of large land masses containing huge populations with materially disparate interests, such as China, the United States, India, and possibly even Indonesia.

Sub-regional economic and political centres of various sizes and structures are likely to develop. The twenty-first century could see a resurgence of local centres along the lines of medieval 'city-states', such as Florence, Venice, and Hamburg, which were as economically powerful as nations. Singapore, ostensibly a country, is in reality a city-state, as is Hong Kong. These two city-states have the highest foreign exchange reserves per capita in the world. Telecommunications may enable populations to form discrete communities sharing common values and with few links with the broader community, beyond the media and the goods provided by the outside world. Some of the large countries in the region — China, India, and Australia, for example — may break up in the next century, as might Canada, as described above, and even the United States.

In Asia Pacific, 'growth triangles' are an important development, not just for the prosperity they bring, but for their effect of eroding borders and drawing Asia's hard-pressed socialist economies into the free trade net. The first of these — the steady economic integration of Hong Kong, Taiwan, China's Pearl River Delta, and Portuguese Macau — is already being billed as one of the region's next 'economic miracles'. Other such economic units embrace Singapore, the southern Malaysian state of Johore, and the nearby Riau islands of Indonesia, as well as the proposed linking up of Malaysia's northern states with northern Sumatra and Thailand's Kra Isthmus. Perhaps the most exciting development of all will be that which will link various Asia Pacific countries with Asiatic Russia — for instance, Asiatic Russia, Chinese Manchuria, the two Koreas, and Japan. Asiatic Russia is rich in natural resources and has the potential to be the Australia of the North. Russia, like India, might have an interesting choice to make. Now that Russia has lost its more Europe-oriented states, there is an internal body of opinion that suggests it should look east to Asiatic Russia for its future, focusing more on its relations with China and Japan than with Europe and the United States. After all, the Russian 'old guard' has a lot more in common with the Chinese authoritarian approach than with the democratic methods employed in the West. Furthermore, its remaining natural resource wealth is largely in the east.

With the demise of the Cold War, people may travel more freely and exercise more choice in where they live. No longer forced to give their proxy to the government, people will have greater opportunity to choose a government that suits their needs. Although governments are the best equipped to run the military, the private sector is best qualified to run business. In late-nineteenth century Japan, state entrepreneurism brought many government corporations to the verge of collapse. When the government transferred state industries into private hands, Japanese industry boomed. State-run corporations in the West have usually operated at a loss; hence, led by the United Kingdom in the late 1970s and 1980s, there has been a worldwide trend towards the privatisation of such companies, which has usually resulted in their becoming much more profitable. In the erstwhile Soviet bloc, where the government tried to run practically everything, the utter collapse of the new state-run economies speaks for itself. Many current reformers in the Soviet bloc recognise this; the same principles apply in India and China.

Whatever the label, virtually all Cold War governments were proactive — acting with the proxy of the people — rather than reactive — acting in response to the people. In communist countries, governments decided where people lived and worked, and where their children went to school. In democratic countries, despite proclaiming that they reflected the will of the people, governments made decisions which affected nearly every aspect of people's lives. Governments set industrial standards which determined what goods people could buy and how safe they were. Governments determined the tariffs set for foreign goods, which affected the selection of goods available and the prices people paid for them. Governments also decided which social programmes received funding — in effect, who would be helped and who not. Even in the United States, where the president is supposed to have approval from Congress before committing any significant military force overseas, it was still possible to invade Grenada and Panama without consulting the American people.

Today, on the other hand, governments are being forced to become reactive, responding to the needs and demands of people freed from a balance of terror. People want more rights for the individual, and businessmen want to be able to trade freely, unobstructed by ideological boundaries. When then President Bush visited Japan in 1992, he was upstaged by Lee Iacocca and other business leaders who insisted on going along with him — the trip became a circus. Bush (and the US government as an institution) lost great face in Asia. Power in most Asian societies is highly centralised and authoritarian, and even where the generals are not in power, democracy, by Western standards, operates only imperfectly. This situation might have been tolerable when people were generally free to make a living without too many restrictions. However, today, three decades of economic growth have produced a large, increasingly well-educated middle class in many Asian countries, which will demand much more of their governments, who will ignore them at their peril. Economic progress has not been matched by the development of mature political institutions. (George Hicks, 'The Likely Pattern in East Asia: the middle class versus the military,' *International Herald Tribune*, 19 May 1992.) The most graphic illustration of the power of this new, assertive middle class occurred during the mid-1992 military crackdown in Thailand. The military forces were unable to contain the demonstrators, as they freely confessed, partly because they failed to allow for the presence in their midst of politically aware and motivated yuppies who co-ordinated the protests using portable telephones.

In Asia, pragmatic, businesslike leadership will replace ideologically-driven autocracies, as a result of pressure from the region's growing middle classes who wish to have at least some 'democratic' say in their future. Confederation offers solutions to otherwise intractable political problems, unblocking local log-jams by removing power to both higher and lower levels, thus avoiding periodic swings between the extremes of dictatorship and anarchy.

The challenge for Asia Pacific, and indeed for the rest of the world, is how best to adjust to these sweeping changes and to the resulting, possibly radical, shifts in attitude. The new middle classes of the countries of Asia Pacific need to harness their new people-power to elect more responsive and visionary governments that are capable of defining and implementing common national and regional objectives, rather than continue to allow governments which concentrate on lining their own and their families' pockets. This will enable the region's countries to be better equipped to deal with this rapidly changing world and their roles within it.

A GENERAL BLUEPRINT
FOR A REGIONAL FORUM

There are no models which could serve as a specific blueprint for Asia Pacific. The Soviet Union has already disintegrated into Russia and the other members of the CIS, and this seems unlikely to survive very long. The United States has always been one country, though it had to go through a bloody civil war to preserve the Union. At the extreme end of the scale, Asia Pacific could follow the example of the American federal system: dividing sovereignty between states and a central government, allowing freedom of trade and movement of citizens, and setting up a supreme court to settle disputes. But a more likely alternative would be a looser association like the original EEC — a confederation of countries which co-operate with one another but in which sovereignty lies with each country. Even the parallel with the now EC can be taken too far, however. It was formed out of the urgent need to avoid further wars in Europe, from countries in close proximity with one another sharing a common political system — democracy — and centuries of cultural familiarity.

What does seem clear are the general principles that will govern whatever structure any regional community decides to create. It will have to work towards an agreement on a wide variety of fronts. These should include, *inter alia*: free trade; free movement of labour within the region; abolition of exchange controls and restrictions on investment; the movement of funds; currency stabilisation; general policy unification regarding different industries, social welfare, transportation, and so on; harmonisation of technical standards and regulations; — and, most importantly, the development of a regional security policy. In effect, these were the goals of the European Commission bureaucrats in Brussels at the end of 1992, which unfortunately, through their drafting of the Maastricht Treaty, appeared to want to turn the EC into a 'federal EC'. This was a far cry from the original EEC confederation, since many in Europe felt the treaty would take away their national sovereignty and identity. Consequently, it was unacceptable. This is a trap the Asia Pacific region must avoid at all costs, especially to begin with.

Some of these goals are impractical in the foreseeable future for Asia Pacific. Although Japan, Hong Kong, and Singapore, for example, are already beginning to suffer serious problems of labour shortage, it is hard to see how these countries, and the other countries of Asia Pacific, could absorb the many millions of Chinese, who, for example, would be likely to move to these countries if their borders were opened. Additionally, of all the countries in the world, Japan is perhaps the least able or willing to absorb immigrants. On an equally, if not more important subject, it is also hard to envisage how the militaristic ambitions of the region's countries — China, India, and North Korea, in particular — and Japan's defensive reactions to them, can soon be brought into alignment. Yet these goals are valuable, if only as ideals, as they reflect the already considerable vocalised concern about the region's security.

Clearly, the first step is likely to be the establishment of a framework for intra-regional, preferential trade. From this point on, integration can proceed step-by-step until an equilibrium is realised with the rest of the world. As a result of the creation of its AFTA, this will eventually happen in ASEAN.

A confederation, however loose, must of course minimise internal disputes. It needs to set up permanent fora with increasing authority to resolve such disputes, with some military clout to provide peacekeeping forces which the region has already shown it needs — and, of course, to resist encroachment from outside. But it also needs a forum to negotiate with the rest of the world on trade and other issues. A country the size of Malaysia, for example, is clearly at a disadvantage when it comes to negotiating with the EC and with the new NAFTA community emerging in the Americas. Even Japan finds it impossible to negotiate on equal terms.

There must be a mechanism to bring together leaders in the region on a regular basis and to enable them to resolve differences of interest in a manner that is credible and generally acceptable. Obviously, the biggest stumbling-block to achievement of these aims is that the key countries in the area have very different political systems. But in the pragmatic, post-communist world, this problem need not be insurmountable.

A regional community can either grow from a core, as in the case of the EC, where the six original signatories to the Treaty of Rome have already become twelve and may become as many as twenty; or it can result from all the countries coming together at one time, which would require a remarkable degree of unity. It is possible that a regional grouping could grow out of a series of bilateral agreements, such as already exists between Australia and New Zealand, for example. But it is hard to believe that such agreements will have sufficient momentum, unless they include the major players in the area, particularly Japan, China, and India. Australasia will (and possibly Asiatic Russia in the future may) also have a constructive part to play.

There are four main questions facing Asia Pacific. First, which countries should be asked, or be allowed, to join the club? How far around the Pacific should it stretch? Should it include countries which are culturally distinct, like Australia and New Zealand? Are countries from the other side of the Pacific to be automatically excluded?

Second, what are the limits of co-operation? Is economic integration the sole *raison d'être*, or should there be political and even strategic co-operation as well? In the long run, it is difficult to have one without the other, as the EC has discovered.

Third, how should members of this putative Asia Pacific community co-operate? What kind of framework would be appropriate? What kind of institutions are required to knit together such a diverse group of nations, and what will the role of these institutions be?

The fourth question, though, is the most important, for without a satisfactory answer, it is not possible to solve the other three. This is the question of *why* the countries of Asia Pacific should want to come together. Is a regional grouping simply meant to be a kind of insurance policy, in case the global trading system breaks down, or a bolthole to hide in during a full-scale trade war? Or is it something more positive?

There are several answers to this question. The negative factors are more obvious: Europe and North America seem to be forming themselves into two potential trade blocs. The crucial world system of 'free trade', as enshrined in GATT, is under serious threat. The dynamic countries of Asia Pacific — particularly Japan and the 'Four Tigers' of Taiwan, Korea, Hong Kong, and Singapore — have every interest in preserving free trade; after all, they have grown on the back of the post-World War II economic freedom. China too has become a dramatic new convert. They may soon be seen to be the champions of preserving free trade in an increasingly isolationist world. But it would be foolish and short-sighted if they were not to make a concerted response to developments in the West which may threaten their future livelihood.

The positive reasons for coming together are much more nebulous and to some extent require an act of faith to summarise. In essence, they involve a recognition that, despite the region's great diversity, Asia Pacific has important things in common: geography, history, culture — but most important, many countries in the region have an economic vibrancy that is the envy of the world. It is also now developing a clear sense of regional identity, which embodies its concerns about the region's future *vis-à-vis* the rest of the world. As I have already dealt with the geographical, historical, and cultural reasons in Part One of this book, it is these two latter points that I will now address in this chapter.

Asia Pacific does not have to start from scratch. Like a child playing with building-blocks, it has been experimenting with different types of regional arrangements since World War II. This experience will stand it in good stead when it comes to the complex task of building a community encompassing one half of the world's humanity. The countries which have taken the most active role in these prototype arrangements will be well placed to take a lead in this evolving process.

Much of the experience of co-operation is to be found in Southeast Asia, where an array of nation-states has found it necessary to come to terms with one another after a centuries-long colonial interlude in which most of them were dominated by powers from outside the region. The integration process has not been easy, for along the way there have been stumbling-blocks, as well as building-blocks. In particular, attempts to form an exclusive Asia Pacific community have met with fierce resistance from outside, particularly from the United States. This resistance fits ill with the United States' own agenda — for example, NAFTA and

Clinton's new Western Hemisphere Community of Democracies.

The organisation with the longest experience of regional co-operation is ASEAN, the Association of Southeast Asian Nations. A regional alliance formed in 1967, its members are Indonesia, Malaysia, the Philippines, Singapore, Thailand, and (since 1984) Brunei. But this was not the earliest attempt to tie the region together. There were three earlier trial runs, from which two institutions survive.

The first, the United Nations Economic Commission for Asia and the Far East, was set up in 1947. Headquartered in Bangkok, its membership extends well beyond the confines of Southeast Asia, containing all the UN members in the region from Afghanistan to the Pacific Islands. Subsequently renamed the Economic and Social Commission for Asia and the Pacific (ESCAP), it has been little more than a talking-shop, with virtually no power to dispense largess. Although rarely in the public eye, it meets every year to discuss matters of mutual concern.

The other survivor is the Colombo Plan, established in 1950 to help co-ordinate economic assistance to the developing countries of Asia. It has been a useful clearing-house for bilateral aid programmes between rich donor countries and Asia's poorer nations, but no more. Japan has developed an Asian Industries Development Plan (AID) which seeks to channel Japan's trade — aid and private capital — surpluses into direct investment into Asia. AID is a powerful force for economic integration. Japanese government agencies have also published papers which foresee the development of intra-Asian trade as the development of a single economy. But in the past the Japanese Economic Planning Agency has reinforced this with clear hints that its goal was the integration of the Asian economies into a kind of greater 'Japan Inc.'. This attitude of domination — regional integration under Japanese economic sovereignty — is dangerous. The Japanese now realise this and have changed their stance. Without the concurrence of the rest of the region, balanced integration is impossible. As the other countries develop, a natural multi-polar leadership should evolve, as it has in the EC. Most probably in Asia Pacific it will be shared between Japan, Greater China, India, Greater Korea, Australasia, and possibly Indonesia, while others will play a smaller but equally vital role.

Countries which have depended on Soviet economic and military help

— such as India, Vietnam, and North Korea — are already having to plan how to get along without that support. The reality is that nobody can afford to give inter-regional aid on the old scale. The countries of Asia Pacific will have to look to one another for help.

Neither ESCAP nor the Colombo Plan has much to teach Asia Pacific about how to co-operate. Nor does the next in the post-World War II history of regional endeavours, the South-East Asian Treaty Organisation (SEATO), established in 1954 under US sponsorship. Of its eight members, only two were from Southeast Asia: Thailand and the Philippines. SEATO was avowedly anti-communist; the protocol to the treaty mentioned Cambodia, Laos, and South Vietnam as three countries protected by its security provisions. In a post-communist world, SEATO would have been irrelevant. In fact, it folded up in the 1960s. Other groupings went the same way. Who today has heard of the Asia and Pacific Council (1966–1971), the Southeast Asia Friendship and Economic Treaty (1959), the Association of Southeast Asia (1961), or Maphilindo (1963)? The most recent new scheme to be floated was in 1992, when former Japanese Prime Minister Yasuhiro Nakasone proposed the 'Grand Pacific Common House for Cultural and Economic Cooperation' — the regional reaction was politely indifferent. Each of these initiatives created a few headlines in the worthier newspapers, and then were gone.

When ASEAN was formed in 1967, few expected it to last much longer than its predecessors. The countries which signed the Bangkok declaration had little in common, apart from their crops and their climates. Four of them had recently emerged from serious disputes with one or more of the others. Yet, politically at least, they have achieved a surprising degree of cohesion, primarily as a result of pressures from outside the group.

Security was ASEAN's main priority at the outset. Britain, the former colonial master of Malaysia and Singapore, had just decided to withdraw its forces from the region. Five years later, the United States was to be badly mauled by its experiences in Vietnam. China was the main communist wolf, along with several trouble-making client states to the south. The then Soviet Union was North Vietnam's chief provider. In 1975, communist victories in Indochina startled ASEAN into action. The new communist masters in Indochina appeared poised to gobble up the rest of Southeast Asia. In February 1976, the first ASEAN summit meeting was hurriedly arranged in Bali. It issued two documents, aimed at giving more political and economic weight to the grouping.

During the years that followed, the ASEAN countries slowly became more confident in facing up to the communist challenge. Partly as a result of internal changes and its own disagreements with Vietnam, China's attitude to the grouping gradually changed from hostility to friendship. In 1978, when the Vietnamese boat people started arriving on Southeast Asian shores, ASEAN foreign ministers were visibly nervous about voicing any criticisms of Hanoi. The following year, after the Vietnamese invasion of Cambodia and the establishment of a puppet regime in Phnom Penh, there was no such reservation. ASEAN became increasingly outspoken in its condemnation of Vietnam's occupation of Cambodia. In July 1982, it was able to persuade three mutually suspicious factions opposing Vietnamese occupation to join hands in an uneasy coalition. Subsequently, ASEAN successfully lobbied the UN to ensure that the coalition, led by Prince Sihanouk, remained the officially-recognised government of Cambodia despite the odium attaching to one of the coalition partners, the murderous Khmer Rouge.

But although the threat from Indochina provided the glue which held ASEAN together during this period, it also served to highlight the underlying differences between the six members. By dint of its location and its history, Thailand took a hard line against Vietnam, and was supported in this by Singapore. Indonesia, on the other hand, has traditionally regarded China as the long-term threat to the region. Therefore, the Indonesians and, to a lesser extent, the Malaysians saw Vietnam as a useful buffer between China and the ASEAN countries.

The glue holding ASEAN together began to unstick after Vietnam withdrew from Cambodia in 1989 and after the subsequent Cambodian peace accord in 1991. A new glue had to be found, and closer economic co-operation was the obvious answer. But this is a tall order for a grouping such as ASEAN. Attempts to encourage economic integration among developing countries usually fail because their members export the same types of goods, mainly basic commodities. ASEAN is no exception: raw materials make up about three-quarters of intra-ASEAN trade. Of the six ASEAN countries, only Singapore is 'newly-industrialised'. In 1989, intra-ASEAN trade comprised 18 per cent of the member countries' entire international trade, or US$22 billion out of US$122 billion. Singapore had a hand in most of it, as befitted an entrepôt.

As countries become more developed, the scope for trade among them increases. Similarly, when oil and gas prices are high, intra-ASEAN trade tends to increase as a proportion of the total. But in 1984, only 17 per cent of exports from ASEAN countries went to other countries in the grouping; the equivalent figure within the EC was 53 per cent. By 1989, the proportion had only increased by 1 per cent, to 18 per cent.

For the first twenty years of ASEAN's existence, no more than minor attempts were made to enhance economic integration. These concentrated on trade liberalisation and industrial co-operation. Trade measures included long-term supply contracts for basic commodities and tariff reductions. The latter have increased until, by 1989, cuts had been granted on more than 18,000 items. Yet their impact has been limited: these items account for less than 5 per cent of intra-ASEAN trade, as most of them have little commercial significance. The Philippines magnanimously reduced for ASEAN producers its tariff on snow ploughs, for example. And Thailand generously cut tariffs on eight kinds of pig's bristles.

Industrial co-operation has proved just as difficult. All the ASEAN nations had industrial plans of their own, some of which duplicated those of their neighbours. One area where they pressed ahead was market-sharing — each member would concentrate on a single, large, state-owned industrial project, whose output would be sold at preferential tariffs throughout ASEAN. In this way, they hoped to avoid damaging competition. The results have not been impressive. No doubt in time, more and more of the industrialisation process will be left more effectively to the private sector, albeit with some state assistance.

Another measure, which proved a flop, was the industrial complementation scheme, in which each country would produce a different set of components of a single product, which would be traded preferentially throughout ASEAN. The frustrated ASEAN chambers of commerce pushed through a third measure in the mid-1980s: industrial joint ventures, in which firms whose ownership was held at least 51 per cent by more than one ASEAN country, qualified for a 50 per cent tariff cut in those countries where the industrial joint ventures were taking place.

ASEAN's economic integration has until recently been painfully slow, but not for want of trying. What has spurred the group into renewed efforts are the events taking place in the wider world, notably the prospect of a protectionist North American trading bloc, as well as a European one. A more immediate catalyst was the establishment in 1988, on the initiative of the then Australian prime minister Bob Hawke, of APEC, which includes all the members of ASEAN as well as Japan, China, Taiwan, Hong Kong, Australia, New Zealand, and South Korea. On hearing of their initiative, the United States immediately strong-armed Hawke into conceding that it should also participate as a member. Canada quickly followed suit. The EC, on hearing of these developments, engineered observer status, using the argument that if the Americans were in, why shouldn't they be. It is now like a mini UN, but without the UN's legitimacy. As a result, in fundamental terms, APEC is unlikely to go anywhere — despite its decision in September 1992 to set up a small secretariat in Singapore. There is probably little effective future for an organisation which tries to marry the incompatible interests of the United States and Canada together with those of Asia, particularly given America's attempts to vigorously pursue its own NAFTA initiative, whose purpose flies in the face of APEC's original purpose. Another example of APEC's naïve and confused aims is its non-exclusivity policy. This is unrealistic because no one else is likely to reciprocate. APEC has its supporters, but they are too close to the trees to see the wood. Like its many predecessors, APEC is likely to have a short half-life as the Asia Pacific region's primary community forum. It is unlikely to achieve much, as for APEC to be really effective, it needs a regional, not an international, membership.

In 1990, after the collapse of the GATT talks in Brussels, Malaysian prime minister Mahathir Mohamad proposed yet another grouping. His proposal was a general one, consisting of a call to the governments of East Asia to begin talks to prepare for the possibility of a collapse of the entire Uruguay Round of GATT trade negotiations. What caught people's attention was the proposed membership of the new club, called the East Asian Economic Grouping (EAEG). All the major East Asian countries were invited to join, including China, Korea and Japan, but not the United States. The Americans were furious. They lobbied their allies not to join the new grouping. Secretary of State James Baker reminded the Koreans, for example, that American lives had been lost in defence of their country, in a reference to the Korean War. No Malaysian blood was spilt, he said pointedly. Singapore's former prime minister, Lee Kuan Yew, was also apparently against the idea initially; he saw a danger of the global trading system dividing along racial lines.

The EC, on the other hand, has not publicly opposed the Malaysian initiative in the way the Americans did. But the crucial question was whether Japan would participate, for without them the grouping would have far less point. As so often happens, the Tokyo government hesitated; it wanted to encourage Mahathir's plan but not to offend its ally, the United States, which was against their participation. However, Tomomitsu Oba, former Japanese vice-minister of finance for international affairs, argued that if NAFTA and the EC are really stepping-stones on the way to greater integration of the global trade system, as their apologists often argue, then Japan should be free to join a consultative body such as the EAEG was originally intended to be, in order to boost a parallel process in Asia. Everyone conveniently chose to ignore the clear logic of his argument.

Japan cannot sit on this fence forever. It will eventually have to nail its flag to a specific mast. While there is risk in doing so, there is more risk in *not* doing so. Europe and the United States have continued to address their trade grievances with Asia on a country-by-country basis. Even Japan has found it difficult to counter this strategy of divide and conquer. Asia Pacific's best defence is to negotiate collectively with the rest of the world. Now that security, for so long the basis of the US–Japan relationship, is no longer such an urgent global issue, America doesn't really need Japan any more, and has urgent problems of its own, which means that its interest in Asia Pacific will diminish substantially. Japan must throw its weight in with Asia Pacific, by all means allowing Mahathir and/or others to make the running — or risk becoming a pariah on both sides of the Pacific, a possible outcome given its cultural xenophobia.

An Asia Pacific dominated by Japan will not work. The spectre of the Japanese attempt to establish a Far Eastern empire in its Greater East Asia Co-Prosperity Sphere is too recent. But Japan can, and must, play a vital co-leadership role. Japan cannot take the initiative without alarming other countries in the region; but if invited to share in a multipolar leadership, it should not decline. An Asia Pacific without Japan is an absurdity, but Japan must be balanced by other countries of equal weight, specifically China and India.

In fact, Mahathir's main mistake was not to invite India or Australasia to join his new grouping. Lee Kuan Yew appears to be changing his mind, recognising that Asia Pacific needs an umbrella organisation to match those elsewhere. The world is not in balance: America and Europe are organising into powerful regional communities, if not blocs, and Asia Pacific should do likewise. Otherwise smaller countries in the region will have to conduct bilateral trade negotiations with giants like the EC, a David facing up against Goliaths, with no secret weapons and without necessarily having a universal moral right on his side.

Faced by a lukewarm response from the rest of ASEAN, as well as Japan, Mahathir gradually watered down his proposal, until by mid-1991 he was describing it as a 'loose consultative forum comprising countries in East Asia'. By the time ASEAN held a summit meeting in January 1992, the initiative was stalled. That summit proposed an ASEAN Free Trade Area (AFTA), something the Thais had advocated all along. It called for the gradual reduction of their current tariffs to less than 5 per cent on fifteen groups of products within fifteen years, i.e. by the year 2008. But there were two important exceptions, agriculture and services, and though AFTA was enacted in April 1992, this has caused some people to wonder about the extent of ASEAN's commitment to the idea. The region's businessmen complained that either the scheme did not go far enough or that it would not go fast enough, particularly by comparison with NAFTA and the EC. Subsequently, however, at the ASEAN summit in October 1992 in Manila, amidst rising concerns about the GATT talks' stalemate, NAFTA, and the EC, it was unanimously agreed to reduce the tariff reduction completion target period from fifteen years to ten years.

As a concession to Mahathir, ASEAN agreed to accept his East Asian Economic Grouping concept, but only if it were to be renamed the East Asian Economic Caucus (EAEC) and only if it would meet as an adjunct to APEC. As one wit described it, a 'caucus without the Caucasians'. This ASEAN response is an evolutionary dead end, and pointless because it confuses the issues — why attach this potentially important initiative to

APEC, which itself is not likely to go anywhere? Maybe ASEAN itself felt threatened by EAEG and wanted to minimise its impact. It is certainly reasonable to take the view that too many conflicting, yet similar, initiatives of this sort will only generate a lack of focus and probably even confusion. However, that being said, ASEAN's response could have been more imaginative.

To overcome the natural fear which smaller countries in the region have of the larger ones, it makes sense for a new regional community to evolve out of ASEAN, perhaps taking its momentum from Mahathir's initiative. ASEAN's combined clout is now substantially increased; combined GNP of the ASEAN countries has risen from US$20 billion in 1965 to US$310 billion in 1992. The major players in the area already need ASEAN to a certain extent, and will do so even more if a more protectionist world develops. Mahathir himself might provide the necessary leadership, especially if he can shake off the narrow-minded touchiness shown several years ago in regard to Malaysia's relations with Australia. Mahathir, though, is handicapped by the fact that Malaysia is a Muslim country, where incipient signs of Islamic fundamentalism are being evidenced. Given the effects of extreme Islamic fundamentalism elsewhere, it is natural that this phenomenon in Malaysia gives the rest of the world cause for concern. The most probable and credible 'Jean Monnet' (the founder of the EEC) of the region is Lee Kuan Yew, a leader of regional and international status. Singapore, in fact, would be an excellent headquarters for such a new community forum, being politically stable, unattached to any other powerful country, and personifying, more than perhaps any other country of the region, a commitment to free trade and order.

However, just as leadership in the new world order cannot be provided by one single country, leadership towards an Asia Pacific community forum probably cannot be provided by one man alone. To build a successful community requires individuals in each of the countries within Asia Pacific to show the necessary vision, and to band together to form a movement which proves impossible to resist. The tide is already flowing in their directon. The ties that now exist in Asia Pacific have come about, not because Australia, Japan, Taiwan, and other countries previously shared a grand vision, but because trade within Asia Pacific has benefited all concerned. The export economies of Asia Pacific have nothing to gain by shutting others out of their markets, lest they be shut out themselves. Fear of retaliation will help to restrain protectionism in regional trade, just as nuclear deterrence kept the Soviet Union and the United States from attacking each other during the Cold War.

In terms of the international economy and how Asia Pacific relates to it, as Kenneth S. Courtis, senior economist with Deutsche Bank Group in Asia, wrote in his broad, excellent, and highly perceptive article in the *Herald Tribune* on 16 October 1992, 'this presents an extraordinary paradox. While much of the world is in recession Asia continues to enjoy explosive growth.' His article then goes on to describe a number of highly relevant factors. More specifically, I share his belief that despite Japan's current recession, the early 1990s will later be seen as a prelude to even higher levels of Japanese performance and influence on the world and regional economies. More generally, he makes the valid point that 'while Asia is becoming younger, is studying, saving, investing and building for tomorrow, much of the rest of the world has matured, taken on debt and aged. The resulting trend is very much in favour of Asia. In 1960 the Asian economies represented 4 per cent of world GNP; today they constitute 25 per cent and a decade from now it will be 33 per cent. [It is interesting to reiterate here that intra-Asian trade, which was worth US$362 billion in 1991, was substantially more than its US$232 billion trade with the EC and for the first time exceeded its trade with North America.] From finance to trade, technology and the vital issues of ecology, health and security, developments in Asia are now of critical importance to the world community. They will be even more so in the future.'

Courtis points out that net saving rates in the six main Western economies have declined from 15 per cent of GNP in the ten years to 1980 to 9.3 per cent in the next ten years. Many of the factors that support savings are trending negatively, particularly budget deficits and declining tax revenues. In contrast, Asia is showing substantial growth. As Courtis stated, 'Asia controlled 16.7 per cent of the worldwide foreign exchange reserves in 1980, while in 1992 Asian central banks controlled almost 40 per cent. With few exceptions, saving rates in Asia exceed 30 per cent of GNP. Even in Japan ... the net savings rate remains almost 25 per cent of

GNP, some two and a half times the average for other industrial countries in the OECD.' He goes on to say with compelling conviction, 'As Asia's savings continue to expand, they will form an even larger portion of world savings. Not only will the balance of economic power continue to shift to Asia, the rest of the world will find capital increasingly available on terms determined by Asia. It means that financial or economic instability in the region will be transmitted to the global economy with a speed and force yet to be widely understood.' I wholeheartedly agree, particularly with his last sentence, 'The tail has begun to wag the dog with a vengeance.' However, what must be recognised is that these regional trends can only continue in either a non-protectionist world and if the countries of Asia Pacific ensure that they develop a greater communality of interests. Even if a protectionist world evolves, such common interests, managed through a common regional forum, will do much to mitigate the region's downside risk.

However, should there be a trade war, it would be naïve to think that Asia Pacific could go it alone, without at least massive economic and social dislocation. But on the other hand, it could probably survive and recover faster than the other two regions.

While there is clear momentum towards developing common economic and trade policies, the question of regional security is beginning to cause considerable regional, if not global, concern. Although Japan's recent participation in the UN-sponsored peacekeeping efforts in Cambodia has more or less been accepted (and in some quarters welcomed) in the region, as well as domestically in Japan, unfortunately this is only the tip of the iceberg. The rest of the iceberg will potentially be either a conventional arms build-up escalation at best, or at worst a nuclear one. There have been considerable sales by Russia and some other CIS members of their advanced military technology and arms to other countries, including to Asian countries and particularly to China. Throughout the region, there has been a substantial revision of military and general security attitudes following the demise of the superpower confrontation, all of which are in a considerable state of flux, if not confusion. Finally, while the spectre of nuclear confrontation on a global scale has materially diminished, this is not necessarily the case in the Asian region — China, India and, possibly, North Korea have a nuclear capability; Japan does not. All these primary factors have caused a considerable increase in the level of concern about security in the region — and possibly even the beginnings of a real, not yet generally acknowledged, security-related tension in the region. This tension could be further exacerbated by North Korea's withdrawal from the Nuclear Non-Proliferation Treaty in March 1993.

For example, in late 1992, China's intention to purchase advanced SU-27 jet fighters and possibly MIG-31s from Russia, its interest in acquiring T-72 tanks, transport planes, aircraft engines, and missile guidance systems, and its stated desire to acquire a nuclear-powered aircraft carrier, will inevitably have a domino effect. Additionally, North Korea's new aggressive, nuclear isolationist stance could have serious ramifications. These events could materially upset the balance of military power in Asia, and Japan and other Asian nations could feel obliged to follow suit in terms of increasing their own military capability. One response has been that in South Korea, a senior military official advised the Korean parliament in October 1992 that South Korea should seek an expansion of its military ties with Japan, including future joint military exercises. In the past, this would have been unthinkable.

In view of China's (and India's) nuclear capability, Japan is likely to be forced to consider seriously the possibility of developing a nuclear capability of its own, despite its current constitution which expressly prohibits such action, if only to avoid future nuclear blackmail or attack. Conversely, if for other future reasons Japan were to develop a strong military capability, China is not likely to allow Japan a military edge. Thus the age-old 'arms-race' cycle could begin once again. This situation could be ameliorated by an increase in Japanese direct investments in China, producing closer trading and other ties between the two countries — in 1991, there was an estimated US$28 billion in bilateral trade. However, in the future, both countries could become competitors on many fronts within the region: political, economic, and militaristic. This could then put the other countries in the region in the invidious position of having to exhaust themselves trying to placate both sides or at worst take the high-risk position of having to choose sides. The more these countries get involved in trade with China and Japan (which trend will be substantially reinforced if the West becomes more protectionist) and, at the same time, the more the United States withdraws its military forces from the region, the more extreme this position could become. However, the flip-side of this equation is that the considerable intra-regional trade could possibly reduce these risks, as it is becomingly increasingly accepted that making money is more productive than making war.

There is also the more general regional concern about the shipping lanes to both the export markets of Europe and the oil supplies in the Middle East. Any disruption of these could result in a major regional conflict. Despite rather optimistic, or even naïve, expectations that the United States can be persuaded to remain a deterrent force in the region, Asia Pacific can no longer count on America to remain the regional policeman.

Thus the Asia Pacific community needs to move forward on a broad front. Trade liberalisation, essential though it is, is not enough in itself. The apparent lack of real substance and positive evolution of the EFTA (probably due to its small size and the competing gravitational pull of its giant neighbour, the EC) helps to illustrate this point. There must be some other political dynamics as well. There should be fundamental co-operation in regional security, but also in many other fields. Asia Pacific needs permanent institutions to guarantee the future: a rotating presidency, perhaps some form of parliament, a council of ministers, a secretariat, and a structure for dealing with legal disputes.

The first stage of trade should be business-led rather than politics-led. The specific creation by ASEAN of AFTA is a concrete demonstration of specific action being taken in this regard. The next stage, or indeed at the same time, is that the highly sensitive issue of 'human rights' should be addressed. Senior members of ASEAN are already beginning to address this issue seriously. They make the fair and valid point that the West focuses first on individual rights, while the East gives equal if not more attention to communal rights — citizens owe certain obligations to their community and society. Both positions are valid, as they derive from different cultural value systems. The same ASEAN countries' emerging initiatives also apply to developing a common position on the environment. Collectively, these are all positive, general signs for future regional co-operation, and none of them need require all the bureaucratic apparatus of, say, the European Commission in Brussels. With the increasing democratisation of the region's countries and the increasing political influence which the middle class is able to wield by virtue of its people-power, the region's governments will have to take more account of their people's views.

The next, and most sensitive, stage will be the question of co-operation on regional security, which will be politics-led. Again, ASEAN is taking some initiative in this area. It is now in the process of drafting a nuclear weapons-free zone treaty for its members and, in the process, consulting with other governments, particularly those with a nuclear capability.

Another important factor affecting these changes is that, although political differences in the region remain enormous, it is fair to say that democracy and capitalism are everywhere in the ascendant and that different forms of democratic government are evolving at an encouraging pace. In a comparative sense, and despite its 'human rights' record and the related endless Western criticism, the same could be said to be true of China. Thus, there will be more cross-linkages between the middle classes of the region's countries. Their common objectives of democracy, peace, free trade, free movement, and so on, should act at least as a partial brake on any excessive militaristic ambitions of their governments.

One must, of course, expect many impractical and compromised proposals as Asia Pacific goes forward. Nevertheless, as has happened in Europe, the concept of a community in the region is gathering a momentum of its own — a *tsunami* (tidal wave) is now just visible. A kind of community nationalism, or regionalism, is taking over. More and more people in the region, led by the educated, increasingly affluent, and more widely travelled middle classes, are recognising what is going on in the world, and are being spurred into action. Now that the former Cold War, superpower-driven security stand-off in the region is over, Asian countries need no longer be client states of Russia or America. Nor, indeed, should they become client states of China or Japan. Nevertheless, they need to be part of something bigger than themselves. Thus, out of the muddle of past regional initiatives, the basis of a powerful community is forming.

It is a huge task which confronts Asia Pacific. So many of the new geopolitical developments in the early 1990s would suggest that the maintenance of existing, or the creation of new, large regional structures will be fraught with difficulty. For this reason, and because of the tribalistic actions of the Serbians, the Quebeçois, the Kashmiris, and others, smaller groupings are the main trend for the future. I believe, however, that they are more a knee-jerk defensive reaction to the past. What is needed is an acceptance that supra-national regional bureaucratic control, even if more in the sense of form rather than substance, is no longer acceptable. This is something which the European Commission in Brussels appears to have forgotten and which, in the second half of 1992, contributed to the rise of widespread *angst* about the Maastricht Treaty and the future of the EC. We really do have to evolve into a true 'new world order', but we are a long, long way from it — there is much to do in the meantime.

What must be recognised is that the new world is breaking down into regional 'clubs'. It is a natural tendency for people who are frustrated with their own 'national clubs', particularly in the West, for all the reasons given above, to want to create new, more effective clubs. The EC now exists and will continue to grow, despite its intermittent growth pains. The Americas, particularly North America, led by the United States, is indisputably moving in this direction. NAFTA is moving towards completion — although it too will no doubt suffer considerable birth pains before it finally comes into official being. Furthermore, Clinton's new Western Hemisphere Community of Democracies initiative, as the *International Herald Tribune* stated, although ambitious, is based 'on a realistic grasp of the new convergence of interests and values drawing the United States and Latin America closer on the objectives of economic integration, the strengthening of democracy and greater social justice.' It went on to state, 'Although NAFTA's ratification takes priority, the Clinton administration should move quickly to transform victory into a hemisphere-wide free-trade club'! This development will no doubt elicit some concern elsewhere as to exactly what Clinton intends by this initiative.

ASEAN's member countries and the other countries of Asia Pacific must take realistic cognisance of these facts.

Wishful thinking, no matter how noble, about the global citizen's right to belong to all clubs, will not wash in any practical sense, as evidenced by the Japanese wanting to be members of both the US and Asian clubs. The world, without the straightjacket of the old superpower stand-off which made the choices much clearer and simpler, now suffers from an excessive multiplicity of choice. It is not surprising, therefore, that the range of available 'clubs' is multiplying almost weekly. It is necessary, first, to establish the base, essential clubs, and then later, after due consideration, to work out the cross-linkages and 'visitor member' rights. Having all these clubs being established in parallel only creates confusion, inefficiencies, faulty structures and, worst of all, considerable friction arising out of fear of what the as yet unknown effects of such clubs might be.

What must also be appreciated is the inherent 'Catch-22' nature of this global equation. If the world finally signs the next GATT Round and free trade is once again enshrined as a global goal, what then? The Catch-22 is that the younger, cheaper, more efficient, more aggressive, more willing to sacrifice now for future gain, and more nationally co-ordinated countries of Asia will continue to develop trade imbalances with the West. This will further exacerbate the already high unemployment rates amongst the Western OECD countries, which problem will in turn be compounded by the much larger 'retiree communities' in these countries. The cost of supporting their out-of-work and elderly will mount to the point where even the OECD countries will find it difficult to sustain the pressure. Inevitably, protectionism will again rear its ugly but pragmatic head. In effect, the world is rapidly arriving at a point where it is 'damned if it does and damned if it doesn't'! Damned if it keeps free trade going and damned if it doesn't. Fear, community tribalism, and all sorts of other viruses will bedevil the process of trying to bring some degree of common sanity and order to this fiendish concoction.

My point is therefore that, without a regional forum in Asia Pacific, how will the region's countries be able to negotiate some semblance of communality of interest with the much larger EC and NAFTA, as well as, very importantly, with their own regional neighbours?

Surely, one doesn't want another *Titanic*, with everyone sailing along in the serene belief that all will be well. Once the collision occurs, it will be devil take the hindmost and to hell with the women and children going first. In terms of aid and general support, isn't this what is happening *vis-à-vis* sub-Sahara Africa? There simply aren't the resources, the will, or the energy to try and deal with it on top of everything else. Further evidence of what I call the '1990s survival factor' is that serious media commentary in early 1993 suggested that a number of senior government officials of EC countries stated they were hoping Clinton's government would decline to become militarily involved in the former Yugoslavia, so that they could follow America's lead and also decline. If the United States went in, they reluctantly accepted that they would have to join them — in the full knowledge that they would all get sucked into an impossible situation, i.e. one which none of them could afford for all sorts of obvious reasons, which would sharply increase tensions between the countries involved, and which had little likelihood of being resolved in the near term.

With an Asia Pacific forum, there will at least be greater equality and general balance around the regional and inter-regional negotiating tables. This should lead to a more balanced and rational response to what could be a global problem of huge proportions in attempting to deal with the above Catch-22 equation.

What is now needed in Asia Pacific is women and men of vision who will rise to the occasion and advocate a structure that provides a framework and forum for the identification and implementation of common goals. It requires the peoples of the region, traditionally inward-looking and xenophobic, to grow out of the Cold War-engendered feelings of hostility towards their neighbours and band together for their common good. The potential benefits are huge, as the region contains more than half the world's population. The region should therefore be able to draw on these immense human resources, as well as on its substantial and varied natural resources. Such a regional community should assist in liberating these talented, educated, and disciplined peoples from the straight jackets of their national identities and systems, the hang-ups of history. Moreover, it could develop into the world's largest and most vibrant common market.

The impatient, whether Asians or Westerners, must not forget that the West took centuries to evolve to its current system of democratic capitalism. Asia has only been at it for the last fifty years or so. Positive, concrete results will be difficult to produce in the sense of catching up with the West and/or mimicking the West — particularly given the West's constant desire for immediate and often precipitate action. Asia Pacific must find its own way to address the real cultural and historical requirements of its peoples without falling into the trap of producing something, anything, that can be temporarily labelled 'progress'. Asia Pacific must, above all, develop a vision for, and a pride in, its regional community, as ultimately it is this form of motivation that will produce the best results in the long term.

The peoples of Asia Pacific and their governments cannot sit back and wait for a regional or new global crisis to force them to come together; this could produce all kinds of expedient, short-lived compromises that would be unlikely to lead to a lasting, well-founded solution. By being proactive and moving strongly forward, they have much to gain — in fact, in the final analysis, they have no option but to try.

Epilogue

EPILOGUE
Are We up to the Moral Challenge?

Looking into the future, say thirty years from now, we are likely to see a 'new confused world order', rather than former President Bush's over-optimistic 'new world order'. Having left the bi-polar superpower world behind us, we are now moving into a 'warring states' interregnum. Yugoslavia, doubts about the Maastricht Treaty, the proliferation of referendums to try and resolve unresolvable political problems (as in Canada), and the chaos of the world currency markets, are all evidence of this. Despite all this confusion, at least it is clear that the world is evolving towards a tri-polar, geopolitical structure consisting of Greater Europe, Greater America (North and South America), and Asia Pacific, together with their 'dependencies'.

Put another way, nothing is static. Democracy as currently practised, which has been held up as the ideal system of government, now risks becoming an inadequate ideology. This development could arise from a number of factors, the most important of which are what I call 'time versus change' and 'information overload'. Democracy, through universal suffrage, has played a vital part in the world's social and political evolution over the last two centuries. However, as governments changed from being proactive during the Cold War to being reactive in the new cold trade war period, the current forms of democracy are proving inadequate to their tasks.

The average voter is simply not equipped to cope with the rapidly changing global condition, nor with the vast amount of information bombarding him day and night. The same could be said for the average politician. We are now in a world where at best it is the half-blind trying to lead the blind. Today, where governments are unable to make major political decisions on such issues as the Maastricht Treaty or the future national character of Canada, a dangerous, though seductive, development of populist democracy is to ask the people to decide through a referendum. Such a solution may make sense in, say, a Swiss canton, where the issues can be defined in relation to people's real experience. However, referendums cannot be used responsibly to deal with the complex issues which have arisen following the increase in trade-driven self-interest, the ghastly aftermath of the demise of the Soviet Union, the new ambitions of Asia, the crisis in the Third World, and the threats to the global environment — and all this during a general world recession. Something is lacking in the existing system; something new has to be developed. This inability of democratic structures to cope may be the main reason why some Middle Eastern governments have been taken over by extreme forms of fundamentalist Islam or are opposing the development of such an extreme ideology in their countries. Egypt and Algeria, for instance, are having to resort to a dangerous level of force and repression in order to prevent this extremist ideology taking hold. Disturbing signs of extremist Hinduism are also being evidenced in India. Such events are not surprising, as a vacuum always attracts attempts to fill it. The world is suffering from a vacuum of purpose and direction. And the increasing focus on trade will not provide a complete solution, as trade by itself provides neither a moral value system nor the basis for any solution to global concerns such as refugees and the environment.

It should be noted, however, that these extremist ideologies are generally only practised in countries where a large proportion of the population lives either below, or just above, the poverty line. Such people may feel they have nothing to lose by subscribing to, and thus supporting, a higher religious force, which gives their lives some sense of purpose. However, such people can be easily manipulated by the unscrupulous, particularly when calls for support of their god, or even calls for a holy war, are invoked. One solution might lie in the expansion of trade, which brings added economic wealth to the countries concerned and thus raises the living standard of its poor. People who have something, and who believe they can get more, become more concerned about protecting, not risking, what they have. Hence, in Malaysia and Indonesia, fundamentalist Islam has been checked by economic success and the new prosperity of the people. If this economic trend, with a concomitant trend towards greater democracy, continues, there is less likelihood that any broadly-based extremist actions will take place in such countries.

Despite all this, I return to my basic view that for the world to evolve in any substantial positive sense, the development of trade as the primary motivating force in the new world order is not sufficient.

U ntil very recently, conflict between different value systems — whether religious, ethnic, or political — has helped to maintain the world in some form of balance. However, today and over the next, say, thirty years, with the demise of the superpower ideological confrontation, with the apparent weakening of religious beliefs (excluding extremist fundamentalist Islam and Hinduism), and with capitalism, particularly in its more extreme free market economy form, becoming the driving force in the industrialised and newly industrialised world, such a defined value system is no longer available. What will provide this new trade-focused, capitalistic world with a sense of moral purpose and a new form of democratic governing process?

This question is elegantly addressed by Hans Küng in his book, *Global Responsibility: In Search of a New World Order* (1991), on p. 25: 'It should have become clear that, at least on negative grounds, the catastrophic economic, social, political and ecological developments of both the first and second halves of the century necessitate a world ethic if humankind is to survive on this earth. Diagnoses of disaster have been of little help to us here. Nor might a pragmatic social technology without foundations for values, of a Western or Eastern tendency, be enough. But without morality, indeed without "global standards", the nations are in danger of manoeuvering themselves into a crisis which can ultimately lead to national collapse, i.e. to economic ruin, social disintegration and political catastrophe.'

Our nascent global society has as yet failed to provide a generally accepted distinction between good and evil. In this capitalist new world order, there appears to be a tendency amongst some towards associating 'good' with being powerful and 'bad' with being weak, or 'good' with economic success and 'bad' (or not worthy of interest and attention) with lack of success. These are the values of Mammon, and are hardly an adequate response to the issues referred to above.

From another perspective, the time versus change equation, which,

over the last few centuries, has become increasingly and almost frighteningly compressed, is a major contributor to the world's confusion.
Additionally, the range and instant accessibility of information have
resulted in an information overload. These two phenomena are often
overlooked. Many people either cannot, or choose not to, cope with the
speed and range of change, and with the information overload. This
situation is further exacerbated by the worldwide recession, which has
forced many people and organisations to retreat economically and intellectually, and to focus on survival, thus giving further impetus to the trend
towards community tribalism.

This tendency is already evidenced by the separatist demands of the
Walloons, Bavarians, Quebeçois, Basques, northern Italians, and Kashmiris.
The same principles apply to the ethnic groups of the countries of the
former Soviet Union, which the developed world, in the form of the
United States (the current uncertain/would-be global policeman), the
confused EC, and the chaotically organised, poorly funded, insufficiently
supported, and monstrously bureaucratic UN, has been unable to assist
in any fundamental way. This inability, combined with these former Soviet
bloc countries' new-found freedom, have led to attempts by tribal groups
in these countries to rebuild their communities almost from scratch. The
most extreme example of this is the Serbs' 'ethnic cleansing' of the other
tribal groups within the territory they have claimed; the rest of the world
looks on in horror, unable to stop the process.

On a larger scale, I believe that the *raison d'être* for a centralised, federal
government in the United States will erode alarmingly in the years to
come — even to the point of causing the federal system to break up — as
a result of local and state communities becoming more self-sufficient,
while the federal government becomes less capable of managing its
constituent parts. It is more likely to evolve into an American confederal
version of the EC system, where the principle of 'subsidiarity' — the
theory that governmental decisions should be taken at the lowest level
consistent with effectiveness — becomes the primary governing mechanism. Thus, it is always incumbent on the federal (or supernational)
authority to demonstrate clearly why it should have governing compe-
tence and authority in a particular field, rather than such authority being
exercised by the state/province (or nation). The same erosion or ultimate

break-up is likely to apply to other federal governments trying to govern large populations spread out over large land masses, such as China and India, and even small populations spread out over large land masses, such as Canada and Australia.

Voters in the developed world, who lack a strong sense of moral purpose, find themselves increasingly confused about the direction in which their governments are trying to lead them. It is not surprising that they are focusing more and more on local community interests or, indeed, on their own interests.

People are drawing in their horns. Communities, including corporate communities, are narrowing their horizons. In the United States, Canada, and Australia, and in other countries where any form of federal government exists, the duplication of effort can be extraordinary, and in many cases confrontational. Federal legal, education, health, housing, transportation, tax, police, and other systems often duplicate state or provincial systems. As local and state communities become more introverted and separatist, there will be increasing concern and even antagonism about the inefficiency, cost, and interference of the federal government system.

There are endless examples of this trend. Prior to the Barcelona Olympics, for instance, advertisements appeared around the world sponsored by the 'autonomous government of Catalonia'. A map showed Catalonia as if it were a separate country. The text emphasised that Catalonia had its own culture, language, and identity — no mention was made of Spain! Independent communities are now being developed in the United States under the legal umbrella of community associations, reported *The Economist* on 25 July 1992. According to the Community Associations Institute, in 1989 there were some 130,000 such associations helping to administer the lives of 12 per cent of the US population. Despite often absurd self-imposed restrictions, such as having to get permission to hold large parties, or limits being imposed on the weight of one's pets, these communities provide their members with a sense of control over their lives. The chaos and violence outside the community is thus kept at bay. As these effectively self-governing communities develop, they will give less support to expenditures by state and, in particular, federal governments. These communities, and others that are evolving elsewhere around the world, bear a striking resemblance to the walled cities of medieval Europe. In this context, it is interesting to note that Siena, Italy, one of the oldest communities surviving as an erstwhile medieval, walled city-state, has the lowest crime rate of any city in Europe. Siena is notable for its sense of community. This is expressed dramatically in the ritual of the 'Palio' horse race held twice-yearly since the thirteenth century in the main city square, the Piazza del Campo. Everyone takes part. This event helps to bind together the people of the city, and gives them a constant common sense of identity.

Concurrently with the tendency towards the creation of smaller socio-political units, there has been a recent movement against giganticism in business units. The corporate raiders of the 1980s acquired large corporations and then broke them up into smaller ones. As separate units, they became more profitable and efficient, and achieved higher values in the stock market. Imperial Chemical Industries PLC (ICI), one of the largest corporations in Britain, took the unusual step of splitting itself into two separate companies, on the grounds that both companies would become more efficient, and thus more valuable to the investors, and less prone to takeover. IBM, the giant US computer company, is taking similar steps, as are General Motors and Rank Xerox. It is likely that more large companies will follow suit. Requirements of cost reduction, greater efficiency, greater flexibility to meet market changes, and a desire to reduce these large businesses to smaller, more motivated groups are the driving force. They, in turn, create a confederation of effort and resources, a form of subsidiarity, as a replacement for the former larger and more inefficient structures. These responses mirror the social changes being evidenced in our global society.

Thus, one of the fundamental characteristics of the current warring states interregnum is the dissolution of old political structures, accompanied by a weakening of the moral and ideological systems that under-pinned them. The larger world is becoming too accessible, too intrusive, too changeable, and thus ultimately too difficult to make sense of. Political, social, economic, and technological changes are accelerating. It is not surprising, therefore, that the 'medieval city-state' concept is coming back into favour. Community tribalism is replacing nationalism on the micro-scale, while regionalism appears to be replacing nationalism on the macro-scale.

It is clear that an apparent, fundamental paradox has arisen. On the one hand, the general reasons underlying the desire for countries to support supranational 'groupings' of one kind or another make sense. They provide a mechanism for the broader implementation of regional goals which are mutually acceptable to the nations involved, while at the same time, as in any club, they provide specific privileges as well as protection from the outside world. Whether the club is the EC, NAFTA, ASEAN (and its AFTA), EFTA, or President Clinton's embryonic Western Hemisphere Community of Democracies, they all have these characteristics in common. On the other hand, there is the current desire of many people around the world to create smaller, more manageable communities within which to live — the existing nation-state structures being deemed too large, inefficient, expensive, and uncaring. It is this conflicting desire that creates the apparent paradox. However, I believe that there is no paradox, as these two apparently conflicting desires are in fact mirror-images of each other.

To begin with, since time began, tribal community cultures have arisen out of people's subconscious, and often conscious, desire to ensure that they had, in general terms, a common value system which, through trial and error, was by and large acceptable to the members of their community. Further, such a system would serve as a binding force to keep the community together. This process was also founded on the basic, instinctive knowledge that a community with a common purpose stands a far better chance of surviving in a hostile world than does an individual on his own. Over time, this process has provided the tribal community with both subconscious building-blocks and a framework, which provided the essential underpinning of such communities. Therefore, in the modern context, in times of repression, or when a tribe within a larger society was being discriminated against, or when the larger world around the tribal community and its parent community (the nation or region) went through a period of confusion or even chaos, the tribal subconscious identity rose to the conscious level to protect it. It provided an easily recognisable framework for basic stability and a common purpose. With the current conditions of global change, recession and, in many areas, chaos, it is not surprising that, as an instinctive reaction to these conditions, community tribalism is on the increase.

However, during periods such as the 1980s, when positive and substantial growth took place on a national and regional level, such tribal communities benefited considerably from being part of the larger whole. During these periods, it was not necessary for them to insist on their own historical and/or cultural independence. More comfort also brought with it a degree of indifference to the antics of their national governments. The tribe could see that its positive participation in, or indeed the subordination of its own traditions to, the larger society would bring it substantial benefits. This gave rise to an awareness that larger groupings had value. One manifestation of this was the evolution of supranational regionalism.

What we have today, in the early 1990s, is probably the most extreme form of tribalism versus nationalism/regionalism in mankind's history. Given the development in the last twenty or so years of the global community through transportation, tele-communications, and the world's media, most of the world's population is aware to some degree of the rest of the world. For the same reasons, much of the world (with the exception of black Africa) has enjoyed, or can recognise the possibility of enjoying in the relatively near future, at least some of the fruits of the world's massive economic expansion since World War II. It is not surprising, therefore, that in this time of global confusion and stress, people around the world are attempting to reduce the size of the communities within which they live to manageable and comprehensible proportions, while at the same time realising that a small community without an association of some description with a larger grouping may not survive, let alone grow, when conditions improve.

This recognition thus provides the resolution of the paradox. This is why extremists Bavaria and Wallonia wish to secede from their respective nations, yet want to have a membership within the EC. They have the history and education to understand that secession alone will not resolve, in the medium or long term, their tribal community desires. The ethnic/ tribal groups in the former Soviet Union, which for decades have suffered often brutal repression, are now emerging with new 'freedoms' amidst a world in chaos. It is not surprising that they are driven by a primitive, almost atavistic desire to re-establish their tribe in its most basic sense, so that they can then rebuild a new community from scratch and with a minimum of internal devisiveness. In doing so, I would argue that such communities will, like the extremist Walloons and Bavarians, come to realise in time that no man is an island. For these communities to survive and grow, they will need to be associated with a larger community, within a region. It is too optimistic to suggest that, at this point in history, such communities should attempt to join the global community directly. After all, even the world's most highly developed countries have given clear evidence that they are not necessarily able to do so. Indeed, outside of the ubiquitous UN, there is actually no definable global community to belong to in any practical sense! Even at the regional community level, member and would-be member countries find it very difficult to develop a clear and focused sense of purpose.

All this having been said, at least the superpower ideologies of the past provided a moral framework. Their absence has created a broad, fundamental problem: a moral vacuum has arisen. Economic association or competition based on self-interest, on an individual, local, national, or global scale, is not enough to satisfy the basic human need to identify with a value system which transcends one's own immediate material interests. A retreat behind a walled community, with its own mutually acceptable value system, while possibly practical in the short term, is not the solution.

'There is nothing against the present-day "self-tendencies" (self-determination, experience of self, self-discovery, self-realisation, self-fulfilment),' writes Hans Küng, 'as long as they are not detached from responsibility for oneself and the world, from responsibility for our fellow human beings, for society and nature; as long as they do not deteriorate into narcissistic reflection on and autistic relationship to self. Self-assertion and unselfishness need not be mutually exclusive. Identity and solidarity are both required for the formation of a better world. ... Human beings must exhaust their human potential in an unprecedented way to produce the most humane society possible and an intact environment.' (*Global Responsibility*, p. 31)

I believe that the East offers something to satisfy this need. In Japan, in particular, the Western notion of individual good is subordinated to the primary concept of community good. In Japan's 'community-first' society, people place emphasis on the survival of society (without necessarily focusing on the 'good'). In the rest of Asia Pacific, with the exception of Korea, emphasis is placed on the survival of the individual and the family, as in the West. Although it inevitably downplays Western values of freedom, individual responsibility, and a higher moral value system, the Japanese system no doubt has something to teach the rest of the world. It has certainly been effective in achieving the country's industrial and economic goals, which, while laudable, are of course not enough.

Perhaps what we need to look for in the future is a new kind of man — not a monkey, as in the selfish Western model, nor an ant, as in the faceless Japanese model — but a combination of the two. In the West, particularly in the United States, we have created an absurd moral paradox — the creation of 'parental' laws intended to govern our behaviour down to the last detail, and the employment of legions of lawyers to get around those laws. To quote Hans Küng again, 'We are all in danger of forgetting the truth of the ancient Roman saying: *Quid leges sine moribus?* — What is the use of laws without morals?'

At some point, it must be our own sense of right and wrong that governs our behaviour. Any balanced adult must have such a moral sense, but for him to develop it, there must be the right environment. It should be provided by the community within which he lives. The community must collectively create and implement a higher moral value system. In many respects, the United States has led the way in this — and yet it has more lawyers than any other country! On top of that, many of them seem to spend most of their time advising their clients how to avoid or evade the various laws set up to enshrine these higher moral values! Additionally, in moral, or indeed spiritual, terms, if the individual or the community is not in a state of balance, then considerable energy is wasted, either in the ultimately trivial pursuit of the desires of the ego or in the exhausting struggle against prevailing norms to achieve some degree of balance on one's own.

In this general context, most of the countries of Asia Pacific, with good fortune and by dint of extraordinary hard work, discipline, focus, and by having the benefits of the West's free trade system, have managed largely to avoid the effects of the current global recession and confusion. It is therefore a highly opportune time for the countries of the region, from a position of strength, to realise too that they need a higher value system in the form of an association with a larger community with regional goals. Such a community could help to introduce and implement such a value system, for the good of the region and, by extension, for the good of the world. While Japan is in the midst of a recession, this probably creates an ideal opportunity for the rest of Asia Pacific to put pressure on Japan to determine where its primary future interests and loyalties lie. By being proactive now, when the region is achieving a form of balance and where, as a result, there is excess positive energy to deal with such important issues, a great deal could be achieved.

If the countries of the region wait for an external threat (such as trade protectionism) and then react defensively by creating a regional forum, or indeed a bloc, much less will be achieved. Additionally, as the trend towards protectionism is likely to be exacerbated during difficult periods of protracted global recession or political confusion, these economic and political factors could, in due course, have a serious negative effect on Asia Pacific. Thus, if Asia Pacific were to become embroiled in such negative global conditions, its response would come from a position of weakness. It would perforce be out of balance and therefore less efficient and objectively rational or correct in its reactive reasoning.

How can the countries of Asia Pacific respond to the stresses, strains, and confusions of this interregnum? Exhortations such as these are not the answer. The answer probably lies in the development of more flexible political structures and a more self-conscious sense of regional identity. There is certainly, and crucially, a need for vision and leadership. For the peoples of Asia Pacific, what is lacking as a pre-condition of these developments is some form of Asia Pacific community forum.

There is already a structure in place out of which such a forum could grow. ASEAN is now finally evolving into a mature organisation. It is now capable of providing the basis for wider regional co-operation by inviting the region's main players — China, India, Japan, and Australia — into a new partnership. Such a move could open the way to the structures of regional co-operation which Asia Pacific as a whole requires and which ASEAN has already started to put in place. It can only be through such new structures that a clear Asia Pacific regional identity can be created and a higher common purpose developed. Such structures, in turn, should enable Asia Pacific as a whole, and on behalf of its constituent parts, to negotiate and co-operate with the other regions of the world — notably North America and the EC.

It is only through such developments as these, that it will be possible for the countries of Asia Pacific to assist in the creation of, and for them to find and develop a constructive role for themselves in, this new world order of tri-polar regional leadership.

Acknowledgements

Without my many friends in Asia Pacific, who in effect developed into my extended family in terms of my affection, respect, and appreciation for their advice and support over the years, I would not have been able to open the many doors to all the different facets of this extraordinary region, let alone feel truly at home in the various countries and within the various friendships. I would therefore particularly like to acknowledge these friends and to offer them my more than grateful appreciation for all they have done for me in their various ways.

Japan

Ishihara Keiko, Hideo, Atsuo, and Miki; Shimamoto Reiichi (deceased); Kida Toshio; Tajima Mitsuru; Akimoto Minoru; Akita Koichi; Funaki Katsumi; Hashimoto Toru; Hazama Kimiko and Koichi; Horie Tetsuo; Ishizaka Nobuo, Itoh Josei; Iwasaki Hiroya; Kakizawa Koji; Kanazawa Kimiko and Koichi; Kawamura Shigekuni; Kobayashi Akira; Kogo Nobutsune; Kurosawa Yoh; Minagawa Eishin; the Miwa family; Nagatani Soji; Nakamura Kenzo; Oba Tomomitsu; Ogata Shijuro; Onogi Nobuo; Owada Hisashi; the Tsubomura family; Tsushima Yuji; Tsutsumi Yuji; Wada Kimiko and Kazuo; Yamada Mariko and Shohei, and so many others in Japan. Collectively, in so many different ways, they allowed me to explore their country and the hearts and the minds of its people, as well as to develop with them a common desire for Japan to become more integrated into the rest of the world.

Hong Kong

K.C. Kwan; Helmut and Anna Sohmen; Alex Adamovich; Tobias Brown; Elsa Wong; Ronald Chao; Endo Shigeru; Hobart Epstein; David Halperin;

Ariane and Charles Joory; Kim Suk; Kirimoto Goshi; Andrew Korner; David K.P. Li; K.S. Lo; Vicky and Alasdair Morrison; Father Yves Nalet; Willie Purves; Barbara and Heinz Rust; Manfred Schoeni; Tang Kok Yew; Sandy Thompson; Father Vincent-Paul Toccoli; Shimada Toshio; France and Bertrand Viriot; Rowena and Eric Winkler; and Tony Yip, who in their different ways, and from widely differing backgrounds, helped to give me an amazing kaleidoscope of perception of what makes up Hong Kong and how it relates to the People's Republic of China and the rest of the world.

Taiwan

Chen S. Yu and W.T. Tsai and his sons Daniel and Richard Tsai, who believed in the sincerity of my attempt to understand Taiwan, its people, and its differences from the People's Republic of China, despite the infrequency of my visits, and who gave me so much of their time.

India

Hemendra Kothari; Biki Oberoi and Mirjana Jojic; D. Basu; S.K. Birla; R.P. Goenka; P.G. Mankad; S.S. Nadkarni; M.J. Pherwani (deceased); and S. Venkitaramanan, who accepted me as an 'extended family member' (members of my mother's family having spent some 150 years in India) and who allowed me the privilege of affectionate and concerned criticism about how, and in which direction, India should evolve.

Australia

Maggie and Derek Denton; Norm Fussell; Dorothy and Geoffrey Heeley; Leo Hielscher; Cam Kerr; Tim Lang; Rhonda and Michael Loftus; Barbara and John Ralph; and Patricia and Philip Spry-Bailey, with all of whom I have a great affinity, no doubt partly because of my Rhodesian background, and all of whom have allowed me to prod them unmercifully on the subject of why Australia should look north.

New Zealand

Gillian and Roderick Deane; Vicky and Tony Ellis; Trevor Farmer; Hugh Fletcher; Jenny and Alan Gibbs; David Sadler; Faith and Keith Taylor; Margaret and Ronald Trotter; Geoff Whitcher; and Judy and John

Wrightson, who made not only myself, but my family as well, so welcome, and who gave us, over the years, such an interesting perspective on New Zealand and its relationship to the rest of the world.

Korea

Yoo Chang-Soon; Song In-Sang; Kim Hong-Suk; Koh Byung-Woo; Chang In-Yong; Choi Dong-Ik; Chung Yong-Eui; Ha Yong-Ki; Kim Sang-Ha; Kim Jae-Yoon; Lee Pil-Sun; Suh Hyung-Suk; Yang Jae-Bong; and Min-Jong and John Wiesniewski, who, with many others, have put up with my enthusiastic probing and have guided me in my 25-year attempt to understand what is Korea, who the Koreans are, and where they fit into the world, in particular *vis-à-vis* their relations with Japan and China.

Indonesia

Arifin Sirigar, who so many years ago started me off on the process of discovering Indonesia.

Malaysia

Tun Ismail bin Mohamed Ali; Tunku Tan Sri Dato'Seri Ahmad Yahaya; and Tan Sri Haji Basir bin Ismail, who allowed me to dream wild dreams with them on the subject of an Asia Pacific community and the possibility of Japan being an important part of it.

Singapore

Ong Beng Seng; Sanjoy Chowdhury; Koh Beng Seng; Ng Kok Song; Sim Kee Boon; and Mary and Patrick Yeoh, who have allowed me again to dream the same wild dreams, all the while allowing me to tease them about the sometimes excessive austerity of the Singaporean approach to its survival.

Thailand

Panit and Varin Pulsirivong; Daeng and Vichit Suraphongchai; Mehta Junhasiri; Nukul Prachuabmoh; and Chatri Sophonpanich and his son Tony, who, together with other newer friends, are still constantly educating me with great patience and affection into the subtleties of the Thai culture and its people.

The West

I also have many close friends in the West, who have taught me so much about value systems in the West. Without their friendship, in the full sense of the word, I could not have made the voyage of the last thirty years. Many of these people were also kind enough to review and frankly criticise parts, or all, of my manuscript as it evolved. In particular, I would like to acknowledge the importance I attach to the friendships I have enjoyed with Kevin O'Sullivan; Niles Helmboldt; Susan and George Ball; Myrna and Theo-Max (deceased) van der Beughel; Madeleine de Brantes; Elizabeth and Dick Bristow; Jeremy Brown; Father Raoul des Cilleuils; Michael von Clemm; Denise and Prentis Cobb-Hale; Anne-Marie and John Edwards; Helena and Per-Olof Eriksson; Bridget and Nick Evans; Barry Friedberg; Maryse and Jean Gabriel; David Gemmill; Don Gershuny; Julian Hartland-Swann; Jayne and Rupert Hughes; Bruno and François Israel; Jerome Kenney; Dominique and Alain Langlois; Andrew Large; Faith and Dick Large; Annie and Georg Lennkh; Daniel Levy; Britta Lloyd; Candace and Peter Luthy; Maria Manetti-Farrow; Arlene and Reuben Mark; Rogan McLellan; Ian Molson; Marli and Babacar N'Diaye; Stella and Christopher Reeves; Sidney Rolfe (deceased); Terry and Michael Sanderson; Bill Schreyer; Philip Seers; Charles Shanock; Isabelle and Jean-Pierre Tirouflet; Manée and Michel Verdet; Roswitha and Philip Wetton; Andrea and Jason Wilson; and Dinny and Stani Yassukovitch.

It goes without saying that there are also a great number of other people throughout Asia Pacific and the West who have in so many different ways helped me and who have been so generous with their time. The language which expresses my feeling most appropriately is the Japanese expression '*minasan no okage de, koko made mairimashita*' — translated loosely as, 'it is thanks to everyone that I arrived at this point'.

T his book would not have been written if, seven years ago, Philip Wetton, after a long and impassioned discussion between his wife, Marie-Thérèse, and myself about Asia Pacific over dinner at their then home in Seoul, had not suggested I put my ideas in a book. The final impetus came, most importantly, from Sanjoy Chowdhury, who also wanted to write a book on the region. We started this book's first draft as co-authors. Unfortunately, as a well-known economist, his more technical and professional economic approach contrasted more and more acutely over time with my rather more general and philosophical approach. This eventually led us to agree amicably that we would each write our own books. I am, however, enormously grateful to him for having been the primary catalyst for this book.

In a more practical sense, I am grateful to Heather Millar for her help over the first two years in doing some of the book's initial research and drafting with me, and to Simon Winchester for having introduced me to her. I am also most grateful to Charles Joory for having introduced me to Margaret and Andrew Hewson of John Johnson Literary Agents in London. Margaret took my original, chaotic manuscript, really read it (unlike some other literary agents) and then gave me an invaluable, initial critique, without which I might have given up the project. She was then kind enough to introduce me to Adam Sisman, formerly the managing, non-fiction editor of Macmillan in London, who, despite the huge workload on his plate, took on, together with his ex-colleague, Susanna Wadeson, the Herculean task of cleaning my literary Augean stables. They reduced my manuscript by a third and completely restructured it. Without their help and, particularly, Adam's solo help in the final stages, no doubt this book would not have seen the light of day.

My grateful thanks go to Stella Holloway for providing considerable background material on a number of countries, specifically those in Southeast Asia and Papua New Guinea, and to Marc Faber for his taking the time to read my manuscript and provide the first professional critique of the restructured draft. Likewise, my grateful thanks go to Jean Cheval; Richard Cole; Nico Colchester; Fritz Leutwiler; Göran Lindahl; Fujii Miwako; Antoine Jeancourt-Galignani; Jeffrey Koo; Kwon Soon-Hee; Keith Lampi; Lee Myung-Jin; Liu Chia Mei; Hazel Moore; Ohnuma Yukio; George Robinson; Onno Ruding; Bob Salter; Peter Smith; Henry Steiner; Philip Tose; Malcolm Turnbull; and Amnuay Viravan, and to so many of my friends listed above for reviewing the manuscript prior to its publication and providing me with many useful comments.

My special thanks go to Tobias Brown, who provided me with

invaluable advice on how to publish and then how to position this book. I also appreciated enormously Michael Blakenham's interest and kindness in not only reviewing the book but also in introducing me to Longman Group (Far East) Limited in Hong Kong and Viking/Penguin in New Delhi, India, who are publishing the English-language editions for Asia and the Indian subcontinent respectively. Finally, I would like to thank Stephen Troth, Nick Wallwork, Catherine Wong, and Clare Hall, of Longman, and Robyn Flemming of Wordswork Limited, for their support and patience.

I must also accept full responsibility for any errors of omission or fact and note that, unless attributed specifically, all the views expressed in this book are my own.

In a more abstract way, I would also like to express my appreciation to the editorial staff of *The Economist*, the *International Herald Tribune*, and the *Far Eastern Economic Review*, all of which publications have provided me over the years with an invaluable source of interesting and perceptive material on the Asia Pacific region.

On a separate note, I would like to extend my apologies once again to Catherine and Peter Cleary, whose dinner party I totally forgot about in the excitement of finishing the book — they had to ring and remind me! Marie-Thérèse and I arrived very late — it was a great dinner. My thanks also to Harold Wong who, at the end of this dinner, left me his cigarettes and lighter, which I needed in order to help calm myself!

Last, but absolutely not least, I would like to express my affectionate and profound gratitude to my associate, Linda Da Cruz, who so often caught in quick succession the many balls I have been juggling during the three years we have worked together and who has enabled me somehow to stay on my feet and to keep up with all my various interests, including the writing of this book.

ORBIS TERRARUM TYPUS DE INTEGRO

ASIA

Polus Arcticus

Circulus Arcticus

AMERICA

ANIAN

MEXICANA

AMER

Tropicus Cancer

Circulus Aequinoctialis

MAR DEL

Oceanus

ZUR

Peruvianus

EL MAR PACIFICO

Tropicus Capricorni

Insulæ Salomonis

TERRA

AUSTRALIS

MAGALLANICA

Circulus Antarcticus

Polus Antarcticus

MAGALLANICA

Terra del Fuego

Corma A.

Aru
Fretu Lupis